Political Culture and the Making of Modern Nation-States

Political Culture and the Making of Modern Nation-States

Edward Weisband

and

Courtney I. P. Thomas

Routledge
Taylor & Francis Group
LONDON AND NEW YORK

First published 2015 by Paradigm Publishers

Published 2016 by Routledge
2 Park Square, Milton Park, Abingdon, Oxon OX14 4RN
711 Third Avenue, New York, NY 10017, USA

Routledge is an imprint of the Taylor & Francis Group, an informa business

Library of Congress Cataloging-in-Publication Data
Weisband, Edward, 1939–
Political culture and the making of modern nation-states / Edward Weisband and Courtney I. P. Thomas.
pages cm
Includes bibliographical references and index.
ISBN 978-1-61205-783-5 (hardcover : alk. paper)
ISBN 978-1-61205-802-3 (library ebook)
1. Political culture. 2. Nation-state. I. Thomas, Courtney Irene Powell, author. II. Title.
JA75.7.W42 2014
320.9—dc23

2014021343

ISBN 13: 978-1-61205-783-5 (hbk)
ISBN 13: 978-1-61205-784-2 (pbk)

This book is dedicated to
Jennifer Renee Pluta, Evangeline Pluta, Genevieve Pluta, Daniel P. Neville, Morgan Elizabeth Snover, Lane Page Snover, Kayla Renee Snover, Alex Vincent Davie

And to
Sonya, Marie, Bettie, and Levi

In hopes that they and succeeding generations live in a world of political cultures where peace, understanding, and reconciliation become so embedded they can be taken for granted.

Contents

Part II The Making of the Political Culture of the American Nation-State

Part III Global Colonialism and the Making of the Modern Nation-State

Part IV The Holocaust, Genocide, and Crimes against Humanity: Political Culture in Violation of Personhood

Part V Nation-Building and State-Building: Future Challenges in the Present

Acknowledgments

We wish to thank the several generations of students who enrolled in *Nations and Nationalities: Cultural Constructions of Collective Identity* offered by the Department of Political Science and by International Studies at Virginia Tech since the course was first offered in 1995. They have been a joy to teach and their enthusiasm for the study of political cultures represents the inspiration for this book. The recent chairs of the Virginia Tech Department of Political Science have demonstrated a deep commitment to the multidisciplinary educational objectives and innovative instructional approaches essential to the study of political cultures. Thus we want to thank Timothy W. Luke, University Distinguished Professor and current Chair of the Department of Political Science, and Ilja Luciak, Professor and former Chair of the Department of Political Science. Distinguished scholars and excellent teachers each in their own right, they have remained on the front lines of support in assigning graduate teaching assistants in sufficient numbers to permit students enrolled in Nations and Nationalities the opportunity to think critically through essay writing assignments. We wish to recognize all our excellent colleagues in the Virginia Tech Department of Political Science for their dedication to research, teaching, and learning. Yannis Stivachtis, Director of the Virginia Tech International Studies Program, in addition to scholarly contributions on normative and strategic studies, has lent critical support to curricular development of international studies and efforts to introduce students to comparative political cultures. In the context of political culture we want to pay tribute to our Virginia Tech colleagues, Scott G. Nelson for his distinguished scholarship on the concept of sovereignty, Bettina Koch for her outstanding scholarly contributions on medieval Islamic and Christian doctrines of war and their relevance to conflict today, and Wayne D. Moore

for his excellent scholarship on American constitutionalism in the making of the United States as a modern nation-state. Several generations of graduate assistants have helped develop the perspectives presented here. We are grateful to all of them. In particular, we want to mention with gratitude Elana Delozier for her wonderful insights and encouragement over many years. We also thank Alec Clott for his contributions to the Alternate Perspectives boxes. We would be remiss not to thank our spouses, Joan Elizabeth (a.k.a. Lisabeth) Weisband and Christopher Thomas, for their understanding and support during the many years while this project took form and matured. Finally, we want to thank Jennifer Knerr and her associates at Paradigm Publishers for their openness to the study of cultural constructions of collective identity and for their willingness to publish this multidisciplinary exercise focused on political culture and identity politics framed in contexts from the communal past to the national present.

Introduction

This book tells the story of the emergence of nation-states from the perspective of political culture. It does so by examining the historical transformations in political culture etched by the dynamics of nation-building and state-building. Nation-states represent a near-universal political formation in modern times. The development of national languages, the emergence of national traditions, and the anchoring of belief or ideological systems in national political culture coincided with economic and technological developments involving the leap from traditional communities confronted by scarcities to mass populations sustained by agricultural surpluses. Agricultural development fostered the rise of societies of strangers particularly in European and British settlements along the peripheries of the Roman Empire. Such societies required forms of governance that gradually became centralized and increasingly extractive. As this occurred they also demanded blood and treasure in the name of these newly established centralized authorities. These processes first became associated with aristocracy and the dynastic kingdoms of classical royalty, but in the course of both time and revolution they fostered the emergence of sovereign nation-states. This book traces these developments in order to demonstrate how political cultures adjusted to these new realities and in turn how cultural dynamics shaped the forms that sovereign state governance eventually assumed in various national locations throughout the world.

In particular, we examine how and with what consequences cultural forms of national self-consciousness arose. Gradual transformations in political affiliations occurred in ways that illustrate how the shifting sands of political governance depended on the changing nature of political cultures. This book traces these pathways. This exploration reveals how cultural constructions of collective

identity created the legitimacies attached to sovereign nation-states as forms of centralized governance. The relationship of nationhood to the legitimacy of centralized state institutions was and continues to be tested. This book demonstrates the significance of political culture for an understanding of the modern world rent by divisions within, beyond, and beneath the nation-state as a political formation. Legitimacy crises, civil strife and insurrections, subnational conflicts, ethno-political violence, and nationalist struggle help to define contemporary international relations and politics. We ask how and why from the perspective of political culture. To understand "failed" or fragile states, for example, requires exploration of the deep divides of political culture that embed the power dynamics of such conflicts. Much political violence is driven by cultural values and meanings, and in particular by conflicts over identity constructions in political culture as they relate to the nation-state and the legitimacy of its governance. Strategic analysis oriented to power structures and dynamics demands prior understanding of the cultural dimensions of political conflict. Such understanding depends on conceptual clarity regarding a range of terms that are too often loosely applied or used with contradictory meanings. Such terms include state sovereignty; nation and nationhood; nationality, citizenship, and peoplehood; nationalism and patriotism; legitimacy and popular consent; and ethnicity and self-determination.

Political culture represents more than an overlay in the study of politics. It goes to the core of the nature of the political, of what grounds human beings in a common faith or commitment to a collective idea, ideal, or ideology. This book thus looks at the ways in which human beings have devoted their lives and anchored personal meanings by creating, sustaining, and even sacrificing themselves on the altars of political cultures and identities. As our emphasis on modern nation-states suggests, political cultures configured around nationhood and nationality developed gradually in the Anglo and European West and became universalized only relatively recently through global colonialism or by means of the contact situation and internal colonialism. These dynamics tended to be devastating to local cultures almost everywhere they occurred and may be seen today in a variety of pathological forms as evidenced by ethnicized kinship violence, ethno-grievances, nativism, patronage, and corruption. But simplistic judgment is neither helpful nor appropriate. This study explores the identity politics or the social constructions of identity group dynamics that emerge from cultures originating in kinship, descent, and segmented lineage. Such cultures tend to be disciplined by codes of honor and shame in ways that bestow legitimacy to patrimonial rule. National political cultures tend to subvert these kinds of traditional and communal forms of legitimacy and governance.

The consequences are varied. They include continuing strife and even genocide as tragically demonstrated by several instances including the case of Rwanda.

Political culture often adheres to processes of essentialization that involve identity group objectifications along various formats: sectarian, religious, racial, class, gender, sexual orientation, etc. The book explores these dynamics across a range of national experiences, particularly with respect to how ethnic categories become racialized according to often tacit or hidden color codes. Once this happens, victim groups also tend to become displaced and dislocated spatially. The present study represents an exercise designed not only to explore identity politics but to place dialogues and discussion of diversity in a comparative political context. Too often so-called diversity education privileges, in a negative way, an American exceptionalism by treating the history of American racial or ethnic histories as if they were definitively apart from the political-cultural histories and experiences of other societies. We thus focus on what we call hyphenated identities in comparative contexts to determine how individuals graft multicultural and multiethnic aspects of their identity to forge unique personalities against the frames of a common nationality, nation-state to nation-state.

Part I
Transformations of Political Culture from Times Past to Future Present

Chapter I
Political Culture

Culture and Continuity

Culture begins in moonlight. As Astronomers Without Borders notes, "every culture on Earth has a view of the moon that is unique to them, their heritage, and their identity as a people."[1] Our earliest human ancestors marked the stages of life and developed cultural values according to their observations of the phases of our closest celestial neighbor. The moon served as a "guide to the natural world" signifying "when to plant crops, when to harvest, when to fish or hunt certain types of animals, when the women were fertile and what type of personality the child would possess upon being conceived under a certain phase of the moon.... [It was] a practical guide to the rhythms of the universe, the cycles prevalent in nature."[2] The moon has been deified in many cultures. It has served as the inspiration for festivals, dances, myths, and legends. It has acted as the centerpiece of the communal experience, the guiding force that provided a sense of cultural continuity against the uncertainties of transient life. For example, Native American cultures have names for the full moons that appear during each month of the year. October's "Hunter's Moon" follows the "Harvest Moon" (the full moon closest to the autumnal equinox) and is named for the moonlight hunts that allow native communities to stockpile food for the winter months. The moon seems to have lent meaning to life in early societies, linking individual persons to the values and traditions that endow human life with communal significance.

Culture: The Silent Codes of Human Development

What is culture and what are its functions? **Culture** refers to the universal human capacity to classify, codify, and communicate knowledge and experiences symbolically and intergenerationally. It inheres in symbolic meanings. These endow human existence with significance. Communities adopt cultural values and meanings in order to communicate, understand, and validate the institutions that regulate their social practices. Culture functions in ways that govern interpersonal relationships, discipline human behaviors, and provide context to collective social and political experiences.

Culture grounds human existence by allowing persons to interpret life from birth to death, from entry into the human condition to passage beyond material existence. It provides moral and spiritual foundation. On such fundamental meanings, human beings, in what we are about to call traditional kinship communities as well as in modern society, situate themselves as members of family, social, or national groups, and today, even as participants in global networks. Our **identities**, the ways that we project ourselves into the world, are products of culture, its traditions, its values, and its meanings. Culture grounds us as we wrestle with questions of association, affiliation, allegiance, and even our own cosmic self-worth. From a traditional communal perspective, culture serves to strengthen the sense of intergenerational continuity. Culture thus, in effect, teaches us how to think about who we are, what is expected of us. It influences how we judge ourselves and others against the normative standards that define what we might, should, and/or must do in life. It guides and shapes our understanding of metaphysical reality, that is, how we interpret the possibilities of a world beyond our own, and it thus facilitates human comprehension and belief as to where we "go" once we pass from this life. Culture thus helps shape our sense of what it is to be a human being among others. Often, it supports the belief that life and living are or can be grounded in elements larger than life, be they conceived in religious, philosophical, or ideological ways.

Cultural cues are everywhere. In some cultures children are taught to "speak only when spoken to" or to "be seen and not heard"; in others, they are encouraged to "speak their minds." Some cultures socialize men to be assertive and women to be submissive while others idealize gender equality. In some cultures it is taboo to make eye contact with a person of a higher social or economic class while other cultures regard the same practice not as a sign of deference, but rather as an indication of disrespect. And because we absorb cultural practices into our behaviors from our infancy, we reproduce them "naturally." In this way, culture

presents itself as given and thus as part of the natural world rather than as a contrivance of human invention. As Terry Eagleton writes, culture is "'history turned into nature' . . . a social order [that] strives to naturalize its own arbitrariness."[3] Yet cultural practices are never completely arbitrary. They are instead invented and reinforced through dynamics of transmission across generations that involve learning and various forms of rational confrontation with the natural world of material circumstances. For these reasons culture is coconstitutive. We are at once the products and the creators of the cultures that anchor and guide our lives. What we do with culture is as important as what culture does through us. We learn to know ourselves through culture. In infancy, we take into ourselves the culture of those who nurture us. From our earliest moments we absorb cultural sensitivities, habits, and modes of relation without self-conscious awareness and without critical analysis. In doing so, we learn without learning. We do not know how we know what we know and yet through culture we become aware of ourselves as knowing persons. We learn not only what to desire but how to desire. Cultural influences instruct us often without our self-awareness, guiding us not merely in what we think but in how we think.

Culture represents the "silent codes" of human bonding and belonging and thus of collective social or political identity. It acts as the root of our communal beliefs, values, and ethical perspectives. It becomes symbolized in our traditions, customs, and norms. Culture surrounds us and we are embedded in it. It is present in our language, our mannerisms, and our habits. It structures our interactions with others and establishes the parameters of social interactions. In these ways, culture reinforces constructions of collective identity. **Political culture** refers to our concepts and symbolic meanings attached to forms of governance. How are we governed? How do we justify or validate governing methods and institutions? How do we convert power through force into authority through rules? What is the meaning of legitimacy and why is legitimacy of government and governing institutions critical to an understanding of the modern world?

Political Culture and the Legitimacy of Governance

When we glance at a map of the world, we see a globe. The planetary universe called Earth is divided into a cartographic design etched by sovereign state borders and the national boundaries that define collective identity. Borders and boundaries are human artifacts. They are not the creatures of nature and do not stem from the natural world. They are the consequence of political history. Nation-states emerge from this history. Each nation-state possesses its own sets

KEY CONCEPTS
Political Culture

Political culture refers to the ideas, beliefs, values, traditions, and practices that provide the foundation for a political system. All culture is **constructed** rather than the product of **nature** or **predestination**. It is the product of history, contingency, environment, and other variables that interact to frame social, political, and economic attachments. For this reason, every country or **state** in the international system has its own unique political culture. States vary widely in terms of leadership, representation, civil and human rights, taxation, entitlements, and rule of law. Even countries in the same region will often have dramatically different political structures and values. For example, democratic ideals developed differently in England, where a strong nobility limited the powers of the monarch, from how they did in France, where the absolute monarch was overthrown by a middle-class revolution.

However, over the past three hundred years the international system has developed its own political culture, one that is defined by **states**, **nations**, **sovereignty**, **nonintervention**, **legitimacy**, **citizenship**, and **self-determination**. These constructions emerged in Europe in the aftermath of the Second Agricultural Revolution and were refined over centuries of revolution, warfare, and diplomacy. They were then exported globally through colonialism, first to the New World and then to Africa and Asia. Today, they are the foundational institutions of international relations. However, as we will see, the imposition of these modern values on cultures beholden to traditional communal values has created challenges for international order that have often resulted in political oppression, instability, and violence.

continued

of narratives and nurtures its own collective stories that indicate the ways of self-understanding within each political culture.

Political geography imposed on the topologies of the earth reveals the contemporary universalization of one particular political form: **the nation-state**. The globe is demarcated by nation-states across the entire globe. This is the outcome of political history and reflects the consequences of political culture over many centuries. The study of **political culture** refers to the examination of cultures and cultural values, meanings, and institutions focused on governance and its legitimacy. Analysis of the **political culture of nation-states** concentrates on what such terms as **nations**, **states**, and **nation-states** mean conceptually from

In recent decades multiculturalism has become an important political value in the international system. As a nation of immigrants, the United States has struggled to create a multicultural society throughout its history. It has tackled slavery, ethnic cleansing, structural discrimination, class bias, as well as gender and income inequality. Various forms of inequality persist in contemporary American society. Many European countries are today confronting multicultural pressures in unique ways. Great Britain, for example, has experienced a large influx of Indian and Pakistani immigrants in recent decades. These immigrant populations have brought ethnic, religious, and linguistic diversity to British society as well as political challenges associated with assimilation and coexistence. Similarly, French society has experienced large-scale immigration from its former colonies in North Africa consisting predominantly of Muslim and Arabic-speaking persons, and thus it has struggled to accommodate cultural and religious differences. In 2010, for example, France passed a law that banned face-covering headwear in public areas. This prohibition extended to traditional Muslim veils such as the *niqab* and *burqa*. This has been a controversial policy as it appears to limit religious expression among devout Muslim women in France. But its legal validity was confirmed by the European Court of Human Rights in 2014 on the grounds that a person's complete social presence constituted a human right that would be violated if females were to cover their full face in society. European societies thus struggle to define appropriate balances between their own cultural ways of life and immigrant traditions and values as they attempt to incorporate increasingly diverse populations into historically homogenous societies. As a result, they are challenged to create new political cultures that emphasize multicultural toleration, acceptance, and support alongside national cohesion.

the perspective of cultural values and meanings. To speak of **political culture in the making of modern nation-states** is to suggest that particular values and meanings arise during the historical development of political culture that make nation-states as a kind of governance even possible.

We ask, therefore, what nation-states are and what they signify in terms of political culture. Not all nation-states share the same forms of political culture. We must review contrasts as well as similarities. Certain political cultures, for example, are more homogenous than others while some suffer from a range of cultural conflicts and debates over the nature of collective identity and state **legitimacy**. All nation-states seek recognition of their legitimacy in two ways: first,

internally relative to governing domestic society; second, internationally in terms of their rights to act as a sovereign agent among other sovereign entities in the international society of sovereign nation-states. **Sovereignty** does not guarantee full and complete autonomy for each and every nation-state. It is a doctrine of international law that attests to the primacy of nation-states as the legitimate form of governance within the international **scapes** of political interaction. Sovereignty also supports the primacy of domestic legitimacy that derives from the people of each nation-state in terms of popular consent. **Popular consent** as a doctrine does not mean that each and every nation-state is governed according to the principles of democracy any more than sovereignty at the international level means that each and every nation-state enjoys full autonomy among other nation-states. It does, however, underscore the fundamental role played by citizens conceived as a single population that inhabits the territory of a sovereign state, a population that in so doing constitutes a nation empowered with the rights and obligations exerted through popular consent. This further underscores the importance of political culture in the making of modern nation-states. For the very concept of popular consent, along with such notions as sovereignty and legitimacy, is essentially a form of political culture that has universal meaning and relevance but that emerges differently in different places at different times.

Traditional perspectives on sovereign states hold to the view that states are centralized political entities, governed by an administrative apparatus and bounded by territory, that enjoy a monopoly over the means of violence and are thus responsible for their own survival among all other states. Often it is theoretically alleged that such states are trapped by a **security predicament**: each must prepare for its own defense and survival; the more each does so, the less each feels secure. Since all states are responsible for their own military preparedness, no state is able to depend entirely on others for their safety. Providential reasoning and prudential judgment call forth a specific kind of rationality or set of rational calculations. As a result, each nation-state acts as a sovereign rational agent among other sovereign rational agents in the name of self-preservation, however defined. The question of legitimacy becomes all the more important as a result. What authorizes or justifies sovereign state action to engage in preparedness for purposes of security and survival? What legitimates state behaviors based on sovereign rational agency if this implies the ever-present possibilities of war and political violence? The immediate answer to questions pertaining to legitimacy is popular consent. Popular consent permits military preparedness in response to the security predicament. But where is popular consent vested? The answer refers back to the citizenry or population of a state that manifests the political culture of **peoplehood** and/or **nationhood**.

Peoplehood represents a cultural kind of belonging in which a population, large or small, recognizes among themselves special features that they share collectively and that render them a singular formation with a unique set of bonds, whether material or metaphysical. If we speak of "the Arabs" or "the Jewish people," we speak of the bonds that tie a people together on the basis of a common language, religion, characteristic, cultural condition, or social circumstance. Nationhood addresses a political and cultural reality relative to mostly centralized and sovereign states. We speak of "the Palestinians" as a people who make claims for the rights to citizenship and bounded statehood, and we speak of "the Israelis," whether Jews or Arabs or those who were formerly Ethiopian, precisely because they enjoy such rights as citizens of the State of Israel.

The historic rise of nations relative to sovereign states is linked to the history of state conflict and the perceived need for centralizing political actors such as classical kings to extract wealth and to place forces under arms for purposes of defense, security, and even, in the course of history, to arm for ostensible reasons that justify acts of aggression against other states and their rulers. As classical kings extracted more and more, especially in the course of European history, the issue of legitimacy arose with greater and greater urgency. The result was a series of extraction crises such as the American War of Independence and the Boston Tea Party, which resounded with the slogan "No taxation without representation." In similar fashion, the French Revolution and the Bolshevik Revolution in Russia contested the rights of rulers to tax and to conscript citizens for purposes of war and military preparedness in the absence of popular consent. Modern political cultures of nations and of nationhood grow out of these episodes of contestation.

Nationhood is a concept of political culture that refers to a kind of peoplehood of those governed by centralized sovereign states but who, as a nation, by definition represent or exercise popular consent with respect to state extraction. The term nationhood is thus rooted in notions of legitimacy. Nationhood as a political-cultural concept refers to a specific common feature of peoplehood, that is, exertion of the legitimacy of sovereign state governance relative to extraction. The "nation" as a concept of political culture speaks to the political values of legitimacy and even accountability with respect to government extraction. Extracting men and women under arms and ordering them into harm's way are state prerogatives that must be legitimated. So too is the extraction of economic wealth from citizens for state objectives. Here again, no concept, however ideal, is meant to imply perfect applications. The existence of nationhood relative to statehood and state extraction does not suggest that legitimacy functions perfectly everywhere and for all time. On the contrary, even democracies on occasion face legitimation crises, as did the United States during the era of the Vietnam War

and interventions in Indochina when a sizable number of draft-eligible youth, including future president Bill Clinton, burned their draft cards and/or moved to Canada to avoid arrest. Nonetheless, nationhood (bottom-up) and centralized sovereign statehood (top-down) represent the two essential valences or value-sets in interpreting the political culture of nation-states today.

Sovereignty thus represents a conceptual kind of political-cultural glue binding statehood and nationhood together. The making of the nation-state as a political-cultural artifact is the consequence of history in which the "hyphen" or linkages between statehood and nationhood occurred. We speak of nation-states precisely to refer to the contemporary significance of the ties that connect nations and states as a result of sovereignty. In a sense, sovereignty is a concept of political culture that refers to the historical bonds that tie nations to states and states to their nations. Ideologies of **nationalism** that extol the specific characteristics of solidarity among citizens of particular nations, or ideologies of **patriotism** that celebrate the specific features of political belief, conviction, or heroism within particular states, reinforce the sense of cultural glue between nation and state. This too is the result of history.

History is not the same everywhere. The cultural cements of sovereignty have not and do not operate the same in all places demarcated today as nation-states. On the contrary, many political cultures struggle both for and against the legitimacy of centralized government, governance, and authority. Often these struggles are associated with forms of **political identity** grounded in cultural values that refer back to political cultures originating in traditional communities beholden to the legitimacies of **kinship, blood ties, tribes, clans, segmented lineage**, and **ancestral land**, all of which are discussed below. Political cultures are not manufactured overnight. They are in constant flux and are subject to change and transformation. The emergence of political-cultural concepts of nationhood bound to the legitimacy of statehood becomes difficult to achieve wherever tradition resists centralization, and when such kinds of resistance become reinforced by cultural values or dimensions such as religion or race. Under such circumstances, peoplehood becomes associated not with nationhood but rather with the values of "otherness" or difference. Various components of difference become purportedly definitive of collective belonging and identity in ways that prevent or impede the political-cultural development of nationhood. Here too we must focus on specific histories and concrete cultures in terms of **nationality** and how it is realized as an integral aspect of collective identity.

Nationality is not a dimension of existential reality because it stems from citizenship, which in turn is a function of legal membership in a national community. Too often nationality is conceived as existential or natural and thus as

having to do with what is mostly associated today with ethnicity. But as the great polyglot nations composed of many ethnicities but one nationality signify, nationality reflects a legal status best symbolized by the right to a passport or to vote. Such cases in point are the United States and India. Much confusion and controversy swirl around the concept of nationality since many seek to conflate nationality with ethnicity, particularly in situations in which specific groups within a state are being systematically suppressed or stigmatized. But the point remains: nationality is a function of law and legal status, not of human nature or cultural difference. Again, the single most direct way to interpret nationality is to suggest that it attaches to those members of a nation endowed with the status of a passport or legal certification as granted by the sovereign authorities of a state. Nationality represents the cultural elements of legal status, for example, the knowledge of language, the acceptance of duty and obligations, and the recognition of rights that stem from legal membership in a nation as determined by state authorities. In political-cultural terms, nationality represents a principle of commonality among citizens in terms of what they share in common by virtue of their citizenship in a nation. Not all citizens share in the same cultural heritage or background in their sense of self or in their attachments to the same subset of identity groups. On the contrary, most populations within nations manifest high levels of cultural distinctions among themselves. Such differences emerge differently depending on the political-cultural history of specific nation-state formations. These differences are described in terms of **ethnicity**, **race**, **religion**, **gender**, **class**, and so on. Some polities reveal high levels of heterogeneity with respect to these differences, others less so. Political cultures and the making of modern nation-states vary accordingly.

The political cultures of nation-states often reveal conflicts between concepts of nationality and difference. In these circumstances, cultural principles and dynamics of commonality vie against principles and dynamics of difference. When such tensions arise, the consequences are sometimes dire. Nationality is systematically distorted as the possession of some and not of others. Nationality becomes objectified as exclusionary and accessible only to some on a discriminatory basis rather than recognized as a measure of common values and shared participation within the political frameworks designed to embrace cultural difference. The result is that some citizens become disenfranchised. The rallying cry of Hutu extremists during the terrifying day of the Rwandan genocide was that Rwanda was for the Hutu alone and not for the Tutsi, although Tutsi citizens had shared in Rwandan nationality since the very beginning of the Rwandan state. The Holocaust against Jewish citizens of Germany revolved around spurious Nazi notions of Aryanism that alleged only those with Aryan blood and

Aryan genetic lines could be of German nationality, this despite the fact that Jews had been loyal citizens of the German nation-state since its very founding. The conflation of nationality with race or ethnicity denies not only the validity of nationality as the very basis for what is culturally common among the people of a nation, but also the validity of what is culturally different as perceived and valued among the citizens of any nation. When taken to extremes this conflation or collapse of nationality with race or ethnicity as the political ground on which to define cultural forms of acceptable or legal belonging in a national culture leads to political violence up to and including genocide and crimes against humanity.

Considerable violence attends the history of political culture in the making of modern nation-states precisely on account of the efforts by some identity groups to dominate or even to annihilate those whose differences become objectified or subordinated. In turn, those whose history is perceived as having been part of an **objectified identity group** sometimes revolt and seek to "capture" the state by making nationality an object of possession. Once this happens, the nation-state becomes torn by the political culture of **nativism**, an ideological expression that yearns for a past that glorifies a group or a cultural heritage in exclusionary and often violent ways, as was the case in Rwanda. This too is the result of historical processes. **Political violence** is often the outgrowth of political cultures that suffer from the consequences of **Anglo-European global colonialism** or from what is referred to as the **internal colonialism of the contact situation**, in which one political culture incorporated others in ways that subordinated them as in the case of Native Americans, African Americans, and Mexican/Chicano Americans. The relationship of political culture to political violence is variegated, as several cases examined below indicate. At their core remains the question of how the legitimacy of governance becomes historically settled or challenged.

Legitimacy of governance thus goes to the core of what we mean by political culture and the making of nation-states. Legitimacy in this context inheres in two sets of relationships: the first between centralized states and peoples who recognize in themselves the commonalities of a nation and nationality; the second between nationality as a cultural principle of commonality and cultural principles of difference. In a sense, the question of legitimacy swirls around statehood-nationhood and nationality-difference. One speaks, for example, of the United States as a sovereign state linked to the American people as a single nation composed of citizens who enjoy American nationality. But one also speaks of identity groups such as African Americans or Chicano Americans as cultural examples of what we mean by the ties between nationality-difference. These two sets of connected or hyphenated relationships represent prototypical examples that have emerged within numerous societies across the globe of modern nation-states.

Indeed, these are the relationships that define the focus on political culture and its significance for an understanding of the making of modern nation-states. The history is manifold and replete with great traditions and achievements. But it is also a story permeated by the tragedy of political violence and brutality and thus by inestimable degrees of human suffering.

Culture Shock

We tend to be most comfortable when enmeshed in the culture with which we are the most familiar. We are at ease when surrounded by people who think and act according to our own cultural norms. We are not surprised by behaviors that conform to our cultural traditions and values. Instead we are comforted when those around us reinforce our own tendencies, what we often call "instincts," relative to culture. When we are confronted by other cultures, however, we sometimes experience **culture shock**. Culture shock is the disorientation that accompanies our immersion in or introduction to a new set of cultural beliefs, traditions, and values. Culture shock can be most disconcerting when it occurs within our cultural "comfort zones," in the places where we least expect to be confronted with challenges to our own cultural roots. When we witness behaviors that offend our cultural sensibilities, even if they are appropriate within another cultural tradition, we can feel the discomfort, frustration, anxiety, and even anger that attend culture shock. We can become overwhelmed with the sense that the behavior is wrong. If we are on our own "turf," we can assume that the person practicing the behavior is an outsider, not an equal member of our community. If, however, we are the interlopers in a different cultural space, we can feel that we are the ones who do not belong. Culture shock can provoke defensive reactions that encourage us to cling to our own traditions and values as if they are threatened by the intrusion of competing cultural beliefs and practices. Or it can force reexamination of our own cultural attachments in ways that can lead to the adoption of altered value systems and norms.

Thus, in a very real sense, we all are the products of the culture in which we have been born and reared but in turn we are responsible for the cultural values we espouse and represent. From our infancy they surround, shape, and secure us. Ruth Benedict writes, "the life-history of the individual is first and foremost an accommodation to the patterns and standards traditionally handed down in his community. From the moment of his birth the customs into which he is born shape his experience and behaviour. By the time he can talk, he is the little creature of his culture, and by the time he is grown and able to take part in its

activities, its habits are his habits, its beliefs his beliefs, its impossibilities his impossibilities."[4] Given this, "no man ever looks at the world with pristine eyes. He sees it edited by a definite set of customs and institutions and ways of thinking. Even in his philosophical probings he cannot go behind these stereotypes; his very concepts of true and false will still have reference to his particular traditional customs."[5] What we do with those customs, and what they do through us, creates the fabric of social interaction and the roots of interpersonal relationships.

Ethnocentrism and Cultural Relativism

When confronted with new or different cultural traditions, values, or behaviors we may fall into one of two traps: ethnocentrism or cultural relativism. **Ethnocentrism** inheres in a set of beliefs or attitudes that assert that one's own culture is superior while all other cultures are, by extension, inferior. Persons gripped by ethnocentric views or opinions tend to judge, sometimes to condemn, different cultures or alternative cultural values through the lens of their own. In this, they perceive traditions, values, and practices other than their own against standards and sometimes prejudices set by their own value systems. In doing so, they risk falling into the traps of prejudgment and, thus, even prejudice. A sign of this is the assertion that other cultures are "primitive" or "backward." This reflects a failure to frame other cultural practices without understanding their motivations, intentions, or purposes.

Unlike ethnocentrism, **cultural relativism** adheres to the belief that cultural practices and traditions can never be judged critically. Cultural relativism is readily associated with **moral relativism**, a set of attitudes dismissive of any universal moral or ethical standard. This assumes that all cultural practices and values, regardless of their substance, are equally valid and thus defensible simply because they are justified within a culture. The problem with this kind of cultural relativism is that it can promote indifference to human suffering in the face of cruelty or oppression. The inferior role and status imposed on women in many cultures represent a set of issues in which relativism veers toward toleration of human subjugation, that is, toward acceptance of forms of brutality that must never be tolerated. Thus, it is one thing to attempt to understand a culture within the frames of its own meanings, but it is another to turn away from social injustices perpetrated by those who validate social practices on the basis of their own cultural values or traditions. As we shall see, many cultural practices—such as female genital mutilation, honor killings, discrimination, racism, sexism, nationalism, and ethnic cleansing—appear to be culturally acceptable but are

morally and ethically deplorable. Relativism does not make them morally right. In our efforts to better understand different cultures and to avoid the dangerous tendencies associated with ethnocentrism, it is essential that we also guard against the moral ambiguities that can attend attitudes of cultural relativism.

Culture, Anxiety, and the Denial of Death

We receive culture much as we receive life: from our bond with nurturing others. The oneness between child and nurturer begins in the womb and continues throughout infancy. Infants do not know how to distinguish between the self and the nurturing other. On the contrary, the self and the world are indistinguishable to the infant consciousness; the infant and the nurturer are one from the infant's perspective. Eventually children develop the capacity for an understanding of themselves as autonomous subjects among others in the world. Separation from the nurturing other becomes an essential project in the development of personhood, a critical moment in the enculturation process. The separation of the self from the nurturing other is inevitable. It is through this process of separation that human beings emerge as independent persons. Infants gradually become aware of a distinction between themselves and their nurturers. As they become aware of the boundary between themselves and others, they begin to develop a pervasive sense of vulnerability. Infants and the very young cannot survive independent of others. And yet, no matter how closely persons intertwine their lives with others, all human beings face life and death in their own skins, that is, as beings separate or distinct from others. One author has observed, for example, that for each of us "loneliness" is a way of life. This points toward a primal anxiety universal to the human condition. As Joan Riviere writes, "helplessness is the deepest source of anxiety in human beings."[6] Rollo May elaborates, "anxiety is the experience of the threat of imminent non-being.... Anxiety is not something we 'have' but something we 'are.'"[7] In that sense, "anxiety strikes at the center core of [our] self-esteem and [our] sense of value as a self.... Anxiety overwhelms the person's awareness of existence, blots out the sense of time, dulls the memory of the past, and erases the future."[8] Anxiety is who we are; it stands as a definitive and fundamental characteristic of the human condition from which no one can escape and with which we must struggle throughout our lives. It cannot be eliminated. As Paul Tillich writes, "it belongs to existence itself."[9] Culture responds to primal anxiety. Anxiety derives from the sense of nothingness, of loneliness in the human condition, of mortality. Culture lends life meaning and embeds

individuals within communities, even to the point that it foments a sense of immortality by means of cultural continuity. Through culture persons can deepen their senses of metaphysical meaning, transcendence, or uniqueness. As Ernest Becker writes, "each child grounds himself in some power that transcends him. Usually it is a combination of his parents, his social group, and the symbols of his society and nation. This is the unthinking web of support which allows him to believe in himself."[10] In this sense, "mankind has reacted [to anxiety] by trying to secure human meanings from beyond. Man's best efforts seem utterly fallible without appeal to something higher for justification, some conceptual support for the meaning of one's life from a transcendental dimension of some kind."[11]

This transcendental dimension lends cultural support for belief in values that vary from benign and benevolent to those that promote violence and various forms of malevolent behaviors especially toward those considered members of outside groups. The aspect of culture that compels ideological conviction adheres to this sense that it is possible to pursue a life that becomes "larger than life." Such cultural illusions appear to foment the personal delusions associated with certain radical forms of violence that are often religiously or ideologically inspired. These dynamics are complex and are often simplistically referred to in terms of "fundamentalism." But, broadly speaking, culture facilitates a sense of personal significance relative to the ways people identify themselves relative to the groups with which they identify. Culture, Becker teaches, conveys a sense of meaningfulness. He writes, "what man really fears is not so much extinction, but extinction *with insignificance.* Man wants to know that his life has somehow counted, if not for himself, then at least in a larger scheme of things, that he has left a trace, a trace that has meaning. . . . It is culture itself that embodies the transcendence of death.... It is the 'religion' that assures in some way the perpetuation of its members.... All [cultures] have in the end the same goal: to raise men above nature, to assure them that in some ways their lives count in the universe more than merely physical things count."[12] Therefore, although we "can never banish anxiety," writes Becker, "what [we] can do instead is to use anxiety as an eternal spring for growth into new dimensions of thought and trust."[13] He concludes, "the child meets the terror of life and aloneness ... by using [culture] as the vehicle for his immortality."[14] Culture is immediate and concrete, but it is also the instrumentality by and through which we create symbols in ways that provide the sense of a possibility to become aligned with the eternal and everlasting. In the power of its immediacy and in the power of its invitation to symbolic transcendence, culture represents the ultimate set of values that guides desire. In so doing it is able to relieve human anxiety. This is especially true of

political culture that grounds collective belonging, governance, and authority. This grounding often entails the symbols and rituals of power and glory.

Symbols and Collective Cultural Meaning

Symbols and rituals serve as mechanisms within social order that reduce anxiety and the pervasive sense of meaninglessness associated with fears of spiritual emptiness and physical dissolution. This further highlights how symbols and rituals help to sustain beliefs in intergenerational continuity. Cultural meanings attached to symbols and rituals allow members of a community to feel and believe that their lives and their deaths are grounded in the continuities symbolized and ritualized through cultural values, institutions, and traditions. Thus culture is to continuity what anxiety is to dissolution. Political culture, in particular, reinforces the sense of bonding and belonging in a collective order that transcends the person. In those cases, where political culture is inconsistent or unaligned with any individual's or group's sense of standing or identity, political culture can fall into the traps of conflict and violence. How, when, and why this happens represent central questions in the study of political culture and the making of modern nation-states.

The word "symbol" derives from a Latin term meaning "ticket." Symbols transport us into a different realm and ground our being in a reality beyond the immediate material world. They represent meanings that transcend immediate and material existence. They are more than utilitarian signs. They evoke deep feelings and convictions. The American flag, for example, may be seen as a symbol of freedom and equal rights by citizens of the United States. Alternatively, it may be seen as a symbol of imperialism and military oppression. Similarly, the Muslim star and crescent moon may be seen as a symbol of a beautiful religious tradition or it may be seen as a symbol of terror and violence. Our interpretation of symbols, much like our construction of them, depends on our cultural roots, political beliefs, and ethical values.

Rituals are repeated, prescribed, and formalized affirmations of cultural values by means of standardized utterances and practices. Rituals demarcate the life of the community in words, music, song, and dance, as well as through symbolic representations. Many cultural rituals deploy the human body as an instrumentality designed to attain a sense of the sacred. Body identification through scarring, tattooing, cutting, and circumcision may be used to reinforce the critical sense of intergenerational continuity grounded in the rites of passage that transform human physicality into the instrument of the "beyond physical" or sacred realm. Rituals and rites of passage that demarcate the passing of a person's

life play an important social role, especially in traditional communities. In many cultures, rituals and rites of passage pertaining to birth, marriage, reproduction, sexuality, transition into adulthood, and eventual death serve sacred purposes designed to ensure the symbolic continuity of cultural survival, despite the ravages of physical decay.

Birth represents the beginning of life and the initial stage in many cultural rites of passage. All cultures develop traditions with respect to birth and childbearing. Who is present during the birth of a child? Is the child born at home or in a hospital? Is the mother permitted to cry out during the birth or is she expected to remain silent? Who cares for the mother and infant after the birth? Are the mother and her child isolated from the community or surrounded by family and friends? What is done with the afterbirth? Is it buried beneath the threshold of the home in order to tie the child to home and community? Is it eaten to represent the continuity of generations? Is it cryogenically saved for use in future medical treatments? Or is it devoid of symbolic meaning and thus discarded as medical waste? Cultures answer these questions in different ways. What is normal for one culture may be wholly foreign to another. For example, in many societies today, colostrum (the mother's "first milk") is believed to be the most nutritious substance that can be fed to a newborn baby. New mothers in these cultures nurse their babies immediately, feeding colostrum until the breast milk comes in. In traditional Sioux culture, on the other hand, a new baby was often not fed the colostrum because it was generally considered to be poisonous. Erik Erikson explains that "the Indian women maintained that it was not right to let a baby do all the initial work only to be rewarded with a thin, watery substance. The implication was clear: how could he trust a world which greeted him thus?"[15] Instead, the child was given the juice of the best berries and herbs while the colostrum was "sucked out of the breast and the breast stimulated to do efficient work by certain older women who had been commanded in their dreams to perform this office."[16] Furthermore, while mothers in modern society often turn to formula to supplement their infants' diets, breast milk in traditional Sioux cultures has tended to be considered communal property and thus women regularly breastfeed others' children on demand.

Thus birth and infancy become a metaphor that grounds cultural continuity. Cultures formulate many ways of confirming membership in a community. Baptism and naming ceremonies are often used to officially welcome an infant into the communal bond. For example, a Christian minister baptizes an infant, symbolizing the child's initiation into a religious community; a Jewish baby is readied for the brit milah, the circumcision ceremony performed on eight-day-old male infants; and a Muslim male receives the ***khitan*** or ***khatna*** circumcision

rite at various ages to underscore the entry of the child into the broader community of the faithful.

Even beyond infancy belonging is manifested in a wide variety of ritualistic forms and institutions. In the next chapter we will explore rituals associated with marriage, reproduction, and child rearing. But, like birth traditions, death rituals are universal to all cultures. Many cultures believe in the soul and immortality, and thus death is often treated as a transition, a rite of passage designed to attenuate that anxiety generated by our inevitable passing. In many cultures, death is not viewed as a single event, but rather as a process whereby the deceased are slowly transferred from the land of the living to the land of the dead. Thus rituals serve as mechanisms that relieve anxiety by indicating symbolically the linkage between cultural continuity and intergenerational meaning. Death throws into relief the most important cultural values by which people live their lives and evaluate their experiences. Some cultures permit weeping while some require calm. Some require the cremation of the body while others require burial or internment. In some cultures a funeral is a boisterous celebration of life lived while in others it is a solemn occasion marking the end of life's journey. From birth to death our lives are punctuated by rituals and rites of passage endowed with symbolic meanings. Together they shape our personal identity construction, grounding us in communal practices and collective cultures. As we learn who we are unto ourselves and within the world, we build on the foundations of cultural traditions, rituals, and values. Thus culture is the essential guide in **identity construction**, the process by which we imbue our lives with cosmic self-worth.

Identities as Projections of the Self in the World

As we move beyond infancy we begin to grapple with the quest for personhood, identities, status, and self-worth. In this process, notions of self and identity frame personhood and self-worth. The **self** represents all of who we are as we live moment to moment, day to day, across the span of our personal consciousness. The self is the "I," the authentic core of personhood. It is who we are for ourselves when there is no one watching. It is the entirety of what we are, known only to ourselves. As Gary Allen Fine writes, the self is "the dimension of personality composed of the individual's self-conception."[17] In contrast, **identity** refers to projections of the self into the world in terms of the multiple public demands that together define the complex array of roles human beings assume throughout a lifetime. Identities represent the many changing public aspects of the self. They are the "social self," the "self directed outward." They speak to how a person

ALTERNATE PERSPECTIVES

Identity

An individual understands his or her identity by asking questions such as "Who am I?" but also "Who are we?" For identity is not only about personal introspection. It is also about group attachments and their meanings. Identities demand to be recognized by others, whether to create a sense of belonging or to establish notions of difference or distinction. For example, Montserrat Guibernau writes about **national identity**, stating that it is a "collective sentiment based on the belief of belonging to the same nation and of sharing most of the attributes that make it distinct from other nations."[18] Furthermore, Guibernau argues that there are various psychological, cultural, and historical dimensions of national identity that shape an individual's understanding of himself and his membership in his community. Along these lines, Ross Poole argues that national identity is the primary form of modern identity.[19] He cites historical patterns of action and discourse that prompt individuals in various contexts and situations to place the nation ahead of the demands of religion, political identification, and even morality.

According to Poole, national identity can make claims on the individual that are unique compared to other forms of identity. Appeals to national identity can legitimate conscription into military service or even prompt citizens to voluntarily enlist in the armed forces. In both cases, individuals are willing to sacrifice their lives, not in the name of God or king, but of their nation.

How people identify themselves as individuals and members of groups depends on the culture in which they live. In primordial communities, understandings of identity are deeply rooted in notions of **lineage**, **ancestry**, **honor**, and **shame**. In modern societies, identities are more often based on individual achievement as well as membership in or attachment to various national, ethnic, racial, political, religious, or economic groups.

"fits into a social location," how we "classify ourselves" and become classified, as well as how we "present ourselves to others."[20] As a result of identity, we say this is who we are in the world at this moment and within a concrete public context. Identity encompasses all social projections of the self. Identity represents the "I" in relation to the "many me's." As we shape our identities, they shape us. They allow us to say "this is who I am" at this moment and in this particular context.

Throughout our lives we construct and convey many different, sometimes conflicting, identities. That is to say, we project ourselves into the world in different ways in different contexts with different groups of people. We may be sons and daughters, husbands and wives, mothers and fathers, workers, laborers, and career professionals all at once, projecting ourselves differently as we act out each of our given roles. And yet each of these identities is constituted through culture. We learn how to behave, think, and be according to cultural rules, values, and traditions.

The quest for cosmic self-worth undertaken by all individuals is embedded in the relationship between the self and its identities. Do my identities reflect my authentic self? Do I like the identities I project into the world? What legacy will I leave behind when I succumb to mortality? Does my life have meaning? How we feel about ourselves and how we project ourselves into the world depend on the relationships we have with others. As Fine writes, the self "develops from relationships.... The self is neither present at birth nor a natural consequence of child development, but emerges from the responses of others. It is because others respond to you that you come to believe that you have a distinct self and that this self is meaningful."[21] As we construct our identities, as we find where we fit in social settings, we are challenged to find balance between two driving forces: direction and passion. Both passion and direction can drive us as we project identities into the world. But lives filled with all passion and no direction or with all direction and no passion are only half lived. When we surrender ourselves to absolute **passion**, we risk falling into the trap of the "**infinity of possibilities**." We imagine so many possible projected identities that we condemn ourselves to fantasy and become paralyzed in the real world. We are unable to make choices and decisions because to choose is to reject one set of possibilities for another and we need to cling to every possibility imaginable in order to give our lives meaning. When captured by absolute **direction**, however, we risk the alienation that comes from assuming the behaviors and actions of the persons we are supposed to be rather than who we "really" are. When we live lives dictated by direction without passion, we go through the motions, doing what we are expected to do, but without inner meaning or significance. What meaning we do find comes from the approval and acknowledgment of others. We feed on accolades from outside sources to validate our choices, decisions, and actions. We feel that we cannot be loved or appreciated for our authentic selves and so we construct identities that call forth the love and recognition that we come to believe we need to survive. We "sell out" for an adored public identity. But while the world loves us, we mourn for our suppressed selves. In both passion and direction we learn that identity is a public, communal construction. Through

culture we create ourselves both as individuals and as members of groups. We learn whom it is we are supposed to love, whom to hate, who belongs to our groups and who does not, and, above all, who we are and how we fit into collective life. Thus, culture grounds our understandings of who we are and who we are in the world. It is through culture that our identities are constructed.

Cultural Constructions of Collective Identity

Self and identity construction are social processes imbedded in culture. As Fine writes, "who you are is a function of how others see you."[22] Much of our individual identity construction, therefore, derives meaning from cultural constructions of collective identity. Often associated with race, ethnicity, class, religion, gender, nationality, and other cultural categories, collective identities situate us within social settings. This informs us about what rules or norms we are to follow. Thus, culture shapes our understandings of the self but also endows the structures of public identity with meaning. **Cultural constructions** refer to the values, institutions, and dynamics through which collective identities emerge. Thus, collective identity reflects the groups to which we belong as we identify with them. Collective identity includes social commitments at deep and intense levels of self-understanding, from our community to our religion, our ethnicity, and our nationality. Collective identities are constructed through shared beliefs, values, habits, customs, norms, and traditions associated with common heritage, background, and lineage. We learn how to act and react in social settings from the culture that shapes our collective identities. As Fine writes, "responding appropriately [to social situations] bolsters your public identity and demonstrates that you appreciate the rules of your community."[23]

In the chapters that follow we trace cultural constructions of collective identity throughout human history. We begin with the earliest human societies—**traditional kinship communities**. We then examine **dynastic** and **feudal kingdoms**. Finally, we study modern sovereign nation-states. In each manifestation of human society we discover a different set of cultural values, traditions, and institutions. **Belonging** is conceptualized differently across the annals of human history as are such political values as **legitimacy, governance**, and **collective identity construction**. As we will see, the making of the modern world transformed traditional kinship communities into a political geography of **sovereign nation-states** with new sets of social pressures and political-cultural demands. This historic process often culminated in various forms of political violence, including civil wars and revolutions.

Chapter 2
Kinship Communities as Political Cultures

Confrontations with Fragility in an Eternal Now

Kinship communities represent the oldest and longest-lasting form of social, cultural, political, and economic belonging and political identity. Encompassing bands, clans, and tribes, these communities are characterized by fragility, resource dependence, and focus on intergenerational survivability and ecological sustainability. Structured, governed, and disciplined to resolve the problem of resource scarcity, kinship descent communities live according to communal rules, rituals, and obligations grounded in blood ties, segmented family lineage, and ancestral descent. These cultural values often emphasize unity, fairness, reciprocal exchange, and mutual support as well as shared property and common fate. Kinship communities stand as an early form of human culture, social organization, and political bonding. Many persist across the globe. From the Australian aborigines to Native Americans and from the Hutu of Rwanda to the Roma of Eastern Europe, kinship cultures continue to have profound impact on the contemporary world and its politics. Much political conflict today stems from the continuing influences of kinship values embedded in traditions of descent, honor, and shame. Often those in the Western world speak of "failed states" when they think they see the inability to form a central government or to govern peacefully across a national territory. But such judgment is facile and often made without sufficient understanding of the lingering hold of traditional legitimacy attached to what we call patrimonial governance associated with kinship and segmented lineage. The making of the modern world includes various forms of cultural resistance to nation-states as a political formation. An understanding

of kinship and of the role that honor and shame continue to play as political-cultural values thus remains a critical aspect of analysis focused on the emergence of modern nation-states.

Each kinship culture is unique, but most require the careful husbanding of resources and the strict regulation of inheritance in order to survive. The political economy of kinship communities varies, but it tends to be dependent on local ecological conditions. Kinship rules, including marriage practices and inheritance laws, often reflect land use patterns and resource dependencies. Village settlements and residential patterns tend to reveal the problems associated with scarcity. From nomadic foraging to horticulture to animal husbandry to small-scale peasant farming, kinship communities attempt to survive in the face of economic scarcity and/or environmental pressures. Ancestrally based governance structures and practices thus often enforce communal disciplines in order to promote intergenerational survival.

Ancestry and Descent in Traditional Kinship Communities

Within kinship communities, power and **legitimacy**, the right to govern or rule, derive directly from the ancestors to whom all good fortune is owed. As Ernest Becker writes, for primordial man, death is "considered the final promotion of the soul to a state of superhuman power and indefinite durability."[1] That is to say, it is "often the dead who [have] the most power. In life the individual goes through ritualistic passages to states of higher power and greater importance as helper of life.... Death is the final promotion to the highest power of all."[2] In this sense, the dead remain a living presence in primordial communities. They act as metaphysical guides and sacred promoters of communal survival. As Becker continues, primordial life is "openly immersed in debt, in obligation to the invisible powers, the ancestors, the dead souls."[3] Thus communities live by "drawing [their] powers from the non-living."[4]

Because kinship communities are embedded in notions and memories of ancestry, each member's identity, belonging, and status in the group are determined by his or her relationship to a specified ancestor through blood or marriage. Whereas the cultures of societies associated with modern nation-states structure social position in terms of economic class, or social and professional standings that in varying degrees reflect achievement-oriented values and institutions, traditional kinship communities, even those that exist today, tend to determine status according to **blood lineage**. In such kinship communities, therefore, economic, social, and political identities are a function of **descent** and are **ascribed** from

birth rather than achieved as a function of individual achievement, creativity, initiative, merit, or other such personal attributes.

To sustain communal integrity and order, descent communities employ a wide range of symbolic interactions that, far from being merely iconic, are aimed at bringing ancestors into life. Through dance, music, and art, ancestors appear as essential forces in determining the fate of the descent group and are believed to confer their strength upon the living members of the community. For example, the use of **totems**, animals, or other natural figures that represent ancestral figures and lineage systems bestows on the dead the mystery of their reincarnated physical presence. **Totem poles** are sometimes meant to document the ancestry of a community and to allow the power of the dead to aid the living. Similarly, many Asian cultures represent ancestors in family shrines or temples, carving their names upon the temple itself and incorporating ancestral worship into their spiritual and religious traditions and rituals. In these cultures, families are understood to be a united group of relatives, that is, both the living and the dead. Shrines to the dead are sometimes kept both in the home and in the clan's ancestral temple.

Because kinship communities are vertically grounded in notions and memories of ancestry, one's identity, belonging, and status in a descent group are often determined by a person's relationship to a specified ancestor. Genealogy is commonly traced through the lineage of blood or ancestors. If genealogy is traced through females, the society is said to be **matrilineal**. If it is traced through males, the society is considered **patrilineal**. Both matrilineal and patrilineal kinship/descent communities, however, tend to be dominated by male tribal elders. Such forms of legitimacy, control, or regulation must confront the problems that arise as a consequence of limited resources in order to promote communal survival, especially in light of fragile environmental sustainability. Marriage serves to resolve a range of issues that emerge with respect to transfers of resources across generations. Such transfers occur as a result of either **consanguineal** (by blood) or **affinal** (by marriage, called by Western cultures "in-law") connections. How resource transfers occur is often determined by kinship rules, practices, and obligations, and such kinship rules are often designed to protect intergenerational survivability. But they can also become obsolete by provoking conflict and by deepening poverty.

Marriage Practices in Kinship and Descent Communities

Regulated marriage and child rearing can become essential cultural "tools" in communities that confront resource scarcity. The rules governing marriage

KEY CONCEPTS

Legitimacy

Legitimacy is the right of a political authority to rule. There are two kinds of political legitimacy—external and internal. A country with **external legitimacy** is one that is recognized as sovereign by other states in the international community. In today's world, this generally means that a state has been invited to join the international community of states at the **United Nations**. In some cases, however, the international community is divided on the question of recognition. Kosovo, for example, declared its independence from Serbia in 2008. By 2013 it had received recognition from 108 countries, including the United States, Australia, Saudi Arabia, France, Great Britain, Germany, Egypt, Pakistan, Japan, and South Korea. It had not been recognized, however, by other major world powers, including Russia, China, India, Iran, and Brazil. These countries still consider Kosovo to be a part of Serbia. Kosovo's status as a sovereign state, therefore, is debatable.

Internal legitimacy refers to the right of political leaders to rule over its citizens or subjects. Internal legitimacy can derive from a variety of sources. For example, in **primordial communities** legitimacy derives from kinship, blood ties, and ancestry. In modern **nation-states**, legitimacy derives from the principles of **popular consent** of the governed. Moreover, a wide array of political systems can be legitimate. Monarchies, dictatorships, democracies, and theocracies can all function with various degrees of support that render them in effect "legitimate" forms of government.

Legitimacy crises have defined the political history of many sovereign states. In 1688 the **Glorious Revolution** in England overthrew King James II and replaced him with William of Orange and his wife, Mary II. This revolution, engineered by Parliament, initiated parliamentary democracy and limited monarchy in England. A year after the revolution, the English

continued

appear to have become adjusted in the course of time to the realities of limited agricultural resources. Kinship communities thus practice a wide variety of marriage and child-rearing practices, but the objective of these diverse traditions is to manage land use and to control resources in ways that secure the survival of the community as a whole. In communities linked by blood where rule and governance are legitimated by ancestry and descent, structures and institutions

Bill of Rights specifically divided power between Parliament and the monarchy and guaranteed basic political rights to all Englishmen. This laid the foundation for the **American Revolution** in 1776. The **French Revolution** in 1789 overthrew the French monarchy and established a republican system of government based on the ideals of liberty, equality, and fraternity or "brotherhood." Based on the political philosophies of the Enlightenment, the French Revolution emphasized the right of the people to choose their system of government and, if necessary, by way of bringing about political change, to overthrow a royal regime, violently if necessary, and thus to destroy the principles of legitimacy associated with classical kings. The Napoleonic Wars that followed the French Revolution spread many of these liberal ideas across Europe thus setting the stage for similar revolutions in Russia, Germany, and the Austro-Hungarian Empire.

Contemporary legitimacy crises include those associated with the **Arab Spring**, a wave of revolutions, demonstrations, protests, riots, and civil wars that began in December 2010. Three years after the revolutions began, leaders had been forced from power in Tunisia, Egypt, Libya, and Yemen while revolutions plagued Bahrain and Syria. Major protests besieged Algeria, Iraq, Jordan, Kuwait, Morocco, and Sudan, while minor protests occurred in Mauritania, Saudi Arabia, Djibouti, Western Sahara, and the Palestinian Authority. Regime changes resulted in several states, often leading to a second wave of crises as nations sought to choose new leaders. This has produced mixed results at best in terms of legitimacy since internal conflicts continue to be waged throughout the region very much as the result of deep cultural divisions over the right to rule and the legitimacy of governance. In Iraq and Syria even the role of centralized authority and the legitimacy of constituted sovereign borders are now being contested. Such threats and challenges point to the very core of what legitimacy crises signify. They also serve to underscore the significance of political culture in examining today's conflicts not only in the Middle East but throughout the contemporary world.

must exist to incorporate nonaffiliated members through marriage ties but in ways that support communal survival.

Optimally, kinship marriages by design or fate work in ways aimed at linking families together in order to maximize available resources and to ensure that these are transferred among communal members and families according to effective and equitable distributions. For this reason, kinship communities may use **arranged** marriages controlled by tribal leaders. In many cases women are

married to older men who in rare benevolent circumstances enjoy some degree of economic security and the social status necessary for responsibilities associated with a wife (or wives) and children. Although women given in marriage must often provide a **dowry**, an amount of money or property that the wife brings to the marriage, men occasionally are made to demonstrate that they are able to support a family before they are permitted to marry. Such dynamics operate differently and with varying degrees of success in terms of the marriage partnership depending on the culture and the extent to which the parties are mired in poverty.

Kinship rules governing marriage tend to revolve around the dynamics of **exogamy** or **endogamy**. "Gamy" stands for marriage. **Exogamous** marriages require that families and groups extend their marriage selection pools outside of the immediate clan toward wider social networks. Exogamous practices promote conflict resolutions among diverse clans within a descent or kinship community and incorporate new economic resources into the community. **Endogamous** marriages, on the other hand, restrict the pools of potential candidates and limit partners to those from within the kinship lines, groups, or regions. Endogamous practices tend to encourage group solidarity and to ensure greater control over what tends to be highly limited resources because such cultures reinforce inclusiveness against those beyond the tribe or clan who might bring new or additional resources to the marriage relationship and thus communal resource base.

In addition, while marriages in the cultures of modern nation-states are almost universally monogamous, kinship marriage rules do include **polygamous** practices. In **polygyny** a man is permitted to take multiple wives. Because polygyny enables communities to replenish their numbers rapidly, it tends to occur in communities in which group survival depends on high birthrates. It is also common when warfare leads to a gender imbalance in which there are many women of childbearing age but comparatively few men. Alternatively, kinship communities can adopt **polyandrous** practices, that is, the marriage of one woman to several men. Although polyandry is far less common than polygyny, it is also used to manage resources in economically fragile societies. Polyandry is common when communities confront extreme land scarcities that require low birth rates to impede the division of land across generations. Under these conditions, intergenerational survival depends on strict population control and inheritance management.

This was the case in Tibet. Tibetan fraternal polyandry worked similarly to the European system of **primogeniture** in which the eldest male offspring would inherit the estate while the younger males would be forced to leave home to seek employment, generally either in the military or in the clergy. But the Tibetan system had the advantage of a single heir, or set of heirs, per generation

combined with the economic security that came from keeping brothers together to work the land. Ernest Van Den Haag describes the economic justifications for Tibetan polyandry, linking the practice to European land divisions and resources transfer. He writes, "Tibetans have too few resources to keep dividing them up. When brothers stay home and share a wife, the family is stable from generation to generation. If no sons are born in a certain generation, a daughter can perpetuate the household by taking husbands. Conservative Tibetans think polyandry is the best system morally, of course. They point out that it works against selfishness, since it stresses the family above the individual."[5]

Kinship marriage practices ultimately revolve around property rights and sustainability across generations. In these ways, arranged kinship marriages may perpetuate communal devotion to the group as a whole. As with all kinship practices, the good of the group is meant to supersede the will of the individual. In the discussion of kinship rites of passage below we shall learn how children are integrated into this communal perspective throughout their lives and how they are constantly tested to ensure that they are willing and able to put the needs of the group above their desires as individuals. For, as we shall see, members of the community who violate the rules of arranged marriage or fail to complete the required rites of passage are sometimes perceived to threaten the practical bases on which the survival of the group depends. As a result, kinship disciplines can be very harsh and include ostracism or even death. Individuals who place their desires over communal unity are no longer deemed members of the group who can be trusted with the fate of the community.

Rites of Passage in Kinship Descent Communities

Kinship cultures combine segmented lineage orders and kinship rules typically designed to preserve the survivability of the group as a whole. Thus, there are cultural practices in the segmented divisions that promote unity across the entire community. The legitimacy of patrimonial rule beholden to various cultures of paternal governance and its prerogatives is ultimately grounded in that sense of unity. Because kinship legitimacy is embedded in ancestry and descent, kinship communities live according to highly symbolic rituals and rules that establish intergenerational linkages and communicate intergenerational meanings. Ritualized forms of the **rites of passage** that are repeated and prescribed represent the formalized affirmations of values communicated by means of culturally standardized utterances and actions. Failure to complete a prescribed rite of passage often results in economic penalties, ostracism, or worse. This occurs because such failures indicate that a group member cannot be trusted on account of

dishonoring the ancestors, who must then be justly compensated since they are directly responsible or at least influential in insuring group survival.

Symbols and symbolic practices demarcate the lives of individuals as members of the kinship communities in accordance with ritualized rites of passage. These occur from birth to death in ways that anchor group members by giving them a sense of who they are in relation to not only the kinship community, but also the ancestors. As Becker writes, ritualized rites of passage, "which [take] place at birth, puberty, marriage, and death," transform communal members by encouraging them to become endowed with the sense of "new states of being ... by means of symbolically dying and being reborn via the ritual."[6] Through ritualized rites of passage, kinship identities, ascribed from birth, are crafted and cemented together as cultural traditions according to which group members live their lives. The rituals that promote kinship unity imbue each member with the conviction that the community is more important than its composite parts. Traditions require that members of kinship communities reaffirm their commitment to their communal identity throughout their lifetimes.

The Maasai are a seminomadic primordial people living in Kenya and Northern Tanzania. Although the governments of Kenya and Tanzania have encouraged them to abandon their traditional lifestyle, the Maasai continue to practice their way of life. After the rite of passage, Maasai men are permitted to marry and become fathers. This is a stage of life that allows warriors to transition to elder status.

Before the rite of passage every warrior must shave his head. They must raise eight bulls to be distributed to the elders at the ceremony. During the event, an animal horn is set on fire and the "warriors are forced to take a piece out before it is completely burned. No one wants to take the piece out, because whoever takes the horn out of the fire will suffer [misfortune] throughout his entire life. However, if warriors refuse to take the horn out from the fire, the entire age-set will be cursed. It is better for one person to be unfortunate than many."[7] This perspective is common to kinship communities: it is essential that every member of the community be willing to sacrifice himself for the good of the whole. Rites of passage focus on self-discipline, communal unity, and the subordination of the individual's desires to kinship rule. Only the elders have the power to govern the community. Again, what is critical is that no member of the clan or tribe assert his own will above that of his elders. Even after a Maasai warrior has completed the ritual circumcision that makes him a man he must defer to his father's wishes. Saitoti writes, "Your father is paramount while he is alive and you are obligated to respect him."[8] A man can rebel against his father's wishes and rules but he will be severely punished for such violation of patrimonial rule.

ALTERNATE PERSPECTIVES

Male and Female Circumcision

For many cultures, circumcision is a ritualized rite of passage. For the male, circumcision involves the removal of some or all of the foreskin. Some cultures practice infant male penile circumcision like the Jewish brit milah (bris), while others, such as the Maasai, use it as a coming of age ritual that bonds the male child to the community. Islamic circumcision does not proceed according to strict rules and traditions as in the Jewish ceremonial rite. The *khitān* or *khatna* is applied at various ages: at birth, at puberty, or at the moment when mastery of the Koran is demonstrated. But it occurs to underscore the relationship of each of the faithful to the entire Islamic community.

For the female, practices of so-called circumcision involve genital mutilation. Female genital mutilation (FGM) involves partial or total removal of external female genitalia by means of incisions, removal of flesh, and, in severe forms, closures of the vagina. As a consequence of such violations, passage of bodily fluids becomes restricted. The physical pain is extreme as is the psychological and emotional sense of humiliation. FGM tends to be applied as a coming of age ritual undertaken at the beginning of puberty, contributing eventually to the pain, risks, and difficulties of childbirth.

FGM has been widely condemned as an abhorrent practice. In July 2014, the British government, for example, announced at a UNICEF conference called the Girls Summit, that parents allowing FGM to occur within England and Wales would be subject to criminal prosecution. We spoke earlier about extending the precepts of cultural relativism too far and of the moral and ethical obligation to condemn practices that degrade the human body and are demeaning to the human spirit. FGM constitutes a systematic violation of the dignity of the human person. It represents violence against women wherever and however it is practiced. It constitutes nothing less than a crime against humanity. It leads to lifelong pain and emotional as well as physical suffering. Nevertheless, FGM is an ongoing cultural ritual routinely applied in at least twenty-nine African

continued

Honor and Shame Disciplines

Honor and shame serve as the foundation of communal disciplines used to secure obedience to traditional practices that promote communal survival and unity. New generations throughout the cultures of descent and kinship communities

and Middle Eastern countries. The vast majority of women in the following countries have undergone FGM: Somalia, Ethiopia, Eritrea, Egypt, Sudan, Burkina Faso, Liberia, Sierra Leone, Guinea, Mali, and Mauritania. It is also practiced within immigrant communities in the United States and Europe. The numbers of women subjected to it are staggering. Approximately 125 million women and girls in Africa and the Middle East have experienced FGM. Despite its demeaning personal consequences, it remains widely supported by men and often by women in the communities that practice it. Many see it as a necessary coming of age ritual associated with purity, modesty, and honor. In many communities where it is considered to be an essential step in the transition from childhood to adulthood, it is treated as a prerequisite for marriage.

The Maasai practice FGM as well as male circumcision. In recent years, however, community leaders have promoted an alternative rite of passage for Maasai girls that celebrates their transition from childhood to adulthood but does not involve circumcision. The first alternative ceremony was held in August 2012. Fifty-two Maasai girls participated. The program emphasizes the importance of health, education, empowerment, and leadership among Maasai girls. At the end of a weeklong workshop, the community gathers to celebrate the girls in song and dance as they make their transition to womanhood. The Alternative Rite of Passage campaign began with Africa Schools of Kenya. Teri Gabrielsen, the executive director of the program, says that it is a model of the eradication of the practice of FGM for the rest of Africa.

Male circumcision, a historically less controversial practice, is also facing increased scrutiny. In 2014 Denmark became the first European country to consider a ban on the circumcision of underage boys. The Danish Society of Family Physicians equated the practice with mutilation while the Danish Medical Association recommended that elective male circumcision should be prohibited until a young man is able to consent to the procedure. In most European, Asian, and Latin American countries, less than 20 percent of the male population is circumcised. According to the World Health Organization, rates of male circumcision are also dropping in the United States, Canada, Australia, and New Zealand.

learn to accept the legitimacy of patrimonial rule grounded in ancestry, the authority of segmented lineage, and the demands of arranged marriages and ritualized rites of passage by means of enculturation processes linked to honor and shame. **Honor** protects kinship traditions and practices against individualistic motivations, desires, and intentions that might undermine or threaten

intergenerational communal survival. **Shame** condemns those who bring dishonor to their families and ancestors. In kinship cultures, honor attaches to the ancestors who are the givers, sustainers, and protectors of communal life. For this reason, family honor becomes valued both as a means to an end and as an end unto itself. The notions of "face" and "saving face" revolve around the need to protect family honor and the family name, often at any cost.

Within kinship cultures, honor is accorded to those deemed loyal to blood and kin. Thus, honor is a communal discipline bestowed upon members of a lineage system whose obedience and triumphs bring glory to the ancestors and to the blood ties that connect successive generations together. It promotes social cohesion as well as cultural conformity. Shame, however, is unleashed upon individuals who violate, undermine, or question the demands of patrimonial rule or traditional values. When confronted by shame, kinship communities must establish mechanisms to restore honor and the order that honor represents. In these situations, shame "faces" the ancestors who "look down" upon the father and his agents to rectify the wrong committed against the communal structure. And because kinship cultures are rooted in the blood ties of segmented lineage, the price of shame must often be paid in blood.

This explains, but does not justify, the ancient practice of **honor killing**, a practice that persists in the modern world. Often exercised against women who violate the presumed moral mandates of kinship rule either by rejecting an arranged marriage or by having illicit relations, honor killings spill the blood of the individual in order to appear to restore family honor. As Suzanne Ruggi writes, "what the men of the family, clan, or tribe seek control of in a patrilineal society is reproductive power. Women for the tribe were considered a factory for making men. The honor killing is not a means to control sexual power or behavior. What's behind it is the issue of fertility, or reproductive power."[9] True to the structure of traditional kinship descent communities, honor killings are a form of communal discipline. Women and sometimes men are executed by members of their own families in order to demonstrate to the community at large that family honor has been restored.

Human Rights Watch defines honor killings as "murders generally perpetrated by family members against women and girls who have entered into a relationship with a man not condoned by the family, or are suspected of so doing."[10] The organization details honor killings in countries around the world. For example, "in 2003, a man fatally stabbed his daughter twenty-five times because she refused to tell him where she had been following a three-week absence. In 2002, a man killed his sister after seeing her 'talking to a strange man during a wedding party.' In 2001, a man killed his sister 'after seeing a man leave her house.'" In

many countries "a woman's life is at risk if she engages in 'immoral or shameful' acts, such as talking with a man not her husband or a blood relative (even in a public place), or refusing to tell a close male relative where she has been and with whom, or marrying someone of whom her family does not approve: in short for doing or being imputed to have done anything that, in traditional terms, is perceived to bring sexual dishonor on herself and therefore on her family."[11] In these societies, "Male relatives may beat, shoot, stab, or otherwise physically harm an accused woman, with the approval of both her family members and large sections of the general population. Police rarely investigate 'honor' killings, seldom take any initiative to deter these crimes, and typically treat the killers as vindicated men."[12] Katherine Zoepf explains that perpetrators of honor killings often use a "colloquial expression, *ghasalat al arr* (washing away the shame), which means the killing of a woman or girl whose very life has come to be seen as an unbearable stain on the honor of her male relatives. Once this kind of familial sexual shame has been 'washed,' the killing is traditionally forgotten as quickly as possible."[13] She continues, "under Syrian law, an honor killing is not murder, and the man who commits it is not a murderer. As in many other Arab countries, even if the killer is convicted on the lesser charge of a 'crime of honor,' he is usually set free within months. Mentioning the killing—or even the name of the victim—generally becomes taboo."[14] Although often associated with Muslim societies, honor killings are prevalent wherever kinship rules and disciplines persist in the modern world. They occur frequently in Africa, the Middle East, and South Asia, but have also been known to happen in Europe and the Americas. They are especially common in India where Human Rights Watch estimates that several thousands of honor killings are committed each year. Often perpetrated against women and men who marry against the dictates of the caste system, Indian officials often pass the deaths off as suicides, natural deaths, or accidents and do not investigate or prosecute the killers.

But the violence is not contained within countries that permit—either by law or by practice—honor killings. In 2002 Fadime Sahindal was killed by her father. She belonged to a family of Kurdish immigrants who had lived in Sweden for more than twenty years. She was killed for having a relationship with a Swedish man, a relationship that violated the rules of her family and clan. In the investigation and court case that followed, kinship rules crashed against modern legal structures in ways that challenged the legitimacy of both. Unlike their Middle Eastern and African counterparts, European legal systems do not reflect the cultural dynamics of honor and shame that come to the fore in honor killings. In this context, "justice" becomes a complicated concept. For many Swedes, justice required that Fadime's father be punished for his crime. For the

Kurdish community, the requirements of justice had been met by the honor killing itself. Tensions between cultures attached to values of honor and shame within traditional kinship descent communities structured around segmented lineage and clans and those cultures attached to values of guilt and merit prevalent across societies of modern nation-states underlie an ongoing struggle. But Fadime's death was not an isolated incident. In the years since, honor killings have been reported across Europe, the United States, and Canada, primarily in immigrant communities still beholden to the demands of kinship tradition and patrimonial rule.

From Kinship Communities to Dynastic Governance

Disciplines grounded in honor and shame represent cultures that live in the "eternal now." Kinship is forever. Honor must be forever. Shame can be forever. Redemptive transcendence is virtually impossible in cultures gripped by notions of honor, saving face, and, ultimately, revenge as a way of justice, that is, returning community standards one perceived as "wronged" back to what is considered "right" according to schemes of putative crime and punishment. Linear time is profoundly irrelevant to the daily routines and conceptions of honor and shame imprisoned in the communal worldview that envisions blood honor as integral to the unfolding of what is now and always the "eternal now." But once honor kinship communities encounter conditions that break the hold of never-ending cycles of birth, life, death, and reincarnation, new conceptions of past, present, and future arise that challenge the communal disciplines of honor and shame.

Despite their fragility kinship communities based on segmented lineage, ancestral legitimacy, and honor and shame discipline have endured for thousands of years and continue to dominate regions of the modern world, particularly in Africa, the Middle East, and Asia. Beginning around 9000 BC, however, a new kind of social order associated with centralization, individuality, and, ultimately, nationality emerged in the midst of kinship order. As a consequence of social, political, and economic dynamics that would undermine the foundation of kinship and patrimonial rule, new forms of governing legitimacy would arise as a cultural frame that challenged and ultimately transformed traditional communities governed by kinship, ancestry, and descent. The consequence was the historic emergence of modern nation-states consisting in national cultures governed by centralized rulers and states. Throughout the world new sets of political, social, and economic challenges arose contrary to descent and kinship as cultural forms of political legitimacy and governance. These challenges were

promoted by increasing levels of agricultural surplus, new settlement patterns, and new forms of division of labor and task sharing. As a result, new forms of governance and cultural expression emerged. This led to two sets of political, cultural, economic, and social dynamics: **state-building** grounded in the political consolidation of central authority; and **nation-building** embedded in the development of political cultures of commonality but grounded in notions of citizenship and personal individuality.

Chapter 3
Dynastic Intermediaries

Culture and Governance between Kinship and States

The Political-Cultural Dynamics of State-Building and Nation-Building

To understand **individuality**, **citizenship**, and **nationality** in the contemporary world one must first understand political and cultural transformations from communities governed by kinship to national societies governed by centralized rulers and states. The explanation requires that we now examine a set of political-cultural concepts that help to explain how traditional kinship communities became transformed by centralized and hierarchical forms of authority. In this we consider how modern nation-states eventually supplanted kinship, descent, and segmented lineage order as legitimate principles on which to ground the political authority of governance. These concepts, including such terms as dynasties, nations, states, and nation-states, permit us to analyze two processes central to the historical development of contemporary constructions of collective, specifically political, identity in the making of the modern world. The first is **state-building**. This refers to the historical and political consolidation of central authority. The second is **nation-building**. This refers to the gradual but steady development of cultures of mass society based on individual citizenship and **popular sovereignty** as a way of legitimating centralized governance. These historical processes occurred wherever increasing levels of agricultural surplus permitted the rise of populations that in many cases posed unprecedented social, economic, and ultimately political challenges.

Kinship rules and practices function more or less effectively to resolve the **problem of scarcity**. As we have seen in the previous chapter, communal

traditions and rites of passage emerged to preserve and to protect the community as a unified whole against the onslaughts of economic fragility and ecological pressure. But primordial forms of division of labor tend to become overburdened by ecological risks and environmental pressures. In addition, agricultural surpluses lead to population densities and new settlement patterns. This promotes the rise of **societies of strangers**, whose members are no longer bonded together by blood ties, clan, or segmented lineage. Such societies confront different challenges and require new, specialized kinds of divisions of labor, governance, and discipline. Thus the very virtues of kinship regulation represent their weaknesses. The rigidities that protect traditional communities from the problems associated with economic scarcity prevent them from responding effectively to the problems of surplus and wealth.

New population densities and settlement patterns first arose in fertile areas enhanced by moderate climates and annual floods. As numerous families, clans, and tribes settled in these fertile regions, they confronted a new set of economic, social, political, and cultural challenges. First, although patrimonial rule legitimated by ancestral descent was a common system of social and political governance among kinship groups, no two groups agreed on the legitimacy of a common set of ancestors. For the first time, groups who shared a common fate but not a common ancestry were expected to live and work together. But they could not readily agree on rules and practices for their society. Where would power rest in these new **societies of strangers**? The answer came initially in the form of **dynastic chiefdoms**, later in the emergence of feudal lords, and finally in the rise of centralizing kings.

Growing population centers necessitated new forms of governance to coordinate increasingly complex systems of specialization, task sharing, and **division of labor**. New rules, traditions, institutions, and decision-making structures had to arise to solve the problems associated with surplus, wealth, and specialized labor. Communities quickly learned that the demands of segmented lineage cut against the development of the appropriate divisions of labor necessary to produce and protect agricultural surpluses. The benefits of surpluses meant an unfolding of new tasks, functions, and risk sharing. Food not only had to be produced, it had to be distributed, stored, and protected in unprecedented ways. Such challenges and the tasks that arose to meet them demanded the development of systems of task distribution and sharing that could only be fulfilled through specialized occupational roles. Ascribed status no longer counted in the same way that it did in traditional communities. On the contrary, what counted was how specialized task performers fulfilled their obligations. Competence and integrity began to emerge as new kinds of social values. And horticultural practices and animal

husbandry in the production and protection of food surpluses signified the need for reform and renewal of cultural values and meanings.

New economic pressures, therefore, eroded the disciplines imposed by segmented lineage and kinship rules. This process, however, led to a political problem for which there was no easy solution. For when rule is legitimated by kinship, it carries the authority of nature. Once there is demand for a kind of authority that is relevant to the surplus economies that sustain societies of strangers, the legitimacy of rule can no longer depend on kinship traditions or the values signified by blood, clan, or ancestors. Segmented orders divided by blood and family lineage no longer function effectively as the basis of collective bonding or social belonging. Divisions of labor and task specialization require mechanisms of coordination. These systems involve the gradual emergence of centralized rule, or what is often referred to as **hierarchy**, that is, centralized authority and legitimacy cultures. Political identity and history were now on the road toward **nationhood** and **royal rule**.

The Production of Surplus and Societies of Strangers

Primordial agricultural systems and the traditional kinship communities that depend on them tend to survive economically by adapting various methods of rudimentary agriculture production. Members of such communities may **forage** for food, that is, they collect available edibles for consumption. In addition, they may employ techniques for **hunting and gathering** that include scavenging and the inclusion of prey in their diets. Finally, they may also develop methods for **small-scale cultivation** that entail planting and harvesting limited ranges of vegetation to supplement their other sources of food. But none of these methods produces a guaranteed yield. Moreover, the food that is produced is consumed immediately. Very little is set aside for future consumption or for times of greater food scarcity due to famine or drought. In such fragile and food-insecure societies, most people spend most of their time working on tasks related to food production.

This economic fragility leads kinship communities to adopt divisions of labor and specialization based on their own versions of rationality. We have already learned that kinship communities rely on **ascribed status** relative to blood, clan, and ancestry to determine task division. Ascription is based on a series of considerations, primarily relationship to the ancestors, age, and sex, but is not necessarily based on consideration of the tasks at hand. In many kinship communities, for example, men hunted while the women foraged, scavenged, or undertook

small-scale cultivation. Tribal elders coordinated such labor based on kinship lineage and ascribed status classifications. Such systems endured for centuries.

The last ice age peaked approximately 18,000 years ago. During the 7,000 years that followed, temperatures rose an average of 9°F. This rise in temperatures had a profound impact on human settlement patterns. Warmer environments supported the large-scale cultivation of cereal grains including wheat, barley, and rye. Families learned that they could harvest enough grain to feed themselves for a year in only a few short weeks, particularly in areas with adequate rainfall and fertile soil.

Ideal conditions for settled food cultivation were found along the banks of the Nile River in North Africa, the Tigris and Euphrates Rivers in the Middle East, the Indus and Ganges Rivers in India, and the Yellow River in China. These **river valleys** were characterized by fertile soils, owing in part to mild climates and the rivers' annual floods. Between 9000 and 7000 BC settlements in **Mesopotamia**, the land between the Tigris and Euphrates rivers, began what is now known as the **Neolithic Revolution** or the **First Agricultural Revolution**, the transition from primordial to more modern forms of agricultural production. Animals were domesticated, and through selective cultivation, cereal grains including wheat, rye, and barley later began to sprout in fertile areas across the world. In each river valley, reliable harvests resulted in new cultural values and led to the transformation of communal organization from kinship to strangers and from blood authority to hierarchical rule. No longer would human culture consist only in small, nomadic tribes. Instead, world populations would become settled in sedentary formations with large numbers of people living not only in small villages, but also in towns and, ultimately, in large urban areas that we know today as cities.

Although small-scale cultivation was common in primordial agricultural systems, the large-scale cultivation of cereal grains that characterized the Neolithic Revolution provided enough food for new settlements to meet their immediate needs as well as to enable them to store supplies for times between harvests. Wheat and other grains became the fuel for the nascent societies of strangers that would transform world cultures politically and economically. This led to the establishment of new governing structures and institutions of authority based not on kinship rule but on dynastic governance.

The benefits of food surpluses generated new pressures on the governance structures of traditional kinship communities. These include population growth, specialized and complex divisions of labor, and trade and exchange with unaffiliated groups. The availability of grain and increased food production per acre of land supported a population boom. While hunter-gatherers needed a great

deal of land to support their populations—approximately 250 square miles per 250 people—agricultural societies required far less land. In addition, surpluses of food made it economically possible and advantageous for people to become skilled workers, specializing in a chosen task. This in turn led to the establishment of **market economies** in which goods and services could be exchanged among specialized workers. Moreover, food surpluses led to new forms of cultural expression. Art, architecture, and theatrical performance were embraced in new and fervent ways by societies that were able to do so on account of permanent settlements. The advent of the written word made it possible to write histories and monographs. Even religion and religious practices associated with ritualized procedures and rites of passage changed in these new settlements. Shrines to grain gods and goddesses, for example, often came to the forefront of the symbolism developed within communities beholden to new agricultural surpluses.

However, for all the advances and opportunities that came from settlement in the river valleys, new challenges and potential problems were also common. Natural disasters, for example, could destroy entire villages. Droughts and floods could ruin crops and wipe out harvests. People who lived close together in towns were more susceptible to disease than those who had earlier survived in nomadic groups. Prosperous villages were vulnerable to attack from nomadic bands or from envious neighbors. And, most importantly, although the groups that lived together in these new societies were linked by a common fate, they were not bound by common blood or ancestry. Fundamental questions arose, therefore, regarding the nature of governance, legitimacy, and conflict resolution in these new societies of strangers. In the end, kinship rules, traditions, structures, and institutions could not sufficiently resolve the challenges associated with new social, economic, and political demands. Thus, gradually but inexorably, kinship legitimacy and segmented clan rule or governance by tribal elders were supplanted by dynastic rule.

Early Societies of Strangers

The Sumerians represent one of the oldest civilizations. Sumer was a collection of separate, independent city-states in southern Mesopotamia that were unified by a common culture and political structure and that shared resources by means of a sophisticated trade network connecting specialized workers. By 3000 BC the Sumerians had built at least twelve city-states that were centers of commerce, culture, and governance. Initially, Sumerian city-states were ruled by priests during times of peace and warriors during times of conflict. However, as conflict

became a more pervasive threat, the most powerful warriors developed into a permanent dynasty that transferred authority from fathers to sons.

Although the Sumerian city-states fell to the Amorites in approximately 2000 BC, many aspects of their culture, including rule by king, written language, and specialized labor, were incorporated into the culture of their conquerors. Building and improving on the Sumerian model, the Amorite civilization reached the peak of its power under King Hammurabi. To govern his empire effectively, Hammurabi developed a written legal system called **Hammurabi's Code**. It included 282 specific laws that dealt with everyday issues, including family relations, marriage practices, and property rights. The laws were carved on a stone column called a **stele**. A stele was then placed in each village so that all individuals living within the empire could know and understand the rules by which they would be governed and, if necessary, punished. Hammurabi's Code was based on three fundamental principles: retaliatory justice, punishments based on sex as well as economic status, and governmental responsibilities for justice and compensation.

Dynastic Rule as a Historical Intermediary

In approximately 1500 BC, the Amorites were conquered by nomadic invaders who were later absorbed into Assyrian cultures. As kinship legitimacy waned because of the rise of agricultural surpluses and the gradual emergence of large settlements in what became societies of strangers, new hierarchies arose in such civilizations as the Assyrian to govern and defend stored resources. As human settlements in the river valleys grew and expanded, they needed rulers who could assign tasks, resolve disputes, punish those who defected on their obligations, and, above all, protect communal resources from attack and conquest. In order to defend against invasion and conquest, new settlements had to organize and maintain armies. This meant that leaders had to **extract** resources from members of the community by means of both taxation and conscription. The overall consequence of these dynamics was the erosion of the legitimacy of kinship rule. The emergence of societies of strangers meant that a new kind of authority had to emerge, one that could legitimately rule by means of the extraction of resources by taxation and by creating larger and larger armies, all in the name of common defense.

The answer, which was forged differently in different places, eventually took the form of **dynastic rule**. Systems of dynastic rule arise to resolve the problems of surplus and wealth once kinship rules and practices become counterproductive

relative to economic survival and to the governance and military demands necessitated by the rise of societies of strangers. **Dynastic rulers**, including kings, emperors, and pharaohs, combined the legitimacy of patrimonial kinship grounded in blood, clanship, and segmented lineage with the centralized hierarchical control necessary to govern and defend societies of strangers. These rulers established legitimacy doctrines based not on the common ancestry of the governed, but eventually on the "**divine right**" of the governors themselves. Such doctrines continued to depend on blood and lineage but in a new way focused on specific bloodlines as justification for what gradually emerged as centralized royal rule. Hearkening to a **metaphysical** or **religious** legitimacy, dynastic rulers asserted the supremacy of their own bloodlines, thus fusing the kinship traditions of both patrimonial rule and ancestral legitimacy, but with the practical demands of centralized control. Thus a dynastic leader could resolve internal conflicts between two or more individuals of different descent, not because of any connection to *their* ancestors, but because of the supremacy of his own blood or clan lineage. Similarly, a dynastic leader could extract taxes and achieve fealty on the fields of battle on the basis of a status that derived from his inherited position as heir of intergenerational authority.

The Role of Trust in Societies of Strangers

Dynastic rulers centralized power and legitimacy from the top toward the remainder of society in ways that made governance of societies of strangers possible. But extraction of resources from members of society, that is, from the bottom, demanded new values. Centralized authority in the forms of dynastic rule that engaged in practices of extraction including taxation and conscription created sets of parallel dynamics that operated both **top-down** and **bottom-up**. The mutual processes of dynastic centralization and extraction did not occur everywhere in the same way, nor did they produce a uniform cultural understanding of what centralized dynastic rule meant in terms of legitimacy or governance. But the emergence of dynastic chiefs bound members of these societies together in new common political cultures. Specialization and divisions of labor in dynastic societies required new forms of centralized governance, but they also required collaboration and cooperation among individual workers. Task **specialization** meant that members of dynastic orders became increasingly **interdependent**.

Specialized workers are at the mercy of other specialized workers. Eventually, this provoked a cultural need for values of **trust**. In traditional kinship communities, trust represents a function of blood and shared ancestry. In very

small communities, trust may be fostered by daily struggles for survival. The role of every member of a traditional community is critical to the survivability of the clan or tribe as a whole. But how is trust created in societies of strangers in which members rely on others whom they have never met and in which all must depend on one another for their survival? Trust beyond blood lineage can only develop when the risks of disloyalty or the corrosive effects of defection from the rigid rules of patrimonial authority cannot threaten the survival of the entire society in part because of surpluses and the complexity of the social order. In societies of strangers, trust stems not from blood or ancestral lineage, but from competence or integrity in performance, that is, in how standards for performing tasks and executing responsibilities are met. This implies the creation of new cultural values, institutions, and systems. Specialized tasks involve personal commitments and require coordination. Cultural values must reflect these new kinds of social requirements. Promises made today bind individuals to future patterns of behavior. This comes automatically when common fate determines how each member of a community acts in relation to all others. But in societies of strangers no such guarantees exist. Centralized dynastic governments arose to resolve such predicaments. They promoted new kinds of cultural values that reinforced the bonds of trust by means of laws, such as those in Hammurabi's Code, and by hierarchical enforcement. In addition to producing, distributing, and protecting economic surpluses, therefore, dynastic governments mitigate risks, generate specific cultures of trust, and resolve conflicts with varying degrees of success. Dynastic governance expanded as societies became more densely populated, more complex, and more distanced from traditional forms of descent or kinship rule. But centralized dynastic authority cannot police or adjudicate every interaction. Trust thus becomes the glue that holds societies of strangers together in contrast to the blood, honor, and ancestral forms of legitimacy so central to the political cultures of traditional kinship communities.

Individuality and Romantic Love as Cultural Transformations with Political Implications

Dynastic governance accompanied a parallel rise in cultural values distinct from the communal tenets that characterized primordial life. Individualism does not exist in kinship communities. On the contrary, kinship rules, rites of passage, and honor and shame disciplines exist in part to erase the individual intentions of community members, teaching them to subordinate their own desires to the demands of communal life.

In societies of strangers, however, people are not solely valued for the legacy of their ancestors. What they can do becomes more important than who they are. Ascribed positions relative to ancestral linkages or clanship no longer operate in ways that automatically determine social status. Individual aptitudes, skills, and merit become the basis of identity construction. In the face of individuality, many other kinship rules and traditions break down. This is true in economic contexts in relation to ascribed status but it also pertains to social relations as illustrated by the contrasts between arranged marriage and marriage based on notions of romantic love. As individuality becomes a prevailing cultural value within dynastic societies, people begin to assert the right to choose their marriage partners based on their own desires and the bonds of romantic love.

The rise of romantic love grounded in individuality ultimately replaces arranged kinship forms of marriage. Emerging first in the age of chivalry, romantic love is based on the passions and selection criteria of individuals rather than the demands of communal life or the intentions of patrimonial fathers. This historical transition is immortalized in three great stories of romantic entanglements that pit the desires of individuals against the rules of their society: *Arthur and Guinevere, Tristan and Isolde,* and *Romeo and Juliet.*

In the Arthurian legends, Guinevere is the queen to King Arthur. She has a romance with Arthur's knight, Sir Lancelot. Lancelot is the personification of medieval virtue. He is loyal, strong, and kind; for these reasons he wins Guinevere's heart. The two try to keep their love a secret, but they are discovered. Guinevere is sentenced to be burned to death for her infidelity. Although Lancelot rescues her from her sentence, the two lovers do not get to live "happily ever after." Instead, Lancelot lives as a recluse, alone in his castle, while Guinevere becomes a nun. Moreover, their love leads to the fall of the Round Table and the end of the idealized Arthurian age. In this legend, romantic love is portrayed as the destroyer of civilization, a warning to individuals who might wish to indulge their desires. This is, in effect, an attempt to reinforce submission to the demands of arranged marriage traditions at the cultural core of kinship communities.

In the story of *Tristan and Isolde,* Tristan is a knight who is responsible for transporting Isolde to King Mark, the man to whom she has been promised in marriage. To seal her marriage to the king, Isolde's mother prepares a love potion. Tristan and Isolde together consume the potion, mistaking it for mere wine. As a result, they are overcome with love for each other. Realizing what has happened, Isolde's handmaiden confronts Tristan by saying, "You have drunk your death." Tristan replies, "If by my death you mean this agony of love, that is my life. If by my death you mean the agony that we are to suffer if discovered, I accept that. But if you mean eternal punishment in the fires of

hell, well, I accept that, too."[1] This signifies a cultural break in the Western world with the traditions of kinship culture, arranged marriage, and lineage love. It is a testament to love as a cultural value chosen as a form of meaning that almost transcends life.

Medieval Christians believed in a literal heaven and hell, and in that context Tristan professes himself willing to accept damnation as the price of his love for Isolde. Here the moral of the romantic tale has changed. No longer are individuals warned to shun their desires in the name of communal survival. Instead they are taught to accept any cost in the name of romantic love and beyond this any sacrifice at the behest of the love above all other love, divine love.

Shakespeare's *Romeo and Juliet* continues the storyline of romantic love. Romantic love, personified in the tragedy of Romeo and Juliet, reveals the tensions in cultural values that emerged in medieval Europe between centralized dynastic authority and patrimonial rule. Romeo and Juliet choose, as individuals and independent moral agents, to marry, but their commitments to each other confront communal values and traditions associated with kinship, blood ties, and patrimonial rule personified by the fathers of each of their families. Romeo is forced into a fight for the honor of his family name and, against his will, kills a blood-kin of Juliet. Both families clamor for justice. In the end, a city prince who represents an early or nascent form of centralized rule and modern legitimacy prevails over the patrimonial rule of both families to condemn Romeo, as an individual citizen, to banishment. Both lovers die precisely because of their determination to be together at all costs.

Merit and Guilt Discipline Supplant Honor and Shame

Romantic relationships based on trust forged between individuals supplanted arranged kinship marriage traditions in regions of the world that were increasingly ruled by centralized dynastic authority and chiefdoms. In interpersonal relationships, trust blends values of cooperation and individual merit in situations in which individual responsibility and personal reliability are devoted neither to ancestors nor to the community as a whole but rather given over to fostering outcomes in ways that require individuals to judge one another in terms of personal merit. Such cultural values supplant the virtues of ascribed status. As communal duties and obligations give way to individual commitments, discipline structures oriented to honor and shame become less effective. Thus, trust cultures must develop new systems of discipline designed to protect and reinforce voluntary standards.

Individual guilt gradually replaces **communal shame**. In **trust cultures**, the primacy of the individual person as a social unit overtakes the dominance of lineage, kinship descent, and ascribed status. Therefore, shame, the demand of saving face in cases of dishonored ancestry, is no longer an effective form of discipline. Shame operates as a public discipline to ensure that the appearance of honor before ancestry and lineage is maintained; it is demonstrated through the implementation of instructional rules in forms that include "saving face" as well as honor killings. The very public execution of shame punishments operates even in the contemporary world as indicated by the stoning of a pregnant woman in Pakistan in 2014 by members of her own family because she dared to select her own mate. Such incidents are carried over from traditional communal cultures in ways that, in the present context, are not only criminal but also dysfunctional as disciplines. However, they nonetheless illustrate how shame disciplines are aimed at "teaching" members of kinship communities to privilege group survival and patrimonial preferences over individual intentions. Once specialized task sharing establishes autonomous individuals as primary social units, however, this cultural privileging of shame as a form of public discipline is no longer effective. Thus, violations of trust in societies of strangers composed of individuals who must collaborate on the basis of specialized role and merit are disciplined no longer by public shaming such as honor killing or public hanging but rather by new cultural disciplines grounded in conceptions of guilt typically associated with sin and various religious paths to redemption as well as contemporary conceptions of personal fault, liability, and criminality. Guilt, unlike shame, ultimately adheres to notions of personal responsibility to and for oneself rather than to members of communal groups as a whole. The feeling of guilt is intensely personal. This aspect reveals its cultural origins in societies of strangers in which specialized task distributions promoted political cultures culminating historically in individualism and, eventually, liberalism.

Guilt is the experience of individual promissory failure, a kind of acid of self-inflicted pain experienced whenever one fails *as an individual* to meet moral, ethical, or normative expectations, including self-expectations, with respect to personal or professional promises within societies grounded in cultures of trust, individuality, and merit. Such promises range from the innermost personal commitments, to the satisfaction of religious ritual, to career goals and contractual obligations. Market economies, for example, function according to a range of cultural values that reinforce commitment rules and practices. Such cultural values encourage individuals to define their sense of self-worth by means of public identities anchored by obligation and merit.

Guilt is thus about **commitment rules and principles** rather than instructional rules. Commitment rules and principles cling to promises made by

individuals to perform in particular ways in the future. This suggests that cultures imbued with promissory principles of conduct tend to become oriented to market exchanges and contractual obligations because such socioeconomic relationships depend on the cultural dynamics of trust since, generally speaking, promises made could not and would not be met in its absence. But the normative discipline in cultural environments that rely on trust tends to be guilt about failure to satisfy obligations or to meet expectations. Along with trust and guilt about failure to meet promises comes the individualism of market exchanges and liberal societies. This stands in contrast to honor and the disciplines of shame so definitive of the normative cultures of traditional kinship communities.

Guilt cultures impose certain kinds of values. In cultures oriented to guilt discipline, there may be space for **mercy**, for forgiveness, or for benevolence. In kinship cultures beholden to normative precepts legitimated by notions of blood and thus "nature" as well as the exigencies of group survivability, mercy may be a luxury, one that would threaten communal survival if allowed to take hold. A kinship group typically cannot afford the risk of individual defections since personal choices or the freedom to exercise voluntary actions might threaten the community as a whole. In such instances, shame punishments can and still do unfold with a vengeance. In kinship cultures, communal shame disciplines often appear as ways to wash away shame in order to restore honor with the blood and humiliation of those who dared to contravene the norms of conformity. Individual desire is publicly sacrificed to protect the entire group. The community as a whole in effect "teaches" through the instructional rules of shame punishments. Instructional rules function in ways designed "to save face" through restoration of honor. Clemency or redemption tends to be alien in cultures in which honor and shame disciplines regulate group membership and thus status identity by means of instructional rules. But in guilt cultures, mercy, derived from the Latin word for "wages," offers the possibility for a second chance, for an individual to make amends and to reconcile with those he has harmed, that is, ultimately, for redemption. This is true within socioeconomic orders defined as market liberalism in which the role of individual responsibility ultimately depends on performance or performative criteria associated with promises and trust. But it applies as well within cultures permeated by belief in original sin and the possibility of redemption through salvation.

For these reasons, guilt disciplines operate in cultures in which personal choice is based on commitment rules and principles of promise and trust rather than on cultural norms that maintain such values as honor and shame. The contrast between shame/honor cultures and guilt/redemption cultures runs deep throughout political history into modern times. Often-cited disparities

between what is deemed "Western" and "non-Western" refer to the divergences in cultural values between instructional and commitment or promissory rules. These differences provoke tensions between cultural values oriented to individual liberty, individualism, trust, and performance obligations based on promises and those oriented to kinship honor, ascribed clan status, and the bonds of segmented lineage. Guilt disciplines regulate individual behavior relative to social orders in which specialization and surplus allow individuals to exercise choices on the basis of their own motivations, desires, and will. Such liberty or freedom of choice does not in principle threaten the survival of the group as a whole in societies of strangers in which surplus rather than scarcity represents a fundamental material factor relative to population growth and sustenance.

Trust cultures and guilt disciplines cohere around concepts of individual identity and personal status. These cultures become beholden to notions of **individualism** because societies of strangers based on surplus and specialization require increasingly complex forms of collaboration and cooperation among citizens who, because of population growth, exhibit weaker cultural obeisance to blood ties and kinship lineage. Thus they are bonded, but as "strangers" who nonetheless must establish collaborative survival mechanisms, unified cultural values, and a sense of solidarity. Interpersonal linkages grounded in blood, kin, and ancestry give way in different places, in different times, and at different paces. Altogether this process is transformative of political identity. Indeed, the very concept of political identity as a social construction emerges in this shift from kinship communities to societies of strangers.

Herein originate modern political-cultural formations and the forms of political identity anchored by such concepts as **nations**, **states**, **nation-states**, **citizenship**, and **nationality**. The emergence of nations represents a historic cultural process that in effect substitutes kinship identities with citizenship identities. The actual processes often involved turmoil and the costs of untold violence. Yet these cultural dynamics appear to have promoted the values of solidarity and the norms of common purpose within societies of strangers in which the primary social unit is assumed to be the "individual" person. The cultural misunderstandings and conflicts that tend to be categorized as the tensions in political cultures between "Western" or centralized states and those sometimes called "failed states" or dysfunctional "non-Western" societies are partially explained by these dynamics. At their core, these tensions derive from the lingering degree to which political culture is still driven and shaped by the legitimacy of kinship and segmented lineage as the cultural basis for governing authority and by honor and shame as disciplines. These contrast with the values of centralized authority and national citizenship linked to the individualism

and guilt disciplines prevalent within societies of strangers once they become economically and politically unified and thus socially transformed by cultures into what modern conceptions associate with nations and nationhood.

On the Cusp of Premodernity: The Roman Empire

The Sumerian city-states were the first human civilizations to make the transition from kinship community to dynasty. In the centuries that followed, societies became increasingly hierarchical. Specialization and task sharing became more predominant. Individuality and guilt superseded honor and shame. Centralized governance replaced patrimonial rule. New cultures and dynastic orders governed increasingly larger territories and complex societies of ever-increasing populations.

Rome was the most advanced civilization to predate modern states. At its height, the Roman Empire stretched across Asia Minor, North Africa, Western Europe, and the British Isles. Because it controlled vast swaths of territory and huge populations, the Roman government was more centralized and more militarized than any previous society. Its culture valued discipline, strength, and loyalty. The Roman Empire supported a series of public works projects, and brutally repressed any revolutionary or insurgent groups within its borders. Although it was premodern in its approach to governance, Rome was still beholden to lingering kinship traditions.

Of particular importance were the cultural values pertaining to honor in Roman society that established a scale of different degrees of honor accorded to military leaders, among others. **Gravitas**, for example, represented the base level of honor; **dignitas** represented the level of honor accorded to those whose military bravery gave them the right to receive gifts and tributes from those of lower status; and **auctoritas** represented the honor earned by outstanding military leaders who had the right to demand gifts and tributes from other citizens. Honor conferred social status as well as political and economic power. Unlike kinship honor, however, Roman honor could not be directly inherited from the ancestors. It had to be earned as a consequence of bravery, a kind of merit.

As in kinship communities, the family was the centerpiece of Roman culture and society. The power to rule belonged exclusively, by both law and custom, to the eldest male in the household, typically a patrimonial figure or the father, known as the pater familias. This authority figure enjoyed complete control over family members, property, and money, and was considered the protector of family members and the chief priest of the household. Even Roman religion was divided by households demarcated by those fathers who were categorized as the citizens

of Rome. Such Roman families or households often had their own gods or deities attached to the role played by the father as the dominant figure in Roman family culture. This represents a kind of traditional carryover of patrimonial rule from communal kinship cultures including that of ancient Greece that continued to operate throughout the Roman Empire. In addition, Roman families inherited different levels of power and status. Although all male Roman citizens could take part in politics, the city was dominated by a small group of upper-class families who claimed that their ancestors had been **patres**, or the "fathers" who had founded Rome. They were known as the patrician class and claimed that their ancestry bestowed on them the right to make laws for Rome and its people. Roman farmers, artisans, and merchants were known as **plebeians**. They were "free citizens" granted a number of rights, including a limited right to vote, but they held less power because they could not hold important political offices. Birth determined the distinction between patricians and plebeians, and the line between the two tended to be rigid. Thus ascribed status continued to determine military service, economic power, marriage traditions, social custom, and political authority.

Roman society also incorporated a system of obligation among citizens based on patronage. If a citizen of Rome owed another citizen the favor of a beneficial exchange including labor, he became that **patron's client**. Clients were bound to fulfill the will of their patrons while patrons were obligated to protect and support their clients. This structure was later incorporated into the feudal traditions of medieval Europe and legitimated noble rule. It also helped to dictate the governance structure of the Roman Empire.

Julius Caesar conquered the fledgling Roman Republic just as it was being wrenched apart by conflict and civil discord. After being appointed dictator by the Roman Senate, Caesar instituted a more centralized system of rule, law, and order. When killed by political rivals, Caesar had great riches and in his will he gave a month's wages to all the powerful patricians and plebeians in Rome. According to the patronage system, therefore, everyone owed Caesar a favor. Octavian, the emperor to follow Caesar, inherited those favors and became the sole ruler of the empire. His legitimacy to rule was thus inherited, not by blood, but because of his succession as patron to Caesar's clients.

Octavian, later called Augustus, led the Roman Empire during its height of power and influence, a time known as the *Pax Romana*. He instituted new trade policies, eliminated taxes throughout the imperial provinces, and introduced a silver coin called the denarius, thus substituting a currency-based economy for a barter market. His government constructed aqueducts to carry water to population centers. It filled Rome with temples and buildings styled around classical architectural designs of enormous influence throughout succeeding centuries. He

also began a program of highway construction designed to connect the Empire's cities and population centers. He put paid civil servants in charge of government projects, elevating individuals on the basis of merit rather than class status. He transformed the Roman military from privatized bands of mercenaries into a fighting force funded by taxes, manned by conscription, and loyal to the Empire. Finally, his government redefined citizenship as a reciprocal agreement between citizens and the Empire, guaranteeing citizens economic privileges, political power, and military protection, but also requiring that citizens obey Roman laws and pay taxes in accordance with Roman statutes. The structures, laws, and institutions his government established made Rome secure and prosperous for centuries, even when it was governed by incompetent and seemingly deranged emperors.

One of Augustus's most famous laws, the *Lex Julia de Adulteriis Coerendis* (17 BC), focused on marriage traditions and sexual relations within the Empire. Because partrimonial rule remained a dominant cultural value, romantic love had not yet replaced arranged marriage within the Roman Empire. Augustus's law codified many kinship marriage traditions including arranged marriage and the ban on adultery. According to the law, those found guilty of adultery were banished to different islands. Fathers were also permitted, but not required, to kill their daughters and their partners for the crime of adultery. Husbands could also kill adulterous partners under some circumstances and were required to divorce adulterous wives. This effort was designed to impose imperial rule over the families of Rome specifically by challenging the legitimacy of paternal authority within Roman households. But the emperor appears to have also entertained an ulterior motive in seeking to impose a single law or normative standard of conduct on Roman women. Augustus, in seeking to determine the behaviors of the daughters of Rome, was simultaneously asserting direct authority over the sons of Rome, the very sons who in time could be impressed into military service. He was thus attempting to construct a direct hierarchical chain of military command under his more or less centralized control by circumventing the status of the traditional pater familias.

Tragically, Augustus's own daughter, Julia, was found to be guilty of adultery. The emperor was faced with an impossible choice—save his daughter or save the legitimacy of his government. In the end, Julia was banished to the island of Pandateria. The Roman historian Tacitus emphasizes that Augustus was ultimately stricter with his daughter than the spirit, if not the letter, of the emperor's law required. Here the power of the fathers and the authority of the government collided in ways indicative of the future to come. One way to envision these conflicts is to interpret them as anticipating the tensions that would arise in medieval Europe and later between royal kings who wanted to centralize authority on the basis of dynastic legitimacy, on the one hand, and

the nobility or aristocracy who wanted to retain as much authority as their own family bloodlines could claim. The struggles between classical kings as state centralizers and the nobility who wanted to maintain the legitimacy of family privilege and prerogative encapsulates the history of European political culture in the aftermath of the Roman Empire. The rivalry between these contending forces occurred not only in Europe but also elsewhere and continues today in a wide variety of ways. As we saw in the case of Fadime in the last chapter, even in the contemporary world kinship and honor traditions can conflict with the cultural values associated with modern institutions, leading to legitimacy crises and conflicts over culture, justice, and human rights. Over and beyond these critical issues is the status of the modern nation-state as a centralized form of governance composed of individual citizens and national polities in the case of contemporary societies rent by divisions over the legitimacy of centralized rule and thus governmental authority. The continuing crises in Syria and Iraq during 2014 serve to illustrate the problem of legitimacy that arises whenever clan divisions become reinforced by sectarian, religious, and/or racial differences.

The Roman Empire would eventually fall to "barbarian hordes" from the east. But the cultural legacy it left behind would have lingering impacts second to none in shaping the world and political identity as we know it today. The cities peripheral to the Roman center would in the course of centuries serve as the nuclei around which modern states and national cultures would develop. Latin, the official language of the empire, would provide a common language. This provided the basis for cultural unity despite the vast cultural differences among the populations throughout the far-flung former empire. They could use Latin to communicate, to engage in trade, and to develop common legal practices. Roman legal conceptions that established inheritance procedures, notions of property, and even early notions of constitutional authority would continue to influence jurisprudence in European cities and early state formations up to the formulation of the **Napoleonic code**. But perhaps the greatest cultural impact of the Roman Empire was that it projected the cultural values linking centralized authority with individualism in ways that proved critical to the emergence of political identities associated with modernity. That this developed in the way it did also reveals the impact of Judeo-Christianity throughout European civilization.

Christianity, in particular, as well as the moral and religious impacts of the Roman Catholic Church contributed to the gradual emergence of a unique combination of values that came to exert a major cultural influence with respect to the status of the individual within society. Much can be said on this topic in light of the role played by religious authorities at different times and in different places during modern European history, a role that often veered toward the

doctrinaire and illiberal. That said, in theological terms, Christian doctrines of sin, the redemptive guilt of individuals, and the abiding emphasis on forgiveness of sins through the good works of the sacraments or by means of divine predetermination all contributed to the emergence of cultural emphasis on the individual person. This bestowed on each member of the faithful a salvific obligation under the auspices of the Church and the aegis of its clerical hierarchy. This association between the individuals as members of a corporate body but responsible for actions relative to their own personal salvation—to be demonstrated by obedience to the laws and doctrines of a new central authority in the Church fathers—paved the way for the gradual flourishing of a revolutionary culture and way of arranging human society. Christian theological doctrines pertaining to God and the Church as an instrument of human salvation thus reinforced the cultural primacy bestowed on notions of central rule and authority reflected in laws meant to be extended down to persons *as individuals*. This too contributed to the gradual but continuing erosion of the status of familial or blood-based lineage as a form of legitimacy in the political culture of European society. Individuals learned that they could bypass authority based on the legitimacy of lineage and turn to centralized authority based on the legitimacy of the new Covenant or Testament embodied in the clerical hierarchy of the Church. Tensions would arise, during what is often referred to as the "Dark" or "Middle Ages," between the Church and both traditional dynastic rulers such as Charlemagne and local authorities including the nobility composed of feudal lords and their knights who challenged Church authority. But a new and fundamental doctrine of legitimacy was being forged as two legal fictions took shape and thereby transformed political order and cultural identity: first, a single **sovereign**; and second, a mass society of strangers composed of individuals who constituted a single body. This formation would eventually turn into modern nation-states. This combination consisting of the doctrine of legal concession justifying the legitimacy of a single sovereign along with the doctrine of legal individualism that eventually endowed the status of citizenship with legal as well as cultural legitimacy would serve as the fundamental cultural artifact on which to build the political cultures and values we associate with sovereign nation-states.

Christianity in the Roman Empire

The Romans were **polytheistic**, inheriting many of their religious traditions, gods, and goddesses from the Greeks. But one province of the Roman Empire, Judea, was dominated by a **monotheistic** religion. That religion was **Judaism**.

The Jews were a constant source of trouble for the Romans. They refused to recognize the legitimacy of Rome, frequently rebelling against Roman law, leading to an almost constant state of martial law within the province. Around 30 AD, **Christianity** emerged from within the Jewish tradition. This would fundamentally alter the Empire and the history of Western Civilization.

Christianity is based on the teachings of the man called Jesus the Christ. His crucifixion and "passion" brought with them a new Covenant between God and humanity. The historical Jesus was seen by Roman rulers as a potential source of instability and trouble. The Roman governor of Judea, Pontius Pilate, was particularly concerned that Jesus would undermine the authority of the Roman government in the province, leading to a new wave of legitimacy crises, revolutions, and military repressions. By crucifying Jesus, the Roman government sought to eliminate the threats of rebellion that emanated from the region, but this had the opposite effect. The death of Jesus did not terminate his influence but, on the contrary, fomented the resistance of converts who spread the doctrines of Christian religious beliefs and practices that were critical to the making of the modern world. Christian apostles, including Paul, spent their lives spreading the teachings of Christ and proselytizing on behalf of the Christian religion. Using both his status as a Roman citizen and the physical infrastructure linking the Roman Empire together, Paul initiated the establishment of churches around the Mediterranean. This facilitated the slow but steady conversion of the people of the region to Christianity. The Roman government was threatened by the spread of this new set of cultural values. In 64 AD Emperor Nero, for example, ordered the first persecution of the Christians. Nevertheless, by 200 AD, approximately 10 percent of the people in the Roman Empire were Christian. Gradually but persistently the Roman Catholic Church gained its own traction and established centralized authority at the Holy See in the personage of the Papal Vicar.

Early Christians believed that Jesus spoke unto the Apostle Peter the following words: "upon thy rock shall I build my Church and thus which you sanctify on Earth so also shall I sanctify in Heaven."[2] This is interpreted to mean that Jesus chose Peter to serve as the head of the Christian Church. Empowered by this **Petrine Doctrine**, Peter chose Rome to be the seat of this new religion and served as the first pope of the Roman Catholic Church. The Church became a doctrinal source of moral authority for citizens of the Roman Empire. In time, loyalty to the Church superseded citizens' loyalty to the Empire, thus undermining the power of the emperor and his agents. In 313 AD, however, the Emperor Constantine attributed a great military victory to Jesus. As a result, he ordered an end to the persecution of the Christians and established Christianity as a religion no longer persecuted throughout the Empire. In 395 AD, Emperor Theodosius

made Christianity the official religion of the Roman Empire. By this time, the Roman Empire was in decline and threatened by Germanic and other tribes. Following the collapse of the Roman Empire, however, the Catholic Church would survive and serve as a unifying political and cultural force across Europe. Its institutions, including its monasteries and priesthood, would safeguard the cultural traditions and knowledge of the Romans throughout the Middle Ages until they would be reborn in the Renaissance.

Christianity, with its doctrines of salvation and redemptive guilt, in combination with the emergence of a clerical hierarchy, promoted a concept of public space that had never existed in classical times. Roman authority never drew the distinction between public space and the private realm. Cultural values associated with doctrines of separation between church and state would not emerge until relatively recent times. Roman society remained familial despite attempts by its emperors to intrude on the domain of the pater familias. This would change in the transition from medieval Europe to the emergence of classical royal kings who brought with them the effort to centralize authority around their own legitimacy in the name of the sovereignty of early nation-states. This too would have enormous impact not only on the political geography of the modern world but also on modern constructions of collective identity.

Feudalism in Medieval Europe

After years of civil war, economic decay, and social strife, the Roman Empire fell to conquering Germanic tribes in the mid-400s. The Eastern Empire split and survived with Byzantium as its center of culture and politics, but the Western Empire collapsed in 476. In its place emerged a new system of dynastic rule far more beholden to kinship rule than Roman law. The Germanic groups that assumed control of the lands formerly governed by Rome were warrior tribes bound by dynastic rule and kinship traditions. They introduced new elements into the cultural formations of early Europe. Throughout the time period we call the Middle Ages, the cultural legacies of Rome and the traditions of the Catholic Church intermingled and influenced both Germanic groups and, to a lesser extent, tribes from the eastern areas of early Europe to form different European subcultures. Thus the cultural uniformity provided by Roman civilization and heritage began to give way to a variety of local dialects, customs, and traditions. This too would contribute to the proliferation of contrasts among cultures and locations with respect to how modern political identities emerged throughout modern Europe.

ALTERNATE PERSPECTIVES

Political Culture and Economic Development

Political culture is tied to economic sustainability. In primordial communities, ascribed status, marriage traditions, rites of passage, and honor and shame discipline confront the problems of scarcity and extreme resource dependence. In dynastic communities, specialization, trust, and centralization evolve to address the challenges associated with surplus. In both instances, political culture and economics are fundamentally linked.

When we discuss the modern world we speak in terms of development and categorize states as developed, developing, or underdeveloped. Lawrence Harrison explains how political culture impacts economic development, both nationally and internationally. In the years following World War II, economists predicted that countries across the world would make great strides in terms of economic development. However, Harrison observes that many countries in Latin America, Asia, and sub-Saharan Africa failed to achieve the expected level of economic progress. This failure is often attributed to the legacies of colonialism or to the proliferation of neoliberal policies in the second half of the twentieth century that stress the role and importance of unregulated markets. However, Harrison observes that some postcolonial states have made significant economic progress while others have not. Colonialism, therefore, cannot be the sole variable responsible for underdevelopment. Instead, he argues, cultural traditions have an impact on the success or failure of economic development programs. Cultures that base economic decisions such as hiring and promotion on kinship ties rather than merit, for example, may struggle to promote growth and development. Here, again, we see the connections

continued

The Germanic tribes held to oral traditions without written languages. In time, Latin became the language of the Church, but different civilizations adopted dialects that combined Latin with Germanic languages. The Romance languages—Spanish, Italian, French, and Portuguese—took most of their structure from Latin, while others—German and English—took their structure from Sanskrit and the Germanic or Teutonic tongues. Although pagan by tradition, many Germanic tribes adopted Christianity into their polytheistic religions. As the head of the Catholic Church, the pope represented the only centralized ruler of all of Europe. In 590 AD, Pope Gregory began expanding the papacy as both a political and a spiritual office. He signed peace treaties, raised revenue

between cultural values emphasizing individualism as well as performance criteria based on merit and the disciplines of promise and guilt in relation to market cultures. Critical debates continue to revolve around the role and influence of government with respect to the efficient functioning of markets, the overall consequences of market structures and exchanges relative to inequalities of socioeconomic conditions, and issues of equity regarding availability of opportunity as means to promote economic freedom.

Harrison is not alone in his assertion regarding the importance of cultural influences in political-economic behaviors. For example, David Landes has examined the relationship between culture and economics, citing changing religious customs in Thailand.[3] Historically, numerous young Thai men would spend years studying in Buddhist monasteries. This appears to have distracted many from participating in pursuits that would contribute to economic growth and productivity. Today, however, it is common for many Thai citizens to spend only a few weeks in religious instruction. This permits them to focus energies on the material world. Economic development has followed this cultural transformation. This case suggests that it is vital that we think about culture not only in terms of its social, historical, or political implications for modern states, but also in terms of economics, development, and distributive justice. To understand a country's economy, one must also understand its cultural predispositions and history. Similar examples include the legacies of apartheid on the South African economy that continue to plague South Africa in terms of massive inequalities, the role of nepotism in the Kenyan economy leading to patronage systems of wealth distribution and the ever-present risks of ethnic conflict, the persisting divisions of the caste system in India provoking a wide range of social dysfunctions, and the impacts of gender bias on the Saudi economy that suppress female activities in the work force.

through taxes, repaired roads, and even maintained his own armies. His vision was for the Catholic Church to replace the Roman Empire in Europe. This ambition pitted him against the dynastic leaders of the Germanic tribes. In time, the **dual legitimacy** of the Catholic Church and the dynastic monarchs would create tensions across Europe and lead to new legitimacy crises.

Charlemagne, or "Charles the Great," was one of the great leaders of medieval Europe. Charlemagne's Holy Roman Empire stretched from modern-day Spain to Eastern Europe. He controlled central Europe as well as Italy. A powerful military leader with enormous land holdings and personal wealth, Charlemagne maintained tight control over the people living in his empire, refusing to share

power with or trust the nobles under his control. By 800 AD Charlemagne was the most powerful emperor in Europe. He took advantage of this position to elevate himself relative to the other dynastic leaders of his era. On December 25, 800, Pope Leo III crowned Charlemagne the Holy Roman Emperor.

Charlemagne died fourteen years later, leaving his only son, Louis the Pious, as king and emperor. Louis, a weak and ineffective king, died in 840 leaving three sons—Lothair, Charles the Bald, and Louis the German. The three sons fought for control of the Empire. When the war ended in 843 AD, the Treaty of Verdun divided the Empire into three kingdoms that would gradually divide Europe into modern France and Germany. Competition between France and Germany for the territory between them would act as a catalyzing force in modern conflicts associated with the Franco-Prussian War, World War I, and World War II.

After the death of Charlemagne, Europe became dominated by a **feudal** system of governance. Feudalism was an economic, military, and political system based on control of the land, local protection, self-sufficiency, and traditions of noble obligation. At the heart of the feudal system was the relationship between noble **lords** and their **vassals**. Lords ceded control of lands called **fiefs** to vassals. In return the vassal would be sworn to defend the lord for the remainder of his life. To protect a fief, a vassal needed a private army. To raise that army, vassals would divide their fiefs into smaller estates creating more vassals and becoming a lord himself. Each lord used investitures of land to tie vassals to military service. At the bottom of the structure were the knights, vassals whose parcels of land were too small to be subdivided.

In theory, therefore, a feudal system was a pyramid. At the bottom were many knights, each with a small fief. Above them were lords who held larger fiefs. At the top was the king who, presumably, could call on all of the knights of his land to come to his aid and defense. Each vassal was also responsible for paying taxes and tribute to his lord, who in turned paid taxes and tribute to the king. In peacetime, knights, vassals, and lords governed their self-sustaining fiefs. Most people in the Middle Ages were neither lords nor vassals. Some were officials of the Catholic Church, but the majority were **peasants** who worked but did not own the land. Most peasants were **serfs**, workers who were tied to the land as indentured servants. They worked on the fief and were governed and "cared for" by the nobles. In principle, this gave them an advantage over **free peasants** who enjoyed greater freedom than serfs but did not receive similar protections.

Medieval fiefs contained their own farmlands, forests, villages, churches, manor houses, blacksmiths, barns, pastures, and mills. Food, clothing, lumber, leather goods, and tools were all produced on the fief. In return for their right to live and produce on the fief, serfs and peasants owed labor, a large portion

of the grain crop, approximately 10 percent of their livestock, and various fees to their lords. In addition, each family was required to give about 10 percent of their income to the Church. As in the ancient Sumerian city-states, the medieval fiefdoms were governed by dynasties grounded in legitimacy based on noble blood. Given this kind of social order, peasants would not allow themselves to adopt the values appropriate to those who might permit the rise of centralized authority. Instead, they thought of themselves as members of an extended "family" defined by relations to a dynastic chief. Each chief had his own warriors who were bound to him, but warriors would not fight for the centralized rulers who were emerging at this time as royal rulers or classical kings. This medieval system of governance based on personal ties made the orderly governance of large territories virtually impossible. Thus, royal rulers set about the task of centralizing state authority around themselves. This would happen differently in different locations. In Britain, the history of constitutional authority beginning with the **Magna Carta** ensured a central role for parliament and would work to reinforce the primacy of decentralized governance throughout the British Isles. The fact that, in the United States, American police forces are so highly decentralized reflects the traditions of local constabulary that began in Britain and reflects cultural values distrustful of absolute authority. The centralized state-building history in France reflective of the role of the Bourbon kings reveals a contrasting process in which King Louis XIV could honestly declare, "L'état, c'est moi" (the state, it is me). It is not surprising that modern France has a national police force, which is unthinkable in Britain or the United States. The point here is to emphasize that classical kings and royalty arose to govern societies of strangers in centralized ways beyond the capacity of feudal lords or nobility. As a consequence, inevitable tensions arose between royalty and nobility. These tensions were resolved historically in ways that reveal more or less centralization in defining the relationship between state and society. But the beginnings of modern identities were about to be forged once royal rulers set about the task of centralizing authority around themselves in the name of their own dynastic blood and to the detriment of all other blood dynasts, including those of aristocratic lineage.

The Rise of Classical States

Feudal governance represents a carryover of kinship governance grounded in blood, honor, and ascribed status. Because feudal lords were loyal to cultural traditions associated with the governance of small self-sufficient communities, they competed for power, legitimacy, and resources with centralizing kings

and classical monarchs. Classical monarchs did not have the authority to extract directly from individuals. Thus, they depended on feudal lords to defend their boundaries and collect taxes. But knights were often more loyal to their lords than they were to royal kings. There was no guarantee knights would actually serve royal kings whenever called. This would soon change as classical kings began, in various ways, to consolidate the legitimacy of the authority to govern populations within specified boundaries of rule unimpeded by obstacles presented by aristocratic lords and their knights. Beginning around the turn of the first millennium, therefore, classical kings sought to assume greater control of their lands and people. This would lead to a political and cultural transformation that would culminate in the establishment of modern sovereign nation-states.

William the Conqueror was among the first to assault the power of the nobles. After the Battle of Hastings, he declared that all of England was his personal property. He granted fiefs to approximately 200 loyal Norman lords and bishops while keeping 20 percent of the land as his personal domain. England thus became centralized but this set in motion the reactions that paved the way to the Magna Carta and decentralized British governance. Other European monarchs followed suit, creating new structures designed to extract directly from the people living on their lands. Their aim was to bypass feudal loyalties and create armies, political institutions, and professional civil servants designed in fact or in aspiration to operate outside of the obligations of the feudal system.

Some, including France, Spain, and Portugal, were very successful. For example, in 1000 AD France was divided into more than thirty feudal kingdoms. In 987 the last member of the Carolingian dynasty, Louis the Sluggard, died, and the French nobles chose Hugh Capet to ascend to the throne. The lords thought that the Capetian kings would be weak and easy to control but in time the power of the French monarchy spread outward from the Capetian fief in Paris. Eventually the Capetian kings would unite all of France under the leadership of a single, powerful monarch, crushing the power of the feudal lords.

Self-determination continues to be a doctrinal influence and powerful ideological force in international politics. During the 1990s, demands for self-determination led to **balkanization** in the former Yugoslavia, a process of devolution that culminated in war crimes, genocide, and ethnic cleansing. Today, stateless nations demand the rights of self-rule and self-determination in the Catalan region of Spain, Chechnya, the Basque Country, Scotland, Quebec, Palestine, Kurdistan, Tamil Eelam in Sri Lanka, and numerous other sites of political and sometimes violent contestation. These demands often fuel separatist movements and have been associated with terrorism, repression, and mass political violence.

KEY CONCEPTS

Self-Determination

Self-determination is the right of a nation to govern itself under the authority of a sovereign state. It is a doctrine that became popular in Europe alongside the rise of nationalism, particularly after the First World War. It was initially used to refer to rights held by those associated with national collectives of Bolsheviks during the Russian Revolution. It was then adopted as a political-cultural doctrine by the Allies during the peace process. In his **Fourteen Points**, American president **Woodrow Wilson** called for self-determination for many of the nations of Europe, citing the importance of legitimacy based on self-rule that would consolidate political allegiance with nationality. For Wilson, self-determination was synonymous with **government by consent** of the governed.

The **Paris system** that emerged after the First World War thus emphasized congruence between nations and states. The end of the war led to the dissolution of the Austro-Hungarian and Ottoman Empires and led to self-determination for Czechoslovakia, Austria, Hungary, Romania, Yugoslavia, Bulgaria, Poland, Turkey, and Yemen. Around the same time the **Treaty of Brest-Litovsk (1918)** extended the right of self-determination to Armenia, Finland, Estonia, Latvia, Ukraine, Lithuania, Georgia, and Poland. However, not every nation gained statehood in the aftermath of the First World War.

continued

To a major extent, the appeals of self-determination in promoting separatist political movements or in creating insurmountable obstacles to centralized rule or national political cultures proved less compelling than national justifications for the legitimacy of the sovereign nation-state. In some cases, the legitimacy struggle between forces of division and centralization would not be decided in favor of national sovereignty until the end of the nineteenth century. For example, Germany continued to be divided by principalities dominated by the nobility who retained the power to elect the king. Power struggles between the German kings and both the nobles and the Catholic popes fragmented Germany and prevented centralized rule until relatively recently. Germany would be one of the last European states, second only to Italy, to make the full transition to a consolidated nation and centralized sovereign state only when it became unified in the late 1800s. Some scholars argue that the reasons that Germany and Italy

Moreover, the doctrine of self-determination did not foster the sense of national unity among many multiethnic societies. Practical problems emerged as nations that were granted self-determination were forced to govern over so-called **minority populations**. This led to many vexing questions of legitimacy, that is, questions about the cultural basis on which political forms of governance would be justified. How would those minority populations be treated? Would they be granted their own states? Would they be granted specific political and cultural rights that would be protected by their new state governments? Would they be deported in the name of national homogeneity? Or would they be the targets of political violence designed to "purify" the nation-state of diverse elements?

International agreements stipulated that minority populations needed protection and required that new states extend that protection as their price of admission to the new family of "civilized nations," that is, the international society of sovereign states. However, in the aftermath of the peace treaties, deportations known as **population exchanges** did occur. In 1919, 200,000 Slavs were moved from Greece to Bulgaria and 170,000 Greeks were shifted from Bulgaria to Greece. In the early 1920s, more than a million Christians were deported from Anatolia to Greece and more than 350,000 Muslims were transferred from Greece to Turkey. These policies of **population unmixing** uprooted communities from their ancestral lands and homes. This led to enormous suffering on the part of those who were made to endure forced migration.

both experienced fascist extremes in part have to do with their late consolidation relative to other European nation-states in combination with memories of their past glory as the seat of either the Roman Empire in the south or of the Carolingian Empire in the north.

However, for the most part governments led by classical monarchs, especially in Western Europe, sought centralized power, influence, and territory since the sixteenth century. To achieve their goals they had to battle the power of the nobility and that of the Church, not to mention competing European monarchs. These campaigns forced monarchs to extract heavily from their people. This in conjunction with social and economic changes promoted new legitimacy tensions that would ultimately undermine the power of the kings themselves. The process we now call state-building requires the emergence of legitimate governance structures and institutions that stand beyond, over, and above blood ties

once and for all. Dynastic rule served as an intermediate step in the transition between kinship communities and modern nation-states because it introduced the acceptance of centralized legitimacy grounded in a single bloodline to cultures previously beholden to governance legitimated by their own ancestors. Later, as dynastic kingdoms made the transition to sovereign states, centralized structures and those royal figures who dominated them were forced to adopt a new form of legitimacy grounded in nationhood, national collective belonging, and popular sovereignty or consent. This eventually led to the deposing of royal monarchy altogether as a form of legitimate governing authority. As cultures became increasingly suffused by cultural values of individuality, merit, and guilt, popular consent became the dominant legitimacy doctrine to justify centralized hierarchical rule. From these cultural values the modern sovereign nation-state would be born. This ascendance represented transformations in political culture definitive of modernity. "Power to the people" became an implicit shibboleth. But extraction for purposes of war and defense did not lessen. On the contrary, once popular consent led to the revolutions and transformations that produced modern nation-states, extraction in the form of massive numbers of citizens under arms, lethality in wartime, and levels of taxation accelerated. As a result, a new form of legitimacy was required to justify these excesses done in the name of "the people." For these reasons, the concepts of nation and nationhood emerged as the basic core of self-determination, and self-determination no longer required cultural homogeneity but rather needed political acceptance of the sovereign legitimacy of state institutions even on the part of a polyglot nation.

Chapter 4
Modern Sovereign Nation-States

Nationality, Citizenship, and Hyphenated Identities

Extraction and Legitimacy

We live in a world of sovereign nation-states, bounded territories that have become the primary unit of analysis in modern political discourse. And as the cultural products of this modern world, we ourselves tend to think of those boundaries and the political units they represent as "natural," as if the world we know were created forever divided into sovereign nation-states. We are familiar with notions of nationality, ethnicity, citizenship, and self-determination; it thus becomes easy to assume that people everywhere construct collective belonging, political identity, governing legitimacy, and moral or ethical disciplines as we do. We evaluate conflicts, crises, and catastrophes through a modern lens, expecting others to conform to our notions of national solidarity. And thus we ignore the continuing influence of kinship governance grounded not in centralized rule and national collective identity, but rather in ancestry, descent, honor, and shame. These cultural values and traditions remain vibrant, particularly in parts of the world "modernized" as a consequence of Western colonialism and imperialism.

The origins of the modern nation-state begin with the political transition from ancestral legitimacy and lineage to centralization and hierarchy grounded in the need to defend surpluses. The extraction dynamics necessary to manage increasingly large and complex societies propelled the rise of centralizing institutions, culminating in the establishment of modern sovereign states. Extraction in the form of taxation and conscription of men and eventually women under arms

required new legitimacy doctrines as soon as rule by blood and ancestry could no longer justify war, taxation, defense, and legal conflict resolution. Rather than the purview of the patrimonial fathers, these became the strategic concerns of dynastic rulers. From the pharaohs of ancient Egypt, to the Roman emperors, to the nobility of medieval Europe, to Europe's classical kings and queens who would ultimately impose their will on the remnants of segmented lineage that threatened to undermine their power, control gradually but definitively moved away from kinship rules and traditions to centralizing doctrines of hierarchical forms of government.

King Louis XIV of the Bourbon dynasty, for example, wanted to make France the model of a modern, centralized state, a cultural, political, and economic leader of the world. This superiority was symbolized by Louis's Palace of Versailles. Versailles was the first European palace to be unfortified. Instead of being surrounded by walls and moats it was surrounded by gardens. The palace was huge, containing a library, theater, ballroom, council chambers, and numerous living quarters. Its most spectacular feature was the Hall of Mirrors, a room for state receptions and parties meant to glorify the power of the French monarchy. All of this excess came at a high cost, both politically and economically, for the nobility, the peasants, and, ultimately, the monarchy alike. In an attempt to limit the power of the French nobility, Louis required that they live at Versailles for the majority of the year. While the nobility basked in the glamour of life at Versailles, they necessarily neglected their responsibilities relative to their manors and fiefs. This allowed Louis to centralize his control over France, bypassing the traditional political power of the aristocratic class and governing the people directly using a network of professional civil servants. Louis was thus known as the first of Europe's **absolute** monarchs, dynastic leaders with complete power. As Louis said, "L'état, c'est moi" (the state, it is me).

Thus Versailles was more than a palace. Its magnificence helped to transform France from a collection of feudal estates into a single, centralized political unit, turning once-independent nobles and land-bound peasants into willing supplicants of the French king and his royal authority. Under Louis's reign, France would create the largest economy, population, and military in Europe. It had 100,000 soldiers in peacetime and nearly 400,000 in war, giving it an army many times larger than any of its fragmented feudal neighbors could possibly marshal or maintain. However, even for a prosperous economy with a large population, the costs associated with this military were a heavy burden on state coffers. To maintain his military, not to mention the lifestyles of the pampered aristocracy at Versailles, Louis extracted heavily from his people. In the name of French honor and glory, he also fought numerous wars to expand his territory and influence.

From 1667 to 1713 he fought to expand France's boundaries to the Rhine River and the Alps. The war bankrupted France, forcing the king to raise taxes on an already heavily taxed population. The civil unrest that resulted from these extraction policies would ultimately culminate in the French Revolution. The French Revolution represents an extraction crisis in legitimacy. The king sought to extract from his people, not in the name of popular consent, but rather in the name of the long-outdated traditions of dynastic blood and kinship.

As we see in France, to solidify their power, vanquish their enemies, and control their populations, classical monarchs would extract more from their people than those subjects were willing to pay. They confiscated disproportionate amounts of surplus from their people to fuel their own ambitions for glory and power. Ironically, the first time the term police is used is not in the context of criminality, but rather in terms of *police des blés*, that is, a quartermaster corps responsible for extracting food from local farmers wherever the king's army traveled. This extraction dynamic in turn led to a series of extraction crises throughout the Medieval and Classical Periods, which in turn led to the rise of collective national political identities. The English Glorious Revolution, the American War of Independence, the French Revolution, and the Bolshevik Revolution represent a series of **legitimacy crises** over extraction that challenged monarchy as the last remaining vestige of kinship authority. In the American political and cultural imaginary this is symbolized by the often-romanticized Boston Tea Party and the outright rejection of any form of taxation—and by implication of conscription—in the absence of mechanisms of legitimacy anchored to popular consent. So strong are these resonances that the symbolism of the tea party has become integral to the political dynamic in contemporary American politics although in highly controversial and politicized ways. In a real sense, the cultural origins of the modern nation-state begin with the social transition from kinship membership to **citizenship** grounded in the need for popular consent and popular sovereignty as political doctrines aimed at ensuring the **legitimacy of state extraction**. Henceforth extraction had to occur in the name of the people as a political-cultural value. Taxation and conscription would, of course, continue unabated. But the legitimacy that justified such extraction would have to be defined in the name of popular consent. This alone would henceforth confer on rulers the rights to extract treasure or men and women under arms within societies of strangers. The concepts of nation and nationhood represent political-cultural values in the history of political legitimacy that emerged once the legitimacy of patrimonial rulership based on blood and kinship and manifested in dynastic chiefdoms, royal monarchy, or imperial authority and their modes of extraction lost its traction. As the nineteenth century dawned throughout Europe the new idea took hold that if governments were to extract

from society it had to be done for and in the name of the people. From this arose the concept of nation and nationhood. Nations are composed of the citizens of sovereign states. They act as a body politic or polity. Nations establish a new form of legitimacy relative to state extraction. This legitimacy consists in a doctrine of popular consent. Today, this serves as the exclusive grounds for justifying state extraction and is the basis for the linkages between nation and sovereign state. The question often arises, what is a nation? Many answers are possible since many different political cultures exist among the many nations in the world today. But what they have in common is their relationship to sovereign states and governments that are typically, but not always, within defined territories. This relationship imposes state obligations in relation to its people but also rights of the people relative to states. At the core of these rights and obligations is the functioning of government and the pursuit of governmental policies in the name of state interests and the interests of the nation including defense. This, in turn, generates the demand for extraction, that is, the deployment of national resources for state purposes by means of taxation and ultimately through military preparedness. How then does state extraction become justified? What is the form of legitimacy applied by modern sovereign nation-states and their governments to justify extraction of treasure or wealth from society, not to mention to justify the forms of extraction that include placing citizens in harm's way in the name of defense, whether through conscription or volunteer military or armed services? The answer derives from the doctrine of popular consent, that is, whenever state extraction occurs in whatever manner, it is done in the name of the legitimacy of the nation who by virtue of their acquiescence bestow popular consent on the sovereign state. In such instances, the term nation applies to the people conceived as a body politic and the agency that alone confers popular consent on the sovereign state. This relationship between sovereign states and nations endowed with the legitimacy of popular consent is not to be confused with democracy or democratic politics and voting. The relationship between nations and sovereign states is not the same as that between a government and a people. Governments come and go. The relationship between a nation and sovereign state represents a historical exercise in legitimacy that is continuous and thus disrupted only at great cost, typically leading to profound crisis. The reason for this is that legitimacy crises threaten the very survival or continuity of the sovereign state itself. When the sovereign state of Iraq becomes threatened by the potential of a tripartite division caused by a sectarian conflict that looms as insurmountable, Iraq may be said to be experiencing a legitimacy crisis in which the doctrine of popular consent no longer exists or applies. The same applies to the Ukraine, where major segments of the population in the east of the country appear to demand the right to secede. Civil wars, separatist

movements, various forms of civil insurrection, and even civil disobedience all represent legitimacy crises in which the existence of a sovereign state becomes threatened or challenged on account of the withdrawal of what is in effect popular consent. This is what is meant by the doctrine of popular consent. Given the threatened breakdown of the state itself, the government can no longer function normally. Popular consent provides a basis for the legitimation of the relationship between nation and state, and thus is the cement between them. Once it deteriorates past the point of providing legitimacy, the sovereign state as a political entity is in jeopardy. Popular consent, therefore, expresses the rights of a nation to extend legitimacy to a sovereign state for purposes of government extraction. The concept of nation is thus embedded in doctrinal understandings of the relationship of citizens to sovereign states and vice versa. The ultimate answer as to what a nation is lies not in naturalistic notions of kinship, ethnicity, race, religion, or even language. Nationhood is a concept that applies to a people with regard to their relationship to a sovereign state. A nation acts as a legitimacy mechanism endowed with the capacity to justify extraction done by governments in the name of the people who collectively compose a nation. The term nation thus represents a legitimation doctrine attached to popular consent. Popular consent does not necessarily mean democracy. It is a regrettable fact that many authoritarian regimes have acted brutally toward their own people and aggressively toward other states all in the name of popular consent. What this demonstrates is that popular consent is a legitimacy doctrine that applies to the relationship between sovereign states and the nation rather than between a people and any single government. It also demonstrates that nations do sometimes follow dictators and fanatical regimes even at times when their civil rights are either threatened or violated, as in the cases of Nazi Germany and Soviet Russia. Legitimacy crises arise when segments of a nation determine that a governmental regime is acting in ways that violate the spirit of popular consent and that there is no recourse but to resist, particularly in nonlegal ways. For so long as a nation demonstrates its willingness to allow a sovereign state to call on it for sacrifices related to extraction, the doctrine of popular consent applies and the legitimacy of nation in relation to state remains in alignment. How the relations between any nation and its government within a sovereign state function differs from nation-state to nation-state. But the principle remains constant: the nation represents a vehicle for the legitimation of state extraction grounded in extraction or sacrifices according to the doctrines of popular consent. Put simply, the nation is an accountability mechanism relative to state extraction. To conceive of self-determination as based on ethnic, sectarian, racial, linguistic, or other forms of homogeneity is to define nationhood or peoplehood in simplistic and naturalistic terms that deny the realities of polyglot nations. If self-determination meant

homogenous forms of nationhood, not all multiethnic and/or multicultural nations would meet this criterion. In fact as well as in theory most nations are composed of peoples who understand themselves as a "nation" but who at the same time manifest an entire range of cultural differences among themselves. To be sure, many issues arise in connection with polyglot, multiethnic, and multicultural nationhood. Some national minorities are suppressed and yearn for a different social and political status within their sovereign state; in other cases, a people may aspire to the status of independent nationhood because they believe that they do not enjoy the rights of citizenship within a sovereign state or authority as it exists. But such examples help to illustrate why the nation as a concept refers to peoplehood in relation to sovereign statehood. A nation is, therefore, a kind of imaginary in political culture. It provides the foundation of legitimacy relative to how modern nation-states justify their calls for extraction and sacrifice. Whenever such calls are made and whenever they are met in the name of the people, that is, whenever the test of popular consent is met, the people of a state may be imagined and defined as a nation. The nation is a principle of legitimation bound by the legal fictions of popular consent, however implemented, from nation-state to nation-state.

This perspective stands in contrast to extraction and its legitimation done in the name of dynastic rulers including classical monarchs. Such calls for sacrifice were done in the name of a mode of legitimation considered "natural." This is illustrated, for example, by the principle of the "divine right of kings." Nations arose historically at different places and at different times but in ways that destroyed the old order based on such political pretensions. As a result, the need arose to justify extraction on grounds other than blood or dynastic traditions. An effective response required a doctrinal and thus cultural move away from naturalistic notions of royal dynastic blood and noble clan. This shift culminated in what we call the nation. The nation is thus a historical formation grounded in the cultural acceptance of legitimacy that does not depend on naturalistic features of a people but rather on their cultural imagination and political solidarity. Nations and the very concept of nationhood represent artificial contrivances or cultural inventions that arose historically once the "natural" form of legitimacy attached to kinship descent and honor became discredited and dysfunctional as doctrines appropriate for the centralized rule of modern nation-states and the kinds of defense and warfare they would pursue.

For these reasons, nation-building as a bottom-up social dynamic and state-building as a top-down process in governance occur concomitantly, especially under those conditions in which the legitimacy of governance has tended to be most durable. The values and meanings of citizenship and nationality arise as new

forms of political identity. Citizenship becomes associated with the individualism of cultures steeped in modernity. But an aspect of citizenship called **nationality** would also arise in order to ensure proliferation of the cohesive values associated with solidarity, cooperation, and unity. Nationality fills the cultural void opened up by cultures of citizenship in societies of strangers governed by centralized state institutions. It generates a need for new expressions, possibilities of popular consent, and mass political representation.

As we have seen, while kinship traditions in governance worked to resolve the problem of scarcity through instructional disciplines of honor and shame, dynastic chiefdoms resolved the problem of surplus and specialization by combining kinship descent with centralized hierarchy. Classical kings, queens, and centralizing state-builders, in turn, resolved the problem of defense and security through extraction. Modern sovereign states resolve the problem of legitimacy through the establishment of political cultures founded on the values of popular consent and nationhood. Ultimately, the doctrine of legitimacy that would vanquish all others in the modern world was nationhood grounded in popular consent in relation to centralized states and sovereign authority. The rise of nations was the direct consequence of the rise of centralized sovereign states. This process transformed the character of political culture forever. Centralized states and rule required extraction but also its justification by state builders in forms that demanded legitimacy grounded in popular consent.

The Second Agricultural Revolution

Just as the **First Agricultural Revolution** led to the transition from kinship communities to dynastic intermediaries, the **Second Agricultural Revolution** led to the transition from dynastic rule to modern sovereign nation-states. New agricultural technologies, combined with increasingly temperate climates, led to a population explosion across Europe that was subsequently followed by mass urbanization in new cities and, as we will discuss later, migration to new colonies. Increased surpluses combined with increased population densities led to the need for increased centralization to coordinate the increasingly complex divisions of specialized labor necessary to produce, store, distribute, and defend even larger agricultural surpluses. This led to an extraction cycle in which greater surplus led to higher levels of extraction but all in the name of classical kings and queens despite increasing individuality within national or trust cultures. Extraction eventually became so intolerable in terms of wars, conscription, and taxation that it challenged the legitimacy of dynastic rulers.

The Second Agricultural Revolution incorporated four major agricultural innovations: enclosure, mechanization, crop rotation, and selective breeding. The Revolution began in Great Britain where the **open field system** had been the norm throughout the Middle Ages. In this feudal tradition farmers would cultivate strips of land in common fields and divide their bounty after the harvest. The **enclosure movement** brought an end to this form of collective agriculture. The open fields were replaced with individually owned and enclosed fields, leaving many farmers unemployed and without grazing or cultivation rights. The movement was based on a new set of efficiency standards or **economies of scale** and **market exchange**. Many of the farmers who were displaced by these dynamics would migrate to cities. They in turn would become the labor force for the industrial revolution. They would also undergo a cultural shift away from feudal values toward nationality that would culminate in the establishment of new forms of political governance and legitimacy.

The larger farms that were created by the enclosure movement benefitted from the economies of scale derived from the **mechanization** of agriculture. The seed drill, iron plow, and other technologies transformed agriculture into an increasingly **capital intensive** industry, increasing yields despite the involvement of fewer workers. Farmers were able to combine the efficiencies generated by technological innovations with those derived from the **selective breeding** of livestock to be larger, stronger, and more productive.

Finally, crop rotation and the three-field system maximized the yield from the land. During the Middle Ages, two crops, usually wheat and barley, were rotated on a three-year cycle with one common field left fallow each year. Gradually, farmers introduced legumes into the crop rotation. Rather than leave a field fallow, the nitrogen-fixing legumes increased the fertility of croplands while yielding an additional harvest of an edible product. Farmers in continental Europe would later introduce a four-field system rotating turnips, clover, wheat, and barley. The clover not only improved grain production by replacing nutrients in the soil, it provided animal feed, thus increasing livestock production.

Together these innovations generated large agricultural surpluses improving nutrition, decreasing infant mortality rates, and extending life expectancies. This led to a population boom, first in England and, thereafter, across the world. But it also led to new social and political pressures. Displaced farmers left the land for burgeoning cities. New demands for textiles would lead to an industrial revolution that would transform the world economy from feudalism to capitalism. And the new class of workers, no longer beholden to feudalism and its obligations, would catalyze populist revolutions across the world leading to the establishment of modern sovereign nation-states.

Nation-Building: New Cultural Constructions of Collective Identity

As the Second Agricultural Revolution displaced agricultural workers and transformed feudal economies into capitalist systems, many individuals migrated to new city centers to find work. These city dwellers became part of a new class distinct from feudal rule known as the **bourgeoisie**. After an individual had lived in a city for one year and one day, he was considered free of feudal obligations. Thus late medieval Europeans quipped, "city air makes you free."

Although feudal fiefdoms were beholden to disciplines grounded primarily in honor and shame, city dwellers were disciplined by merit and guilt. Over time, city dwellers became members of communities with common cultural constructions of collective identity. They lived together, worshipped together, were governed by the same rules, and were interdependent on one another for the goods and services they needed to survive. The new political formation was the **nation**, and its collective identity **nationality**.

Thus the rise of nations and nationality represents a reassertion of individualistic trust cultures once dynastic rule becomes delegitimated. The concept of nation links trust culture, individual merit, citizenship, popular consent, and disciplines of guilt based on commitment rules to the "promises" of market exchanges associated with the "promissory" values of legal contract, obligation, liability, or tort. A nation supports the legitimacy of a single centralized government empowered to extract, but only in the name of the people as a unified entity or political order. The concept of nation, therefore, applies to a wide range of political cultures that ground national collective identities or the sense of peoplehood across a spectrum of differences in race, ethnicity, language, religion, and class.

Benedict Anderson described "nations" as "imagined political communities." They are imagined in the sense that "the members of even the smallest nation will never know most of their fellow-members, meet them, or even hear of them, yet in the minds of each lives the image of their communion."[1] Unlike kinship groups, in which citizens are connected not only through personal knowledge of one another but through ties of blood and marriage, nations are connected by desires to belong, to be a part of something greater than the self. Nations are not naturally occurring and they are not born. They are created. And they are limited in the sense that even the largest nation "has finite, if elastic, boundaries beyond which lie other nations."[2] Key to the idea of nationality is the concept of collective belonging grounded in exclusion. Nationality is about who we are and how "we" are different from "them." And it is about governance, for at its core nationality is, as Ernest Gellner writes, "a theory of political legitimacy, which requires that … all nations have their own political roof."[3] For Gellner,

therefore, the notion of **self-determination** is central to nationality itself but as a doctrine of legitimacy grounded in popular consent.

Notions of nationality emerged as the Enlightenment and the Protestant Reformation "were destroying the legitimacy of the divinely-ordained, hierarchical dynastic realm."[4] Vernacular languages replaced Latin. Protestant religion challenged the Catholic Church. Political philosophers elaborated political values stemming from the Enlightenment such as political liberty, the separation of powers, and the social contract. All the while, **nationalist revolutions** overtook Europe as European nations sought to create new forms of legitimacy and political consolidation. **Nationalism** took hold as a form of political culture. In order for governments grounded in the legitimacy of sovereign states to rule effectively, the concepts of the **nation** and **nationhood** had to transcend the political imagination of kinship and become concrete as the foundation of all political cultures associated with the sovereign state. But, for all that, the concept of nationhood remains an "imagined" or invented form of subjectivity.

Beginning with the Glorious Revolution, English monarchs agreed to power-sharing demands made first by the nobility and later by the bourgeoisie. British monarchs held power, but that power was limited by the Parliament, and both institutions worked together toward social, political, and economic goals. Although only 5 percent of English citizens were permitted to vote in Parliamentary elections, over time Parliament gained authority relative to the English monarchy. After the fall of the Stuart dynasty, a series of German kings inherited the English throne. George I and George II, the first of these Hanoverian kings, did not speak English, live in England, or engage in English politics. Power thus shifted from the monarch to the prime minister, the chief member of the Parliamentary cabinet. Later Hanoverian kings, including George III, tried to exert greater authority and influence over English affairs but faced opposition from the Parliament. After facing an extraction crisis in the form of the American Revolution, which was catalyzed by attempts to tax American colonists without extending to them representation in Parliament, England underwent its own political revolution. This further limited the power of the monarchy. Today England remains a limited monarchy. Political authority and legitimacy rest in the hands of the Parliament, the Cabinet, and the prime minister. While the English monarchs capitulated to pressure from the nobility and the bourgeoisie to accept limited powers, the French monarchs clung to their absolutist pasts. Since the Middle Ages, France had been divided into three groups called **estates**. The First Estate comprised the Catholic clergy; the Second Estate comprised the nobility; and the Third Estate included everyone else—the bourgeoisie, the urban poor, and the peasant farmers. By far the largest of the three estates, the Third Estate,

constituting nearly 98 percent of the population, was also the most fragmented and the least unified in its political objectives.

This created a crisis in **collective action**. The vast majority of the members of the Third Estate were either absent or indifferent to the processes in which their interests were determined, whereas those with the narrowest interests were deeply engaged in political dynamics. The three estates met in the **Estates General**, the medieval version of a French legislature. Although the nobility constituted only 2 percent of the population, it owned 20 percent of the land and held the highest offices in both the army and government. In addition, the nobility wielded great influence over the Catholic clergy since the younger sons of noble lords often joined the Church as priests. Most importantly, neither the nobility nor the Church paid taxes to the king. Thus the entire tax burden rested on the shoulders of the Third Estate.

The Estates General required a two-thirds vote to carry any motion and each estate was allocated a single vote. Because the clergy and the nobility shared social, political, and economic interests, they voted as a block, effectively shutting the Third Estate out of political power. But members of the Third Estate, particularly the wealthy bourgeoisie, were inspired by the ideas of the Enlightenment. They wanted social and political power to match their economic status. The urban poor demanded secure access to food within the cities where they worked and lived. And the peasants, who paid nearly half of their income in taxes and also owed the corvée, a labor tax to be paid in work on government projects, demanded tax reform. When Louis XVI needed to raise taxes to cover the aid he provided to the leaders of the American Revolution, he decided to tax the nobility. The nobles demanded that he call the Estates General to approve this new extraction plan, expecting to use its influence with the Church to shift the tax burden onto the already over-taxed Third Estate. But when the groups met, the Third Estate demanded that each delegate's vote be counted separately so that its 610 votes could outnumber the First and Second Estates' 591 votes. When the king ordered that the Estates follow the old rules, Abbé Sieyes suggested that the Third Estate form a National Assembly to pass laws and reforms in the name of the French people. The delegates agreed and on June 17, 1789, they declared an end to the French monarchy and the beginning of a representative democracy. Although Louis tried to appease the Third Estate by promising reform and representation, the revolutionaries refused to compromise. Fearing that the French military would side with the National Assembly, Louis called for an army of mercenary Swiss Guards to defend France. In response, the people of Paris revolted, stormed the Bastille, and defended against the Swiss troops. This victory of the French people against the foreign

defenders of the monarchy became a symbol of the **French Revolution** that then spread from Paris into the countryside.

On August 4, 1789, the National Assembly eliminated the ancient privileges of the nobility and the clergy, thus effectively abolishing feudalism within France. It adopted a set of revolutionary ideas known as *A Declaration of the Rights of Man and Citizen* that stated that all men were born equal in natural rights including life, liberty, property, security, and resistance to oppression. It granted equal justice, freedom of speech, and freedom of religion to all members of the French nation and stated that the French people were **sovereign**. This meant that the people alone had the authority to make law. By 1791 the National Assembly had created a new constitution with a limited monarchy and an elected assembly. The monarchy had the power to enforce and execute laws but only the elected Legislative Assembly had the authority to make laws in the name of the French people. In addition, the National Assembly stripped the Catholic Church of both its lands and its political status. The government took church lands to pay off French debts. The National Assembly also cut ties with the pope and demanded that the Catholic officials swear an oath of loyalty to the state instead of the Church. Thereafter, Church officials and priests were elected by French property owners and paid as state officials.

In both England and France the centralization of power in the hands of the monarchy associated with early **state-building** prompted a reaction from the governed. These reactions provoked different historic processes and thus different outcomes associated with nation-building. In England, the reaction came first from the nobility, and in France, it came from the Third Estate. As Anderson writes, having imagined themselves as a community, both the English nation and the French nation brought new imagined realities into being: "nation-states, republican institutions, common citizenships, popular sovereignty, national flags, and anthems, etc., and the liquidation of their conceptual opposites: dynastic empires, monarchical institutions, absolutisms, subjecthoods, inherited nobilities, serfdoms, ghettoes, and so forth."[5] In the case of Britain, given its constitutional history, state-building led to highly decentralized forms of governance. In France, the opposite occurred since it tended to remain governed from Paris and thus in relatively centralized ways. But in both cases the people sought statehood. As Gellner writes, "there is one particular form of the violation of the nationalist principle to which nationalist sentiment is quite particularly sensitive: if the rulers of the political unit belong to a nation other than that of the majority of the ruled, this, for nationalists, constitutes a quite outstandingly intolerable breach of political propriety."[6] To be governed by a power outside the nation, be it the monarchy, the nobility, the Church, or a foreign power, is unacceptable

to a people since they often take this as an assault against the legitimacy of their authority based on popular consent. For this reason, the Glorious Revolution, the American Revolution, and the French Revolution bring to life a new form of political culture, one that links legitimacy with governance and grounds this in the popular consent of nationhood. A new political culture thus emerged, one based on the legitimacy of rule or authority stemming from the people, in relation to government, namely, the **nation-state**.

States, Nations, and Nation-States as Political Cultures

A modern sovereign **state** is a bounded political unit that exercises authority through centralized political institutions. It has territory, a system of law and justice, structures to enforce contracts and promissory agreements, and the ability to extract from its citizens. In the modern world, the state holds a monopoly on violence. Only the state can raise and maintain an army. It can declare war, institute martial law within its boundaries, and legally require the people living within its boundaries to act according to its rules. In the international society of states, a state is **sovereign** and enjoys legal rights to **nonintervention**. This means that there is no authority above the state that can legally compel it to act in ways contrary to the policies and decisions of a national government. In terms of international law, no international institution or global force can demand that a sovereign state undertake any action it does not choose to do. Furthermore, state intervention in the domestic affairs of another is considered tantamount to aggression, even an act of war.

Until the end of World War II, sovereignty and nonintervention were considered to be absolute. Having witnessed the gross human rights violations that attended the Holocaust, however, several governments within the international system began to reconsider these two pillars of international rule and order. Today, most major sovereign states have promised to intervene in the domestic politics of other sovereign states to prevent massive violations of human rights. In the aftermath of ethnic cleansing in Kosovo and genocide in Rwanda in the 1990s, states in the international system agreed to a set of international norms called the **Responsibility to Protect (R2P)**. According to this set of normative principles and structure, sovereign states and their governments have the primary responsibility for protecting their own citizens against gross violations of human rights and mass political violence. If they are unwilling or unable to do so, however, the responsibility to prevent humanitarian crises, to stop mass political violence, and to rebuild failed states is transferred to the international

community. At present, however, states remain hesitant to violate the sovereignty of other states on account of human rights violations alone lest they risk the threat of challenging the legitimacy of their own sovereignty by acting beyond the bounds of popular consent with respect to populations other than their own. Sovereignty thus remains the core characteristic of the international society of states in the modern world.

As we have learned, a **nation** is an imagined political community of individuals who seek to govern themselves on the basis of a kind of legitimacy associated with popular consent. Although it is widely assumed that high degrees of homogeneity must exist among those who constitute a nation, the empirical or objective facts of nations around the world reveal heterogeneity, diversity, and difference. Many if not all nations comprise people who enjoy cultural differences in race, ethnicity, language, religion, and class. Thus the term nation must be able to extend to heterogeneous and multicultural populations that nevertheless constitute a single national identity.

As we will soon see, nation-states generate cultures of **citizenship** and **nationality**. The cultural strength of a nation-state as a political culture is a measure of the extent to which national cultures bind individuals as national collectives to the legitimacy of centralized state authority and rule. Strong nation-states as political cultures can be, and often are, multicultural, multiethnic, multireligious, and multilingual. Nationhood does not require racial, ethnic, religious, or socioeconomic homogeneity. Instead, collective identities grounded in nationality permit citizenship and legitimate centralized institutions to function in ways that are congruent and mutually reaffirming across a range of nation-states as political cultures—from the most culturally homogenous (Japan) to the most culturally diverse (India).

The concept of the nation, therefore, differs from those of race, ethnicity, and religion. It refers to the dynamics of legitimacy and popular consent as the basis for state sovereignty, political governance, and nation-state congruence. A nation is a historical, political-cultural invention or creation that represents the collective identity of a group of people who believe that they hold a common destiny if not a common history. For example, the American nation, like many other national political cultures, exists not only because its citizens recognize that they share a common past or set of material markers, but because they understand that they partake of a common future.

A **nation-state** operates as a political culture whenever and wherever a unified nation is governed by its own sovereign state. Within nation-states, rule of law is exerted in the name of the people as the exclusive source of political legitimacy. The hyphen in nation-state represents **congruence** between top-down

centralizing state institutions and bottom-up national legitimacy. Within modern sovereign nation-states, the popular consent of the governed permits the state to rule. Individuals' **patriotism**, or loyalty to the state, is linked to their membership in the nation.

Popular consent does not necessarily conform to democratic or republican practices. It may be populist as in Venezuela, monarchical as in Great Britain, or authoritarian as in the People's Republic of China. So long as political institutions represent the will of the nation, popular consent can be said to exist.

Stateless Nations and Nationally Divided States

Modern legitimacy crises occur whenever and wherever there is a lack of congruence between the state as a form of government and authority and a nation as a political culture unified by a sense of common destiny and solidarity or community and grounded in popular consent. This leads to various kinds of crises in political culture, one labeled as **stateless nations**, another as **nationally divided states**. A stateless nation exists whenever or wherever an imagined political culture that functions in ways that permit a people to conceive of themselves as a nation finds itself lacking its own sovereign, independent state. In modern political cultures, stateless nations often become transformed into disaffected minorities with memories of collective cultural loss, and are never fully integrated into the national society of the sovereign state that governs them. Modern examples abound: the Palestinians in Israel and Occupied Territories as well as Gaza; the Kurds in Iran, Syria, Turkey, and Iraq; the Tamils in Sri Lanka; the Chechens in Chechnya; the South Ossetians in Georgia; the Basques in Spain and France; the Tibetans in China. These are representative of national aspirations on the parts of those who as a result often seek **self-determination** through the establishment of their own sovereign nation-states under the doctrine of popular consent.

In many instances, these political cultures exist as a source of domestic tension, often culminating in political violence. In 2008, for example, a legitimacy crisis in Georgia led to armed conflict between Georgia on one side and Russia and the separatist government of South Ossetia on the other. Several hundred combatants and civilians were killed in this struggle for South Ossetian independence. In the end, Russia recognized South Ossetia as an independent republic and Georgia lost control over approximately 40 percent of South Ossetian territory. But the situation is not resolved and tensions continue over the question of self-determination for this stateless nation.

ALTERNATE PERSPECTIVES

Sovereignty

The relationship between the **nation** and the **state** is grounded in legitimacy and sovereignty. While there is debate over the definitions of both concepts, many arguments revolve around the purposes of state sovereignty. Naeem Inayatullah highlights the general advantages and disadvantages of sovereignty in its modern use. The work of Scott G. Nelson illuminates these issues as well. Currently, sovereignty is crucial in discussions of international security due to its encouragement of nonintervention. Regardless of relative power or size, sovereignty discourages the use of force in international relations. In theory, the principle of nonintervention allows a wide variety of national governments to coexist peacefully without conflict. However, sovereignty can be seen as an obstacle to human rights and humanitarian intervention. There is a tension between the rights of states as sovereign actors and the rights of individuals as human persons.

Thomas J. Biersteker and Cynthia Weber, in *State Sovereignty as Social Construct,* argue for a distinction within the discussion of sovereignty as a socially constructed phenomenon. Their stipulation is that while territory, population, and authority are important aspects of state sovereignty, they are also socially constructed in combination with the modern state system. Biersteker and Weber indicate that the current system revolving around sovereignty is not a natural or necessary outcome of the past, but instead the product of social, political, and economic events and forces. The modern sovereign nation-state is a product of social interaction and construction—a historical development that emerged from the cultures of primordial communities and dynastic kingdoms.

South Ossetia is not the only stateless nation to make recent news. After decades of political repression of and violence against the people of the Darfur region of Sudan, the southern region of the country voted to secede from its former state. A referendum was held in January 2011 to determine whether South Sudan should declare its independence from Sudan. With nearly 99 percent of the population voting in favor of independence, South Sudan declared its formal independence on July 9, 2011, making it one of the world's newest nation-states. After decades of ethnic cleansing and brutal violence, however, South Sudan faces a number of challenges to its legitimacy and sovereignty. It is constantly under the

threat of violence and tens of thousands of civilians have been displaced. In July 2014, the United Nations announced that no fewer than seven million people required humanitarian assistance on account of continuing conflicts in South Sudan, especially in the Darfur region and on account of massive movements of refugees fleeing the conflict, overwhelmingly on foot. Such international and regional tensions thus undermine the new government.

An additional example is the Palestinian claim to nationhood and their application for recognition of sovereign statehood. In 2011 the Palestinian political leadership requested that the United Nations General Assembly recognize Palestine as a sovereign state. The issue remains highly contentious. Serious questions arise concerning international stability and the treatment of people under conditions in which state sovereignty and nationhood do not reflect the congruence of a nation-state and thus the doctrinal legitimacy of popular consent. The conflict between Israeli and Palestinian peoples over land, power, control, authority, and legitimacy represents one of the most complex and inflammatory antagonisms besetting the international community, one that defies peaceful resolution year after year. Many aspects of this persistent dispute appear to elude resolution. But the most intractable of all issues concerns the disposition of land and the demarcation of boundaries, in particular the future control over Jerusalem that both sides claim as capital. This speaks to the symbolic nature of confrontations between Israel and the Palestinians, a symbolism rooted in conflicting versions of political culture and communal heritage.

A **nationally divided state** is a centralized state that lacks a unified nation within its boundaries. Often divided by lineage, class, or sectarian loyalties that defy the legitimacy of centralized forms of state governance, nationally divided states struggle to achieve the popular consent necessary for stable and peaceful rule. Contemporary examples include the Democratic Republic of the Congo and Somalia. As we will see in our discussion of colonialism, nationally divided states are often the consequence of colonial dynamics that violated the political and cultural boundaries of kinship groups and dynastic kingdoms. Today, nationally divided states are characterized by illegitimate central governments, political turmoil, and, often, mass political violence.

Many of the **Arab Spring** protests that have dotted the North African and Middle Eastern landscapes since late 2010 center around the dynamics of **nationally divided statehood** and have resulted in legitimacy crises across the region. As a result rulers have been forced from power in Tunisia, Egypt, Libya, and Yemen, while civil uprisings have occurred in Bahrain and civil conflict has assailed Syria to the point where the very existence of civil society within established

borders is threatened. Although state governments legitimated by primordial, feudal, and dynastic principles or merely in terms of corrupt power have been overthrown, the continuing turmoil in the region bespeaks the difficulties of creating national political cultures based on the legitimacy of popular consent that would extend across the sectarian and religious as well as ethnic divides. The end result of these revolutions remains unclear. A venomous Islamic caliphate has been declared across large swaths of Iraqi and Syrian territory, making the boundaries between these two sovereign entities virtually indistinguishable in some areas. Iraqi sovereignty remains threatened by a tripartite division along sectarian and ethnic lines. The timeline and eventual outcomes of such conflicts remain unpredictable. At their very core, however, they reveal the depth of feeling provoked by conflicts over legitimacy, popular consent, the role and status of state sovereignty, and the meanings attached to nationhood, all of which are central to political culture and the making of modern nation-states. Both stateless nations and nationally divided states represent episodes of contemporary conflict grounded in the disconnect between centralized sovereign statehood and collective political culture constituted by nationhood.

Nationally divided states sometimes veer toward extremes by becoming virtually ungovernable. When this happens they fall into the traps of what are sometimes referred to as failed states. Under these political-cultural conditions, clashes arise between political cultures beholden to kinship and segmented lineage and those oriented to modern sovereign authority attached to specific nation-states. Contemporary theorists who explain events in such places as Sudan, Iraq, and Afghanistan emphasize the lack of historical congruence between nationhood and sovereign statehood throughout many parts of the modern world. **Failed states** appear to lack the capacities to generate sentiments and ideologies of national popular consent. The reasons point toward the continuing grasp of the patrimonial legitimacies and the cultural disciplines of descent, honor, and shame discussed earlier. The long history of transition from kinship communities through dynasties to nationhood and statehood sometimes translates into the development of political cultures that resist nationhood or the political imaginary configured around conceptions of unified nationality in relation to sovereign statehood. The reasons are manifold, including sectarian, religious, kinship, and ethnic considerations, but the origins often stem from the lingering grasp of segmented lineage and subsequent disavowals of the legitimacy of the sovereign authority of centralized states. Thus the cultural divisions that impede nation-building relative to statebuilding in the modern political cultures of failed states tend to reflect historical, cultural legitimacies grounded in patrimonial rule and kinship honor.

KEY CONCEPTS

Sovereignty, Nonintervention, and Human Rights

The **Peace of Westphalia (1648)** ended Europe's Thirty Years' War and established sovereignty as the foundation of interstate relations. In its aftermath, states became the supreme agents of international politics. **Sovereignty**, sometimes called **Westphalian sovereignty** after its origins, is constituted by the prime authority of the state over a specific territory. Sovereignty endows state political formations with the rights of succession so that changes in governments do not imply alterations in the status of sovereign status or governance. Sovereignty revolves around international state recognition, a process that occurs among states designed to underscore each of their rights to exist and to undertake actions on behalf of their people and interests. Sovereignty is also a doctrine of domestic legitimacy that empowers nations acting through states to choose their political and economic institutions, their system of leadership and administration, and their own interpretations of justice and rights. Sovereignty is thus a doctrine in international law that recognizes the continuity of statehood, the role of governments in pursuit of state interests, and the primacy of national law and legislative machinery within the territorial jurisdictions of sovereign borders.

Sovereignty is thus associated with the legal principles of **nonintervention.** This obligates sovereign states not to interfere in the internal affairs of other sovereign states. In theory, sovereign states enjoy the legal right to govern in the absence of intervention on the part of other states in the international system. Traditionally, sovereign states were the only subject of international law and, for such reasons, sovereign states appeared to possess the right to deny civil rights to their citizens or to engage in practices that included gross violations of the human rights of citizens without fear of interference from any other state, group of states, or multilateral organization.

As we saw earlier, strict doctrines of absolute sovereignty and nonintervention underwent a transformation in the second half of the twentieth century. Norms associated with international human rights law and humanitarian intervention gained increasing acceptance in the international system. In the aftermath of the Holocaust, the international society of sovereign states recognized that genocide or crimes against humanity within the domestic

continued

borders of a sovereign state warranted intervention even if such actions appeared to violate the legal sanctity of another state's sovereign borders. In 1948 many states signed the **Universal Declaration of Human Rights**, which committed them to respect the human rights of citizens. For the first time, individual citizens within the domestic borders of sovereign states became the subject of international law and procedures. The Universal Declaration included no enforcement mechanisms. Thus it did not technically infringe on the sovereignty of the states that were signatories to the Universal Declaration or other states in the international system. Nonetheless this was progress toward developing a concept of state sovereignty delimited by international obligations dedicated to the promotion and protection of human rights laws and practices. In 1948 many states also acceded to the so-called **Genocide Convention**, which made genocide and crimes against humanity subject to criminal procedures in ways that also required intervention in the domestic politics of sovereign states in cases in which such violations appeared. Article II of the 1948 United Nations Convention on the Prevention and Punishment of the Crime of Genocide defines the crime of genocide as "acts committed with the intent to destroy, in whole or in part, a national, ethnical, racial, or religious group, as such."

Even with that, however, and a variety of subsequent international treaties and conventions, the question remains: What happens when a domestic government or their agents become the perpetrators? Human rights are essentially adjudicated in terms of international or regional law over and beyond strict normative standards posed by state sovereignty. To the extent that they represent the development of new normative standards, they provide evidence of the progression of political and cultural acceptance of collective or quasi-universal standards regarding the proper treatment of human beings, as individuals and in groups. For international human rights law to exist at all it must establish multilateral tribunals and international human rights jurisprudence. In recent years, recognition of the importance of international juridical structures to apply human rights jurisprudence in cases of extreme violations has led to the impaneling of several major tribunals. These include the International Criminal Tribunal for Rwanda (ICTR), the International Criminal Tribunal for the Former Yugoslavia (ICTY), Extraordinary Chambers in the Courts of Cambodia (EECC), and the International Criminal Court (ICC). The latter was established by the Rome Statute that came into force on July 1, 2002.

Nationality as a Bulwark against Exclusivism and Hate

Sovereignty establishes the nation-state as the primary object of international law and bestows legal legitimacy on centralized authority. Sovereignty is thus a legal doctrine that establishes the primacy of singular centralized governmental authority within the internal affairs of nation-states bounded by territorial borders or demarcations. A crucial attribute of sovereignty is the singularity that attaches to the authority of central government within nation-states.

There is an important distinction between the legal doctrine of sovereignty and the political dynamic of legitimacy. Sovereignty is a legal doctrine that grounds the relationship between a so-called nation and a singular centralized political or governmental authority. It establishes the legal authority for singular centralized states to function within bounded territories. Legitimacy, on the other hand, refers to the political process by which a singular centralized government functions relative to the popular consent of a people deemed a nation. The extent to which governments rule according to the practices of freedom, accountability, democracy, openness, responsiveness, and, ultimately, popular consent of all members of that society or every group within that society represents an important but ultimately separate issue that does not define the nature of legal sovereignty within nation-states.

National governments confer nationality on citizens by virtue of their being legal members of a sovereign nation-state; nationality is not a function of racial, ethnic, linguistic, religious, or other such naturalistic or identity differences. Such contrasts may or may not be found within any society. They may or may not be a matter of tension or lead to conflicts. Nationality also does not depend on homogeneity among the citizens of a state or members of a nation. Nationality is the outcome or a function of citizenship per se. It represents the cultural dimensions of citizenship. It is based on legal membership in a national community and is grounded in the capacities of those who enjoy the legal status of citizenship in a nation-state to participate in and to benefit from the dimensions of a national culture. Simply viewed, nationality inheres in the cultural facets of collective belonging, including language, political values that grow from and out of citizenship, and the legal right to carry a passport as issued by the government of the sovereign state in which one is a citizen.

Sovereign states alone decide the criteria necessary for the conferral of citizenship and thus the **nationality** of their citizens. **Nationality** depends on but it is not the same as **citizenship**, since the latter is attached to legal status whereas the former involves the cultural requirements or standards on which citizenship depends. Thus, nationality is a culturally constructed artifact of citizenship. Na-

tionality as a cultural concept is readily transformed into an ethnic identity once a citizen of one sovereign state moves into another for whatever reasons. This is the meaning and significance of what in American parlance is called "naturalization." Immigrants into the United States, once naturalized as citizens, take on not only the legal status of an American citizen but also American nationality, whatever their origins. In these cases in which individuals are exchanging citizenship from one to another nationality, their past nationality becomes a form of ethnic or identity difference within the frames of American nationality. Nationality thus represents a cultural concept that stresses the commonalities among members of a specific nation despite all other identity differences among them. Nationality is not the same as ethnicity, race, religion, kinship, class, or any other cultural classification that differentiates among the people of a single nation. On the contrary, nationality refers to cultural solidarities among citizens of a nation by emphasizing the cultural features that make members of a nation conceive of themselves as a single people or at the very least act in conformity with the requirements of citizenship. Nationality exists in the cultural values and dispositions that reflect the legal status of citizenship based on the individuality of persons as citizens in relation to a sovereign state. Kinship belonging does not entail nationality as such unless it is integral to formal status in relation to legally defined state citizenship. Individuality of citizens, once anchored to nationality, enables members of a nation to transcend the kinds of group contrasts that might fracture the sense of commonality among all citizen members of a nation whatever their identity differences. There exists, however, no guarantee in this regard. If and when racial, ethnic, sectarian, or religious categories and the like become conflated with concepts of nationality or become equated with standards of citizenship, intense ethno-political conflicts tend to arise. During the Rwandan genocide, for example, the Hutu engaged in a frightful attempt to exclude Tutsi citizens from Rwandan nationality as justification for their annihilation. Accordingly, whenever a central authority or sovereign state appears beholden to a particular racial, ethnic, or religious group in ways that marginalize other groups within the nation, there tend to be high levels of domestic struggle and conflict. Thus, cultural efforts and campaigns to racialize or ethnicize nationality represent dangerous political episodes fraught with risks to major segments of a national population and are by implication utterly destructive of any sense of nationhood.

Modern nation-states grounded in legal conceptions of sovereignty thus give rise to the importance of cultural constructions or classifications of nationality that are **hyphenated**. Hyphenated identities emerge in multicultural and multiethnic cultures in which citizens of common nationality maintain ethnic,

racial, sectarian, religious, etc., differences but in ways anchored to a single political culture. Many polyglot nations exist in which citizens or permanent residents embrace identity differences all the while living within political cultures defined by nationality. In such cases we speak of hyphenated identities such as African American or Chicano American. These are figures of speech that signify how individual citizens combine various forms of identity and heritage but in ways linked to nationhood. Hyphenated identities are not to be taken literally in the present context. Rather, they represent identity categories consisting in the multiple ways that citizens of any nation combine identity differences with nationality. Polyglot political cultures embrace the values of **nationality** as a principle of **commonality** and/or political solidarity, on the one hand, and the particular features of **individual and group cultural identity** on the other. These features may vary across a range of distinct differences including those that derive from race, ethnicity, and religion, among others. Thus nationality **anchors** racial, ethnic, and religious differences in the commonality of citizenship while individuality and citizenship become anchored in commonality of peoplehood as it celebrates difference. In nationality, differences among individuals and groups do not threaten the cohesion of nations so long as they are grounded in the solidarity of nationality and citizenship. Nation-building represents the rise of political capacities to anchor difference in conceptions of legal citizenship and conceptions of common nationality. If nations are to consist of individuals rather than members of traditional groupings defined by segmented lineage and their contemporary legacies, citizens of modern nation-states must have the right to enjoy hyphenated identities constructed collectively and personally that connect the cultural commonalities of nationality with personal features of social, cultural, or political difference. The hyphenated forms of collective political culture that ground nationality and difference within modern nation-states are as varied as they are distinct. They arise wherever national political cultures exist. Within the United States we speak readily of African Americans, Latino/Hispanic Americans, Jewish Americans, Italian Americans, Catholic Americans, and a host of other hyphenated identity constructions. British citizens may speak of Irish British, Scots British, English British, Welsh British, Pakistani British, or Indian British. In the African country of Kenya, where hyphenated forms of personal and political identity are still being forged and the unity of nationality is beginning to overcome the divisions of segmented lineage, we may perceive the cultural identity of Kikuyu Kenyan, Kamba Kenyan, and Meru Kenyan. In each example, cultural, religious, ethnic, racial, and even tribal difference is grounded in the progressive politics of national collective belonging and the possibilities of national unity based on cultural recognition of the meaning and significance

of nationality that derives from citizenship. This process defines "modernity" within the context of culture and the making of the modern nation-state.

Historically, American society has used the terms **melting pot** and **salad bowl** to describe commitments to **multiculturalism** and **hyphenated identity**. The term melting pot came into common use in the late 1700s and referred to the homogenization of American society. It was a metaphor for the melding together of the distinct racial, ethnic, and cultural differences found throughout the United States as waves of immigrants assimilated into mainstream Anglo-American culture. By the 1970s, however, proponents of multiculturalism and hyphenated identity began to use the term salad bowl instead of melting pot to indicate that the cultural differences found within American culture were not eliminated by the unity of American nationality. Instead, racial, ethnic, and cultural differences remain at once distinct, as the ingredients in a salad, as well as complementary parts of a whole, as in the salad itself. The salad bowl metaphor, far more than its melting pot predecessor, captures the importance of hyphenated identity in modern nation-states: the freedom to preserve and express diverse cultural histories grounded in the unifying force of common nationality.

Therefore, the strength of a nation-state as a political culture may be said to derive from the degree to which it successfully anchors **cultural difference in nationality**. As we will see, to do so is never merely given but requires political determination and commitment relative to a specific set of cultural values. Even the world's oldest nation-states struggle to balance their commitments to cultural diversity on the one hand, and national unity or solidarity on the other. In Great Britain, for example, a Scottish independence movement persists. Many British citizens of Scottish descent believe British nationality to be dominated by English culture, excluding Scots from equal participation in the British nation and from the full enjoyment of British citizenship. Similarly, the French government is currently facing a national identity crisis with regard to its Muslim and North African populations. The French government's ban on the Muslim head scarf in publicly supported educational institutions indicates a way of eliminating conflicts that might arise among citizens who share French nationality but who also experience sectarian differences. This approach contrasts with that in the United States since American conceptions of freedom of religion permit citizens to wear religious and sectarian symbols at will. Throughout Europe today, immigrants and recently admitted citizens of foreign origins confront various forms of discrimination while European governments, societies, and political parties and movements seek to adjust, sometimes successfully, at other times dismally, to the new cultural realities created by the presence of citizen populations originating from abroad. The quest for total integration of immigrants into the mainstream

of European national cultures depends on its capacity to forge nondiscriminatory hyphenated identities country to country, a task seemingly made more difficult by the absence of full employment across Europe. The consequence is the rise of anti-immigrant and even far right parties that often promote rejection of European institutions as a whole. That said, many European societies now provide higher living standards for multitudes of foreign-born persons now admitted to citizenship who in their own lifetime are working to create the kinds of hyphenated identities that inhere in the privileges of full citizenship and nationality. Even the United States, a country that has struggled throughout its history with the balances between difference and unity and exclusion and commonality, continues to face numerous tensions regarding nationality, immigration, and the road to citizenship. The quest for citizenship and nationality is still characterized by the divisive power of exclusion and marginalization in many nation-states. And the tragedy of the human costs of immigration continues to mount. This is symbolized by the so-called boat people who leave the shores of Africa en route to European entry points, risking their lives and those of loved ones. Even those who arrive safely face years in detention camps and thus lives of abject emptiness. This pertains to other coasts and jurisdictions including those of Australia. Across the southern border of the United States, thousands of Mexican and Central American immigrants attempt to enter illegally. US failure to create a new immigration law and set of procedures exacerbates the human costs by leaving many former immigrants in limbo, residents but not citizens, ethnically integrated into American life and culture but in terms of citizenship and thus nationality considered as alien. These tensions with respect to immigration and emigration highlight the political-cultural landscape created by the movement of peoples across the terrains of the nation-state leading to hyphenated identities within the frameworks of nationhood and common nationality.

Part II
The Making of the Political Culture of the American Nation-State

Chapter 5
Internal Colonialism and the American Experience

Hyphenated Identities American Style

America is a nation of immigrants. For centuries waves of immigrants have passed through the main immigration building on Ellis Island in New York Harbor in search of better lives as citizens of the United States and members of the American nation sharing in American nationality. They are welcomed by another national landmark on nearby Liberty Island, the Statue of Liberty, whose inscription reads, "Give me your tired, your poor, your huddled masses, yearning to breathe free, the wretched refuse of your teeming shore, send these, the homeless, tempest tossed, I lift my lamp beside the golden door." A gift to the United States from the French people, the Statue of Liberty is a representation of Libertas, the Roman goddess of freedom that stands as a powerful symbol of the American nation and all it is presumed to mean.

The American nation is replete with hyphenated identities. These represent vast differences in language, culture, ethnicity, race, and religion, but they are grounded in a common nationality. Yet the immigration experience has been far from ideal. For many, the American experience has been defined not by freedom, opportunity, and acceptance, but by exclusion, discrimination, and outright rejection. The challenges of hyphenated identity have defined American history, punctuating the cultural landscape with such events as the Trail of Tears, the American Civil War, the Asian Exclusion Act, Japanese internment, and the Civil Rights movement. Even today, the record-high number of hate groups in

America indicates that the balance of ethnicity and nationality in hyphenated identity is a tension the American nation has yet to resolve. American history thus remains an unfinished project.

The Contact Situation and Colonized Minority Groups

Much of American history may be viewed from the perspective of **contact situations**. A **contact situation** represents an initial phase of interaction between cultures that represent themselves as "white" and "civilizing," such as the European colonial powers, on the one hand, and kinship or segmented lineage cultures, such as those native to Africa, Asia, and the Americas, on the other. During the contact situation, the chains of knowing and belonging central to kinship communities are devalorized and subordinated.

The colonial experience in the United States witnessed contact situations that resulted in the forcible incorporation of three sets of indigenous peoples: Africans, indigenous Mexicans, and Native Americans. These represent the **colonized minority groups** of the American experience, the groups that became incorporated into the American nation, not by choice, but by conquest. Their incorporation was framed by an ideological justification called **Manifest Destiny** grounded in a notion of **American exceptionalism**. Manifest Destiny referred to the belief that the American nation, and, more specifically, the Anglo-Saxon "race" that dominated it, was destined to expand across the North American continent, controlling all of the lands between the Atlantic and Pacific Oceans. It was based on the idea that the American nation had a divine destiny: to civilize the North American continent and its native peoples by settling the continent with people who believed in liberty, egalitarianism, individualism, and popular consent. This mission-based logic would justify not only the enslavement of African populations, but also the conquest, displacement, dislocation, and cultural subordination of indigenous Americans and the occupation and annexation of Mexican territories and peoples.

American history is also the story of the voluntary incorporation of numerous racial, ethnic, and religious groups. Waves of immigration from Europe, Asia, Africa, and Latin America have added rich cultural diversity to the tapestry of the American nation. And yet American culture and nationality are, as they have been since colonial times, dominated by Anglo-American values associated with English settlers in the original thirteen colonies. Today non-Anglo minority groups within the United States struggle to become equal members of the American nation and to have equal rights under US law. While the challenges

are different for groups that were forcibly incorporated versus those that were voluntarily incorporated, the forging of the critical hyphen between ethnicity and nationality, between difference and commonality, remains an ongoing project in American cultural life.

Debates continue today regarding multiculturalism, the status of immigrants, and the nature of American society against the background of lingering forms of discrimination. Some of the worst forms of discrimination in American society have been directed at the three groups forcibly incorporated into American nationality: Africans, Native Americans, and Mexicans. But immigrants to the United States who have come on a voluntary basis have also been subjected to discrimination and geographic confinement.

Spatialization on the Basis of Group Identity

The relationship between immigration and the American nation reveals deep-seated cultural concerns over the presence of newcomers despite American social history characterized by successive waves of immigration. As a result, recent émigrés find that their ethnic differences become objectified. This appears to generate political and social pressures to confine them to specific locations. Such confinement pressures represent how certain kinds of social constructions dealing with difference or otherness become manifested by a social geography we call **spatialization**. Spatialization on the basis of group identity assumes various forms—**ethnic enclaves, ghettos, internment camps, refugee** or **immigrant islands, detention centers, plantations**, and **reservations**—but the effect often remains the same: cultural difference and the immigrants who represent it become confined and all too often isolated for indefinite periods of time. In the American experience, spatialization of difference from ghettos to internment camps underscores the anxieties and projected forms of dread and resentment that objectify ethnicity and race. This process of objectification in American cultural experience is manifested in a kind of **color code** that reveals the patterns of spatialization with respect to subordinated difference. The history of spatialization demonstrates how mainstream American culture objectifies the complexity of ethnic differences by transforming them into categories of racialized identity groups. The color code represents this racialization of ethnic differences and the experiences of objectifying cultural difference in response to immigration into the United States:

- **Black:** Slavery and Forced Labor Migration (1600–1865)
- **Red:** Native American Displacement and Dislocation (1700s–1800s)

- **Brown Episode I:** Mexican American Forced Territorial Incorporation (1840s)
- **Yellow:** Asian Immigration and Its Exclusion (late 1800s)
- **Green:** Anti-Arab and Anti-Islamic Sentiment (contemporary)
- **Brown Episode II:** Chicano and Central American Immigration (contemporary)

The critical component in American social history relative to ethnic difference has been the imposition of **majoritarian** mainstream Anglo culture symbolized by **whiteness**. As we will see, the unspoken privilege of whiteness has been the key to acceptance, social integration, economic mobility, individual freedom, and legal equality in the American nation.

The dynamics of cultural subordination may be understood as a form of **internal colonialism**. Internal colonialism involves two sets of dynamics: first, **displacement** and **dislocation**, and, second, **push** and **pull** factors. **Displacement** is a spiritual, emotional, imaginative, and/or psychological emptiness that is experienced both individually and communally whenever beloved traditional values appear stolen or lost. It throbs as a trauma, a pain experienced in the hearts and minds of those who are or who come to believe that they are the victims of a cultural imperialism that seeks to replace their traditions and values with a new and disorienting set of practices and attachments. **Dislocation**, on the other hand, occurs when a people are physically removed from the environment, land, or geography to which they have been traditionally attached. It is a physical phenomenon in the material world rather than a metaphysical loss in the imaginative spaces of communal belonging.

Thus, forced displacement and dislocation tend to destroy the intergenerational linkages necessary to nurture communal ties and the sense of kinship belonging. Because kinship and belonging anchored by ancestry are grounded by devotion to land, dislocation and displacement destroy the faith and certainty of cultural belonging. Displacement is an imaginative detachment from the sacred land of ancestry and kinship. It erodes the cultural foundations of community and communal order in the here and now as well as in an imagined past. It even corrodes the possibilities of an imagined future. Taking land away from indigenous peoples robs them of their credo of time past and time future that lie at the heart of their confidence in communal belonging. This leads to grief and an everlasting feeling of loss driven by the pervasive memories of what is forever taken to represent communal humiliation.

Dislocation through forced marches and displacement to reservations represent assaults against kinship cultural modalities, in terms of both space and time.

KEY CONCEPTS

Citizenship

Citizenship is a modern legal status defined by political, economic, and social rights that is granted by a state to people living within its borders and/or under its protection and care. States can grant citizenship on the basis of ancestry or **jus sanguinis** (the right of blood). This means that if one's parents are citizens of a given state, one inherits the right to citizenship within that state. Many sovereign states allow both parents to transfer citizenship to their children but some limit that right exclusively to fathers. Alternatively, sovereign states can grant citizenship on the basis of birthplace or **jus soli** (the right of soil). This means that persons are citizens of the sovereign state in which they were born. Many states confer citizenship based on a combination of land and blood, meaning that citizenship can be granted either by virtue of parentage or on account of the location of one's birth.

In addition, some states establish different classes of citizenship. A **second-class citizen** is one who is denied the full benefits of citizenship and is instead discriminated against by the state. States may disenfranchise second-class citizens or limit or restrict their access to civil and human rights including the freedom of movement, property rights, religious freedom, cultural expression, or access to the rites of formal and/or legally sanctioned marriage. In some cases, second-class citizenship is **de jure**, or based in law. This was the case in South Africa under apartheid and in the United States during the era of racial segregation. In others, it is **de facto**, or based in practice. Sovereign states will often deny de facto differences in citizenship. However, examples include Germans of Turkish descent in modern

continued

Wherever and whenever it occurs it projects the aims of the colonial experience to demean and to destroy the cultures of kinship descent on the part of those who purport to represent Western or European "superiority" and "whiteness." Severing present generations from the traditions of segmented lineage and from ancestral lands, which they deem sacred, through processes of dislocation works to destroy the capacities of traditional kinship communities to function in the "real" as well as metaphysical worlds. Once memory of the past becomes threatened in the present it is difficult for a people imbued with traditional communal understandings to envision a collective cultural future. That is to say, once a

Germany, Kurds in modern Turkey, ethnic Maya in modern Guatemala, and the Tamils in Sri Lanka.

In the modern world we assume that every person is the citizen of a sovereign state, but this is not always the case. Some people lack or are denied the rights associated with citizenship. They are thus considered to be **stateless**. In many cases, stateless populations have been purposefully stripped of their citizenship by their governments on the basis of their race, religion, ethnic, or cultural differences. In Nazi Germany, for example, Jews and Gypsies, among others, were denied citizenship both in Germany and wherever the Nazis gained control of the government as a prelude to their attempted annihilation. In other cases, **state succession** can result in statelessness. When **Yugoslavia** ceased to exist as a sovereign state, its people were rendered effectively stateless unless they could be reassigned citizenship by one of its successor states, a process that took on dramatic immediacy. In still other cases, statelessness results from the limitations built into a country's citizenship laws. Countries that require that citizenship pass from father to child, for example, create stateless individuals when either the identity or the citizenship of a child's father cannot be documented. Finally, determining the citizenship of individuals who live in transnational nomadic communities, such as the Maasai, can be a legal and practical challenge. The Maasai migrate throughout Kenya and northern Tanzania as if the boundaries did not exist. This makes it sometimes difficult to determine the citizenship of each individual member of the kinship community. Stateless populations are inherently vulnerable. International agreements such as the 1954 Convention on the Status of Stateless Persons seek to protect them from deportation, discrimination, and annihilation, but in the absence of the protection of any sovereign state such persons confront inordinate risks to well-being and physical integrity.

group is forcibly incorporated as a subordinated minority it is very difficult for them to assimilate, to accommodate to foreign ways of life, or to achieve equal status in the mainstream. This explains why immigrant minority groups tend to assimilate with greater success than those colonized minority groups that result from the dire circumstances of dislocation and displacement and thus as the consequence of contact situations.

Dislocation and displacement are fueled by **push** and **pull** factors. **Push** factors are exerted by force whenever sets of subordinated individuals and traditional clans are made to live as **subaltern** groups by being forced to live in the

"containers" of **spatialized** difference. Native American reservations exist as a consequence of push factors. **Pull** factors are exerted by incentives that serve to entice people by means of the promise of a better life. Such experiences often end instead in misery and sadness. Immigrant ethnic enclaves emerge because of pull factors. Historically, a parallel arises in the African American experience. While African Americans left southern rural locations to migrate to the American North and Midwest as a result of incentives, a **pull dynamic**, Native Americans were displaced and dislocated as a result of force, a **push dynamic**. As a consequence, African Americans were **displaced** and **dislocated** from rural agriculture as a result of **pull** factors during the early 1900s. On the other hand, Native Americans throughout the 1800s were **displaced** from communal sites and traditional values and found that they were consistently **dislocated** from sacred land as a result of **push** factors, often by brutal force. Together these push and pull factors help to explain the unique historical character of what retains its significance as American nation-building.

Slavery as a Forced Incorporation Process

Slavery stands as the first and prototypical episode of the forced incorporation of an immigrant population into US society. Slavery was a form of forced labor that existed as a legal institution in North America long before the founding of the United States in 1776 and that continued until the passage of the Thirteenth Amendment to the Constitution in 1865 following the American Civil War. Virginia, the first English colony in North America, acquired its first African slaves from the Dutch who dominated the slave trade in the New World. The Dutch captured slaves in East African colonial holdings. Although the vast majority of African slaves ended up on sugar plantations in the Caribbean and Brazil, a small number went to the British colonies in North America where they primarily worked on cotton, tobacco, indigo, and other plantations. The slave trade was part of the **triangle trade** between Europe, Africa, and the Americas: slaves were sent from Africa to the Americas; raw materials were sent from the Americas to Europe; and manufactured goods were exported from Europe to Africa and the Americas.

Slavery is an institution as old as civilization itself. However, slavery in the Americas took on two unique characteristics. First, slavery was **racialized**. European colonies and, later, the United States codified slavery according to nefarious notions of white supremacy. By the early eighteenth century, colonial courts and legislatures had established a system in which slavery applied nearly exclusively

to people of African descent. In time, even free Americans of African descent would be denied equal status or equal protection in the United States. Second, slavery in the Americas was **intergenerational**. Children inherited the status of their parents. A child born to a slave would be born into forced servitude. This system is known as **chattel slavery**, that is, a form of slavery in which a human being and his or her descendants are considered property that is physically owned by another human being. An estimated 645,000 slaves were brought to what is now the United States during the sixteenth through the nineteenth centuries. By 1860 the American slave population had grown to four million.

Through slavery the body becomes a dehumanized object. Chattel slavery treated the slave as if the person were without a cultural past or personal future. In slavery the body was transformed into chattel property without ancestral history, present family, or future blood connection. The bonds of lineage and communal order and tradition were systematically and cruelly assailed. As a consequence of slavery, the agency of the slave was viciously restricted. Disobedience was often punished by mutilation of the body from scarring to flogging. This domination of the slave required repressive forms of identity construction to separate the physical activity of slaves from any opportunity for mental or spiritual growth. The pain and suffering of slavery was not only implemented by means of physical brutality. At a spiritual and emotional level it occurred by means of a psychological process of degradation involving **dehistoricization**. In slavery, a person's cultural heritage became systematically detached from his or her life or autobiography. As a consequence of chattel status, and in order to dominate the slave in total ways, slave owners made certain that their slaves would become culturally divorced from any sense of continuity or connection with kinship order. One mechanism was the **slave auction**. People were bought and sold with complete disregard for their family ties. The chain of belonging that links generation to generation, particularly in terms of segmented or kinship lineage, was severed. To destroy one's sense of past is to destroy the hope of a future; and in the absence of a vision of the future, all courage disappears. Abraham Lincoln may well have been right when he declared in his second inaugural address that the pain and suffering of the American Civil War may well have been a form of divine retribution for the inhumanity of slavery.

Slavery was a point of contention in the United States throughout its history. It influenced the drafting of the Constitution, a document that mandated an end to the international slave trade and that counted a slave as three-fifths of a person for purposes of representation. By the mid-1800s it dominated the national discourse as **abolitionists** demanded an end to the institution while pro-slavery voices advocated its expansion into newly incorporated territories. The rights of

a state to permit slavery and of individuals to own slaves were critical issues that led to the American Civil War. Only one in ten Southerners owned slaves, but the institution of slavery was popular even with non-slave-owning Southerners in part because it established a social hierarchy in which an individual of European descent was, however poor or marginalized, necessarily considered superior to one of African ancestry. After the Union army defeated the Confederate forces, however, slavery was made illegal throughout the United States.

In 1821 the American Colonization Society established the colony of Liberia as part of a movement to return Americans of African descent to Africa. Although thousands immigrated to Liberia, most Americans of African descent did not want to be repatriated. They had, after all, been born in the United States, their kinship-based cultural traditions had been replaced, and they had experienced little to no direct connection to Africa or its peoples. They instead wanted full rights as American citizens. But that status was a long way off.

After the Civil War, freed slaves were legally guaranteed American citizenship. They were not, however, treated as equal citizens, particularly in the South where years of institutional racism persisted into the postwar period. Legal and social structures, including **Jim Crow laws**, enforced racial **segregation**, white supremacy, and legal disenfranchisement throughout the South until the Civil Rights movement of the 1960s. Not only did African Americans face legal discrimination, they were also the victims of violence and persecution. Across the South, groups such as the **Ku Klux Klan (KKK)** terrorized, tormented, and killed African Americans to prevent them from exercising their civil rights as American citizens and to prevent them from achieving equal membership in the American nation. Across the South, hundreds of African Americans were lynched as part of an organized campaign against them. As Elliot Jaspin writes in his history of racial cleansing in America, "whites feared that [African Americans] would become citizens. They feared blacks were a danger to the community. They worried that blacks would take jobs. . . . In the end these were justifications for a cleansing rather than their cause. Blacks were targets for a cleansing because, while they lived in a community, they usually did not belong to the place where they lived."[1] In dozens of counties across numerous states, the KKK and other racist organizations ethnically cleansed communities of all African Americans, expelling them and warning them never to return. These realities **pushed** many African Americans to migrate north to industrial centers, particularly in the Midwest in search of work, fair wages, and equality. They quickly learned that life in the North was also harsh and discriminatory and in this sense not altogether different from life in the South. Rather than acceptance, African Americans in the North faced resentment, racism, and discrimination, particularly as competition for jobs pitted different social subsets

of workers against each other. Even after the Civil Rights movement of the 1960s legally secured an end to segregation and disenfranchisement, African Americans continued to struggle to overcome centuries of cultural, social, economic, and political repression, particularly in the face of persistent racism.

The Contact Situation and Native Americans

When the British, French, Dutch, and Spanish colonists first arrived in North America, they did not find an uninhabited territory. Hundreds of traditional kinship/descent communities beholden to the patrimonial legitimacies of ancestors, sacred land, and segmented lineage inhabited the continent of North America from the Atlantic to the Pacific. Prior to Anglo-American white settler contact, Native Americans lived in traditional kinship communities. They hunted according to tribal traditions and cultivated a number of stable crops including corn (maize), beans, and squash. They lived in segmented lineage orders in which ancestry legitimated rule and, as we have seen elsewhere in the world, in which honor and shame as cultural values functioned to promote intergenerational survival. Contact with Anglo-Americans and Europeans, however, proved disastrous for these native cultures.

Scores of Native Americans died of European diseases to which they had no acquired immunity in the immediate aftermath of settler contact. Epidemics of smallpox, measles, chicken pox, and other European diseases decimated indigenous populations. Surviving communities were often enslaved and forced to work for Anglo-American and European landowners. So-called civilizing projects often imposed forced assimilation on indigenous tribes requiring them to renounce the legitimacy of their kinship values and traditions on the pretexts of "superior" Anglo-American and European ways of life.

From the early 1800s lands belonging to many tribal peoples were subject to annexation by the US government. As settled territories became US states, state governments continued to work to dissolve the autonomous boundaries of Native American communities. Gradually, many native traditional communities that had maintained control over their tribal lands found themselves subject to dislocation and displacement on account of the implementation of the internal colonialist doctrine familiarly known as **Manifest Destiny**.

In 1830, the United States Congress passed the Indian Removal Act in order to facilitate European American expansion into western territories. This authorized the government to relocate Native Americans from their homelands to lands west of the Mississippi River. The Cherokee, Creek, Seminole, Chickasaw, and Choctaw, known collectively as the **Five Civilized Tribes**, were removed from

their lands in the southeast and forced to walk to "Indian Territory" in present-day Oklahoma in a relocation dynamic known today as the **Trail of Tears**. Many Native Americans died of exposure, disease, dehydration, and starvation along the way, including 4,000 of the 15,000 relocated Cherokee. The removal process opened twenty-five million acres of land in the American South for settlement and cultivation by Anglo-Americans.

In the 1860s, the US government's plan to build a transcontinental railroad and settle the West necessitated the removal of native tribes from lands slated to be used in its construction. In addition, as Anglo-American settlers pushed west, they continued to remove indigenous populations from traditional lands, forcing them to live on ever-smaller and less sustainable reservations. For example, the Navajo were deported from their traditional territory and forced to walk at gunpoint to reservations in eastern New Mexico. Known as the **Long Walk**, this policy removed the Navajo from their ancestral homeland within the borders of the four sacred mountains from northeastern Arizona through western New Mexico.

Several tribes, such as the Sioux and the Cheyenne, forcibly resisted the US intrusions into their lands. A series of Indian Wars in which native peoples were systematically slaughtered by the US Army thus followed the American Civil War. Ultimately, the army's superior firepower all but eradicated native populations forcing them to relinquish their territorial claims and to relocate to government-run reservations. Not only did this practice of relocation sever the indigenous peoples from their cultural lands, it also undermined their economic sustainability. Native American tribes from time immemorial had lived in a symbiotic relationship with their natural environments. The religious and cultural traditions, on which their survival depended, were tied to the lands. Land was critical to intergenerational communal survival. Cut off from the buffalo and other herds and confined to reservations with poor soil quality for cultivation, many tribes became dependent on the US government for food. The overall consequence was the loss not only of their cultural autonomy and communal independence but of their economic security as well.

Many of these militarily contrived reservations were not sustainable. They impoverished the people made to live on them. Native American communities, now dislocated according to white settler notions of security through containment on territorial reservations, became subjected to policies associated with **Americanization**. US officials systematically worked to eradicate kinship cultures and the legitimacy of segmented lineage. Galvanized by doctrines associated with the **white man's burden** and the white or Anglo "civilizing process," the US government sought to impose "modern" values, traditions, and practices on Native Americans. Tribal religious ceremonies and communication and the teaching of

native forms of knowledge were prohibited. Boarding schools were established in which students were taught to speak, read, and write English and to practice Christianity in ways that forcibly demanded immediate assimilation and thereby the rejection of kinship traditional religious or metaphysical cultural traditions.

In the spirit of Americanization, the US government shifted its policy emphasis from isolation by means of containment and began to embrace a policy of **Indian termination**. From the mid-1940s to the mid-1960s, the United States pursued policies guided by the conviction that Native Americans would be better off if they became part of mainstream American society than if they were to continue to remain on reservations. The policies selected to accomplish this proved harsh and often dysfunctional if not counterproductive. Congress eliminated federal aid to Native American peoples, forcing them to become economically self-sufficient but under sparse and nearly impossible conditions. From 1953 to 1964 the US government terminated recognition of 109 formerly independent tribes. Approximately 3 percent of the indigenous population renounced their tribal affiliation to become US citizens. Approximately 2.5 million acres of reservation land were removed from protected status and sold, primarily to nonnative buyers. Although some native tribes were able to have their federal recognition and independence reinstated toward the latter part of the twentieth century, for many Native Americans, the policies implemented under Indian termination served decisively to sever their lingering efforts to maintain ties with kinship roots.

Eventually, reservation life and law imposed private land ownership on many traditional communities. This too has often proved devastating by working to diminish the functionality of traditional communal agricultural and horticulture systems and thus by eroding cooperative forms of farming. As a consequence, Native American peoples today tend to live in circumstances of intense poverty and struggle with identity crises relative to their relationships to each other, to their ancestors, and to the American nation.

Incorporation of Mexican Americans

The contact situation with Mexico dates to the Mexican-American War (1848) and the forced incorporation of large numbers of Mexicans into the Anglo-dominant culture of the United States. The United States acquired territories formerly belonging to Mexico as a result of the annexation of Texas, the Treaty of Guadalupe Hidalgo, and the Gadsden Purchase. The resident Mexican population throughout this region thus became in effect a conquered and colonized

minority group. Mexicans now incorporated into the territory of the United States became subjected to economic pressures. Newly acquired Mexican lands were gradually transformed into homesteads and ranches by Anglo-American settlers. In 1836 Texas declared its independence from Mexico, forming the Republic of Texas as a free, independent, and sovereign state. Mexico contested this secession, however, as well as the 1845 annexation of Texas by the United States. In 1846 war erupted between Mexico and the United States, beginning the Mexican-American War. US forces quickly occupied New Mexico, California, and other Mexican territories. The war ended in a US victory when American troops captured Mexico City in 1848. The Treaty of Guadalupe Hidalgo that ended the Mexican-American War forced Mexico to sell the territories known as the Mexican Cession to the United States for $18 million. This victory seemed to fulfill the promise of American Manifest Destiny as the United States now controlled continental territory from the Atlantic to Pacific Oceans. However, surveyors quickly learned that the Mexican Cession did not include a feasible route for a transcontinental railroad connecting to a southern port. For this reason, the United States and Mexico agreed to the Gadsden Purchase of 1853, a purchase that secured US ownership of railroad-friendly land.

Many of the people living in the territories covered by Texas, the Mexican Cession, and the Gadsden Purchase were indigenous Mexican, Spanish, and Hispanicized European settlers who settled the lands after the Spanish conquistadors had made first contact with native Mexican civilizations. People of these political cultures did not necessarily think of themselves as "Mexican." Instead, they were primarily loyal to regional authorities. Social status, political power, and economic influence in these communities derived from land ownership. At the top of the social pyramid was a landed elite known as **patróns** who owned large ranches and raised large herds of cattle. Small landowners were next in the hierarchy. Often called **rancheros**, they owned small homesteads where they raised small herds of horses and cattle. Finally, there was a lower class of landless **peóns** who were free but bound to the land. Landowners and peóns enjoyed a semifeudal relationship in which the peóns worked for the patróns and were under their legal authority and care.

By the early 1800s, Anglo-American settlers outnumbered Mexican residents by a ratio of ten to one. In the aftermath of the Mexican-American War, that ratio continued to increase. The question became how to deal with the native Mexican population composed as it was of people who had been Mexican citizens before the war but were now subject to the authority of the US government. The Treaty of Guadalupe Hidalgo promised that landowners in the newly acquired territories would be guaranteed the property rights and protections of

US citizens. This might have left the traditional social, economic, and political structure intact. However, in practice, many Mexican Americans lost their lands to Anglo settlers. As a consequence, the Mexican minority was transformed into a landless, stateless population that resented the people and authorities responsible for its dislocation. Many individuals and groups sought judicial redress through the US legal system. But they often resorted to violence against Anglo settlers once legal means proved unsuccessful or too expensive. This in turn prompted Anglo communities to seek to further subordinate the Mexican population. In many cases legal obstacles, like the Jim Crow laws of the American South, denied Mexican Americans equal social, political, and economic rights and privileges. Violence against Mexican Americans was common. An estimated 600 Mexican Americans were lynched between 1848 and 1928. During the Great Depression the US government sponsored a repatriation program. This encouraged Mexican Americans, many of whom were descendants of people forcibly incorporated into the United States, to move "voluntarily" back to Mexico. Throughout this period anti-Mexican repression by state authorities, including the Texas Rangers and mobs of settlers, was also common, reducing Mexican Americans to the status of **second-class citizens**. As a consequence of widespread discrimination in the American Southwest, many Mexican Americans sought work in other regions of the country. They found jobs in agriculture, meatpacking, and manufacturing plants. But they did not escape discrimination. As they moved away from the American Southwest, many left behind their own sense of cultural roots and traditions and struggled with issues of assimilation into mainstream American society.

Today, like so many other groups in the United States that maintain a sense of rich cultural heritage or belonging, Mexican Americans seek to balance life in the United States while maintaining adherence to their own unique cultural, religious, and linguistic traditions. Many have become fully integrated into American social, economic, and political life and make enormous contributions to US cultural life. For some who have partially secured labor, voting, and education rights, struggle for full acceptance and integration remains. For example, vast numbers of Latino/Hispanic illegal aliens, **Chicano Americans** included, provoke issues pertaining to resident status and the meaning and impacts of American nationality. This results in widespread conflicts over cultural identity. Such conflicts persist in painful and poignant ways relative to the majority culture. This is partially because waves of new immigrants, both from Mexico and from Latin and Central America more generally, have generated new challenges with respect to what it means to share in the political culture of the United States. The interests of recent immigrants often differ from the interests of those,

particularly Mexican Americans, who have been American citizens or residents in the United States for generations. Disagreements abound, for example, over what to call members of these groups—are they Chicanos, Latinos, or Hispanics? How do descendants of Mexican Americans who have been resident citizens of the United States for decades relate to more recent immigrants and vice versa? Given widespread concerns regarding émigré populations living the United States illegally who are mostly Mexican, Chicano, and Latino, and continuing debates over immigration reform, many social issues emerge that bear on the nature and future development of the political culture of the United States. In particular, questions relate to the social and political dynamics of hyphenated identity and the quest for social justice on terms that protect the integrity of US cultural integrity.

Richard Rodriguez, in his discussion "On Becoming Chicano," confronts some of these critical issues. He writes first of self-objectification saying, "Does the fact that I barely spoke any English until I was nine, or that as a child I felt a surge of self-hatred whenever a passing teenager would yell a racial slur, or that I saw my skin darken each summer—do any of these facts shape the ideas which I have or am capable of having?"[2] He goes on to explain that his parents were encouraged by grammar-school nuns to speak English in their home and to avoid their Spanish language in order to give their children a better chance at assimilating into American society. He writes, "Heroically, they gave up speaking to us in Spanish—the language that formed so much of the family's sense of intimacy in an alien world—and began to speak a broken English. . . . Gradually, Spanish became a sound freighted with only a kind of sentimental significance. . . . Just as gradually, English became the language I came not to *hear* because it was the language I used every day, as I gained access to a new, larger society. But the memory of Spanish persisted as a reminder of the society I had left."[3] He then explains how his assimilation distanced him from his family and his culture. He writes, "I knew that education had led me to repudiate my race. I was frequently labeled a *pocho,* a Mexican with gringo pretentions, not only because I could not speak Spanish but also because I would respond in English with precise and careful sentences. . . . For my grandmother, the least assimilated of my relations, the changes in her grandson since entering school were especially troubling. She remains today a dark and silently critical figure in my memory, a reminder of the Mexican-Indian ancestry that somehow my educational success has violated."[4] However fully he could reject his past and assimilate into mainstream Anglo culture, he could not change how others viewed him. Rodriguez concludes, "I became a Chicano in the eyes of students and faculty members. My racial identity was assumed for only the simplest reasons: my skin color and last name."[5]

His experience is not unique but, at the same time, Rodriguez's degree of successful assimilation is rare. Many Chicanos, Latinos, Hispanics, and Mexican Americans struggle to assimilate into Anglo-American culture. Today many Chicanos lag behind the rest of the US population in every measure of socioeconomic well-being from level of education, to occupational success, to employment status, and to family income. They are increasingly the victims of hate crimes on an individual level and systemic discrimination on a social or collective level. Demands that English legally become a national language and structural barriers against Spanish-speaking populations in education, the workforce, and civic life remain common. Despite this, Latino/Hispanic Americans remain an integral component of cultural life in the United States and are highly influential in transforming American political culture. The increasing numbers of successful Latino/Hispanic American figures, especially in politics, business, and entertainment, bode well for their future. They are gaining increasing influence at all levels of American politics, from presidential to local within many communities, especially in the South. This is especially important given the fact that Latino/Hispanic Americans are on the cusp of becoming the single largest minority population in the United States.

Manifest Destiny, the "Yellow Peril," and the Transcontinental Railroad

Manifest Destiny was an American ideology that justified Native American removal, and the annexation of lands previously held by Mexico. The notion that it was the right of the American nation to settle the entire North American continent had major consequences for all three of the groups forcibly incorporated into the American nation by subordination or colonization. Although Manifest Destiny acted as a push factor relative to Native Americans and Mexican Americans, it served as a pull factor with regard to Asian Americans. Manifest Destiny encouraged transcontinental movement across North America from the Atlantic to Pacific Oceans. Essential to this project was the construction of a transcontinental railroad system linking established population centers in the East with new settlements in the West. The construction of these railroads presented enormous economic and engineering problems and required major commitments of manual labor. From 1820 to 1890 waves of Asian immigrants flocked to the United States seeking to meet the challenges of transcontinental railroad construction. Their role and impact proved critical to the creation of a national economy in the United States throughout the nineteenth century. They

readily became the primary source of labor for building the transportation infrastructure fundamental to the establishment of an economic powerhouse. More than this, the completion of transcontinental railroads facilitated the flourishing of a sense of a united American nation. American nationalism emerged during this time as a new and potent ideological component of US national political culture. The immigrants from Asia who built the transcontinental railroads, often under duress and at great personal costs, made a unique historic contribution to this visionary project.

Chinese immigrants constituted the first wave, arriving in California in time for the 1848 Gold Rush. Initially they were welcomed as a source of inexpensive labor, particularly during the early stages of the Gold Rush. Later, as the supply of gold ore appeared to diminish, competition for jobs in California increased. This resulted in increased animosity toward the Chinese population. Chinese were excluded from the gold mines. In time, the influx of Chinese immigrants to the West Coast cities provoked **jingoistic** fears that the United States would be overrun by "hordes" of Chinese immigrants. Groups such as the **Supreme Order of Caucasians** promoted ideologies that objectified individuals of Asian descent as a threat to the American nation. This fear pervading American culture at this time was communicated by the term **yellow peril**.

Concerns over the so-called yellow peril led to the implementation of a series of federal laws designed to restrict Asian immigration to the United States. The **Page Act** of 1875 was the first federal immigration law. It prohibited the entry of immigrants who were considered "undesirable." Furthermore, it classified as "undesirable" any Asian immigrant who was coming to the United States in order to be contracted as a laborer. The law was designed to protect "the fate of white men, white families, and a nation constructed as white" from "immoral" Asian cultural traditions and values.[6] In 1882 the **Chinese Exclusion Act** became the first US immigration law targeted at a specific ethnic group. It allowed the United States to suspend Chinese immigration to the United States. The act excluded all Chinese laborers from emigrating from China to the United States. Amendments to the law passed in 1884 applied exclusions to ethnic Chinese regardless of their country of origin. The Act was renewed in 1882 for another ten years as well as in 1902 with provisions that extended it indefinitely. The Chinese Exclusion Act was finally repealed in a 1943 statute but permitted a national quota per year of only 105 Chinese immigrants. Eventually Chinese families were forced to settle in ethnic, mostly urban enclaves familiar to many Americans today as **Chinatowns**. The dynamics we associated with spatialization took a different form than the one that led to Native American reservations. But the effects were to contain Asian residents in particular locales so as to have

them live together within highly restricted areas. One positive side effect of this is that it has permitted such groups to support one another economically and to benefit from a wide variety of cultural supports.

Although Chinese immigrants represented the majority of Asian immigrants to California during the nineteenth century, numerous Japanese men immigrated to the West Coast of the United States seeking work and opportunities especially in the aftermath of the Chinese Exclusion Act. However, Japanese immigration further fueled national anxieties that in turn provoked calls to contain the yellow peril. In 1907, the United States and Japan entered into a **Gentlemen's Agreement**. The United States promised that it would not impose legal restrictions on Japanese immigration; in turn, Japan promised that it would prevent further immigration to the United States. The impact of this was to curtail Japanese male immigration to the United States. In 1913, the United States enacted the **Alien Land Act** prohibiting Japanese immigrants from land ownership in the United States. This represented a particularly difficult hardship since Japanese immigrants tended to settle in rural agricultural areas rather than in urban centers in contrast to Chinese immigrants. Finally, the 1924 **National Origins Act**, repealed in 1965, excluded all Japanese and other Asian immigrants from obtaining naturalized American citizenship.

While Chinese immigrants preferred urban work, Japanese immigrants often established rural ethnic enclaves in order to pursue profitable small-scale farming often using sustainable agricultural methods. Such orientations to farming often led to their voluntary isolation on farms in rural districts. This tended to reinforce Anglo-American stereotypes of the Japanese as clannish and even as anti-American. Such stereotypes later came to haunt Japanese Americans since they were applied in ways that appeared to justify institutional forms of discrimination, particularly after the 1941 Pearl Harbor attack. On December 7, 1941, the Japanese Imperial government attacked the United States naval base at Pearl Harbor, Hawaii. Three hundred fifty-three Japanese fighters, bombers, and torpedo planes were launched from six aircraft carriers to carry out the attack. All eight US battleships were damaged and four were sunk alongside three cruisers, three destroyers, and several smaller vessels. One hundred eighty-eight aircraft were destroyed in a battle that killed 2,402 Americans and wounded 1,282 others. The assault precipitated US involvement in World War II and had profound consequences for Japanese American citizens, particularly those living on the West Coast. The attack on Pearl Harbor came as a shock to the American people, particularly since it occurred with no formal declaration of hostilities between the United States and Japan. In the immediate aftermath of the conflagration, Americans began to speculate that the Japanese government would have had to have domestic collaborators in the United States for it to have been so successful

in destroying Pearl Harbor. American citizens of Japanese descent living in the Western United States became increasingly suspect but without any corroborating evidence. Nonetheless, collective American anxiety over the Pearl Harbor attack led many Americans to objectify Japanese American citizens as US security risks. This perceived vulnerability generated a pervasive sense of national hysteria about the stranger within, which was symbolized by the presence of Japanese Americans. Fantasies of distrust generated a certain line of reasoning that, even if most Japanese Americans were loyal to the United States, a few collaborators could undermine the security of the nation.

This led to the internment of Japanese Americans during World War II. In spite of data collected by naval intelligence and the FBI that in effect documented that Japanese Americans were of no threat to the United States, President Roosevelt signed Executive Order 9066 in February 1942. This led to the forced mass evacuation of Japanese Americans from the coasts of California, Washington, and Oregon. Executive Order 9066 resulted in the internment of Japanese Americans in concentration camps where they were placed under guard. In *Korematsu v. United States* (1944) the Supreme Court ruled 6–3 that the forced dislocation of Japanese American citizens did not exceed the constitutional powers of the United States government. This decision had the effect of legitimating the mass incarceration of more than 110,000 Japanese American citizens.

Mary Matsuda Gruenewald writes of her experience in an internment camp in her book, *Looking Like the Enemy.* She declares, "while my parents wanted us to adapt to some American ways, they were also sure about the importance of Japanese values.... As the second generation, the *Niseis,* [my brother and I] became more American through our school activities, friendships with non-Japanese students, and exposure to the media."[7] In the aftermath of Executive Order 9066, her family was warned to "Get rid of anything that can incriminate you, anything that can tie you too closely to Japan.... If [the government authorities] find anything, they might take your [father] and send him off somewhere far away, or some other terrible thing." So that night she and her family

> started looking at everything in our home. We went through every drawer, closet, cupboard, and shelf looking frantically at everything that could possibly threaten our future. . . . We gathered all our mementos of Japan and put them together in several boxes, ready to be burned after dark. We had to get rid of these things because the risk of being labeled even faintly "disloyal" was just too great. That evening after dusk while we still had our work clothes on, we brought out the boxes with all our treasures. . . . We stood in front of the table

> looking at all of our cultural treasures. Papa-san took a deep breath and said, "This is it. Let's get this difficult task done."[8]

Although they burned their treasures, they were not safe from persecution and internment. As Gruenewald goes on to indicate, "*After all we have done to protect ourselves, nothing has changed.* My hair was still coarse, straight, and black. My skin was yellow, and my bespectacled eyes were small and slanted. We tried to erase our Japanese history by destroying all those precious things, but we couldn't escape from the way we looked. Nothing could change that. And in the end, all that mattered to the United States government was what we looked like."[9] A few weeks later the evacuation order came for alien and nonalien persons of Japanese descent. Although many of those evacuated were full-fledged American citizens, they were legally reduced to the status of an alien and subsequently were denied the legal status that was their birthright. Gruenewald's family, numbered 19788 by the US government, was sent to Pinedale Assembly Center, an internment camp built just outside of Fresno, California. Upon arrival her family was greeted by the sight of "soldiers with machine guns [standing] in twenty-foot-high guard towers situated at strategic points along the perimeter of a huge camp. The area was encased in steel-wire fencing topped by three rows of barbed wire. Large searchlights next to the towers rotated continuously. Black tar-papered barracks were laid out in regimented form along the flat terrain. Gray dirt or lava gravel completed the menacing scene. Impatient soldiers yelled at [them] to move forward, into the camp."[10] They were taken to a small, bare room with six army cots. There was no other furniture, no running water, no storage space, and no kitchen facilities. They were required to share the space with another family. They ate foods prepared by the camp officials in communal dining rooms. They had no privacy and no freedom.

Throughout the war, groups such as the Native Sons of the Golden West and the American Legion supported a permanent evacuation of all persons of Japanese descent from the West Coast. Some went further and argued that all detainees should be sent back to Japan. But by 1943 American leaders realized that they needed Japanese labor, particularly on farms that would feed the country and its troops. As previously mentioned, many Japanese immigrants had settled in rural areas and had been farmers before the evacuation. Although their own lands had been effectively seized in the aftermath of their evacuation and internment, Japanese detainees were encouraged to work as agricultural laborers on farms in eastern Oregon, Washington, Idaho, Utah, Montana, and Wyoming. Others worked as nurses or enlisted as soldiers. But the harsh reality was that, no matter what they contributed to the war effort on behalf of the American nation, they

were by virtue of their objectified Japanese ethnicity excluded and thus rejected by American society. After years of internment Gruenewald wrote, "I still longed for my life on Vashon—free. It was always hardest at night when I was alone with my thoughts. . . . I often tossed in bed, unable to sleep, my stomach aching, and my feet cold. Shame and anger kept crowding in as we faced the daily indignities of being imprisoned. These thoughts and feelings threatened to overwhelm me. I was now convinced, *America will never accept me as a full-fledged American. . . .* The injustice of it all haunted me: They had declared me guilty without giving me a chance to prove I had been a loyal and patriotic citizen—but loyalty to the government meant the betrayal of myself."[11]

When the war ended and the camps closed, internees faced new problems. Many had lost their homes and property and had nowhere to go. They had become dependent on the government for food and shelter and were without assets with which to begin new lives. Many of the first generation immigrants, the *Issei,* were not citizens and thus had no civil rights. Those who wanted to return to their communities on the West Coast did not know how they would be received since the fears and contempt that had appeared to justify internment in 1941 had not evaporated entirely with the end of war. But for many Japanese Americans there were other, perhaps less pragmatic but equally pressing issues in the postwar world, particularly with regard to ethnic and cultural identity. As Gruenewald writes, "the evacuation came at a time when I was struggling with my identity. The pressure to appear 'loyal' to the United States caused me to bury my Japanese self for decades. . . . It has taken me sixty years to come to terms with who I am. The country of my ancestors is no longer my enemy."[12] Neither, in time, was the country of her birth.

In 1988 President Ronald Reagan signed the **Civil Liberties Act** that acknowledged that a "grave injustice was done both to citizens and permanent residents of Japanese ancestry by the evacuation, relocation, and internment of civilians during World War II."[13] Each survivor received a formal letter of apology as well as $20,000 in compensation. This triumph was the achievement of grassroots efforts by Japanese Americans nationwide to bring closure, restitution, and public attention to the suffering of Japanese Americans during the war. For many third- and fourth-generation Japanese Americans, the institutional discrimination and political repression endured by their parents and grandparents are distant memories of a nearly forgotten past. Today Japanese Americans are integrated into mainstream American society. But as Gruenewald reminds us in the conclusion to her story, collective hysteria and fear led to unfair treatment of Japanese Americans and it can happen again to others in similar ways. She decided to write her story in the midst of the anti-Muslim sentiment that swept the country in the aftermath of the September 11 terrorist attacks. She wrote as a warning, "Perhaps if I share my

experiences, this will be one more convincing piece of evidence against the possibility of internment camps in the United States ever happening again."[14]

The Invisible Privilege of Being White

Those who live according to what we have figuratively referred to as hyphenated American identities—African Americans, Native Americans, Mexican Americans, Latino/Hispanic Americans, Asian Americans, and many others with similar rich cultural backgrounds—historically have confronted a wide variety of inequalities, for example, in wealth and income distributions. In addition to inequality they also experience a wide range of social exclusions composed of limited or discriminatory access to various socioeconomic advantages including lack of socioeconomic opportunities. They thus experience not only inequality but also inequity. Whereas **equality** and **inequality** measure how certain values are distributed among members of a group or society at any given point, that is, as an end-state condition, **equity** and **inequity** provide a metric or standard for gauging the extent to which access to benefits including material goods and services thought desirable, such as education and medical services, as well as values enjoyed symbolically, such as prestige or recognition, are open to all groups and individuals on anything like a fair basis. Fairness itself may be considered as a criterion that measures not only conditions of equality but also the structures and dynamics of equity. Unfairness and injustice may well grow out of attempts to impose conditions of socioeconomic equality since what members of any group and certainly of any economy may deserve at any give time may differ for all sorts of reasons. How to determine who deserves what and on what basis often provokes controversy and often leads to a discussion of entitlements. Entitlements are benefits given on the basis of what a person or groups of persons have earned and in that sense deserve. Various societies measure this differently. Standards of equality may apply to an entire population facing starvation since it is morally plausible to argue that all persons are deserving of protection against famine or chronic malnutrition. In this sense, they are entitled to protection. But the danger of making equality an end in itself is that it works to punish those who genuinely deserve, for whatever "fair" reasons, a larger share of the "pie." Thus the additional standard of equity also applies. This criterion allows us to also assess the fairness of the extent to which the opportunities that stem from economic freedom as well as political and social liberty are available to all groups. Standards of equity take into account questions of structure or positioning relative to group social interactions and economic activities. This means that equity standards permit us to recognize

that some groups are positioned in ways that unjustly block them from fair access to opportunities whereas others are positioned in ways that grant them undue advantages. This often occurs on account of class structures that position certain groups in relation to one another in ways that grant excessive advantages to some while producing disadvantages for others. In such instances, inequity derives from the class structure itself, particularly the socioeconomic structures that disadvantage certain groups by preventing full participation in society or by maintaining the kinds of institutional discriminations that maintain lack of access. That said, individuals and groups embodying hyphenated identities tend overwhelmingly to be subjected to the effects of inequity or unfairness with respect to access to socioeconomic opportunities. Such inequities in the course of time reinforce inequalities of condition that sustain a wide range of poverty or substandard economic conditions. These work in various ways to strengthen not only the structures of inequity but also the kinds of prejudice and discrimination against those who are poor and who are made to experience various forms of contempt and rejection. It also obscures the importance of ensuring that equitable structures operate in the lives of those with hyphenated identities and backgrounds. Again, the issue is not so much the achievement of equality imagined in simplistic terms; the essential issue is how any society, including that of America today, proceeds through policies and attitudes toward the realization of equitable standards and structures that benefit all members. However, mainstream or majoritarian American prejudice and discrimination target racial and ethnic minorities within the United States and also those from abroad. American ideologies infused by **xenophobia**, or fear of foreigners, and/or various kinds of American **nativism**, in forms that include blank opposition to immigration, emerge among segments of the American population. These attitudes have traditionally targeted persons and groups whose cultural heritage appears distinct from the **WASP** (**W**hite, **A**nglo-**S**axon **P**rotestant) mainstream. Justifications for such discriminatory ideologies often contend that immigrant groups are hostile to the United States or that their members cannot be assimilated into American society. In 1798 President John Adams signed the **Alien and Sedition Acts**, which made it difficult for non-Anglo immigrants to gain full political rights. The term **nativism** was first used in this context to refer to **Native American political parties**. Here the term **Native American** does not refer to the indigenous tribes who lived on the American continent prior to Columbian contact but rather to descendants of the inhabitants of the original Thirteen Colonies. The **Know Nothing Party**, active during the mid-1800s, fought for numerous anti-immigrant policies including laws to require a longer waiting time between immigration and naturalization as full US citizens. Anti-immigrant ideologies initially targeted Roman Catholic

immigrants, particularly those from Ireland and Italy, under the assumption that their fealty to the pope precluded loyalty to the American nation-state. The tendency of Catholics to settle in ethnic enclaves, to found their own parochial schools, and, of course, to worship outside of the mainstream Protestant religion, became part of the discriminatory American universe virtually up to the time that President John F. Kennedy was elected. His election finally brought to an end the worldview that suggested that an individual could not be simultaneously Catholic and an American president.

Similarly, anti-German sentiment became common in the United States from the mid-1800s through the end of World War II. German Americans were distrusted for some of the same reasons as their Catholic counterparts—because they spoke a different language, lived in ethnic enclaves, and founded German-language schools, they were seen as separate from the American nation. This is indicative of the problem we have previously discussed of confusing nationality with ethnicity. What this lack of acceptance of German American hyphenated identity at the time demonstrates is how German American ethnicity became falsely conflated with their American nationality in ways that were detrimental to their status as American citizens. Anti-German fervor reached new heights during the First World War (1914–1918) when the United States fought the Second German Reich. Some German Americans were tried, convicted, and imprisoned on charges of sedition because they refused to swear allegiance to the American war effort. During this time, numerous German American schools and newspapers were forced to close, and public libraries burned German American books.

To prove their patriotism, many German Americans bought war bonds and volunteered for military service. Others actively denied their German heritage, Anglicizing their names and rechristening their towns after Anglo-American heroes. In New Orleans, Berlin Street was renamed for General Pershing, the head of the American Expeditionary Force. Some went as far as to rename sauerkraut "liberty cabbage," hamburgers "liberty sandwiches," and dachshunds "liberty pups." However, for German Americans in the World War I era, denying German ancestry was relatively easy. German Americans, particularly second- and third-generation German Americans, could pass as Anglo-Americans with no real difficulty. This is suggestive of the invisible privilege of **whiteness** or of white skin. As we have seen, Japanese Americans during World War II were not so fortunate.

Exclusion, oppression, prejudice, and discrimination have targeted Italian, Russian, Polish, Hungarian, Greek, Jewish, Arab, Muslim, African, and Hispanic as well as many other immigrant groups during the social and cultural history of the United States. This is the dark and chastening lesson that emerges from the unfortunate aspects of American nation-building. Immigrant generations

ALTERNATE PERSPECTIVES

Ethnicity, Nationality, and Nation-Building

Ethnicity and **nationality** are concepts that initiate numerous alternate discussions within the fields of political science and international studies. For instance, **ethno-nationalism** is a term often used to describe nationalism that is based in ethnic identity. However, Walker Connor argues that, if properly used, nationalism and ethno-nationalism are interchangeable. For Connor, a nation is a group of people who believe that they are ancestrally related. Therefore, nationalism is identification with a national community whose solidarity depends on perceived blood, lineage, and ancestral linkages. Here, common ancestry, rather than a sense of common political belonging, becomes a prerequisite for membership in the nation. Connor uses this distinction to argue that nationalism does not necessarily align with state loyalty. That is, a group of people can strongly identify with a national community but not with the state government under which they live.

Another common distinction in nationalism as it relates to ethnicity is between the concepts of civic and ethnic nationalism. Rogers Brubaker suggests that this distinction is often explained by "civic nationalism, characterized as liberal, voluntarist, universalist, and inclusive; and ethnic nationalism, glossed as illiberal, ascriptive, particularist, and exclusive."[15] Civic nationalism is synonymous with notions of nationalism that base identity in shared ideas and values, whereas ethnic nationalism is synonymous with ethno-nationalism. However, Brubaker indicates that this dichotomy insufficiently describes nationalism and also applies inappropriate normative evaluations.

Discourse and research on nation-building highlight varying forms of nationalism in the making of the modern world. Andreas Wimmer categorizes three major methods of nation-building: incorporation, amalgamation, and emphasis shifting. Each reflects how "state elites" pursued different policies for transforming the self-identification of people in the process of nation-building. The process of incorporation works to endow an ethnic group with the belief that it now shares in the nationality of the majoritarian culture; amalgamation functions to ensure that various ethnic groups identify with the nation; and emphasis shifting appeals to a "higher level of categorical distinction that supersedes existing ethnic distinctions."[16] While not all attempts to build a strong, cohesive nation are equally effective, the methods and policies adopted to promote nation-building among preexisting ethnic groups undoubtedly alter the subsequent political and social circumstances within the national society.

are readily transformed into identity group objects and suffer discrimination and worse as a result. With every successive wave of immigration, hate groups promoted the "purification" of the American nation and the expulsion of foreign or alien influences. Today the Southern Poverty Law Center reports that there are more than one thousand active hate groups in the United States. These groups include active chapters of the Ku Klux Klan; neo-Nazi organizations; white nationalist groups based on white supremacist or white separatist ideologies that focus on the alleged inferiority of nonwhite groups; racist skinhead groups; Christian identity organizations that are based on fundamentally racist or anti-Semitic doctrines; neo-Confederate organizations that seek to revive the racist principles of the antebellum South; black separatist groups whose ideologies include tenets of racially based hatred; and general hate groups that emphasize antigay teachings, anti-immigrant sentiment, Holocaust denial, racist music, extremist traditional Catholic teachings, and other abhorrent doctrines. In addition, nearly 200 "nativist extremist" groups—many associated with the Minuteman Project along the US-Mexican border and the Federal Immigration Reform and Enforcement Coalition—and nearly 1,300 antigovernment militia groups were active in 2011 throughout the country.

Thus, for Americans, nation-building is an ongoing process. As Peter Behrens wrote in 2012,

> for many Irish-Americans, including me, St. Patrick's Day isn't really about Ireland. It's about our ancestors leaving that country, often in bitter circumstances, and risking everything on a hazardous journey and being met with fierce hostility and scorn. It is about immigrants struggling, and mostly succeeding, in their new life, or making success possible for their children and grandchildren. . . . Before the mass exodus from Ireland provoked by the great famine of the 1840s, new arrivals to North America were either settlers or slaves. The Catholic Gaelic Irish were the first cohort consistently labeled as "immigrants" in the modern, quasi-pejorative sense, and their experience established a stereotype, a template, applied ever since to whichever national or ethnic group happened to be the latest impoverished arrivals: French-Canadians, Chinese, Italians, Eastern Europeans, Hispanics. . . . It's embarrassing to listen to prosperous 21st-century Americans with Irish surnames lavish on Mexican or Central American immigrants the same slurs—"dark," "dirty," "violent," "ignorant"—once slapped on our own, possibly shoeless, forebears. The Irish were seen as unclean, immoral and dangerously in thrall to a bizarre religion. They were said to be peculiarly prone to violence. . . . Soon it was another people's turn. During the 1890s, when hundreds of thousands of French-Canadians were quitting rocky farms in Quebec for jobs in New England textile towns, *The New York Times* wrote, "It

> is next to impossible to penetrate this mass of protected and secluded humanity with modern ideas or to induce them to interest themselves in democratic institutions and methods of government."[17]

He explains, "Since we have all been more or less constantly on the move since our ancestors decamped from the old neighborhood in Ethiopia, 195,000 years ago, you'd think that, as a species, we might have worked through our hostility and suspicion of newbies by now. But we haven't."[18]

Although non-Anglo immigrants of many religions, colors, and ethnicities have been targeted for exclusion and oppression by the Anglo-American mainstream, those of European heritage possess an advantage over the others: **white privilege** that derives from looking Anglo-American. While first-generation immigrants from Ireland, Poland, Italy, Germany, or other European countries may struggle to adapt to American customs, language, and society, second- and third-generation immigrants easily assimilate and, on account of their white skin, are often assumed to be equal members of the Anglo-American majority. This status provides them with a series of often invisible privileges such as those enumerated by Peggy McIntosh:

- I can go shopping alone most of the time, pretty well assured that I will not be followed or harassed.
- When I am told about our national heritage or about "civilization," I am shown that people of my color made it what it is.
- I can be sure that my children will be given curricular materials that testify to the existence of their race.
- Whether I use checks, credit cards, or cash, I can count on my skin color not to work against the appearance of financial reliability.
- I do not have to educate my children to be aware of systemic racism for their own daily physical protection.
- I can swear, or dress in second hand clothes, or not answer letters, without having people attribute these choices to the bad morals, the poverty or the illiteracy of my race.
- I can remain oblivious of the language and customs of persons of color who constitute the world's majority without feeling in my culture any penalty for such oblivion.
- I can criticize our government and talk about how much I fear its policies and behavior without being seen as a cultural outsider.
- I can be pretty sure that if I ask to talk to the "person in charge," I will be facing a person of my race.

- If a traffic cop pulls me over or if the IRS audits my tax return, I can be sure I haven't been singled out because of my race.
- I am not made acutely aware that my shape, bearing or body odor will be taken as a reflection on my race.
- I can take a job with an affirmative action employer without having my co-workers on the job suspect that I got it because of my race.
- I can choose blemish cover or bandages in "flesh" color and have them more or less match my skin.
- I will feel welcomed and "normal" in the usual walks of public life, institutional and social.[19]

America is a nation of immigrants, but whiteness remains as a cultural form of unspoken discrimination leading to prejudice and even to hate crimes against those who do not pass as white. But, as we shall see, the political culture of the United States is hardly alone in nurturing cultural forms of subordination aimed at identity groups as objects. The political culture of numerous modern nation-states foments similar dynamics and challenges. In recent years the British nation has had to confront its own problems with respect to the integration of Pakistani and Indian cultural groups into the mainstream of British nationality and way of life. France struggles with the integration of its North African citizens. Germany confronts prejudice against the full integration of its Turkish citizens. Japan, historically one of the world's most homogenous nations, faces increasing diversity within its borders and the subsequent set of challenges in accepting different racial, ethnic, and religious groups into its national community. For their part, postcolonial political cultures face complex challenges when it comes to nationality, ethnicity, and the grounding of difference in the unity of the nation. For, as we shall see, nation-building dynamics in postcolonial states are often encumbered by postcolonial pathologies that too often culminate in hate, exclusivist ideologies, and mass political violence.

Chapter 6
Groups as Identity Objects in American Political Culture

A Story of Blue Eyes and Brown Eyes

What do we mean when we refer to groups as **identity objects in American political culture**? Let us begin to answer this with the following story. On the evening of April 4, 1968, Jane Elliott, a third-grade teacher from Riceville, Iowa, learned of the assassination of US civil rights leader Dr. Martin Luther King Jr. Although Elliott had discussed racism with her eight-year-old pupils, she noticed "that they weren't internalizing a thing. They were doing what white people do. When white people sit down to discuss racism what they are experiencing is shared ignorance."[1] So the next day she decided to give her all-white, all-American class of third-grade students a taste of discrimination in America.

Elliott asked her pupils what they knew about African Americans. Although many of her students had never met or even seen an African American, aside from the occasional photograph or television appearance, "a pattern developed from their answers."[2] This pattern revealed in child after child the very essence of prejudice based on delusion. "Negroes weren't as smart as white people. They weren't as clean. They fought a lot. Sometimes they rioted. They weren't as civilized. They smelled bad."[3] Elliott reports, "None of [this] was said in a vicious way. There was no venom, no fear, no hate, but rather a sort of disapproval, a sense of disdain."[4] Realizing that her students had no real understanding of discrimination, prejudice, or racism, let alone of individual African Americans, Elliott embarked on an experiment that would challenge her students, her

community, and eventually the entire nation to think differently about groups and categories of groups as identity objects.

Elliott created a sense of identity object by dividing her class according to eye color. In her class there were seventeen blue-eyed children and eleven brown/green-eyed children. So she proceeded to misinform her pupils, "Brown-eyed people are better than blue-eyed people. They are cleaner than blue-eyed people. They are more civilized than blue-eyed people. And they are smarter than blue-eyed people."[5] Immediately a conflicted hierarchy emerged. Elliott reports,

> The brown-eyed children began to look at each other in wonder. They sat up straighter in their chairs, waiting to hear more. The blue-eyed children frowned, stirred uneasily, not understanding. One blue-eyed boy slumped way down in his chair. "What color are your eyes?" [Elliott] asked him. "Blue," the boy said, straightening up. "Is that the way we've been taught to sit in class?" "No," the boy said. "Do blue-eyed people remember what they've been taught?" [Elliott] asked the class. There was a chorus of "No's" from the brown-eyed children as they began to see how it would work. The blue-eyed boy now sat bolt upright, his hands folded neatly in the exact center of his desk. A brown-eyed boy near him, one of his close friends in the room, gave him a withering, disdainful look. It began that quickly.[6]

Elliott went on to enumerate the rules for the day: "brown-eyed children could use the drinking fountain in the room as usual. Blue-eyed children were to use paper cups. The brown-eyed children would have five extra minutes of recess. They would go first to lunch, could choose their lunch-line partners, and could go back for seconds. The blue-eyed children could do none of these things." When asked, "Who should sit in the front of the room?" the brown-eyed children answered, "The brown eyes!" When asked, "Who should be our row leaders?" the answer came again, "The brown eyes!" Elliott went on, "Blue-eyed people are not allowed to play with brown-eyed people unless they are invited. They may not play on the big playground equipment at recess. And they may not take the small playground equipment out of the room."[7]

By recess, Elliott was shocked and heartbroken by her third-graders' behavior. She said,

> The brown-eyed children were happy, alert, having the time of their lives. And they were doing far better in their work than they ever had done before. The blue-eyed children were miserable. Their posture, their expressions, their entire attitudes were those of defeat. Their classroom work regressed sharply

> from that of the day before. Inside of an hour or so, they looked and acted as though they were, in fact, inferior. It was shocking. But even more frightening was the way the brown-eyed children turned on their friends of the day before, the way they accepted almost immediately as true what had originally been described as an exercise. For there was no question, after an hour or so, that they actually believed they were superior. The fact that we were going to change roles on Monday was forgotten. Everything was forgotten in the face of the undeniable proofs that the blue-eyed children were inferior to them. It was as though someone had pointed out to them something they simply had not noticed before. Weren't the blue-eyed children making more mistakes than they were? Of course. Wasn't the teacher finding fault almost exclusively with the blue-eyed children? Of course. Wasn't it clear that she liked the brown-eyed children better? Of course. What better proof did you need?[8]

On Monday, Elliott reversed the roles. She told her students, "I lied to you on Friday. I told you brown-eyed people are better than blue-eyed people. That's not true. The truth is that blue-eyed people are better than brown-eyed people. They are smarter than brown-eyed people," and so on.[9] Once again, she saw an immediate impact. "I had not expected that the brown-eyed children, knowing full well after their experience on Friday that it was all an exercise and that it would last only a day, would react as intensely as the others had to the experience of discrimination. But they did. Within minutes, they had become nervous, depressed, resentful."[10] Near the end of the day, Elliott ended the exercise and told the class that it had all been a lie. She was overjoyed to watch her once-divided class reunite and to hear her students' resounding "No!" in response to her question, "Does the color of your eyes have anything to do with what kind of person you are?"[11]

The following day, Elliott and her students explored what they had learned and applied it to racist attitudes prevalent in the United States. They learned that "discrimination not only hurt, it affected the way you behaved. The way you behaved, the kind of work you did, and the way you felt about yourself—all these affected the way you appeared to other people; in fact, they could affect the way you actually were. Discrimination could change the kind of person you were if it went on long enough. And there was another conclusion: it was no better—and no more accurate—to judge a person by the color of his skin than by the color of his eyes. Neither told you anything important about the person."[12]

Jane Elliott's third-grade class thus learned a powerful lesson about the modern social and political culture into which they had been born, particularly about treating groups and cultural groupings as identity objects. While kinship

communities categorize individuals by blood, ancestry, and lineage, modern cultures develop classifications of difference in collective or group identity. These center on both objective and subjective characteristics. The categories of difference include such features as **race**, **ethnicity**, **class**, and **gender**. Although they often masquerade as natural, these classifications represent the cultural constructions of a postkinship world in which meaning and belonging become associated with the political culture of nation-states.

Group Identity in Nation-States

The **political culture of nation-states** creates and sustains categories of group identity. At times, these categories become objectified. Once this happens, individuals in groups can become treated as objects. This represents the great danger of categorizing groups as identity objects. Group categories differ from nation-state to nation-state. In some cases, these categories reflect personal or subjective self-understandings. In such instances, they support human dignity, the sense of personal worth, and equitable possibilities in political freedom. Group identifications define who we are, how we interpret who we are, and how we express and experience the values and meanings of belonging. Value systems oriented to the modern nation-state anchor citizenship and rule of law within group identities. The participation in the life of identity groups represents an important human and civil right.

Within the political culture of some nation-states, however, a tendency to not celebrate group identifications occurs, leading to attempts to objectify group differences. This happens in ways that establish fixed, frozen, and naturalized categories. Often this leads to extremism and hate. In such instances, people and the groups with which they identify or become identified are transformed into the equivalent of objects. Political culture then works to demean human dignity and freedom.

The political cultures of modern nation-states shape how cultural constructions of group identity are objectified into a series of fixed and naturalized categories. Individuals and groups in modern nation-states are often classified on the basis of naturalized features, that is, social characteristics that are culturally formed but that are treated as if they were the consequence of genetic, biological, or physical "nature." When this occurs, viewing groups through the lens of identity objects leads to perspectives on difference configured around **binary oppositions**. These are composed of parallel notions of superiority and

inferiority. Categories that draw their meaning from binary oppositions define individuals and groups, not in terms of what they are, but, just as importantly, in terms of what they are not. Groups as identity objects involve binary oppositions in relation to race, ethnicity, gender, class, etc. Such features tend to assume value-laden, adversarial, and naturalized status such as male/female, white/black, and young/old. In each case, there can exist a certain unspoken but powerfully prejudicial set of cultural assumptions that imply one set of identity objects is superior while the other is subordinate.

Naturalized binary categories tend to privilege and to subordinate on the basis of difference. This often occurs in invisible or unspoken ways according to codes of cultural meanings, associations, and symbols. As Jane Elliott learned in her classroom experiment, individuals in groups are sometimes quick to internalize, accept, and perpetuate the privileges and subordinations that take form and emerge through categories molded around binary oppositions, particularly those reinforced by cultural values and social structures.

As Elliott discovered, members of groups internalize notions of superiority and inferiority very quickly. In the 1940s, African American researchers Kenneth and Mamie Clark demonstrated that attitudes shaped by binary oppositions were integral to American culture. The Clarks conducted the doll experiment. In this exercise children were presented with two dolls. Both dolls were identical in every feature save one—race. One doll was white with yellow hair while the other was brown with black hair. The children were then asked a series of questions regarding the dolls: Which doll would you rather play with? Which doll is the "nice" doll? Which doll is the "bad" doll? Overwhelmingly, children, black and white alike, preferred the white doll to the black one. The Clarks found that children of both races identified the black doll as the "mean," "bad," "lazy" doll. In 2006, fifty years after the Supreme Court ordered the desegregation of public schools, Kiri Davis repeated the Clarks' doll experiment. In her experiment, fifteen out of twenty-one African American children chose the white doll over the black saying that the white doll was "pretty" and "good" while the black doll was "ugly" and "bad." Objectified categories of group identity shaped by binary tensions may thus strengthen ways of thinking that work to reinforce prejudice.

Binary oppositions, once transformed into cultural values and personal attitudes, act as a simplifying force by working to erase cultural ambiguities. Attempts to carve out a middle ground in political cultures of modern nation-states confront this tendency to sort human beings into the mutually exclusive categories of groups as identity objects. As the dynamics in Jane Elliott's class demonstrated, green-eyed children were never perceived as a third category but instead were lumped together with brown-eyed children. Thus binary oppositions,

once imposed on individuals and groups, limit the capacity of people to develop their own unique sense of who they are in the world and of their culture. In political cultures beholden to categories of groups as identity objects grounded in binary oppositions, a child born of interracial parents often does not have the freedom to consider himself/herself "white" or even "biracial." Such a person readily becomes objectified as "black." This cultural practice is known as **hypo-descent**, that is, the practice of culturally perceiving and categorizing children of a union between members of different racial, ethnic, or cultural groups as belonging to the group treated as an identity object. Once "nature" is substituted for "culture" individuals and groups are robbed of the freedom to be, to change, or to be different from what stereotypes require that they be, that is, to be emancipated in terms of self-definition.

Race and Modern Nation-States

Individuals living in modern nation-states no longer think exclusively in terms of kinship identity. This is critical to the making of the modern world and thus to definitions of modernity. But there is a major consequence in the present context. Group identifications in national cultures often emphasize group characteristics focused on race, ethnicity, class, sex, etc. These features represent the principles of difference. These stand in contrast to the values of nationality, commonality, unity, and even of conformity and solidarity that are presumably embedded in the political cultures of sovereign nation-states. Both principles of commonality and difference situate the political cultures of citizens within nation-states tied together by virtue of nationality rather than the "natural" bonds of kinship lineage. Group identity and nationality represent social, cultural, and political constructions unique to the history of each nation-state although they often masquerade as "natural."

Racial distinctions, for example, grounded not in biology but in cultural attitudes and perceptions, often break down into classification schemes that categorize identity groups based on a misleading range of characteristics including **phenotype, geographic ancestry**, and **physical appearance**. Largely based on the color of an individual's skin and physical, in particular facial, features, racial categories applied to identity groups represent cultural constructions. Racial classifications thus vary widely across modern nation-states.

Social constructions of identity groups in the United States often **ethnically lump** individuals together who identify with distinct cultural backgrounds. This is evident in the misleading ethnic categories adopted by the US Census

Bureau. In the United States, a wide range of cultures—Japanese, Chinese, Thai, Burmese, Korean, Laotian, Vietnamese, Mongolian, Malaysian, Indonesian, Philippine, and others—are ethnically lumped together as "Asian." This serves to deny the significant differences that distinguish one from the other. Ethnic lumping may also involve racist constructions that transform group affiliation and identifications into identity groups as objects. Whatever the case, ethnic lumping of diverse cultural groups collapses principles of cultural differences into categories that subordinate cultural variations in favor of a kind of demeaning cultural conformity. When this occurs, we are witness to the dynamics of binary opposition in which identity groups become represented or treated as objects that are "naturally" inferior or subordinate.

In the course of US history, conceptions of race have changed dramatically. In 1850 the US Census recognized three racial groups: whites, blacks, and mulattos. In 1870 it added "Chinese," a category that included all East Asians as well as American Indians. In 1930, the Census Bureau added "Mexican" as a racial category. That classification was eliminated in 1940; thereafter all individuals of Mexican descent were counted as among the white population. Until the mid-1900s, individuals who were as little as 1/32 African were counted as "Negro," a nod to **hypodescent** in the American experience often reflected in the saying that "a drop of Negro blood" was sufficient to make an individual black. In 2000 the Census listed five racial categories:

- **White**: A person having origins in "any of the original peoples of Europe, the Middle East, or North Africa including those who classify themselves as Irish, German, Scottish, Italian, Lebanese, Near Eastern, Arab, or Polish.
- **Black or African American**: A person having origins in any of the Black racial groups of Africa. It includes people who indicate their race as Black, African American, or Negro or provide written entries such as Kenyan, Nigerian, or Haitian.
- **American Indian and Alaska Native**: A person having origins in any of the original peoples of North and South America (including Central America), and who maintain tribal affiliation or community attachment. It includes people who indicated their race or races by marking this category or writing in their principal or enrolled tribe, such as Rosebud Sioux, Chippewa, or Navajo.
- **Asian**: A person having origins in any of the original peoples of the Far East, Southeast Asia, or the Indian subcontinent. It includes people who indicated their race or races as Asian Indian, Chinese, Filipino, Korean, Japanese, Vietnamese, or Other Asian or written entries such as Burmese, Hmong, Pakistani, or Thai.

- **Native Hawaiian and Other Pacific Islander**: A person having origins in any of the original peoples of Hawaii, Guam, Samoa, or other Pacific Islands. It includes people who indicated their race or races as Native Hawaiian, Guamanian or Chamorro, Samoan, or Other Pacific Islander or written entries such as Tahitian, Mariana Islander, or Chuukese.[13]

In an attempt to be more precise, the 2010 US Census listed the fifteen racial categories and, in addition, left space to write in specific races not listed on the form. It also permitted individuals to mark more than one race, an option added in 2000.

Although the United States defines race narrowly, albeit less narrowly than it did historically, other countries use less exclusionary categories with regard to race. Brazilian culture, for example, is similar to that of the United States in the sense that it has native populations, European immigrants, and a history of slavery. It differs, however, in that it does not recognize hypodescent. Instead, Brazilians use many more racial labels—more than five hundred in the 1970s—than Americans. While race in American society is generally ascribed by hypodescent at birth and does not change over the course of an individual's lifetime, Brazilian racial constructions are far more flexible, allowing individuals to change their race over time. For example, a Brazilian may self-identify with one race in the winter and a different one in the summer when the sun's rays tan the skin and bleach the hair. This more fluid approach to racial categorization severs the pseudoscientific linkage between skin color and race, the linkage that in many contexts naturalizes racial divisions within societies. It is also emancipatory in that it allows individuals to self-identify with respect to their own cultural and ancestral heritages.

The difference between American and Brazilian racial constructs hearkens to the history of these two countries. Given the history of slavery in the United States and its painful historical aftermath, including segregation and institutional discrimination, there continues to be a cultural tendency to conceive of race in collective opposition terms such as "black/white." Given the historical dynamics of interracial marriage in Brazil, however, a complex vocabulary has emerged that labels racial distinctions across a wide spectrum of physical markers including skin pigmentation, cultural origin, and personal preference. In Brazilian society labels such as "black/white" seem crude and irrelevant. In this sense Brazilian culture, although class bound, appears to avoid what American culture on the basis of its history cannot: an exclusivist approach to race relations. In the United States the question "Is it possible to be a white African American?" can be both controversial and adversarial.

Thus race represents a highly complex social construction treated differently in many nation-states according to the history of racial relations within it. The so-called biology of race upon which exclusionary racial classifications are constructed denies the vast commonality in the physical biology of humankind that renders racial variations and differences, seen and unseen, relatively minor. Nonetheless, race and racial distinction have in many national settings been socially constructed to represent major concepts of identity, belonging, status, and difference.

Cultural Constructions of Group Identity: Ethnicity in Modern Societies

In addition to race, groups within modern nation-states often become distinguished in accordance with a range of physical, cultural, and spiritual features associated with **ethnicity**. The word ethnicity derives from the Classical Greek *ethnos* meaning "foreigner" or "stranger." Thus implicit in the notion of ethnicity is the idea that members of the same ethnic group belong together while those from other ethnic groups remain foreign or strange. Ethnicity lends itself, therefore, to constructions centered on the binary opposition us/them. Ethnicity can include differences according to both **subjective** and **objective** criteria. Subjective features center upon communal linkages based on home country (German American), religion (Catholic American), language (Arab American), or cultural heritage (Latino/Hispanic American). For example, the term Catholic American emphasizes religion as ethnicity. The term German American distinguishes country of origin as ethnicity. Arab American is a term that stresses the cultural importance of the Arabic language in the traditions of those who identify as such. As in the case of race and racial identities, ethnic features and concepts of ethnicity often become misconstrued and thus transformed into the binary categories of identity groups as objects.

This process of labeling identity groups as objects operates according to a wide range of labels and terms. Sometimes members of groups differ among themselves as to the appropriate ethnic name by which they wish to be identified. A prime example is the disagreement that arises over the terms "Latino American" and "Hispanic American." "Hispanic American" tends to apply to those who identify themselves as from those regions that historically were colonized by the Spanish empire. The term Hispanic thus privileges the continuing influences of Iberian Spain's era of imperialism. Some members of these identity groups reject this label on account of these connotations, others accept it however reluctantly, and many appear either unaware or indifferent. Perhaps a more neutral term, Latino is also applied to many in this subset of ethnic groupings and refers merely to Latin cultures based in Romance

languages, including those of Spain, Portugal, France, and Italy. Labeling political cultures grounded in the use of Portuguese such as Brazil as "Hispanic" represents a profound misunderstanding. Portugal, an imperial power in its own right and therefore never colonized, was never "Hispanic." Ethnic groups originating in Portuguese and Brazilian cultures are Latino, not Hispanic. Since both Portuguese and Brazilian cultures were especially influenced by African cultural motifs, the misapplication of the term Hispanic to them and their ethnic groupings operates in denial of this history of cultural intermingling. Thus, how ethnic groups are imagined, categorized, and distinguished reflects historical confluences of cultures over periods of time. These might differ from nation-state to nation-state. Such distinctions spin around different cultural constructions of national, cultural, and group identity. In modern nation-states, for example, populations may be divided according to linguistic groups, sectarian or religious affiliation, cultural heritage, or racial origin. Ethnicity thus represents a broad and encompassing category of group identity. Ethnicity as a form of group identity is shaped by the history of belonging in the political culture of any specific nation-state. Such political culture reflects the history that emerges in the contrast between how individual citizens adopt principles of difference in terms of group identity and how citizens adapt to the principles of nationality and citizenship in any given nation-state. This history differs from nation-state to nation-state. The cultural history of each nation-state requires intense scrutiny, particularly with respect to ethnic minorities and their relationship to majority or mainstream culture often represented by nationality itself.

To a degree, ethnicity can be understood as the modern successor of kinship culture. In many nation-states ethnicity is associated not merely with kinship descent communities, but with immigrant groups or identity groups based on conceptions of difference or constructions of belonging. To speak of Irish American or African American ethnicities is not to speak of groups linked by kinship, tribal belonging, or marriage to a common ancestor. Such terms of group affiliation refer to identity groups that share a broad range of cultural features. In postcolonial nation-states, on the other hand, the linkage between ethnicity and kinship may be experienced in a more concrete way. To speak of Hutu Rwandan or Kikuyu Kenyan group identity is to refer to kinship loyalties that existed prior to colonization that became **ethnicized** during the cultural history of the postcolonial period. In either case, the cultural challenge in all modern nation-states is to anchor racial and ethnic differences, whatever their subjective or objective grounds, in the unifying conceptions and traditions of nationality and thus in ways informed by principles of commonality. This again refers to the significance of forging principles of difference with respect to group identity with principles of commonality or nationality in the political culture of modern nation-states.

KEY CONCEPTS
Group Rights

Group rights are rights that attach to groups of people rather than to the individuals in those groups. Group rights may apply to racial, ethnic, religious, or national groups. They first emerged as an international issue in the aftermath of the Paris Peace at the end of World War I. As the old European empires were broken into new sovereign states, some nations were granted autonomy on the basis of self-determination. Each new state, however, had substate minority groups within its borders whose rights needed to be protected by governments that were dominated by majority interests.

Today group rights are represented by **cultural security**, an international norm associated with **human security**. Cultural security requires that sovereign states and the international community protect substate groups from the loss of traditional relationships and values and from sectarian and ethnic violence. Cultural security is an important international norm to reaffirm. Throughout the world, minority communities, many maintaining kinship traditions, face the risk of annihilation, either because of ethnic cleansing or genocide, or because of efforts by centralized governments to assimilate them into majoritarian culture. Protecting the rights of groups to practice their own religious, ethnic, and cultural traditions, and even to exist, encourages expressions of diversity within the tapestry of nations. Cultural security, therefore, seeks to advance multiculturalism within the contemporary political-cultural frameworks of the making of modern nation-states.

Group rights and cultural security are controversial norms, in part because they potentially conflict with individual rights and other aspects of human security. For example, personal security requires that states protect individuals within their borders from physical violence from their state, external states,

continued

Class in Modern Nation-States

In addition to race and ethnicity, **socioeconomic status**, often called **class**, represents an important cultural construction of group identity in many modern nation-states. In the present context, class refers to certain cultural differences across socioeconomic groups. It is not an objective classification based upon wealth alone. Thus it is not defined by distributions measuring degrees of equality or

violent individuals, substate actors, domestic abuse, and predatory adults. What does this mean for groups that practice male circumcision or female genital mutilation? Honor killings? Arranged marriage? Body scarring? In many kinship and descent communities, these centuries-old practices, which are legitimated by patrimonial traditions and segmented lineage, have been fundamental to survival and persist into the modern age. To protect group rights and cultural security states must, in theory, allow groups to continue these traditional practices. However, to protect personal security, states must protect individuals from harm. The two are at times, if not mutually exclusive, certainly contradictory. How does a government protect a young girl placed in an arranged marriage from what Western values would call sexual exploitation and abuse while also respecting the rights of groups to practice traditional marriages? This question remains pertinent in many places in the world today including south Asia and the Middle East.

This is a question that the international society of sovereign nation-states cannot resolve with a single response or policy initiative, and yet it raises significant issues directly pertinent to questions that must be considered when we discuss group rights and human security. Which is more important—the individual or the group? In kinship and descent communities disciplined by honor and communal shaming, the answer is always the group, and the traditional values those communities practice are designed to reinforce that norm. In the modern world, however, the answer is the individual, and modern civic, economic, and human rights attach specifically to individual citizens. Balance between the two, particularly in modern states with political cultures that subscribe to the continuing practice of traditional values and rituals as well as in those nation-states that have growing minority enclaves devoted to traditional communal practices, the social and cultural balances elude simple solution and often remain fraught with tensions.

inequality alone. It is reflected in shelter and residence, levels of education, livelihoods, and access to health and security as well as availability of opportunities for social and economic advancement. It thus pertains to equity and to the role played by political culture, specifically identity constructions and categories as they relate to class distinctions. Class is generally an intergenerational classification that has wide-ranging effects in terms of education, language, employment, lifestyle, and marriage practices. An individual's class can have a significant impact on his or her educational opportunities. This underscores the importance of access to educational

opportunities relative to standards of equity. In societies without public education, education itself can become an exclusive privilege of the wealthy. Even in societies that make some level of public education available to most or all citizens, class can determine the quality of education. In the United States, for example, poor school districts, such as those in rural areas or inner cities, are notoriously overcrowded, understaffed, and underfunded. A poor school system may struggle to provide textbooks, let alone computers, to its students while a middle-class school district may have the resources necessary to enrich its students' education with diverse extracurricular activities and advanced technological accessories. And for students in the wealthiest class, elite private schools offer educational opportunities that allow students to access the skills, knowledge, and, often most importantly, professional networks and contacts that open doors of advantage and ultimate privilege. For such reasons, class distinctions tend to become reinforced by class structures that position some to gain as they compete while others are positioned in ways that place the burdens of disadvantage on them. As Ruby Payne learned in her study of intergenerational poverty in the United States, children from poor families are often educationally stunted from the beginning. They begin school knowing fewer words than their middle- and upper-class counterparts, they are less likely to have pre-K educational experiences, and they are less likely to pursue higher education and advanced degrees.

Beyond education, an individual's class has a significant impact on his or her physical health. Class often dictates a person's access to preventative medical care, emergency medicine, and even proper nutrition. For these reasons, class can impact life expectancy. Poor communities are plagued by high infant mortality rates, low life expectancy, and chronic illness. Moreover, lower-class or working-class individuals tend to work in hazardous conditions, such as meat-packing plants or coalmines, but have less access to health insurance and medical care when compared with middle- and upper-class workers. Employment is often both a reflection and a product of socioeconomic class status. In many cultures class distinctions represent the boundaries of social interaction. In the United States, the term **new money** is used to refer to those individuals whose wealth grants them access to upper-class neighborhoods, social clubs, jobs, retail establishments, restaurants, and educational institutions but whose pedigree, upbringing, and heritage nevertheless exclude them from full membership in upper-class society. Overwhelmingly, people tend to associate socially with members of their own socioeconomic class. In many modern societies this impacts marriage selection pools and practices. Although there may not be laws that dictate who may marry whom in modern societies, class plays a role in identifying individuals who are or who are not selected as appropriate life partners.

There are often hidden rules that govern social interactions within and among class groups. Ruby Payne defined hidden rules as "the salient, unspoken understandings that cue the members of the group that this individual does or does not fit."[14] To successfully interact with another class or to move from one class to another, Payne writes, it is essential to have a mentor to model and teach you the hidden rules. This is especially important, she argues, with regard to language. To be successful in American schools and jobs, individuals must speak and write in the **formal register**, standard American English with proper sentence structure, grammatical syntax, and word choice that relies on complete sentences, the absence of profanity, and language specificity. However, this is not the register most commonly used in working-class and poor American households where the **casual register** is ubiquitous and nonverbal cues are often more important than verbal instruction. For children born in poverty to succeed in school and work, therefore, it is essential that they learn how to use the formal register, the form of speech that children born in the middle class "know without learning." And class education does not end with language. From the right clothes to wear to the proper way to set a table, the hidden codes of class culture can be just as exclusionary as those associated with race or ethnicity.

Although class is its own cultural construction of collective and individual identity, it is often linked with race and ethnicity. In many political cultures, wealth is concentrated in the hands of a particular racial or ethnic group while racial and ethnic minorities become relegated to lower-class status. In the United States, for example, poverty rates for "blacks and Hispanics greatly exceed the national average. In 2010, 27.4 percent of blacks and 26.6 percent of Hispanics were poor, compared to 9.9 percent of non-Hispanic whites and 12.1 percent of Asians."[15] In addition, "poverty rates are highest for families headed by single women, particularly if they are black or Hispanic. In 2010, 36.1 percent of households headed by single women were poor, while 15.8 percent of households headed by single men and 6.2 percent of married-couple households lived in poverty."[16] Finally, "there are also differences between native-born and foreign-born residents. In 2010, 19.9 percent of foreign-born residents lived in poverty, compared to 14.4 percent of residents born in the United States. Foreign-born, non-citizens had an even higher incidence of poverty, at a rate of 26.7 percent."[17] This is not only true of the United States. In countries around the world, racial and ethnic minorities are often associated with lower class status. In Great Britain, for example, "around two-fifths of people from ethnic minorities live in low-income households, twice the rate for White people."[18] More specifically, 20 percent of white people, 30 percent of Indians and Black Caribbeans, 50 percent of Black Africans, 60 percent of Pakistanis, and 70 percent of Bangladeshis live

in poverty. Here, as elsewhere, race, ethnicity, and class are linked. These class distinctions influence political cultures since they help to determine the political access critical to political power and influence. This again underscores the importance of ensuring application of equity standards and policies, especially in ways that counter rigid class structures. This is a moral and ethical imperative. But it also ensures greater economic productivity, social peace, and tolerance within any nation-state.

Sex and Gender in Modern Societies

In addition to race, ethnicity, and class, group identities often result in tendencies to categorize individuals with regard to **sex** or **gender**. **Gender** identity constructions are even more complex than those associated with sex. Gender focuses on the difference, not between male and female in terms of sexual traits, but between **masculine** and **feminine** attributes. Masculinity, when associated with identity groups as objects, becomes objectified and thus linked to such features as physical strength, rationality, independence, aggression, dominance, competitiveness, and confidence. In this process of objectifying specific identity groups, certain features become "naturalized," that is, as we have already seen, they are assumed to be the result of biological nature rather than an invention of culture. When this happens femininity is typically subordinated. It readily becomes objectified. Thus it is often associated with dependence, emotionality, passivity, sensitivity, submission, compassion, innocence, empathy, weakness, grace, nurture, and acceptance. **Gender roles** emerge from these kinds of objectified behavioral norms as if the masculine and the feminine were mutually exclusive and in binary opposition.

Gender roles differ widely across societies and throughout time. In the United States until the mid- to late-1900s, for example, gender roles established hard boundaries between men and women with regard to their legal rights, personal freedoms, and social expectations. Women were expected to remain in the **private sphere**, the home where they would care for their husbands and children and tend to household affairs. Men, on the other hand, were expected to operate in the **public sphere**, to hold jobs outside of the home, to earn the wages necessary for the family to survive, and to participate in civic and political affairs.

During the Second World War, however, the United States needed women to enter the industrial workforce to replace male workers who were deployed to fight in Europe and the Pacific. **Rosie the Riveter** became a cultural icon beckoning women to abandon the private sphere to enter the factories that produced

weapons and war supplies. Government advertisements targeted women asking, "Can you use an electric mixer? If so, you can learn to operate a drill." Millions of women entered the workforce in traditionally male-dominated industries to support the war effort. After the war, however, women were expected to return to their housekeeping and child-rearing activities. Although some were willing to do so, others continued working in factories and became the leaders of the **sexual revolution** that redefined gender norms in American culture.

ALTERNATE PERSPECTIVES

Feminist IR Theory

Feminist IR (International Relations) Theory provides an alternate standpoint that is applicable in a variety of fields, not only international studies. At a basic level, feminist discourse seeks to include gender as a prominent variable when discussing or analyzing political culture across many contexts and frameworks of analysis including comparative and international politics, social psychology, and international sociology. Feminist scholars have suggested that global political affairs have traditionally been dominated by masculine discourses, which leads to specific kinds of emphases relative to interstate power and conflict that have tended to ignore or downgrade the relevance of minority or disadvantaged voices or that discount the relevance of a range of qualitative methodologies and perspectives including recognition of the importance of storytelling or narrativity in the study of politics. For example, J. Ann Tickner notes that, throughout the past, diplomats, military officials, and academics in security studies have primarily been male and have emphasized masculine issues such as war and conflict. Some feminist scholars criticize realism, a prominent theoretical perspective in the study of international politics, as often skewed by masculine-oriented viewpoints that ignore or deny various complexities in examining social and political interactions within and across sovereign nation-states. Tickner argues that a close examination of current discourse and the inclusion of feminist perspectives allows for an ungendered, or more broadly human, discourse in which men and women are equally represented and respected in the field and discipline of political science. Alternatively, feminist-oriented research has highlighted otherwise invisibilized issues such as war rape, human trafficking, wealth disparity, and social justice. It has also focused on the often dire impacts of international politics on subordinated groups such as women, children, the disabled, and the elderly.

Gender roles have changed significantly since that time, but gender constructions within American society place heavy burdens on women. Scholars refer to this as the **double burden of "invisibilized" housework and underrewarded career work**. Moreover, women continue to crash against the **glass ceiling**, the unseen yet nearly impossible to breach barrier that keeps minorities and women from rising to the upper rungs of the corporate ladder with regard to professional advancement and earning potential, regardless of their qualifications or achievements. In April 2012 Wisconsin repealed its Equal Pay Law because, according to State Senator Glenn Grothman, "You could argue that money is more important for men . . . because they expect to be a breadwinner someday."[19] Throughout the United States today, women continue to be underrepresented in positions of political, corporate, and social power, although some evidence exists as of 2013 of a counter trend, such as the number of women in the US Senate. Violence against women, including domestic abuse and rape, continues to be a widespread problem in American culture as everywhere. The objectification of women in advertising and other media leads to a disproportionate number of body-image issues and eating disorders among women.

Stereotypes, Prejudice, Discrimination: Identity Groups as Objects

Modern cultures classify individuals by race, ethnicity, class, sex, and gender. It is one matter, however, to recognize differences among human beings, but it is quite another to judge, condemn, or subordinate individuals and groups on the basis of difference. In many modern societies, stereotypes, prejudice, and discrimination divide people from one another and distort their relationships and interactions along racial, ethnic, socioeconomic, sectarian, and gender lines. Identity groups result from the various ways that individuals become objectified as members of groups. Such processes often include stereotyping. When this social and cultural dynamic occurs individuals are categorized according to certain features or characteristics attributed to them on account of their imputed membership or association with a particular group as perceived by those doing the stereotyping. The phenomenon of stereotyping thus works to transform individuals and the groups to which they allegedly belong into identity objects. Such processes of objectification often follow along predictable lines when engaged in stereotyping: in such cases, the person doing the stereotyping typically says, "You see one of them, you see them all." Thus the behavior of any one person identified as a member of an identity group is prejudged according to the distinguishing markers associated with the group, while the group itself and its members are in turn judged by the behaviors

of one individual, however idiosyncratic the personal conduct of such individuals perceived to be representative of the identity group may be.

Stereotypes embed attitudes and perceptions about members of a group and how they behave. Individual members of groups are judged not as individuals but on account of their perceived membership. But, in turn, groups are prejudged on the basis of the perceived behavior of one or a small number of individuals so that one person's behavior becomes the behavior of a "them," that is, how all members of their identity group now objectified are presumed to behave. Derived from the Greek words *stereos*, meaning "firm" or "solid," and *typos*, meaning "impression," stereotyping is a way of judging individuals based on what others purport to know about identity groups as objects. Once stereotypes take hold within a society, **prejudice** becomes a functional basis of division and conflict. Prejudice includes preconceived judgments about individuals and groups based on objective and subjective characteristics such as race, ethnicity, class, age, sex, gender, sexual orientation, or religion. On account of prejudice, some people assume that members of an identity group necessarily behave according to stereotypes. Stereotypes and prejudice devalue individuals and groups on the basis of their assumed behaviors, values, capabilities, or attributes. For this reason, stereotypes and prejudice often become the basis for discrimination against individuals and groups within modern societies.

Discrimination is the prejudicial treatment of individuals and groups on the basis of difference. It refers to policies and practices that harm a group and its members by means of unfair mechanisms designed to prevent access to goods and values of benefit to them. Discrimination might be de jure, sanctioned by law, or de facto, practiced without legal authorization. Mandatory racial segregation in the American South was an example of de jure discrimination; any tendency of employers to prefer potential workers with Anglo or white-sounding names over those of certain minorities represents an example of de facto discrimination. Discrimination restricts the freedom of individuals and groups by excluding them from the opportunities that are made available to members of other groups. Particularly invidious are practices associated with institutional discrimination. This arises whenever institutions pursue policies that lead to discriminatory decisions with malevolent effects on the lives or well-being of individuals or families on account of their presumed membership or association with an identity group. Institutional lending policies in the US and several European economies have been found to be discriminatory against applicants with names associated with particular identity groups, including African American and Hispanic/Latino American. What makes institutional discrimination so profoundly troubling is that it proceeds quietly in ways that are difficult to discover or investigate. For

these reasons, oversight and accountability mechanisms play an important role in ferreting out such practices that reinforce inequitable class and distributive structures. Over time, prejudice, stereotypes, discrimination, and institutional discrimination appear as "natural" rather than as culturally produced forms of socially constructed objectifications. The assumption that cultural categories of identity and difference are determined by nature rather than historical contingencies allows the political culture of entire nation-states to evade a collective sense of moral responsibility for how individuals and identity groups become objectified.

The socially constructed binary opposition between "straight" and "gay" has led to the cultural and legal subordination of homosexuals in some modern societies, including the United States. Members of the Lesbian, Gay, Bisexual, Transgender, Queer, Questioning, and Allied (LGBTQQA) community have historically enjoyed second-class citizenship in the United States on account of brutal, hate-motivated violence—symbolized by the murder of Matthew Shepard—as well as because of institutional discriminations based on laws permitting employment prejudice on the basis of sexual orientation. This subordination has been institutionalized by bans on same-sex marriage across the United States. While some states permitted "civil unions" reminiscent of the "separate but equal" rhetoric of the segregated South, America's same-sex couples were systematically, legally, and almost universally denied the full rights and privileges of marriage until the 2010s. In recent years, however, social and legal changes have swept across the nation and states. Discrimination in employment on the basis of sexual orientation is now prohibited by federal statute. As of July 2014, nineteen states had legalized same-sex marriage. In twelve others, prohibitions of gay marriage have been overturned by court decisions. On the whole, policy changes signify changes in social norms and attitudes that have become progressively more open to sexual and gender fluidity in recent years. This represents a process of social transformation. Cultural values that are socially constructed by means of identity group objectification and thus in ways that promote prejudice and discrimination are being reconstructed in ways that advance civility and equal respect as well as equity in terms of equal protection and opportunity.

The Physicality of the Human Condition and the Scourge of Objectification

People embody physical and physiological differences. Socially contrived cultural and social constructions are shaped in part by that physicality we call the **materiality of difference**. Materiality allows us to celebrate cultural differences among

individuals and groups, grounding racial, ethnic, sex, and gender differences in the unity of the human condition. Openness to the materiality of each and every human person fosters a broad compassion for others and willingness to share in and experience difference. This contrasts, however, with the dynamics of **objectification**. Objectification represents a way of interpreting cultural principles of difference according to determinist explanations. They deny the possibilities of human complexity and freedom; they reject the exigencies of history as relevant to explanations of intergroup relations; and they ignore the structures of class and inequity that so often control the contingencies of individual lives by reducing or even devastating what are called life chances. In this sense, objectification denies the possibility that individuals and identity groups can transcend their perceived "nature." Identity groups become objectified things. Objectification represents a way of seeing the cultural world through the political lens of a fixed, materialist, and determinist nature. Those who engage in the practices of objectification might claim that identity group categories represent the genuine principles of difference. This is essentialist in that it bases prejudgment of others according to materialist determinations and naturalist categories. The ultimate failing of such perceptions and reasoning is that they sever what is most human in all persons from what is most personal in each individual. Essentialism reduces individuals to objects and confines their cultural heritage and associations within the boxes or categories of identity objects. This denies the role and significance of identity constructions grounded in cultural heritage within the lives of so many persons and groups. Objectification in the context of political culture thus illustrates how power and class structures function in ways that can and do deny the possibilities of individuality, spontaneity, growth, and renewal by means of nurturing the richness of cultural diversity in all its myriad forms. In such cases, everyone's lives, especially those given to such objectification and stereotyping, are diminished.

Part III
Global Colonialism and the Making of the Modern Nation-State

Chapter 7
Colonialist and Postcolonial Political Culture

Global Colonialism and Its Lingering Dysfunctions

The world as we know it is the creation not of "nature" but rather of political culture and its historical contingencies. This is the case especially with respect to the establishment of modern nation-states throughout the Americas, Asia, and Africa. Anglo-European cultures invaded and in many cases occupied the land and territory on which traditional kinship peoples and communities depended. When such colonialist occupation occurred it happened in ways that were exploitative, dominating, and often brutal and inhumane. During the age of colonialism, European powers conquered much of the world and imposed their political culture on peoples and cultures that were dedicated in one form or another to the legitimacies of kinship and segmented lineage. Overall, in doing so colonialist influences transformed global political geography in ways that overwhelmingly favored the nation-state as a political formation. But the political culture of such nation-states reflected and did not mirror that of the European nation-state. The reasons for this underscore the political history of the modern world, in particular the political history of **contact situations** in which cultures that regarded themselves as "civilized" subordinated the kinship and segmented lineage or tribal cultures they regarded as "primitive." These dynamics happened differently in different regions. The broadly devastating result lives on today in the disastrous inability of numerous modern states to form political cultures that manifest the functional features of the nation-state. They are beset by fragile, fractious, and conflict-ridden nation-building and dysfunctional processes of state-building. As one looks at the globe today, one sees the near universal

political geography of the modern sovereign nation-state. But within numerous internal boundaries, the process of nation-building and state-building continues unabated given the deep divides gripping such societies in no small measure due to the lingering footprints of colonial history in the postcolonial era.

Internal colonialism emphasizes how displacement and dislocation, alongside push and pull forces, destroy the linkages between people and land necessary to sustain and nurture kinship ties and belonging from one generation to another. A similar cultural devastation occurs as a consequence of **global colonialism**. Culturally invented categories of difference reflective of the power dynamics inherent within the contact situation become constructed and accepted as equivalent to natural reality. The specific incursions due to global colonialism and the contact situation often retain their influences on developmental processes of nation-building and state-building even today. These impacts bear directly on identity constructions, in particular how the various groupings struggling with the contingencies of unity and nationality perceive and relate to one another. But these postcolonial influences and their consequences often become obscured or denied altogether. The way such denials occur tends to assume a particular mode of reasoning: that this intergroup conflict had existed in times past even before the colonial experience; that it is part of the very "nature" of indigenous groups to engage in conflicts against one another. For the most part, this line of reasoning is fallacious. Case after case throughout the postcolonial universe reveals first how the identity groups that emerged within contemporary political-cultural formations did so under the historic pressures of colonial occupation and settlement. Second, this history, encapsulated by the notion of global colonialism, unfolded in ways in which the clans of kinship descent and segmented lineage become transformed into what we will call ethnicized identity objects. As this happened they became perceived and in many instances perceived one another as no different in their origin than aspects of the "natural" world. Colonialist contact situations generated cultural constructions that were contingent on the unequal power relationships between European states and the peoples they conquered and/or occupied as settlers. In time, the cultural constructions that emerged seemed to appear as "natural" although they represent the continuing effects of the contact situation in the postcolonial era. This is not to say that the colonialist contact situation is exclusively responsible for all the dysfunctions of developing nation-states throughout the world today. But it does suggest that the political culture of modern nation-states emerged historically as a consequence of dysfunctional processes. This is demonstrated in particular by three **postcolonialist disorders**: **clientism**, **dysfunctional mimesis or imitation**, and **nativism**.

The story of global colonialism varies from region to region, but its main vectors involved economic and resource exploitation, political domination, and cultural subordination. As a consequence of global colonialism, resources were extracted throughout Africa, Asia, and the Americas for use in European economies. This historical transfer of resources tended in time to have unfortunate consequences for the economies of the colonized, but it enhanced the prosperity of the colonizers. Especially in cases in which colonizers became settlers within the colonized locations, power relations delegitimated kinship or patrimonial rule associated with ancestral descent and segmented lineage. The overall aim—and certainly the historical consequence—was to replace kinship rule and dynastic governments with what we know today as the political culture of centralized administrative nation-states. As indicated earlier, the political culture associated with kinship communities became objectified as "inferior." European states took on *la mission civilatrice* (the "civilizing mission") or the white man's burden to bring "civilization" and "culture" to the "savage" and "primitive" peoples of the non-European world. The indigenous peoples of segmented lineage and kinship descent became suborned and subordinated. Their widespread cultural commitments to honor and shame disciplines became devalued. But this colonialist process of cultural devalorization only partially succeeded in many places. Cultural residues of honor and shame remained, as evidenced by their continuing demonstration around the globe by the formerly colonized. Colonialist political cultures transformed the complex cosmos of communal traditions into a postcolonialist universe of subaltern "otherness." This generated a series of predominant perceptions regarding the political culture of the postcolonial world. Henceforth, the characteristics of subordinated political cultures would no longer be measured simply in terms of their internal values of honor and shame, but would rather be judged according to external meanings and value systems. In keeping with the tendency toward binary oppositions, universal political culture consequently would be perceived as divided into two: Western and non-Western political culture. Often the assumptions behind this division would remain unspoken. But the implications for Western political culture were clear. The civilizational values of the Western world were considered "good"; all things non-Western associated with patrimonial and kinship legitimacy and values were perceived as "bad." As ever, binary oppositions were not "neutral" in their import and significance. The silent code of meanings that attended the split between Western and non-Western was assumed to represent a division between, on the one hand, political cultures of the nation-state that functioned effectively and, on the other hand, political cultures of former colonies doomed "by nature" to fail without Western colonialist interventions. These perceptions

that often operate in denial of the complicity of Western involvement ignore the role played by global colonialism in generating the dysfunctional pathologies that affected and continue to affect the political cultures of fragile nation-states in the postcolonialist world.

European states colonized and in many cases settled Asia, Latin America, and Africa in ways that exploited their resources and dominated their territories in order to glean economic advantage. But often their self-understanding turned on the benefits of civilization they were bringing to the "heathens." What European political cultures assumed was that their civilizing project was altogether beneficial and progressive. The realities on the ground, then and now, remain much more complex. In terms of political culture, the corrosion and even destruction of communal traditions produced weak forms of governing legitimacy that altered how modern nation-states emerged. This is demonstrated by the range of ethno-grievances and internal struggles that continue in many areas among ethnicized kinship groups. The impacts carried by the historical erosion of the legitimacy of traditional patrimonial rule vary from region to region and culture to culture. But certain general outcomes are discernible. Colonizing political cultures transformed kinship identities and meanings in ways that subordinated segmented lineage and kinship. The consequence was that kinship became transformed into **"ethnicized"** divisions. As a result, identity group cultures formed and became organized around conflictual values, meanings, and institutions. Once kinship became devalued in favor of ethnicity, resentments and hostilities developed and grew in ways that had never existed before. As kinship became transmuted into ethnicity, kinship was typically represented as "inferiority" relative to the colonizing political culture. Kinship was perceived as "backward," "primitive," and "infantile." The emergence of postcolonialist ethnicity as a form of political and social identity, therefore, has been historically associated with the subordination of kinship traditions and legitimacy. Colonialist and postcolonialist political cultures further subordinated kinship values and traditions by processes that in effect **racialized** divisions based on kinship or segmented lineage. The involuntary Westernization of kinship communities—peoples beholden to ancestral or segmented lineage—historically signified sets of cultural dynamics in which the transformations of kinship into makeshift kinship ethnicities would also culminate in cultures that were politically divided into racialized kinship groupings. This complex set of historical dynamics in the transformations of political culture that were wrought by global colonialism demonstrates how contemporary political-cultural divisions that result from the contact situation are perceived as "natural" characteristics of objectified identity groups. Kinship groups, once transformed into adversarial ethnic groups, often

relate to one another within national political formations in ways that are driven by competition for status if not conflicts over power and distributions of wealth. These conflictual dynamics tend to become exaggerated once kinship ethnicities become racialized. This very process of racialization represents another version of transforming the contingencies of historical process into the necessities of nature. To racialize identity groups is to attribute fixed and frozen qualities to their nature now and for all time. Racialization of kinship ethnic groups transforms political culture by objectifying difference. It leads to perceptions of identity group objects in which their features become essentialized. This sets the stage for political conflict and even violence.

Colonialism and postcolonialist political cultures created new territorial boundaries across the kinship topologies of segmented lineage. These colonial boundaries anticipated the establishment of sovereign and independent nation-states, but the ultimate result was the creation of nonhistorical states. In the postcolonial era this would lead to new kinds of identity constructions, tensions, and conflicts. Nonhistorical states across the world would be forced to contend with a range of political dysfunctions and cultural disorders. These include

- conflicted legitimacies between colonialist centralizers and the patrimonial authority of traditional elders or tribal rulers;
- tensions between kinship honor and political cultures grounded in notions of nationality;
- postcolonial violence among kinship groups as a result of having become "ethnicized" and "racialized" in terms of political culture;
- territorial discontinuities between the geographies created by global colonialism and the geographies of kinship allegiance that remain culturally vibrant;
- difficulty in developing political cultures grounded in the legitimacy of popular consent and the values of nationality in nation-states that were created as a result of colonialism and postcolonialism.

Colonialist competitors established territorial boundaries in accordance with their own interests. For this reason, modern nation-state boundaries often defy the political cultures once indigenous to these territories. The cultural effect is to dislocate traditional values and meanings by imposing national territorial configurations on sacred land in ways that divide members of kinship communities. These dynamics displaced traditional communities by imposing cultures of nationality on them in ways that distorted the very process of citizenship as an aspect of political culture. Citizenship meant risk, fear, and danger. It

implied cultural disorientation rather than political solidarity and communal cultural strength. As Frantz Fanon wrote, postcolonialism "does not establish a reassuring State for the citizen but one which is troubling. Instead of inspiring confidence, assuaging the fears of its citizens and cradling them with its power and discretion, the State, on the contrary, imposes itself in a spectacular manner, flaunts its authority, harasses, making it clear to its citizens that they are in constant danger."[1]

Colonialist competitors tended to establish territorial boundaries in accordance with their own interests, often ignoring the traditional geographies of segmented lineage orders and kinship groups. Modern political boundaries are not congruent with ethnic demarcations. Thus modern territorial boundaries defy the political cultures indigenous to these territories. The political cultures of postcolonial nation-states struggle for popular consent grounded in nationality and national collective identity against the background of territorial disarray. The making of the modern nation-state centers around the creation of a political geography demarcated by sovereign state boundaries and legitimated by national polities. The geographic universalizing of the nation-state occurred as a consequence of the colonial contact situation in which colonialism and the competition among Anglo-European powers for colonial territory imposed boundaries onto traditional cultures and tribal communities without the "organic" historical transition that attended the development of cultural meanings, values, and institutions in the European and Western world. **Nation-building**, **state-building**, and **nation-state-building** in Europe and America developed over the course of several centuries. These sets of political-cultural dynamics reflected changing economic realities and the gradual development of legitimacy attachments to specific nation-states over a wide period of time punctuated with many periods of acceptance and turmoil. When nation-state boundaries were imposed on non-Western political cultures by the global forces and trajectories of colonialism they represented foreign and illegitimate cultural exports. For these reasons alone, the political cultures of modern postcolonial nation-states are fundamentally different from the political cultures of nation-states that developed without a colonial history.

The involuntary "modernization" of peoples beholden to kinship honor and shame in many instances subordinated indigenous peoples, reducing them to "primitive" "races." This subordination was done in the name of "Westernization." The consequence was to leave a historical and communal memory of humiliation in the communities of those whose traditional cultural realities were now transformed into various forms of subaltern existence. Yet again we see that postcolonial projects produced political cultures that were deformed

by the dynamics through which kinship was transformed into ethnicity and ethnicity changed into racist identity constructions. Identity groups become objects unto one another within the parameters of postcolonial political cultures, leaving residues of deep resentment toward not only the former colonialists but also each other.

Native groups often sought to imitate the "superior" culture of postcolonialist settlers by rejecting kinship values and traditions. Anglo-European political culture was largely artful in the self-delusions that it appears to have cultivated, namely, that its ways and attitudes brought civilization everywhere it went. As a result of postcolonialism and the universalizing of political cultures linked to modern centralized nation-states, the legitimacy of kinship institutions, values, and traditions are denied historical validity. What is foreign becomes desired; what is local becomes undesirable and subject to rejection. As Fanon writes, "every effort is made to make the colonized confess the inferiority of their culture, now reduced to a set of instinctive responses, to acknowledge the unreality of their nation, and, in the last extreme, to admit the disorganized half-finished nature of their own biological makeup."[2] The result often proved devastating for the political cultures of the recipient society in that the postcolonial impacts of such Westernizing/modernizing projects favored the cultural devices of ethnic identity, the **social constructions of otherness** grounded in ethnic conceptions of belonging, and the emergence of **racialized distinctions** based on naturalized beliefs in human and communal **difference**. The vector that spread these cultural distortions was a kind of **dysfunctional mimesis or imitation**. Traditional kinship communities adopted the political cultures of the settler in the name of "progress." But "progress" brought racialized distinctions or differences that were color coded according to kinship, blood, and ancestral lineage. The color codes of difference transformed traditional kinship cultures into **ethnicized divisions**. These were built into the very cultural fabrics of nationality once independent nation-states emerged from under the yoke of colonialism.

Ethnicized divisions exaggerated cultural difference in ways that combined subordination for some racialized identity groups and domination over the power of the nation-state for others, especially those previously supported by colonialists. This left a legacy of **clientist** groups to imitate those who represented the "superiority" of the West. Clientist groups nurture networks of patronage and payoffs between those who control the power of the nation-state and its bureaucracies and those among the electorate who are of the same ethnic identity group. Clientism thus operates as a kind of "Tammany Hall" political ward system, payoffs and all, and represents a dysfunctional form of democracy. Some become advantaged by and in such a system of payoffs while others languish in

marginalization and **nonrepresentation**. It is often the case that the patronized group formerly privileged by the colonialist powers comes to dominate the political and economic administration of the postcolonial nation-state in ways that favor, reward, and thus **patronize** "their own" on the basis of kinship loyalties. **Clientism** represents an attack against the unifying solidarity of nationality. It demonstrates the continuing hold of kinship loyalties and honor disciplines within the political-cultural frameworks of nonhistorical centralized nation-states. Because of postcolonial clientism, nationality becomes constructed as the preserve of a single, privileged (often ethnicized and racialized) kinship group rather than the right of all citizens who live within the boundaries of the particular sovereign nation-state. This is dysfunctional democratic nation-state-building and it appears across the political geography and culture of postcolonial nation-states often as the indirect result of the colonial experience.

On account of the history of subordination and exploitation, attempts to imitate the political cultures of centralized nation-states with their values of popular consent and individualized citizenship lead to racialized cultural divides within numerous nation-states that, as a result, are often referred to as "**failed states**." In the postcolonial era, racialized conflicts arise among identity groups that had been kinship communities but now represent ethnicized and racialized objects for one another. These dynamics transformed cultural constructions of nationality and ethnicity in the postcolonial world with devastating consequences, especially for subordinated peoples who often seek a return to the legitimacies of kinship rule, frequently with vengeance toward privileged elites. This sense of vengeance is integral to the dynamic in political culture whereby kinship becomes transformed into ethnicity and ethnicity becomes racialized. Thus, postcolonialism represents a historical phase in which formerly colonized peoples contend with the impacts of their cultural and political subordination. It is a period characterized by the establishment of independent nation-states throughout previously colonized territories. But the creation of modern nation-states implies certain capacities for political congruence and nationality that did not occur in political cultures where legitimacy continued to be anchored to kinship and tribal governance. As a consequence, as Fanon so poignantly observed, "instead of being the coordinated crystallization of the people's innermost aspirations, instead of being the most tangible, immediate product of popular mobilization, national consciousness is nothing but a crude, empty, fragile shell. The cracks in it explain how easy it is for young independent countries to switch back from nation to ethnic group and from state to tribe—a regression which is so terribly detrimental and prejudicial to the development of the nation and national unity."[3] Nationality as a cultural construction of solidarity and collective identity could not emerge in postcolonial

nation-states where the hold of legitimacy continues to attach to tribal division or segmentation. As a result, many postcolonial states remain politically **underdeveloped**. Because of colonial domination and the lingering legitimacy of kinship forms of governance, the crucial **double congruence** between nation and state and between **nationality** or political commonality and **ethnicity** or cultural difference cannot develop in ways that foster the establishment of nation-state legitimacy.

KEY CONCEPTS

Failed States

A **failed state** is a sovereign nation-state that functions in name only and not in the fullness of the legitimacy founded on the bedrock of popular consent. It fails to satisfy the basic criteria of statehood and/or does not meet the conditions of nationhood on account of the inability of a population bounded together within a defined sovereign territory to establish the kinds of political consensus necessary for the operations of a unified nation-state. It is typically assailed by various conflicts. These work to prevent the emergence of political-cultural values that are supportive of nationality based on principles of commonality and anchored by the recognition of shared peoplehood within the boundaries of a sovereign state. Failed states are chronically unable to fulfill the minimal responsibilities of a modern sovereign nation-state. A failed state represents a political formation in which the impediments to legitimate centralized authority and administrative government tend to be powerful. Many criteria and characteristics may be adduced in describing what failed states are, do, and represent conceptually. Over and beyond any stands the basic issue of political culture. The US-based Fund for Peace[4] defines a failed state as one that no longer presides over the political dynamics occurring within its territory; no longer maintains sole legal or legitimate use of violence within its boundaries; experiences the erosion of legitimate authority to make centralized decisions; demonstrates an inability to provide public services; and is typically unable to interact with other nation-states as a fully engaged member of the international society of states. A failed state tends to be afflicted by a weak or dysfunctional central government that is ineffective with respect to basic services but still capable of violent repression. A wide range of deficient and inefficient dynamics plagues failed states, from corruption and criminality to economic and political instability. Many living in failed states seek to emigrate to other nation-states, but typically without success.

European Nation-States and the Age of Exploration

The centralization dynamics historically associated with state-building emphasized economic prosperity as well as social and political stability. During the sixteenth century many European powers adopted economic policies associated with **mercantilism**. **Mercantilists** favored the establishment of overseas colonies, the accumulation of gold and silver, export subsidies, domestic economic self-sufficiency, and trade barriers between sovereign states. States dedicated to the pursuit of mercantilist policies competed for resources, and valued positive balances of trade so that in every exchange a gain had to accrue to the sovereign. Economic policy was thus deemed subordinate to the political interests of the state measured in terms of national wealth defined as the amount of gold possessed by the national treasury. Trade policy thus became subservient to aims of national glory. State independence was considered paramount rather than interdependence among trading partners.

Mercantilism encouraged the excesses that generated many of the intra-European wars during this era. French wars with German kingdoms for control of Alsace-Lorraine, for example, can be understood as mercantilist struggles for the iron and coal resources of that region. However, mercantilism also explains why European states sought control over Asia, Africa, and the newly discovered Americas. Control of colonial empires gave European states access to raw materials and resources that empowered them in conflicts with their neighbors, filled their domestic coffers, and conferred national glory upon the emerging state bent on extraction for purposes of war and royal power. In the early days of the Age of Exploration and Discovery, as early monarchies were consolidating their power around centralized forms of government, royal navies took to the seas in search of a resource prized across Europe—spices. But this history is long and originates, in part, in the political-cultural conflicts between Christianity and Islam.

Between the eleventh and thirteenth centuries Classical monarchs across Europe called forth militants to pursue a series of religious wars known as the **Crusades**. In 1095 the Byzantine emperor Comnenus asked Western Christians to join in a military campaign against the Muslim Turks who had conquered Baghdad, Jerusalem, and Asia Minor. In response, Pope Urban II called upon all the knights in Western Europe to join the expedition to free the Holy Lands from Muslim rule. Though grounded in religious justifications, the Crusades were a product of ambitions on the part of four leading European social groups—the pope and the Catholic Church, royal state builders, the landed nobility, and the incipient merchant class. The pope wanted to unite all of Western Europe into a single political, cultural, and economic unit, known as Christendom, over which

he would rule. He also hoped that by sending an army to liberate the Holy Lands he could reunify the Catholic and Orthodox Churches. Royal rulers and noble knights, each for their own reasons, sought the power of domination through the glory of battle, the riches of plunder, and the commutation of sins. And the merchants looked to the Crusades to establish new trade routes between Europe and the Middle East and, from there, India, Southeast Asia, and China.

Although the Crusades did not unite all of Western Europe into a single pope-ruled empire nor did they release the Holy Land from Muslim rule, they did result in a series of lingering impacts upon European society. First, papal power and legitimacy waned as the Crusades became less and less successful during the twelfth and thirteenth centuries. Second, the Crusades weakened the feudal nobility. Thousands of knights died as a consequence of the Crusades while others sold their properties to fund their expeditions. Classical monarchs took advantage of this weakening of the aristocracy to consolidate their own power. Finally, the Crusades stimulated trade between Europe and the Middle East. Moreover, Crusaders returned to Europe with new tastes for the food, clothing, and spices that they had purchased in Arab markets. The growing demand for exotic goods created opportunities for ambitious merchants who imported sugar, pepper, cloves, cinnamon, plums, watermelons, apricots, dates, pistachios, lemons, silk, Persian rugs, and cotton cloth to Western Europe. Initial trade routes were monopolized by merchants in Italy. This led to tensions with other mercantilist states including Spain, Portugal, France, and England. As a result of their mercantilist ambitions, they pursued new trade routes to the Middle East, India, Indonesia, and China that would circumvent the trade routes dominated by the Italian city-states. Out of this competition grew the increasing efforts of the mercantilist state to find new trading routes and expanded forms of trade with the east. This fueled the Age of Exploration and, ultimately, the Age of Colonial Domination.

In 1420 Portugal's Prince Henry organized voyages along the western coast of Africa. On the islands of Madeira, the Azores, and Cape Verde the Portuguese found such commodities as gold and ivory. But their most significant and cruelest exploitation was aimed at the inhabitants themselves whom they immediately began to impress into servitude as slaves. In 1497 Vasco de Gama rounded the Cape of Good Hope and landed in India, thus giving the Portuguese control over the Indian Ocean and access to trade with China and the Spice Islands. However, the Spanish claimed to have their own route to India—a route west across the Atlantic Ocean.

King Ferdinand and Queen Isabella of Spain needed funds for their state-building projects designed to unite Spain under their centralized authority. In

1492, therefore, they financed Christopher Columbus's voyages west in search of the Indies. Instead of the Indies, Columbus found the New World and initiated an era of European control over North and South America. Spain continued to send explorers and **conquistadors** to the New World and proceeded to conquer much of modern-day South America, Central America, Mexico, and the southwest United States. Here, too, utter devastation of the indigenous populations occurred. And the Spanish also proceeded to adopt slavery as a form of self-aggrandizement.

Portugal, however, was not content to allow Spanish domination of the New World, particularly when the Spanish explorers returned with boats full of Aztec gold, spices, and other riches. The rivalry between Spain and Portugal for control of the Americas became so intense that in 1493 Pope Alexander VI ruled that the two must divide the new lands along the **Line of Demarcation**. The Spanish would hold all lands west of the line while the Portuguese would control the territories to its east. As officially Catholic states both government authorities acknowledged the legitimacy of the pope to make such a determination. But in 1492 the Treaty of Tordesillas moved the line of demarcation farther west giving Portugal additional territorial holdings. This treaty explains why modern-day Brazilians primarily speak Portuguese while the dominant language across the rest of Central and South America is Spanish. These historical events also suggest why the blanket term Hispanic is so misleading. It denies both the Portuguese heritage that resisted Spanish influences throughout the New World and the important set of African cultural influences within the Portuguese and Brazilian cultural environments.

European Colonialism in the New World

Spanish and Portuguese conquest of the Americas was, in a word, brutal. Both objectified the native New World populations as not only savage and inferior, but even subhuman. These early political cultures carried with them the oppressive freight of assumptions that helped to establish the lingering cultural binary oppositions between the native and the European, the colonized and the colonizer, and the primitive and the modern. With their dark skin, primordial kinship descent traditions, and often dynastic governments, the pre-Columbian indigenous American peoples appeared as the antithesis of the post-Enlightenment Europeans, at least to the Europeans. The conquistadors became the very conquerors they were by first objectifying native populations and labeling them as inferior. When Columbus landed in the Bahamas in 1492, he was met by the Arawak of

whom he wrote, "They would make fine servants. . . . With fifty men we could subjugate them all, and make them do whatever we want."[5] The indigenous peoples were no match for European weaponry and were quickly subdued. Additionally, native populations, having no natural immunity to European-based diseases such as measles, influenza, chicken pox, and smallpox, died en masse in the years immediately following Columbian contact. It is estimated that post-Columbian populations were decimated by 90 percent as a result of war, disease, and enslavement at the hands of the Europeans. The demographic impacts were so great that the Europeans turned to importing African slaves to serve as labor on their New World plantations.

The Spanish and the Portuguese also eradicated the agricultural and traditional cultures of the native peoples. Both the Spanish and the Portuguese were committed by Vatican decree to convert the natives to Catholicism wherever they maintained colonial holdings. Indigenous kinship practices were considered idolatrous and were prohibited by the European religious, military, and civil officials. For these reasons, many indigenous cultures were destroyed by European conquerors. In their attempts to "civilize" the natives and then to subordinate them into lives of servitude, the Spanish and the Portuguese oversaw the almost complete eradication of kinship culture in Central and South America.

Native populations did not fare better throughout French, British, and Dutch holdings in North America. As we saw in the previous chapter, British colonists and early Americans dislocated the indigenous tribal communities to reservations where they endured systematic cultural annihilation. Although the Dutch, British, and French powers were willing to use native knowledge and resources when it advanced their colonialist/imperialist interests, the natives were, in the end, expendable. Nor were the resident indigenous peoples living in colonial America prior to the American War of Independence exempted. On the contrary, entire indigenous settlements, composed of kinship descent groups and living west of the eastern seaboard in areas recognized today as New England and the industrial heartland, were devastated by settler incursions long before those against Native Americans in the American far west occurred.

Gradually, European settlers replaced native populations across the American continents. Small pockets of kinship communities remained but the European drive to conquer American land and resources succeeded, supplanting indigenous agricultural cultures. In other examples of European colonialism, however, colonizers sought not to settle the lands of dislocated and displaced natives, but rather to extract valuable resources through a system of indirect governance. Although the populations of these colonies were not devastated to the same extent as those in the Americas, the impact upon their cultural traditions was no less shattering.

The British Raj and Colonialism in India

India is home to one of the world's most ancient civilizations. Along the banks of the Indus and Ganges Rivers, India's first settlements were similar to those of Mesopotamia and Egypt. Early south Asian Indians built cities along the rivers, using the fertile soil deposits from annual floods to sustain agricultural communities. Dynastic hierarchies stored and protected grain surpluses, distributing resources to members of the community as necessary. Farmers domesticated animals both to eat and to employ in their agricultural systems. Craftsmen made pottery, dyed cloth, and forged gold, silver, copper, and bronze into tools. Trade among the cities facilitated by a written language contributed to the overall prosperity of the region.

In approximately 1500 BC nomads from central Asia traveled through the Khyber Pass and into the Indus River Valley. Called **Aryans**, these nomads were herders who counted their wealth in cattle and conquered larger human settlements as they trekked across the Indian continent. The Aryans were a kinship culture that passed traditions, values, and practices intergenerationally through an unwritten or **oral tradition**. Eventually the Aryans and the Indians intermingled, creating a new and unique culture on the Indian subcontinent.

The Hindu religion is a product of that cultural heritage and mélange. When the Aryans migrated to India they brought a rich **polytheistic tradition**. Aryan priests memorized long poems and hymns suited to religious rituals that were gathered into four collections called **Vedas**. Beginning in 400 BC, teachers began to interpret and explain the hidden meaning within the Vedas. Their explanations were recorded in a collection of essays called the **Upanishads**. These teachings, which included notions of **karma** and **reincarnation**, became the dominant cultural tradition of the Indian people and a binding devotion in the political culture of modern India.

Hinduism includes a complicated set of social divisions between groups of people known as the **caste system**. According to this tradition, four different groups of people were created from the body of a Hindu god. The Brahmins were created from the god's mouth and became the priestly cast. The Kshatriyas came from the god's arms and became the rulers and warriors. The Vaishyas were created from the god's legs and became the landowners, merchants, artisans, and farmers. The Shudras came from the god's feet and became the servants or slaves. The most marginalized members of Hindu society were those who were outside of this system altogether. These **outcasts** or **untouchables** were isolated from Hindu society.

Hindus were taught only to associate with members of their own caste. Status was ascribed by birth and children inherited their professions from their parents.

Intermarriage between castes was prohibited. And because Hinduism taught that one's caste placement was determined by one's actions in a previous life, social mobility in one's succeeding life depended on perfect obedience to the demands of caste. Each caste had its own social obligations known as **dharma**. To be reincarnated as a member of a higher caste required perfect obedience to those rules and practices. The individual's wishes did not matter. It was better to do one's own duty badly than to do someone else's duty well. These influences remain alive and well in the political and social culture of modern India.

The Indian civilization was conquered several times in its history. It was incorporated into the Persian Empire and later into the Muslim Empire. Traditional Indian culture survived nonetheless. But in the early seventeenth century, India was again conquered, this time by an imperial state, Great Britain, seeking to incorporate India into its global colonial dominion on which its wealth and power seemed to depend. The British ruled India until 1947. They did so in exploitative and highly discriminatory ways that devalorized Hindu cultural traditions but never to the point of extinguishing the sense of commonality among the many linguistic groups and minorities composing traditional Indian society.

From the early 1600s through the middle of the eighteenth century the English East India Company dominated the trade in Bengal. The British did not seek to rule India at this time and instead merely co-opted the existing native governance structures to suit their economic needs. The rivals to the British were not indigenous peoples but rather the French and Dutch who challenged British control of the lucrative spice trade in the region. From the mid-1700s until 1857, the East India Company increasingly shared its control of India with the British crown. From child-rearing practices to land rights to inheritance rules, the East India Company replaced primordial traditions of the Indian people with their own system of centralized, merit-based governance. In 1857 a rebellion of the **sepoys**, Indian troops who had been incorporated into the East India Company's army, catalyzed into a broader rebellion of Indian nobles, rural landowners, and peasants. These groups revolted against the East India Company's violations of feudal and kinship traditions. Ultimately the British crown intervened, crushing the rebellion. Although the rebel leaders became national heroes as part of an Indian nationalist movement, in the aftermath of the rebellion the British established direct control over the colony, quashing domestic nation-building initiatives.

The British government continued the East India Company's policy of "modernization" in India. Although the Indians' kinship traditions and cultural practices were too imbedded to change quickly, the British ran roughshod over India's social, political, and economic structures. In 1858 the British government

replaced the East India Company with administrative civil servants who were British by birth. Although members of the Indian caste hierarchy kept its ceremonial status, real power was transferred to agents of the British crown. The British government also modernized the Indian legal system, introducing a new penal code of civil and criminal procedures based on British law. It modernized Indian agriculture, industrialized Indian provinces, built railroads across the subcontinent, and reformed the Indian economy to include mercantilist policies. It established universities as hubs of modern education that emphasized European history, government, and cultural studies and that served to sever feudal linkages across the subcontinent. This ultimately worked against the British. Indian students were educated in notions rooted to the **Enlightenment** including the values of limited government, popular consent, and self-determination. University communities readily became proponents of **Indian nationalism** and independence. In the aftermath of the Second World War, these movements would culminate in the creation of two sovereign nation-states out of the Indian Raj. India would be a predominantly Hindu state while Pakistan would be predominantly Muslim. Both would govern themselves having been transformed culturally, politically, economically, and socially by the British rule.

When the British came to India they found a feudal society dominated by the caste system. Most Indians were farmers and craftsmen. Indian society was ruled in accordance with kinship rules and practices that were heavily influenced by Hindu and Islamic teachings. However, during the years of British rule India was forced to leave its traditions of primordial kinship and dynastic government behind, adopting instead modern systems of political, economic, and social organization. While the British brought industry, advanced agriculture, schools, hospitals, sanitation, and infrastructure to the subcontinent, the Raj stripped away Indian political culture, replacing kinship values with those associated with individuality and nationality. Those who imitated the political-cultural values associated with modern nation-states rose to power and prestige. This ultimately led to the independence movement of Mahatma Gandhi and the successful creation of a modern sovereign nation-state in the place of the colonial Raj. But India, a modern nation-state, still struggles with sectarian violence, honor killings, the trappings of the caste system, brutal poverty, and massive levels of corruption flowing through the pipelines of patronage and clientism left over from the days of traditional kinship cultures. India today is the world's largest democracy, but it confronts problems such as tensions with Pakistan over the disputed Kashmir and Jammu regions where the majority of people are Muslim but governed by a sovereign nation-state manifestly dominated by a Hindu majority. Finally, a great irony pervades the political culture of modern India, namely, that its unifying

national language, the vernacular of its political class, is English, the very language of its historical colonial settler. By some estimates modern India is a nation that includes nearly two thousand linguistic minorities who would find it difficult if not impossible to communicate with one another but for the widespread adoption of English as an official language of the Indian national state.

Modernizing Africa: The Berlin Conference

European colonialism was not limited to the New World and Asia. At the Berlin Conference in 1884, European powers met to discuss the imperial race to conquer the African continent. Although trading posts and seaports along the African coast had long been used to facilitate trade, particularly in exporting slaves to the New World, the interior of the continent had attracted little colonialist/imperialist attention. Beginning with Belgian king Leopold II's conquest of the Congo, however, European competition for African land and resources pitted European states against one another. This colonialist fervor threatened to undermine the European balance of power system that German chancellor Otto von Bismarck had carefully crafted in his attempt to build a strong and unified German nation-state under the leadership of the Prussian principality. Bismarck thus hosted the Berlin Conference to give European powers the chance to divide Africa among themselves and in order to prevent conflict among the European states, as well to advance German diplomatic interests in Europe.

The meeting produced the **General Acts of the Berlin Conference**, which stated that (1) the Free State of the Congo (today the Democratic Republic of the Congo) would remain the private property of the Congo Society under the leadership of King Leopold II and would remain open to all European investors; (2) all signatories would enjoy the privileges of free trade throughout the Congo basin; (3) the Niger and Congo Rivers would remain open for shipping; (4) European powers would have the exclusive rights to pursue ownership of the land (relative to other European states) within their designated **spheres of influence**. To claim a colony, a European state had to practice the **Principle of Effectivity**. These were the rules of the game that competing European powers had to follow in relation to potential colonies across the African continent. That is to say, European nation-states could only claim as colonies those lands that they actually "possessed" or controlled. The colonial power had to establish an administration in the territory replete with military or police forces to keep order and had to make use of the colony economically. Otherwise another nation-state could take over the territory in question. As a result of this set of understandings,

the lands that European powers claimed throughout Africa before the Conference became the site of what is now recognized as the **scramble for Africa**. This scramble is demonstrated by the heated competition among European settler states for control of particular portions of the African land mass and their peoples that occurred within a relatively brief period especially in the aftermath of the Berlin Conference.

By 1902, 90 percent of African lands were under European control; this resulted in the deepening of systematic subordination of kinship descent cultures across the continent. Three historical episodes emphasize the multifaceted dynamics of global colonialism and demonstrate how and why postcolonial pathologies tend to confront nonhistorical states across the African continent: the Belgians in the Congo, the British in Kenya, and the Germans in Namibia.

Belgians in the Congo

The Berlin Conference confirmed that the lands currently known as the Democratic Republic of the Congo belonged to the Belgian king Leopold II both in fact and in law. When Leopold first sent agents into the Congo as explorers, they found that "the peoples of this vast territory were as diverse as the land. They ranged from subjects of large, organizationally sophisticated chiefdoms to the Pygmies of the Ituri rain forest, who survived in small bands with no chiefs and no formal structure of government. The dynastic chiefdoms, with large towns as their capitals, tended to be in the savanna, where long-distance travel was easier. In the rain forest, where paths had to be hacked through thick, rapidly growing foliage, communities were generally far smaller. These forest-dwellers were sometimes seminomads: if a group of Pygmies, for instance, killed an elephant, that site became a temporary settlement for a week or two of feasting, since it was easier to move a village than a dead animal."[6] The people of the Congo, therefore, represented several different stages of cultural development. Some lived in small kinship groups. These were the nomads who dwelt in environments where resources, particularly food, were scarce. Others lived in more fertile regions where settled horticultural agriculture was possible. These adopted dynastic forms of centralized chiefdoms tantamount to royal kingdoms designed to coordinate their economic and communal lives.

Adam Hochschild writes of the Congo's primordial peoples, "Many practiced slavery and ritual cannibalism and were as likely to make war on other clans or ethnic groups as people anywhere on earth. And traditional warfare in this part of Africa, where a severed head was sometimes proof of an enemy killed in battle,

was as harsh as warfare elsewhere. In some areas of the Congo all women were maimed, as still happens today, by forced clitoridectomies, a practice no less brutal for being a cultural initiation rite."[7] He goes on to write, "like many indigenous peoples, inhabitants of the Congo basin had learned to live in balance with their environment. Some groups practiced what was, in effect, birth control, where couples had to abstain from sex before the men left on a hunting expedition, for example, or as long as the woman was breast-feeding a baby. Substances found in certain leaves and bark could induce miscarriages or had contraceptive properties. All these means of population control, incidentally, were strikingly similar to those which had evolved in another great rain forest an ocean away, the Amazon basin."[8] These primordial kinship and descent people produced beautiful artwork. Baskets, pottery, copper, ironwork, and woodcarvings served both functional and symbolic purposes. As Hochschild indicates, "The art sprang from cultures that had, among other things, a looser sense than Islam or Christianity of the boundaries between our world and the next, as well as those between the world of humans and the world of beasts. Among the Bolia people of the Congo, for example, a king was chosen by a council of elders; by ancestors, who appeared to him in a dream; and finally by wild animals, who signaled their assent by roaring during a night when the royal candidate was left at a particular spot in the rain forest."[9] For their part, the Belgian colonialists "treated the Congo as if it were just a piece of uninhabited real estate . . . an expanse of empty space waiting to be filled by the cities and railway lines constructed through the magic of European industry. To see Africa instead as a continent of coherent societies, each with its own culture and history, took a leap of empathy, a leap that few, if any, of the early European or American visitors to the Congo were able to make. To do so would have meant seeing Leopold's regime not as progress, not as civilization, but as a theft of land and freedom."[10] The Belgians had discovered that the Congo was replete with economic resources including rubber, copper, ivory, gold, and other minerals. To extract these resources so that they could be sold in European markets, Leopold II instituted a system of forced labor throughout the Congo. George Washington Williams, an American who wrote about the abuses in the Congo, observed that Belgians destroyed Congolese primordial cultures in an effort to extract economic resources. Rather than providing "wise government and public services," they did not establish schools or hospitals in the colony. The civil servants did not know the native languages. Europeans and Africans were held to different legal standards. Traders and state officials kidnapped African women and used them as concubines. Officers shot villagers to capture their women and impress survivors into forced labor regimes. Across the Congo, Africans were enslaved to expedite the extraction process. In many cases women

were held as hostages to force their husbands to work on plantations in exchange for their freedom. Hochschild estimates that ten million Africans died as a result of the Belgian abuses in the Congo.

Williams's observations were echoed by other witnesses including Protestant and Catholic missionaries in the Congo. Even state officials documented the abuse, writing that "there were about a hundred [workers], trembling and fearful before the overseer, who strolled by whirling a whip. For each stocky and broad-backed fellow, how many were skeletons dried up like mummies, their skin worn out ... seamed with deep scars, covered with suppurating wounds."[11] A Belgian senator described workers as

> black, miserable, with only a horribly fitted loin-cloth for clothing, frizzy and bare head supporting the load—box, bale, ivory tusk ... barrel; most of them sickly, drooping under a burden increased by tiredness and insufficient food—a handful of rice and some stinking dried fish; pitiful walking caryatids, beasts of burden with thin monkey legs, with drawn features, eyes fixed and round from preoccupation with keeping their balance and from the daze of exhaustion. They come and go like this by the thousands ... requisitioned by the State armed with its powerful militia, handed over by chiefs whose slaves they are and who make off with their salaries, trotting with bent knees, belly forward, an arm raised to steady the load, the other leaning on a long walking-stick, dusty and sweaty ... dying along the road, or, the journey over, heading off to die from overwork in their villages.[12]

Eventually other observers exposed the conditions in the Congo to the public in the early 1900s. In 1904 Leopold II allowed an international commission to enter the territory to assess his practices. They found still more abuses. By 1908, public pressure enticed Belgium to annex the Congo as a colony, ending Leopold II's ownership of the Congo Free State. For the people of the Congo the transformation of the territory from a private holding to a Belgian colony brought few changes. Forced labor practices would continue although the Belgian government claimed that some of the earlier excesses were curbed. However, the primary objective of the colonial government was to extract valuable mineral resources from the Congo and corporations were given wide latitude to achieve this end. Tens of thousands of workers were dislocated from the interior of the colony to the copper belt in the south. Others were displaced from their traditional economic systems by colonial mandates. Peasants were forced, for example, to grow cash crops including cotton and coffee for sale in European markets while their traditional forms of agriculture were abolished. During the

Second World War, workers were sent to rubber plantations to supply rubber to the Allied Powers and to uranium mines to supply the United States with the raw materials necessary for its nuclear project.

In the aftermath of World War II, Belgium ratified the United Nations treaty, a document that required **self-determination** for former colonies. In 1960 the Congo became a free, independent, and sovereign nation-state marking the end of the colonial period. However, the ravages of colonialism were not left in the past. In the years since independence the Congo has struggled with political instability, civil war, ethnic violence, and genocide. Belgium left the Congo a **nationless state**, a centralized political formation without the bottom-up legitimating force of a single, unified national culture and collective political identity. Today the Congolese government struggles against a de facto state of anarchy and the challenges presented by ethnicized militias in control of various regions of the country. As was the case during its colonial past, the Congo today is the site of important mineral wealth. Within its borders are large deposits of so-called **conflict minerals**. These key resources include columbite-tantalite (necessary to extract tantalum), cassiterite (necessary to produce tin), wolframite (necessary to extract tungsten), and gold. These minerals are essential in the production of consumer electronics including cellular phones, laptops, tablets, and MP3 players. Often extracted using exploited and abused labor and the abuse of child laborers, the minerals are sometimes sold to generate the profits that fund widespread violence in the region. The militias that have partially controlled the mines have used rape, violence, and terror to control the workers and their families. Much can be said regarding the contemporary history of the Democratic Republic of Congo including a political history of secessionist movements and the egregious avarice of several of its leaders. The pathological inability to engage in constructive processes of state-building and nation-building until very recently has generated an insufficiently recognized genocidal dynamic in which millions of Congolese have been murdered and subjected to inhuman brutality. The pain and trauma suffered by women and children on account of rape and the sheer cruelty of sporadic but widespread sexual torture at the hands of numerous militias have afflicted millions of fellow (and sister) citizens, particularly in eastern Congo. And even the camps of internally displaced persons are dangerous. The perpetrators of these outrages often act in groups of organized armed militia that appear to want to take revenge against innocents. A major mode of operation is to kidnap young boys and to force them into becoming quasi-militia killers. The reasons for this are clearly complex. But one cannot and should not ignore the heavy burden carried by the dire history of Belgian occupation and the destruction of kinship throughout the Congo as a means to

Belgian self-enrichment. The Belgian Congo stands as one of the most sordid of histories in the already dismal history of the contact situation within the frames of global colonialism. The pathologies of modern day society in the Democratic Republic of Congo reflect the historical impact of decades of colonialist cruelty and oppression that destroyed the essential fabric of communal traditions. Such pathologies illustrate the plight of the postcolonial world struggling with the requirements of legitimacy, popular consent, nation-building, state-building, etc. To place the failed state label on the political disarray facing the people of the Congo is a beginning toward understanding their plight. But it is only a beginning. Genuine understanding requires recognition of the difficulties the people of the Congo face in reconstructing themselves as the Congolese in a political environment in which centralized state institutions are so weak and carry so little legitimacy. This is the postcolonialist carryover and it illustrates the problems of postcolonial nation-states almost everywhere. The pathologies of the past are not eliminated instantly nor do they disappear on the day that sovereign independence is announced. This underscores the heavy burden carried by political culture during the present-day postcolonial conditions of specific nation-states that struggle with "failure" as a consequence of the history that was not entirely of their own making.

The British in Kenya

In 1920 the East Africa Protectorate was transformed into the British colony of Kenya. The British campaigns in Kenya began in the late 1800s with the construction of a railroad throughout its East African territories. The British financed the project and imported over 30,000 workers from India to complete it. In the course of construction, no fewer than 10,000 workers were killed or wounded. Once the railroad was complete, it fell to the commissioner of the British East African Protectorate to generate the funds necessary to repay Britain for its investment.

To do so the British colonial government decided to base the Kenyan economy on the production of export commodities. Thousands of British settlers migrated to Kenya, determined to make it a modern **White Man's country**. The settlers acquired large estates in the fertile highlands of central Kenya. But as Caroline Elkins writes, "These wealthy families did not come to Kenya to work, but rather to take advantage of the British government's offer of land, labor, and capital, an offer which the settlers interpreted rather generously. . . . On their estates or farms or in European neighborhoods in Nairobi, every white settler in

the colony was a lord to some extent, particularly in relationship to the African population."[13] Elkins continues,

> Settler self-interest was predicated on a sense of entitlement that resulted not only from the shared aristocratic pedigree of many British immigrants but also from a perception of profound racial superiority that infused every rung of the colony's white socioeconomic ladder. By virtue of their skin color, whites of all classes were the master race and therefore deserving of privilege. To the settlers there was nothing noble about the African "savage." Many believed the African to be biologically inferior, with smaller brain sizes, a limited capacity to feel pain or emotion, and even different nutritional needs, requiring only a bowl of maize meal, or *posho,* to maintain their health. African men had to be controlled; they were unpredictable and sexually aggressive, threatening both white women and the maintenance of their idealized chastity as well as the racial purity of the colony's European community. Virulent racist ideology grew more intense over time as the so-called native was moved along the racist spectrum from stupid, inferior, lazy and childlike to savage, barbaric, atavistic, and animal-like. This shift in characterization would correspond closely to the Africans' increasing unwillingness to be exploited by the colonial economy, and with their desire to reclaim land they considered to be rightfully their own.[14]

Although all of Kenya's kinship descent groups experienced the effects of British colonization, the impacts were particularly devastating to the Kikuyu. The Kikuyu were a communal people engaged in traditional forms of agriculture and governed by patrimonial councils of elders, the representative heads of segmented lineage. The British dislocated many of these small-scale farmers by removing them from ancestral lands to make way first for the railroad, and later British or European settlers. Not only did this threaten the economic survival of the Kikuyu, it threatened their culture as well. Here again we are witness among traditional kinship communities to the cultural significance borne by the intimate connections of land, ascribed status, and the liminal processes definitive of stages of life. For a Kikuyu to progress from childhood into adulthood required access to land. As Elkins writes, "a man needed land to accumulate the resources necessary to pay bridewealth for a wife, or wives, who would in turn bear him children. Land and family entitled him to certain privileges within the Kikuyu patriarchy; without land a man would remain socially a boy. A woman needed land to grow crops to nurture and sustain her family; without it in the eyes of the Kikuyu she was not an adult. A Kikuyu could not be a Kikuyu without land."[15]

Since the Kikuyu were agriculturalists they were particularly vulnerable to exploitation by the British. British settlers needed African labor to produce the cash crops on which the colony's export economy was based. The British colonial government recruited African labor, drawn primarily from the Kikuyu population, and forced them to work as virtual slaves on their formerly tribal lands. The British also recruited workers by forcing native kinship groups to either work on British plantations or live on reserves throughout the country that had limited land and resources. For example, Kikuyu lived in the Central Province, the Maasai in the Southern Province, and the Luo in the Nyanza Province. Many had no choice but to look for work on British farms since the land reserves could not adequately sustain their populations.

The Kikuyu were also the victims of a "divide and conquer" strategy. The British sought African collaborators who would be able to assume an authoritative role in the colony. The goal was to administer the colony by "co-opting local African leaders, using them to enforce discipline and control over local populations."[16] The system was based on the European assumption that African tribes had chiefs at the top of a hierarchical system. But the Kikuyu did not have chiefs. Instead, the Kikuyu chiefs that were created to govern Kikuyu territories were the creation of the colonizers. They were illegitimate in the eyes of the Kikuyu people but they acted as the clients of the British regime, enforcing British law upon the Kikuyu population. As Elkins writes, "the introduction of chiefs brought with it a bitter internal conflict within the Kikuyu community, a conflict that only intensified over time."[17] However, because of the willingness of the Kikuyu "chiefs" to collaborate with the British, they quickly became the British clients in charge of other African groups. These clients would become the greatest African beneficiaries of colonial rule, incurring the wrath of other tribal groups.

In the early 1950s, the Kikuyu established an anticolonial group known as the **Mau Mau**. The British saw the Mau Mau as a savage, primitive, violent form of perverted tribalism determined to recreate a precolonial, premodern Kenyan civilization. For the Kikuyu and other Kenyan tribes, however, the Mau Mau represented a nationalist movement dedicated to self-determination and popular consent. Though it built its legitimacy on a traditional past and, specifically, upon a Kikuyu segmented lineage past, its rebellion against the British represented a modern legitimacy crisis.

The Mau Mau resistance turned violent in October 1952 when Senior Chief Waruhiu, a Kikuyu chief who served as an agent of the British government, was assassinated. The British declared a state of emergency and began actively fighting the Mau Mau insurgency. Their Kikuyu clients facilitated their military plans by

identifying Mau Mau members and supporters. Seeking to decapitate the movement, the British arrested 180 alleged Mau Mau leaders and began attacking suspected Mau Mau supporters. Rather than deter people from the movement, the British reaction convinced many moderate Kikuyu that the Mau Mau were their only hope for self-government and justice. But the British response escalated in 1954 in ways that decimated Kenya's Kikuyu population.

First the British conducted a military purge throughout Nairobi, capturing and interning tens of thousands of suspected Mau Mau supporters and sympathizers. The Kikuyu were thus removed from Nairobi and deported to Kikuyu reserves outside the capital. Detention centers were established to contain the suspected Mau Mau members, supporters, and sympathizers. The British established a system called the **Pipeline** to organize the detainees. Each was given a color classification. **Whites** were cooperative prisoners who were sent back to the Kikuyu reserves. **Greys** were sympathetic to the Mau Mau. They were sent to work camps before their release. Lastly, **blacks** were the core of the Mau Mau movement. They were sent to special detention centers for incarceration. While in transit to detention centers, individuals were denied food and water. Once in the camps, they were subjected to forced labor projects and encouraged to submit to reeducation and rehabilitation programs run by the British military. Sanitation in the camps hardly existed, often resulting in epidemics. Thousands died as a result.

In addition to these programs, the British undertook a rural resettlement program designed to crush remaining support for the Mau Mau. More than one million Kikuyu were dislocated to "protected villages" behind barbed-wire fences, spiked trenches, and watchtowers. Called concentration camps for Mau Mau sympathizers, these villages were ostensibly used for rehabilitation but were actually used to break the nationalist spirit of the Mau Mau rebellion. Cut off from their homes, their ancestral lands, and their families, the Kikuyu interned in these villages combatted disease, famine, and abuse at the hands of the British troops. By 1956, after tens of thousands of deaths, the Mau Mau rebellion was successfully crushed by the British and their Kikuyu collaborators. Here again we find yet another example of geographic containment on the basis of racialized or essentialized differences. As kinship communities become transformed into constellations of ethnicity by means of colonialist oppressions, they begin to be perceived as identity objects that must be contained spatially according to colonialist strategies of survival and superiority. This leads to a spatialized political geography separating the realms of socioeconomic growth and prosperity from one assaulted by underdevelopment and exploitation. But the ultimate costs include the damage done to the development of political culture. Once identity groups are formed out of the past of colonialist experiences and are made to

reside within the confines of spatialized reserves or reservations, the competition among identity groups takes on a reality of its own. Yet again it becomes all too easy to see this as the result of age-old conflicts nurtured in the souls of patrimonial or traditional kinship communities. The truth, as we see in the case of British colonial rule in Kenya, is much more complicated.

British rule over Kenya retreated in 1964 as the father of postcolonial Kenya, Jomo Kenyatta, assumed control over the country as the representative of a Kikuyu-Luo alliance. Today, Kenya continues to grapple with the tensions represented by the linkages between nationality and ethnic kinship identity. The political culture of an emerging Kenyan nationality vies against the continuing grasp of kinship loyalties that erupt at critical junctions, particularly at times of national elections. Presidential candidates tend to be viewed from the perspectives of kinship affiliations. In the December 2007 presidential election the incumbent Kikuyu candidate, Mwai Kibaki, was challenged by a popular Meru candidate, Raila Odinga. President Kibaki was declared the winner despite widespread allegations of election tampering, many of which were confirmed by international observers. This resulted in a legitimacy crisis as well as ethnic violence against Kikuyu people throughout the country. The Kikuyu retaliated and the country faced a serious political and humanitarian crisis. Approximately 1,300 people were killed, many more injured, and 600,000 displaced. In February 2008 a peace sharing agreement created a coalition government and put an end to the violence, but instability continued. Moreover, a resurgence of ethnic or tribal identity among Kenyan youth emerged from the crisis. To reestablish political and social order, a new constitution was passed in 2010, and the first elections under its authority were held in 2013. Such outbreaks reflect the history of competition that undergirds the process of state-building and nation-building even in contemporary times. Also involved are competing interests over land ownership and land use, especially with respect to areas associated with specific kinship communities but now controlled by overlays of other groups or interests. So the struggle for postcolonial nationality in Kenya continues and marks how the politics of nation-state-building in Kenya play out from region to region and from kinship group to kinship group. The core issue from the perspective of political culture is how nationality as an attitudinal or social construct emerges in the hearts and minds of the Kenyan people who, as in the case of all nationalities, are caught in the struggle over how to recognize, in themselves and one another, the commonalities and even the solidarities of a peoplehood. These tensions within the ideological and attitudinal frames of political culture are illustrated by the comments of a current generation of Kenyan youths who confront these conflicting values in political culture in intensely personal ways.

A story published in the *Washington Post* in 2005 indicated that perhaps Kenyan political culture was "growing beyond the pull of the tribe"[18] but slowly and with setbacks. The analysis reported that Kenyan students believed that "tribalism in Africa, it's still very much there. But do we really want to be like our grandparents, quarreling over such tired ways? Aren't we all Kenyans at the end of the day?"[19] Kenyan students who were interviewed confided that "hiring based on tribe is very much there. It's the way people are raised—your tribe is still the priority. It's bad, but it's life."[20] When asked, "Would you offer me the job since I was your desk mate and you know my merits and how hard I studied? Or would you give it to a Meru tribes member, who may know your parents?" the response indicated, "I don't really know what I would do. I have to be honest and say I would think about it a lot. But even now, I know it won't be that easy for me to refuse my own people."[21] Thus we return to one of the central themes that arises whenever political culture and the making of the modern nation-state are discussed: hyphenated identity. Some scholars speak of "hybridity" in this connection and the efforts to graft multiple forms of belonging, affiliation, and allegiance onto a single identity. As we have also seen, such a process can be and often is intensely personal. But it is also interpersonal since it involves intergroup relationships. Thus the hybridity of multiethnic, multicultural identity constructions represents a subjective phenomenon in terms of how individuals perceive themselves. It also involves social constructions in terms of how others in the society of any political culture perceive those whose identity is said to be "mixed." Such issues and concepts feature the sociological implications of identity construction within the context of society and social construction. But emphasis on political culture and the making of modern nation-states introduces an additional dimension to this inquiry: the problematics of nationality. The main focus of our examination relates to the question as to how different political cultures function regarding the baseline or common denominator of nationality. In the present context, how do postcolonial societies that have emerged out of the colonialist histories that transformed kinship identities into ethnicized categories forge the hyphenated identities in which nationality and the legitimacy of popular consent complement ethnicized groups' loyalties, attitudes, and constructs? This is the critical issue confronting most so-called failed states. This leads to a further question as to the possibilities of chosen exogamous marriage across tribal or ethnicized identity groups in favor of multiethnic and multicultural identities grounded by a common core of commitment to the values and meaning of nationality bound by the legitimacy of a modern sovereign nation-state. Favored by some, anathema to others, this issue and others similar to it provoke profound reactions. Kenya serves as an important example with its own idiosyncratic features. But such

issues cut across most so-called failed states that are not necessarily failures to the extent that traditional loyalties retain their legitimacy. The question is not failure or success in some simplistic sense. The issue concerns how any political culture creates meaningful bonds of belonging that enable and empower its members and citizens to enjoy the benefits of civil association to the extent possible.

The Germans in South-West Africa or Namibia

Germany's colonial holdings in Africa were limited but included German South-West Africa, the territory known today as Namibia. As Avraham Burg writes, "German colonial energy, late to emerge, was directed at the very few territories that remained free. . . . An empire without colonies launched a drive to settle an empty, uninhabited territory—not that it was without humans, but 'humans' at the time meant white people, especially German."[22] The German perspective was that the indigenous groups were "beasts. . . . They slaughter innocent white settlers. Africans tear out women's intestines while they are still alive and hang them on trees. . . . The negro is a wild beast. . . . It can be taught to be respectful only under the gaze of the tamer and his whip."[23]

Among the kinship groups living in German South-West Africa were the Herero and the Nama (or Namaqua). The Herero were a Bantu-speaking tribal or kinship community. They were a pastoral people who also largely survived by husbanding livestock. Status was based upon the number of cattle a Herero herder owned. Within Herero society, land was not owned but rather shared among all members of the community. Belonging was linked to a system of **bilateral descent** in which ancestry was traced through both the mother and the father. The Nama were a nomadic people roaming and foraging in southern Namibia. The Nama lived in nine clans on communal lands throughout Namibia. Their main cultural expressions included oral traditions emphasizing music, poetry, and storytelling. Both the Herero and the Nama nurtured rich cultural traditions devoted to intergenerational continuity, ritualized rites of passage, arranged marriage, and honor discipline.

Namibia was rich in mineral resources including diamonds, gold, copper, and platinum. In an attempt to build a prosperous colony, the Germans displaced the Herero and Nama from their traditional lands. The Germans confiscated their cattle and drove both groups into the desert. As Burg writes, "The Herero, the largest African tribe in the region, were no obstacle in the Germans' view. But the 'non-human' natives rebelled ferociously against the German occupation and the result was expulsions, settlements, confiscations, abuse, and humiliation."[24]

Again, the colonialist strategy turned to displacement, dislocation, and spatial containment of a kinship order now brutally transformed into an identity group. At first, German settlers forced the Herero and Nama into slave-labor camps and mines. However, in 1903 the Nama revolted against the German colonial regime. A year later, the Herero joined the rebellion. Some of the primary grievances cited by the indigenous peoples were land rights. The Herero had ceded over a quarter of their territory to the Germans but had learned that the Germans intended to evict them from their remaining lands in order to relocate them to concentration camps as part of a design to build a railroad that would open Namibia to increased German settlement. In August 1904, German general Lothar von Trotha ordered the annihilation of the Herero people. Burg writes, "As a good, organized German general, he left his hot-blooded enthusiasm at home. Everything was done in cold blood, with detailed planning and murderous efficiency. . . . 'I will wipe out rebellious tribes with rivers of blood and rivers of money. Only following this cleansing can something new emerge,' he wrote in his diary."[25] Thus began a genocidal policy that included ethnic cleansing in Namibia. As Burg continues, "The Germans ... surrounded about thirty thousand Herero—men, women, and children—together with their cattle, in a place called Watterberg, shelling and shooting them for hours. The only escape was to the arid Kalahari Desert. The German forces then surrounded the desert, erected watchtowers, and poisoned wells inside and around it." Von Trotha then declared the following principle: "Any Herero found within German borders, with or without a gun, with or without cattle, will be shot."[26] The German commander wrote of the battle, "I believe that the nation as such should be annihilated. . . . This will be possible if the water-holes from Grootfontein to Gobabis are occupied. The constant movement of our troops will enable us to find the small groups ... and destroy them gradually."[27] Many survivors from Watterberg were immediately killed and dumped in mass graves. Others, primarily women and children, were sent on death marches to concentration camps and forced to work as slave labor. Many died of disease, hunger, and overwork. Violence in the camps, including shootings, whippings, and hangings, was common. One observer recalled,

> There are hundreds of them, mostly women and children and a few old men.... When they fall they are sjamboked [whipped] by the soldiers in charge of the gang, with full force, until they get up.... On one occasion I saw a woman carrying a child of under a year old slung at her back, and with a heavy sack of grain on her head ... she fell. The corporal sjamboked her for certainly more than four minutes and sjamboked the baby as well.... The woman struggled slowly to her feet, and went on with her load. She did not utter a sound the whole time, but the baby cried very hard.[28]

Other Herero and Nama were sent to extermination camps where they were systematically killed.

Some survivors were used for medical experiments. Eugen Fischer, a German pseudoscientist, conducted medical experiments on racial and genetic features in the concentration camps using Herero and Herero German children as subjects. He ran tests including head and body measurements and hair and eye examinations before decapitating the victims and sending their skulls to Germany for further study. He also experimented with sterilization techniques and germ warfare and exposed numerous Herero adults to smallpox, typhus, and tuberculosis.

In total, approximately 65,000 Herero and 10,000 Nama died before the violence ended in 1907. When the camps closed, the surviving Herero and Nama were dispatched throughout the German colony as laborers. All Herero within the colony over seven years of age were forced to wear a metal disk with their labor registration number. They were also prohibited from owning land or cattle, thus keeping them from returning to their primordial livelihoods and traditions.

In 1985 the United Nations classified the program as an attempt to exterminate the Herero and the Nama peoples, one of the world's first genocides. As Burg writes, "Four decades before the Holocaust in Europe, Germany perfected the model in Africa. Namibia was the introduction to the Shoah; the Herero were Africa's 'Jews.'"[29] The ravages of colonialism took on a genocidal bent in southwestern Africa as they did in other parts of the world, including Australia, in the course of globalism. One of the triggers of violence on the part of colonialist settlers toward indigenous populations is native resistance to the incursions of colonialism. It is as if those engaged in the colonial project were so convinced of their cultural and thus moral superiority that any means, however cruel or lethal, seemed appropriate whenever kinship groups dared to place obstacles on the road to their complete subjection and displacement. That German occupation and domination of the Herero and Nama peoples was brutal beyond description speaks to the dignity and courage of those native peoples who suffered outrageous forms of inhumanity done in the name of German civilization and progress. This too is suggestive of the capacity of collective ideology to create frames of self-delusion. Germany and German representatives not only brutalized the kinship groups they ultimately attempted to decimate, they legitimated (at least to themselves) their actions on the basis of racial and genetic justifications. The political culture of German-style global colonialism thus turned to the human body, the body of the Herero and Nama, and inscribed onto it the torments of subhuman markers by branding it incapable or unworthy of human sensibility, feeling, or pain. Those who lived in such bodies were deemed entirely expendable thus dispensable at the will of the German settlers and their agents. For

the Germans it did not matter whether the indigenous peoples were displaced, dislocated, beaten into submission, systematically tortured, beheaded, used as subjects of pseudoscientific and racially informed experiments of inordinate cruelty, or if they were simply annihilated. What counted was the vainglorious victory of German expansionism in the name of an incipient German nationalism.

We have emphasized the basic significance of nationality as a dimension of political culture in the making of modern nation-states. Nationalism is distinct from nationality in that it represents a collective belief in the unique qualities of peoplehood shared among those of common nationality. Such uniqueness is often a matter of collective celebration undertaken by means of anthems sung, flags waved, and other rituals performed at the behest of modern nation-states. Taken to extremes, however, this sense of uniqueness readily translates into attitudes and convictions of superiority. Such beliefs can lead to a series of justifications that legitimate malevolent and/or violent behaviors on the grounds of national superiority, including in the present example of Germany in southwestern Africa, which exhibits the extreme cruelty and domination of others on the basis of a superior nationalist political culture. Nationalism, to the extent that it is grounded in the vanity of self-glorification, runs the risk of collective self-delusions including the right of one people to dominate others by means of violence, aggression, and even war. Extreme forms of nationalism tend to feature naturalist explanations. These conflate ethnicity with nationality in the guise of extreme ethno-nationalism. This results in claims of ethnic superiority but in ways that assert the exclusive right to dominate sovereign state institutions. Ethno-nationalist fervor is often articulated in racist ideologies that tend to stress the "nature" of ethnic "purity." The precepts of ethnic purity once converted into a form of extreme nationalism can be applied to justify almost any set of outrageous acts, including those of the German settlers during their colonialist destructions aimed at the Herero and Nama. Some scholars see the foreshadowing of the Holocaust in the ideology of ethnic purity and nationalism of German colonial practices. Certainly many of the techniques applied by General von Trotha would reappear during the Nazi regime in Germany. Such historical parallels are complex and need to be studied carefully and with due diligence in relation to the historical record and its interpretation. That said, the assumptions that appear in political cultures with respect to identity constructions and identity group objectifications are repeated over the course of time. They become part of the cultural fabric that informs political beliefs, attitudes, and behaviors. This certainly seems to the case here. German political culture perceived indigenous kinship groups under their control in Africa to be inferior genetically, less than human in terms of phenotype. That any human being

could be categorized in this manner, however fraudulent and vicious, appears to have retained influence within aspects of German political culture. In time, these self-aggrandizing delusions would reappear, this time closer to home in Germany and aimed at German Jewish citizens whose right to nationality was rejected on the basis of their ethnicity. The process of objectification in German political culture was similar in southwestern Africa as it was during the Holocaust: first, eliminate the distinctions between ethnicity and nationality; second, define nationality in terms of ethnic purity; and, third, annihilate those deemed unworthy of nationality on the grounds that they did not share in the purity of ethnic identity.

For these reasons, conceptual clarity becomes critical in the study of political culture and the making of modern nation-states. Let's summarize the conceptual distinctions we have been making. **Nationality**, **nationalism**, **ethnicity**, and **ethno-nationalism** are not identical. Nationality is a phenomenon in political culture that is distinct from nationalism. Nationality is a function of citizenship and its full civil enjoyment. Nationalism represents a form of collective belief and attitude that celebrates the uniqueness of any political culture associated with nationhood, peoplehood, and collective solidarity or belonging. But it is amenable to manipulation and extremes on account of its inherent assumptions regarding the unique superiority of any nation. It becomes especially dangerous when applied as justification for war, violence, or conflict in cases in which ethnicity becomes conflated with nationality and both are combined in ways that objectify a sense of nationalism on the grounds of natural purity. The illusions of ethnic purity in cases of extreme nationalism slip into various forms of racism. This was the case during the German colonialist era in southwestern Africa; it took on the form of racist fascism during the Holocaust. Ethnicity is a form of identification that is both subjective in terms of personal self-understanding on the part of an individual alone or as a member of a particular group. It also represents a category of identity used and applied to individuals and groups on the basis of certain markers. It often generates the social or cultural constructions we have labeled hyphenated identity. This permits us to emphasize the linkages forged among multiethnic and multicultural amalgamations in relation to examples of nationality in cases of polyglot nations such as the United States, India, and other highly heterogeneous national political cultures. Ethno-nationalism represents the extremes in political culture that often emerge as the result of ethnic conflicts or ethno-grievances with respect to the legitimacy of state government or control. Ethno-nationalism in political culture presents a challenge to the legitimacy of state institutions in ways that harken back to the appeals of self-determination and the demand for transformations in who governs the state or how it is governed

relative to the doctrine of popular consent. As such, ethno-nationalism can lead to ethnic conflict and wars of independence, partition, or separation. Finally, we are confronted by the question as to what is the meaning of patriotism. Clearly, patriotism is about loyalty to a nation-state in the very specific sense of a willingness to make sacrifices for the sovereign state. Patriotism celebrates the history of sacrifice and thus the sacrifice made by others in the past as well as in the present to ensure the security of the state. Days of commemoration, monuments to unknown soldiers, military cemeteries and parades, flags lowered to half-mast, and other forms of collective mourning and celebration all evince the deeply felt experiences that compose patriotic sentiments, attitudes, and behaviors. Patriotism is a way of transforming mere belonging into bonding. It converts societies of strangers into nations. It helps to transfigure a collectivity of individuals into the singularity of peoplehood. Patriotism represents another way of interpreting the legitimacy of modern sovereign nation-states and the critical dynamics of extraction and sacrifice. Patriotism is a form of sentiment and ideology grounded in the sense of popular consent and the obligations of sovereign states to extract from their nations for purposes of national security in a universe of international politics and power. Herein arise the risks of infusing patriotism with the ideological constructs of extreme nationalism. Although nationalism and patriotism represent distinct concepts, they too can become conflated. When this occurs, the celebration over past and present sacrifice for the sovereign state combines with celebration over the superiority of the nation. This represents a powerful and dangerous mix in political culture. War and aggression are some of its symptoms, as are far right and/or fascist ideology and the violence these pathologies in political culture perpetuate.

Three Postcolonial Pathologies

The end of World War II helped to initiate a global decolonization movement. In the decades that followed, colonial empires were dismantled. This led to the historical process that extended the domain of sovereign nation-states to the point today of near-universal presence across the globe. But unlike the nation-states that emerged over decades through the convergence of **top-down state-building** and **bottom-up nation-building** dynamics across Europe, postcolonial nation-states often lacked the crucial congruence in political culture between nation and state. Certain terms are applied to them such as "nationless states," "nonhistorical states," or "failed states." This terminology represents a nod to the absence of a unified national community to legitimate state rule. It also provides

ALTERNATE PERSPECTIVES

Failed State Index

Each year the Fund for Peace and *Foreign Policy* publish a **Failed State Index (FSI)**. The Fund for Peace, an independent organization dedicated to research and educational awareness, promotes **sustainable security** by using the FSI to analyze contemporary conflicts in an effort to prevent hostilities before they begin. The organization encourages a wide variety of actors to use the FSI to bring attention to those states most susceptible to conflict and instability. The index and an analysis of its methodology and applications can be found at http://ffp.statesindex.org/.

The FSI scores nation-states in the international system on the basis of a set of twelve key indicators and over 100 sub-indicators. These encompass social, economic, political, and military criteria. Nation-states are scored from "alert" (10) to "sustainable" (1) for each of the key indicators. The sum of the twelve indicators produces a state's overall score. Countries with higher scores are classified as "alert" states with low degrees of social, economic, and political stability. States with lower scores are considered "sustainable" with high degrees of stability.

In 2013, Somalia, Democratic Republic of Congo, Sudan, and South Sudan were the four highest-ranking nation-states and were thus categorized as high alert. Switzerland, Norway, Sweden, and Finland were the lowest-ranking states. The Fund for Peace also analyzes trends based on the FSI. In 2013 the organization evaluated nation-states based on trends from 2008 to 2013. Some countries, such as Turkmenistan, Lebanon, and Moldova, had shown improvement in their rankings. However, many others, such as Libya, Yemen, Tunisia, Senegal, and Mali, were found to be facing rising pressures, diminished capacities, and increasing levels of instability.

Most of those besieged by features leading to an alert status, that is, those scoring highest on the failed state index, were to be found in sub-Saharan Africa. As of 2013 failed states designated by alert status in addition to the ones mentioned above included Chad, Yemen, Afghanistan, Haiti, Central African Republic, Zimbabwe, Iraq, Ivory Coast, Pakistan, Guinea, Guinea-Bissau, Nigeria, Kenya, Niger, Ethiopia, and Burundi.

Many of these fragile political formations are postcolonial states that gained their independence in the mid-twentieth century, but despite their late establishment, or perhaps on account of it, they lack political-cultural

continued

congruence between nation and state. In some cases, they have seen the rise (and fall) of **secessionist** movements within their countries, some of which led to failed states within failed states.

For example, Nigeria became independent from Great Britain in 1960. However, the borders of the Nigerian state did not reflect the ethnic boundaries of the people living within it nor did the people think of themselves as belonging to a "Nigerian" nation. After seven years of coups, widespread ethnic tensions, and political instability, the southeastern region of Nigeria seceded to try to form its own state, the Republic of Biafra. The secessionist population was primarily **Igbo**, a people with a strong sense of ethnic identity, one that made claims to sovereignty on the grounds of popular consent and the legitimacy of the right of self-determination. Biafra was formally recognized by Gabon, Haiti, the Ivory Coast, Tanzania, and Zambia and received support from Portugal, Israel, France, Rhodesia, South Africa, and the Vatican. However, its declaration of independence led to a war with Nigeria known either as the **Nigerian Civil War** or the **Nigerian-Biafran War**. The war lasted for two and a half years. During that time the central Nigerian government based in Lagos used food deprivation as a weapon of war and systematically starved the Biafran population into submission. More than one million people died in battle or from starvation. The Biafran military was defeated in late 1969 and in January 1970 Biafra was reintegrated into Nigeria. However, demands for a separate state persist. The **Movement for the Actualization of the Sovereign State of Biafra (MASSOB)** continues to advocate for self-determination for the Igbo people. The Nigerian government accuses MASSOB of violence, but MASSOB maintains that it is dedicated to peaceful secession from a state that systematically discriminates against the Igbo population. The political and ethnic tensions between the Igbo and the Nigerian government are thus ongoing. Despite this, most world attention has turned to the sectarian conflict in the north of the country centered on the Nigerian city of Kanu in which Christian and Muslim communities are often victimized by those claiming to act on their behalf. In particular, the extremist organization that calls itself Boko Haram (Western Education Is a Sin) has campaigned violently against settlements and villagers with lethal success and has also succeeded in kidnapping dozens of girls and young women. The Nigerian central government remains powerful and the political-cultural sense of a Nigerian nation-state appears to be strong and well entrenched among Nigeria's many kinship ethnic groups despite various tensions. But the question arises as to the capacity of the central government to sustain national unity against the background of fractious conflicts and tensions.

a conceptual perspective that underscores the "ethnic" violence that characterizes their postcolonial political cultures today. Without a political culture based on national solidarity or conceptions of common nationality, virulent forms of postcolonial pathologies foment "ethnicized" and "racialized" differences among objectified identity groups. The **postcolonial pathologies** demonstrate how the impacts of colonialism continue to plague societies across the globe. These present major challenges for the building of political cultures imbued by sentiments and ideologies that consolidate nationality and sovereign statehood in the anchors of popular consent.

The anxieties provoked by a sense of ambivalence and cultural loss within nonhistorical states sometimes lead to a glorification of the kinship past and mythological memories of tribal loss in order to justify modern forms of ethnonationalist conflicts grounded in objectified constructions of difference. The consequences are manifested in collective frenzy in which **nativist** narratives **totalize** political reality around the scapegoated objects of hatred and contempt.

When mass political violence erupts in nonhistorical states, therefore, it tends not to be about "ancient hatreds" or "age-old animosities." It is instead about the return to kinship honor with a vengeance toward the postcolonial clientist face of modernization. In **nativism**, segmented kinship groups that lived together according to traditional kinship and descent rules and whose identities relative to one another became racialized under colonial domination seek a return to the lost glory of kinship. Colonial practices included divide and conquer strategies that favored certain kinship groups over others in a variety of ways. As these groups changed to accommodate the colonial experience, they became ethnicized in terms of their identities as social groups linked together by means of a centralized colonial administration that was often cruel. Such modes of state-building did not necessarily signify nation-building. On the contrary, as kinship groups became ethnicized for purposes of colonialist state-building the resentments among them often became exaggerated on account of the favoritism or rejection asserted by colonialist rulers. This bred hatred and resentment, which led to the dynamics of objectification and essentialism among ethnicized kinship identity groups. These processes culminated in what we call the racialization of difference among ethnicized kinship identity groups. The differences among such objectified identity groups thus come to represent features or characteristics associated with racial stereotypes and prejudice. This sometimes leads to outbreaks of conflict up to and including genocidal violence. In the political cultures of many postcolonial nation-states, subordination of kinship values and traditions reinforced by the dynamics of **clientism, patronage** or **favoritism**, and **dysfunctional imitation** can provoke vengeful attempts to reassert the legitimacy of traditional forms of

honor based on blood, kinship, and ancestry on the part of kinship groups that were rejected or marginalized by colonial powers.

Because European powers represented their cultures as the core of modern civilization, they provoked the dynamics of mimetic desire on the part of primordial communities who confronted the power and legitimacy of the colonialist nation-states from the now subordinated perspectives of honor and shame. A profoundly dysfunctional form of imitation grew out of the binary relationship between the dominant colonizer and the subordinated colonized. As a consequence of mimetic dynamics, the kinship institutions, values, and traditions that governed indigenous peoples almost everywhere for centuries were denied historical legitimacy. The political cultures of modernization denied the legitimacy of the oral traditions important to intergenerational continuities among kinship communities. Once the oral histories crucial to segmented lineage and ancestral legitimacy became devalorized, the essential tragedies of the postcolonialist era—anomie and alienation—soon took hold in many cultures. Local legitimacies became devalued in favor of external cultural forms of governance and legitimacy. This reflected the power realities advanced by Western or non-segmented cultural traditions.

As we have seen repeatedly, Anglo-European powers promoted their political cultures as representative of civilization itself. In so doing they created the illusion of a binary opposition between the superior (modern) and the inferior (primitive) political culture. This often provoked the dynamics of **mimetic desire** on the part of the members of kinship or traditional communities seeking to escape from the power and legitimacy of postcolonial political cultures not by rejecting them but rather by means of imitating them. This process of dysfunctional imitation and desire for modern political culture often provoked indigenous scorn in relation to indigenous values and traditions. The deep sense of honor in kinship blood and bonding now turned against itself and became awash with shame. The cultural superiority represented by the political culture of postcolonialist powers became mystified in ways that provoked mimetic desire on the part of subordinated kinship groups who sought also to be "modern." Subordinated groups rushed to imitate those who appeared to be superior, but this process whereby kinship groups became ethnicized took a toll in terms of political culture and development of political legitimacy. A dysfunctional set of ideologies and attitudes spewed forth, stemming in part from the kinds of political-cultural imitations reflective of historical **inauthenticity**. The dominant colonizer and the subordinated colonized rarely, if ever, developed identical political cultures since their histories, geographies, and cultural experiences had been so different and especially since the power valences throughout their

mutual histories had been so unequal. In wanting what the "Other" had and in seeking to become what the Other was or appeared as, the political cultures of kinship groups in effect ran the risk of renouncing their own traditions, values, and beliefs. The loss of kinship roots and lineage honor eroded the communal sense of cosmic significance, particularly in the case of those whose cultural identities were anchored by ancestry and segmented lineage. As we have seen, the historical loss of cultural roots is often devastating.

The cultural traditions and values of societies configured around segmentation and kinship honor tend to underscore the importance of group belonging and collective identities defined by blood and lineage. The colonialist transition to modern political cultures associated with postcolonialist nation-states eroded these traditional values and superimposed on them sets of institutions that were not of their own making. The basic problem of political-cultural development revolves around these combinations of kinship and ethnic identity within national contexts or frameworks that seek to rob the past of its legitimacy by privileging a future based on imitation and cultural inauthenticity. This leads to a series of legitimacy crises. Individuals and groups who deny the past in an attempt to hammer out a political culture deemed necessary for a modern future can fall into the trap of desiring the very values that corrode their sense of political-cultural identity. This leads to the worst of both worlds, neither traditional nor modern, merely corrupt, or worse still, violent.

The cost and consequences of such cultural renunciations and rejections readily become manifested in terms of objectified forms of identity and division. Subordinated groups imitate the political cultures of modern centralized nation-states but long for a return to kinship honor disciplines, values, and traditions. The past thus becomes a mirage glorified by nativist calls for return. Nativist outbreaks of mass political violence can be the consequence of attempts to restore "honor" through the relief of "shame" by spilling the blood of those whose "face" mirrored the face of the agents of modern political cultures.

To comprehend the dynamics of **nativism** we must first understand kinship values, traditions, identities, and disciplines as well as modern values, traditions, identities, and disciplines. All represent the elements of political culture relevant to postcolonial nation-states. Nativism is a form of yearning for the return to kinship identity but with an objectified and racialized vengeance aimed at postcolonial scapegoats who are taken to represent the humiliations and other outrages experienced during the colonialist period. Nativism is a form of extremist ideology conceived in hatred and resentment over colonialist histories of suppression and brutality. But it also inheres in a sense of resentment toward one's own group or history for having conceded too much to notions

of colonialist or Western superiority. In addition, nativist ideologies spin exclusionary understandings of nationality in order to eliminate the hyphenated identity constructions separating ethnicity from nationality. Nativism played out with horrific consequences during the Rwandan genocide. Extremist Hutu elements came to the view that the Tutsi, who had been favored by the Belgian colonialist settlers, were Hamitic intruders on the lands of Rwanda and no longer deserved to live in Rwanda or be considered as Rwandan citizens with rights to enjoy Rwandan nationality. Just as Hutus were excluded from the colonial and postcolonial power structures, Tutsis became excluded—legally and physically—from the Rwandan nation.

Nativism thus represents a one-two punch. First, it adheres to a kind of socio-pathological reassertion of the legitimacy of kinship rule but in terms of the racialization of segmented lineage that had been fostered, promoted, and imposed upon kinship peoples by colonial powers. Second, it thrives on a renunciation of hyphenated identity in national political cultures. Nativism represents a postcolonial cultural return to the primacies of segmented lineage that had been disciplined by kinship honor and shame. But now its cultural and ideological forms become extreme and exclusivist and thus tempered by the fires of vengeance aimed at the objectified identity groups that stand as the mirror images of the colonialist settler and intruder. Throughout the colonial experience, kinship identities become transformed. In postcolonial political cultures caught in the throes of nativism, extremist groups objectify other identity groups as material targets of contempt. Nationality becomes divided into "us" and "them" as it was during the heydays of the colonialist experience, but the struggle is now internecine and all the more dangerous and prone to violence. Nativist dynamics also occurred in Uganda during the genocidal regime of Idi Dada Amin, a member of a relatively small and powerless kinship group who, once in power, in effect waged a war against those favored by British colonialist settlers, namely, the Baganda.

Nativism thus represents a return to the values, cultures, and traditions of kinship but with a vengeance against the face of the objectified Other. In nativism, kinship loyalty becomes perversely distorted into an ethnic supremacy that demands the degradation and even the annihilation of the objectified and targeted identity group all in the name of the return to honor in the form of revived ancestral lineage. Honor becomes a subterfuge for the objectification of the identity group object that now represents conflicted desires: the desire to be modern by controlling the power of the nation-state and in so doing realizing the desire to return to the values and traditions of kinship. But there is no honor in shame. To relieve shame through violence and contempt is never honorable; to

take up a machete to mutilate and slaughter others can never be considered an act of honor, and to annihilate the face of colonialism by attempting to eradicate the surrogate face of the colonialist in a postcolonialist era can never recreate the mysteries of the totemic past or conjure the forgiveness of the totemic ancestors for what has been renounced and can never be retrieved.

For these reasons, nativism represents a phenomenon characterized by a range of violent episodes manifested in crimes against humanity that totalize political reality around objectifications that end, ultimately, in genocide. Identity groups caught by the dispirited doctrines of nativism battle against the social-psychological pathologies of love and hate within themselves and in relation to the targeted identity groups. In this they want what the political culture of nation-states requires: nationality framed by the recognition of difference. But they despise what the political culture of modern sovereign nation-states imposes upon them: hyphenated identities combining citizenship and the concepts of nationhood, that is, the need to ground nationality and nationhood in principles of difference anchored by commonalities of political belonging attached to the legitimacy of sovereign statehood.

In nativism the face of the modernizing and colonizing collaborators becomes the scapegoated and ultimately dehumanized Other. It is significant that some segments within modern India attempt to project discrimination, exclusion, and objectified forms of disdain not on the British colonizers, but upon the Sikhs who are objectified as collaborators and clients of the colonial regime.

Clientism refers to a set of postcolonial political dynamics in which a single kinship group comes to dominate the political and economic apparatus of a sovereign state in order to favor, reward, and patronize "their own" on the basis of traditional kinship loyalties. The clientist group is often one that collaborated with and was thus privileged by the colonial regime. In postcolonialism, clientism represents an attack against the unifying solidarity of nationality. It demonstrates the continuing hold of kinship loyalties and honor disciplines within the political frameworks of nonhistoric but centralized sovereign states. It embodies political-cultural sets of values that socially construct political identity in ways that reinforce and naturalize the ethnicization of kinship that occurred during the colonialist period. Clientism represents postcolonial patronage systems and often functions in ways that use the auspices of the sovereign state to aggrandize the benefits accruing to specific kinship groups or networks. As in the case of nativism, clientism operates in the political cultures caught in between the postcolonial and the modern. In such circumstances, the centralized state exists, as does a nation, but the pipelines of power and reward flow in accordance with traditional lineages and loyalties.

Sovereign States and the Modern World

As a consequence of colonialism we live in a world governed by modern sovereign nation-states. While certain nation-states are products of hundreds of years of anthropological and political change, many are the artificial creations of brutal domination, oppression, and cultural delegitimation that wreaked havoc upon traditional kinship communities across Africa, the Middle East, Asia, and the Americas. As we have seen and will continue to see, mass political violence is often a consequence of these postcolonial dynamics.

Chapter 8
Ethno-Political Violence and Subnational Conflict

Identity Construction and Global Conflict

Throughout modern history there have been numerous episodes of ethno-political violence in subnational conflicts that have revolved around questions of both land in relation to nationality and citizenship relative to political authority. In these circumstances, subnational conflicts transform political imaginaries and cultural understandings of state and nation into battles for territory, representation, or autonomy. During these conflicts victims become caught in political struggles rooted in failures to build a **congruent legitimacy** between nation and state. Political violence and mass brutalities result whenever nation and nation-building or **nationality** and **nationalism** do not align with state and state-building or **citizenship** and **patriotism**. **Nationalism** is an aspect of political culture that adheres to a sense of exceptionalism in the identity constructions of **peoplehood**. It thrives whenever a nation elevates the primacy of the common features that bind them together. Nationalism extols, even glorifies, the meanings of those unique dimensions of solidarity that lead members of the nation to recognize in one another what can be seen in no one else. It can be felt or experienced in a variety of ways according to political culture as a set of ideological convictions, as an attitude or sentiment, or as a protocol made present through rituals. At its extreme it turns toward essentialized or objectified forms of national superiority. When it does so, it is amenable to manipulations that can involve political violence. **Patriotism** represents an aspect of political

culture that adheres to the legitimacy of the sovereign state and to the abiding significance of its security and of the obligations of sacrifice, whether measured in blood or treasure as calls above other values. It sometimes calls forth the kinds of heroism under conditions of war or duress that are honored across political cultures of modern nation-states. Generally speaking, nationalism and patriotism represent manifestations of the political cultures that are central to the making of modern nation-states.

Political culture examines the values that nurture, sustain, and sometimes challenge relations between state and nation. Modern sovereign states represent a political-cultural form of governance; nations provide the basis for governance on account of political cultures that legitimate sovereign states. Nations and states come together in a kind of marriage in which political culture plays a critical role. Nations are composed of people who for reasons of history and culture recognize, in themselves and in each other, a degree of commonality and belonging that is not shared among those deemed outside. Nationality is the cultural dimension that derives from citizenship and membership in the nation. Nationality reflects a way of life, a sense of belonging, a legal status that derives from citizenship. Nationality is thus a term that refers to a culture of "peoplehood" once peoplehood becomes attached to a particular sovereign state within defined borders. Political culture that aligns peoplehood and statehood in a kind of glue referred to as the sovereignty of nation-states underscores the fundamental significance of legitimacy as a political-cultural value. **Legitimacy** represents the primary value of political cultures given over to the modern formations of sovereign nation-states. It validates the sovereignty of the nation-state by embedding the congruence between nation and state in doctrinal notions of popular consent.

In the absence of legitimacy, the cultural attachments between nationhood and statehood cannot become forged or at the very least are impeded in ways that often provoke crises of legitimacy. Legitimacy crises are costly and dangerous. They often lead to violence, especially during the postcolonial political stages of history. Some legitimacy crises are resolved through power and military might. Most leave deep historical scars. We have examined the emergence of nation-states as a specific political formation that arose in Europe and in North America. We have seen how the nation-state became universalized during the history of colonialism and postcolonialist struggles for independence. The development of political cultures of legitimacy has served as the essential ingredient whenever these historic processes have entailed conscription of men and women for purposes of military might and extraction of wealth from society in the form of taxation. Often, **legitimacy crises** have turned on conflicts over taxation. This is signified by struggles to achieve a certain representation in the name of

ALTERNATE PERSPECTIVES

Ethnic Conflict

Ethnic conflict is a frequent and widespread problem in the modern world. Although it is often discussed only in terms of sub-Saharan African countries, ethnic conflict based on kinship, clan or tribal configurations, sectarian or religious divisions, or other forms of identity construction plagues nation-states in many regions on nearly every continent. But how does ethnic conflict differ from economic or political conflict?

Stefan Wolff first defines conflict as a "situation in which two or more actors, who interact with each other, pursue incompatible goals, are aware of this incompatibility, and claim to be justified in the pursuit of their particular course of action."[1] Ethnic conflict, however, has an added dimension. In ethnic conflict, the goals of at least one party are defined exclusively in terms of ethnic identity and the primary fault line of the confrontation centers upon an ethnic distinction in political culture. Ethnic conflicts are thus essentially conflicts rooted in political culture and occur among subnational groups or between the government of a sovereign state and a minority population within the territory of a sovereign state.

But what causes ethnic conflict to erupt in some places but not in others? Monica Toft argues that territory is a key variable in answering this question.[2] Territory is essential to survival for both states and ethnic groups. In cases in which multiple groups desire the same territory, an increased potential for violent conflict arises. An ethnic group's settlement pattern also provides the conditions for potential conflict. Specifically, wherever ethnic groups form a concentrated majority in a particular region of a sovereign state, especially if that region is considered their homeland, calls for secession, autonomy, or independence spark possible ethnic conflict. For this reason, competition for territory is particularly prevalent in states with strong secessionist movements. The Chechens in Russia; the Kurds in Iraq, Turkey, Iran, and Syria; the Tamils in Sri Lanka; and the Palestinians on the West Bank and Gaza live under the sovereign jurisdictions of states against whose legitimacy they have fought and opposed. In this limited sense, they may be considered stateless peoples that in various ways and to varying degrees have made claims for a nationhood linked to a different sovereign legitimacy. These claims arise as a consequence of the fact that each has sought to preside over bounded territory as part of its campaign to achieve sovereign statehood or some derivation thereof. Their lack of success derives from the fact that they were unable to accomplish full control over the territory they claimed by virtue of not being able to assert the power or the legitimacy to make a sovereign jurisdiction exclusively their own.

popular consent so that when state extraction occurs it is done in the name of the people. As we learned earlier, this is the core meaning of the concept of a nation. A nation is precisely that formation in political culture that refers to the relationship of a people to a sovereign state with respect to extraction. When extraction occurred under the devices of dynastic rule, whether chiefdoms or royal kingdoms, it was legitimated by reference to nature, bloodlines, ancestors, or divine will. Nations, on the contrary, represent not natural phenomena but artificial contrivances used to justify sovereign state extraction once the natural bonds of attachment in dynastic rule became both historically and ideologically discredited. Nations thus stand for the dynamics of legitimacy based in popular consent that enable extraction to occur at the behest of sovereign states but on behalf of the collectivity of citizens joined together in peoplehood. Such historical dynamics between nation and state or people and governance are the core of what we mean by nation-state-building. This process is similar but different everywhere it happens. How different nations have achieved a sense of legitimacy relative to a particular state or form of governance reveals various national political histories. This is the very nature of comparative political history in cultural contexts. We refer to this as the "hyphenated relationship" between sovereign state governance (top-down) and nations or nationalities (bottom-up). This alignment represents an indispensable element in the process of establishing the legitimacy of modern nation-states.

As we have already seen, a secondary relationship in political culture exists within the nation itself. Nationhood is a direct relation to a specific sovereign state, but the grounds of this relationship depend also on the political-cultural identities associated with nationality. Nationality represents a principle of commonality. All citizens of a sovereign state share in it in virtue of being a citizen. But not all citizens of modern sovereign states share in the same cultural heritage. They differ among themselves as a matter of sociology and social identity. These identities readily become politicized in ways that can and do lead to fractures in political cultures of legitimacy. In extreme cases, this leads to legitimacy crises in which the very meaning of nationhood and the very definition of peoplehood become unraveled. At such critical junctures the possibilities for collective and extreme violence become great. Once nationality as a principle of commonality gives way to fragmented interpretations of what it means to belong to a collective culture, the potential for ethno-political violence in subnational conflicts becomes immediately threatening, as can be currently witnessed in Syria.

In another example, stateless nations can seek self-determination, potentially through liberation movements and/or terrorism. Chechnya is a federal republic of Russia that demanded but did not receive its independence after the fall of the

KEY CONCEPTS

Nationalism

A **nation** is an identity construct among those who justify to themselves and one another the presence of unique features that enable them to believe and/ or to recognize openly or tacitly a common political culture. The nation as a concept represents the experience and expression of legitimacy relative to sovereign states especially with respect to extraction, in particular conscription and taxation. Members of a nation who enjoy nationality attached to legal citizenship are not necessarily homogenous in any ethnic, religious, or racial sense. The modern world is characterized by a number of **stateless nations**, including the Chechens, the Tamils, and the Palestinians. Although stateless, their claims to the rights of sovereign legitimacy prompt considerations of them as nations according to standards of nationhood, although this remains highly contested for political rather than cultural reasons. There are also **transnational nations**, including the Kurds and the Pashtun. The key to defining such peoples as nations is their deep commitment to the possibilities of sovereign statehood despite, or perhaps on account of, their widespread settlements across several sovereign jurisdictions. This works in various ways. To the extent that the Kurds in Iraq accept the legitimacy of the sovereign state of Iraq, they represent Iraqi nationality but retain their Kurdish ethnicity. The same applies to the many Pashtun clans in Afghanistan who may remain true to Pashtun ethnic and kinship loyalties but, to the extent to which they act within the political-cultural frameworks of sovereign Afghanistan, reaffirm their Afghan nationality that derives from being a citizen of that sovereign state. This becomes a matter of major controversy since a number of Pashtun clans traverse the borders separating Afghanistan from Pakistan as if they enjoyed dual citizenship and thus dual nationality, which they do not.

USSR. The population of the republic is predominantly ethnic Chechen with a Russian minority, and the Chechen people believe that they have a right to **self-determination** and **sovereignty**. From 1994 to 1996 the Chechens fought a war for independence against the Russian state. The Russian military was unable to establish permanent control over the region. The conflict ended when Chechnya was granted de facto independence from Russia. However, in 1999 a series of apartment bombings blamed on Chechen separatists launched a second war and the Russian army took control of the region. Throughout the 2000s,

Chechen forces continued to fight the Russian military and attacked numerous civilian targets, including schools and hospitals. Russia responded by installing a new regime and brutally reintegrating Chechnya into Russia. Struggles between the Russian government and the Chechen forces are ongoing.

Nationalism represents a belief in unique features of a people conceived as a unified political culture capable of maintaining high levels of commonality and solidarity appropriate to nationhood or peoplehood and patriotic loyalty and sacrifice. When taken to extremes it devolves into a fanatical devotion to the nation in ways that demonstrate ideological notions linked to exclusion and sometimes to purity. This leads to a number of political dysfunctions. In some instances, sovereign states will adopt nationalist policies that deny subnational groups the full benefits of citizenship on the basis of identity constructions marked by characteristics such as race, ethnicity, religion, and even class. For example, the Sri Lankan government dominated by a Sinhala majority has been accused of systematic discrimination against the state's Tamil minority. The government has adopted Sinhala symbols and traditions, including the language and flag, as national symbols and traditions while attempting to devalorize Tamil culture. It has been alleged that it has attempted to colonize predominantly Tamil territories with Sinhala people and of **ethnically cleansing** certain regions of its Tamil population. In such instances, nationalist ideologies and policies lead to political instability, legitimacy crises, and violence. Unlike **nationality**, which encourages difference and diversity grounded in nationhood, nationalism in extremist forms promotes exclusivist policies that are often justified in ideological terms that revolve around notions of political-cultural purity. The results are politically disastrous.

The postcolonialist legacy has generated rifts across many political cultures among identity groups who perceive ethnic, sectarian, or racial differences in one another that they hold to be irresolvable except through eradication or violent transformation. As a result, the contemporary political history of the postcolonialist nation-state includes the tragedy of ethno-political violence that revolves around **essentialized group identity**. Identity groups become objectified or marked by cultural perceptions of difference and otherness. The features of otherness vary. In some cases, kinship, ethnicity, and region are principle features of conflict; in other instances, sect, religion, class, or race becomes the major factor in subnational conflict. The combinations of cultural features as factors in political violence depend on historical memory and on the ways people as individuals and in groups choose to perceive and relate to one another.

Characteristics of social and political identity tend to be regarded as part of human "nature" but they are historically derived and thus part of the cultural

heritage of any political formation. The **"naturalizing" of human identity** provides a means in political culture for the impositions of power, especially on subordinated or subaltern groups. But the cultural dimensions of political identity are not given by nature. They are the collective outcomes of history and thus are highly dependent on myriad factors and multiple causes and trajectories. In effect, political-cultural identities are inventions. They represent choices over time, the products of human values and meanings as interpreted by means of intergenerational influences that bond people together but also separate them culturally, sometimes in seemingly intractable ways. This is the very power of political culture: to bind peoples together, but also to promote division, distrust, and sometimes even violent hatred or contempt. Here "nature" plays no role, but political culture certainly does.

Our discussion of political culture and the making of the modern nation-state, therefore, must focus on the critical relationships among collective identity construction, the legitimacy of governance, and subnational conflict. Often subnational conflict arises as a consequence of how the identity of specific groups is constructed within specific political cultures in relation to nationality. At moments of ethno-political violence nationality often becomes objectified. It becomes associated with one identity group. Nationality no longer is considered as a legal status linked to citizenship. It becomes "naturalized" as if it belonged to particular individuals as members of a group on the basis of their nature. Often this nature is characterized according to difference rather than commonality and thus linked to ethnicity, kinship, race, class, or sectarian group identity rather than to legal and cultural affiliation embedded in nationhood. The nation thus becomes essentialized, objectified, and even naturalized. Difference is no longer tolerated. The status of those deemed outside the natural condition of the nation is made insecure. The political-cultural conditions thus emerge that help to explain why and how ethno-political conflicts occur within subnational conflicts. Once such tensions develop, the secondary "hyphenated" set of political-cultural formations between nationality as a principle of commonality and identity group otherness as a principle of difference in nationhood can no longer operate. The nation becomes a kind of political possession of only those powerful enough to possess it to the disenfranchisement of the less powerful. Here, again, we see the making of subnational conflict based on status insecurity in which political culture conflates nationality with difference in ways that systematically disadvantage particular groups.

The consequence is a legitimacy crisis based on **status insecurity**. Status insecurity on the part of identity groups invariably causes legitimacy crises to occur. But how events in the field unfold differs from legitimacy crisis to legitimacy

crisis. Power relations help shape how political cultures function during crises. History, historical memory, the influences of colonialism and of postcolonialist relationships, and the specific contours of religion, race, kinship, and patronage systems all represent factors at work in determining if, when, and with what effects violence breaks out including the often-horrendous human costs.

Any classification of these complex histories of ethno-political violence in subnational conflicts during the contemporary era must reduce certain sets of specifics to what they bear in common. The story of ethno-political conflict may be told in terms of **three subsets or kinds of ethno-political violence**. All three represent major legitimacy crises that attend modern states and all bear witness to the terrible violence that occurs once statehood as a form of governance over a people within a territory is no longer regarded as legitimate among those whose willingness to accept it is critical, especially in terms of taxation and conscription. The history of legitimacy crises also demonstrates the political-cultural role of collective or group identity constructions and the dangers of conflating nationality with a single form of group identity. This involves the dynamics of **objectification** or **essentialization** that naturalize differences and make otherness appear unacceptable to national formations or nation-building. These dynamics fall heavily on those excluded or on those who exclude themselves from the principles of commonality in nationality on the basis of objectified and/or essentialized identity constructions in political culture.

Legitimacy crises in the making of the modern nation-state demonstrate at least three basis patterns in how violent transformations occur due to conflicts over values and meanings in political culture. They are **sectarian separatist/exclusionary**, **communist class/totalitarian**, and **fascist extremist/inclusionary**. The primary factors at work during these upheavals tend to revolve around identity constructions involving religion, class, and ideology in various formats and combinations. Together they represent crucial factors in provoking ethno-political violence during subnational conflicts. Identity constructions and political culture play a significant role in influencing behavior along the pathways taken within these three patterns. For this reason we speak of the role of ideology. Ideology may be defined in multiple ways, but in the present context we represent ideology as the ways in which political-cultural ideas and concepts represent social and political reality in relation to identity constructions. We pursue this within the frames of subnational conflict. We are interested in how ideological ideas, beliefs, and assumptions regarding political culture serve to justify violence at subnational levels. Ideologies can be deployed as justifications for violence, especially during struggles over the legitimacy of governance. Ideology thus provides context for the study of political culture with emphasis on the relations

of identity constructions to ideological programs regarding the meanings of nationality in circumstances when the legitimacy of the nation-state is in question.

In cases of ethno-sectarian and/or religious conflicts leading to sectarian separatist/exclusionary violence, group identity constructions transform religion—spiritual or metaphysical belief—into ideological justifications for the violent political breakup of sovereign legitimacy and institutions. In such circumstances, legitimacy conflicts often become converted into a struggle over the nature of divine will and the superiority of one way to salvation over all others. At the time of writing, such a struggle is being etched in the sands of Iraq and Syria in which numerous armed organizations and militia vie for control over the sovereign territories of both sovereign states, not in their own name alone but rather in the name of a higher will or truth. The consequence is often severe violence, as in this case. Ideological religiosity burns itself on altars of self-immolation when fueled by virulent hate against those deemed infidels, apostates, and nonbelievers. Hate becomes exclusionary once the territorial borders of sovereign states become ideologically constructed as the exclusive property of particular sectarian and religious identity groups and as off limits to all others. This tendency readily congeals into justification for violent subnational conflict. This proclivity becomes exaggerated especially if sectarian belief and identity become the ideological basis for partition of sovereign territory into exclusionary zones as well as the basis for identity group objectifications. Whenever this happens, political culture becomes transformed into a political geography of exclusive spatialized difference. Gerard Toal and Carl T. Dahlman call this **ethnoterritorialism**. It fosters a kind of depletion in the capacities of political culture to promote nationality across sectarian divides within the frames of a modern sovereign nation-state.[3]

Examples include the conflicts in the Balkans leading to the sectarian divisions among the Serbs, Croats, and Bosnians in the aftermath of the demise of the former Yugoslavia. Here ethnicity mattered less in the ethno-nationalisms causing the conflict since all parties were ethnically Slavic. What counted most in the sectarian divide at least in terms of political culture were religious affiliations distinguishing Serbian Orthodox, Bosnian Muslim, and Croatian Catholic. The partition of India and Pakistan separating Hindu India from Islamic Pakistan and the creation of Bangladesh from eastern Pakistan also revolved around religious and sectarian differences. In these cases conflicts led to mass atrocities and genocidal levels of ethno-political violence. Still other instances include the civil wars in Sri Lanka, Sudan, and East Timor, all examples of excruciating levels of violence and atrocity used during instances of sectarian separatist/exclusionary conflicts embedded in political culture. Identity constructions turn on ideological

visions of exclusivist superiority in cases when legitimacy becomes not a matter of popular consent but a way of executing God's will on earth as seen through the interpretive frames of sectarian and/or religious fanaticism. The moderations and partialities of hyphenated identity critical to the historical evolution of what is often referred to as liberal political culture in the making of modern nation-states are thus rejected.

Sectarian separatist/exclusionary legitimacy crises stem from religious or ethnic status insecurities. Religious beliefs and ethnic practices become transformed into ideological struggles over what bestows legitimacy on governing institutions within sovereign territorial boundaries. This results in intense conflict over who is eligible to enjoy national citizenship. Ethnic affiliation defined by religious or sectarian identity constructions and nationality are made to appear exclusive of each other. Such legitimacy crises often lead to political violence, especially when specific sectarian or religious groups engage in political campaigns or movements aimed at territorial separation or the fragmentation of an already constituted sovereign state. Such separatism or secessionist political movements tend to provoke intense forms of hatred and contempt. Violence results from such a constellation that combines emotion and ideology in identity construction with strategic military and political objectives. This is the case whenever an identity group seeks either the breakup of the sovereign state in terms of ethnic purity or cleansing, or to maintain the territorial integrity of the nation-state in ways that would allow one insurgent identity group struggling to form their own autonomous political entity to dominate over others. An example of the former is the breakup of the former Yugoslavia. An example of the latter is the war between the Sinhalese majority and the Tamil minority in Sri Lanka. Darfur, the home of the Fur people, also provides an illustration of tormenting violence waged against a kinship group occupying traditional lands subject to ethnic cleansing at the behest of agents acting with the consent, if not direction, of those who were at the time in the central government but of different ethnicity. These examples are discussed below.

The territorial dimensions of nationhood and statehood ground sentiments of national belonging in ways that bind a people together. No resource serves to consolidate a sense of unity, common destiny, and national glory more than land. The demarcations of national space delimit the political realm in material, and even more significantly in cultural and ideological, ways. Modern conceptions of sovereignty and patriotic attachments to flag and country all denote the collective desire to assert proprietary claims to territory as the basis for a way of life that is distinguished by nationality and conceptions of existential or group identity. For such reasons, challenges to the integrity of territorial or spatial understandings

of what constitute statehood appear to provoke profound responses and, under certain conditions, nationalist forms of rage that make mass political violence possible. This occurs whenever counternationalist aspirations for autonomy become galvanized into secessionist action. Separatist movements assume a wide variety of names: Liberation Fronts, People's Parties, National Fronts, Liberation Armies, Democratic Popular Fronts, National Movements, Civic Alliances, Autonomous Movements, or Solidarity Movements. These struggles have provoked some of the most brutal conflicts in modern history. Disputes over the legitimacy of centralized governance and the solidarity of national belonging revolve around the particularities of historical state- and nation-building. But they erupt over the right of a people to constitute themselves as a nation bounded by a territory and governed as a sovereign state legitimated by and through the doctrines of popular consent. This combination of forces and factors can evoke responses on the part of "mother governments" in the form of long, smoldering wars of attrition punctuated by outbreaks of violence that involve a steady unfolding of inhumanity.

Tamil Separatism and Sinhalese Nationalism in Sri Lanka

Any disjuncture between **peoplehood, nationhood** (bottom-up), and **statehood** (top-down) results in crises of legitimacy. In many cases, long-term oppression against an objectified racial, ethnic, religious, or kinship minority erupts in political violence. Especially volatile are those instances arising from conflicts over sovereignty and citizenship when national unity appears to be threatened or undermined by the presence of **separatist** or **secessionist** subnational groups. The political alignment of state relative to the cultural configurations of nation thus becomes challenged by an unwillingness of certain groups to accept citizenship or nationality in a sovereign nation-state from which they wish to leave or that they wish to redefine. For decades the Sri Lankan government unleashed massive violence upon the Tamil minority within its state. On May 17, 2009, the Sri Lankan Ministry of Defense announced that "Sri Lankan armed forces have militarily defeated the *Liberation Tigers of Tamil Eelam (LTTE, a.k.a. the Tamil Tigers)* and freed the nation from three decades of terror."[4] Since its independence from Great Britain, Sri Lanka has been ruled by a Sinhala majority, one accused of ethnically cleansing the nation-state of its Tamil minority. According to Tamil advocates, "the intent and goal of al Sinhala governments (without exception) has been to secure the island [of Sri Lanka] as a Sinhala Buddhist Deepa.... The Sinhala Buddhist nation masquerading as a multi-ethnic 'civic' 'Sri Lankan'

nation set about its task of assimilation and 'cleansing' the island of the Tamils, as a people, by depriving a section of Eelam Tamils of their citizenship, declaring the Sinhala flag as the national flag, colonizing parts of the Tamil homeland with Sinhala people, imposing Sinhala as the official language ... [and resorting] to murderous violence in 1956, in 1958, in 1961, and again in 1977 directed to terrorize the Tamils into submission."[5]

Civil war and armed Tamil resistance to the Sri Lankan government began after the July 1983 government-sponsored anti-Tamil pogroms. Memorialized as "Black July," the violence carried out by Sinhala mobs killed at least 400 Tamil people, destroyed tens of thousands of houses, and began a diaspora known as "the scattering" of Tamil people who fled the carnage for other countries. For the next twenty-six years the LTTE waged a violent secessionist campaign that sought to establish an independent Tamil state in the north and east of Sri Lanka. Though the Tigers have been accused of numerous atrocities against civilians, including abductions, suicide attacks, assassinations, piracy, the use of child soldiers, and ethnic cleansing of Sinhalese and Muslim inhabitants from areas under their control, many attacks and many civilian deaths have been attributed to the Sri Lankan military. Allegations suggest that the Sri Lankan army, navy, and air force engaged in "state terrorism" against Tamil civilians, supporters, and sympathizers. As noted in an August 2007 report released by Human Rights Watch, "the Sri Lankan government is responsible for unlawful killings, enforced disappearances, and other serious human rights violations since the resumption of major hostilities with the LTTE."[6] The Asia Director for Human Rights Watch went on to acknowledge that "the Sri Lankan government has apparently given its security forces a green light to use 'dirty war' tactics.... Abuses by the LTTE are no excuse for the government's campaign of killings, 'disappearances,' and forced returns of the displaced."[7] According to Yael Danieli, author of *Trauma of Terrorism,* Sri Lanka transformed "state terrorism" into a "mechanism of government." In Sri Lanka, murder and terror became extensions of politics in the face of an ethnic secessionist threat. This continued until the government officially defeated the Tamil Tigers in 2009.

Balkanization and Ethnic Cleansing: The Remaking of Bosnia as a Nation-State

Mass political disruptions originating in sectarian separatist/exclusionary violence characterized the **balkanization** of the former Yugoslavia throughout the 1990s and early 2000s. Named for the Balkan region and its political-cultural

dynamics, **balkanization** refers to the fragmenting of a larger political entity such as the Austro-Hungarian Empire or a sovereign nation-state such as Yugoslavia or South Slavia into a number of small sovereign entities. Often these struggle against one another for recognition and legitimacy. Balkanization thus stands as a metaphor designating the failures of political culture to prevent dysfunctional forms of fragmentation in the making of the modern nation-state. Yugoslavia was a sovereign nation-state carved out of the Austro-Hungarian Empire after World War I. From the beginning, despite the many ethnic groups within the country, it was dominated politically and militarily by Serbia. The Yugoslav government privileged Serbs over other groups including the Slovenes, Bosnians, Croats, Kosovars, and Albanians. This postimperial nationless state was held together by a brutal dictator, Josip Tito, during the Cold War, and began to crumble in the early 1990s after Tito's death. The devolution and eventual demise of Yugoslavia provides an example of **balkanization**. First to go was Slovenia in the north, which voted overwhelmingly for independence in 1990. Slovenia was able to control its borders and appeal to international recognition from the European Community. It eventually seceded with little resistance. However, when Croatia declared its independence in March 1991, the Serbian army invaded, committing crimes against humanity as it attempted to subdue the Croatian population. In 1992 Bosnia and Herzegovina declared their independence. Here the Serb army and quasi-armed militia attacked, ultimately committing near-genocidal violence against the Bosnian Muslim population. Finally, in 1999 the Serb military attempted to ethnically cleanse or purify the southern province of Kosovo of its ethnic Albanian population. The North Atlantic Treaty Organization (NATO) intervened with a bombing campaign. This stopped the violence but the status of Kosovo as an independent country remains contested in the international community.

In the former Yugoslavia, therefore, balkanization led to the creation of Slovenia, Croatia, Bosnia-Herzegovina, Montenegro, Macedonia, Serbia, and Kosovo. Violence was particularly brutal in Bosnia-Herzegovina where Serbian military forces attempted to maintain control of Serb-dominated territory and ethnically cleanse it of minority populations. Gerard Toal and Carl T. Dahlman explain that "ethnic cleansing, in short, is a form of geopolitics. The 'geo' and 'politics' can be parsed to signify two interrelated practices: first the attempt to produce a new *ethno-territorial order of space,* and second the attempt to build an *ethnocratic political order* upon that space. The remaking of Bosnia through ethnic cleansing involved both."[8] During this ethno-political subnational conflict involving ethnic cleansing, the Serbian objective was to transform Bosnian nationality into the possession of those who shared in Serbian ethnicity to the exclusion of

others, particularly Muslim Bosniaks. The solution to the conflict, negotiated in Dayton, Ohio, rewarded Serbian perpetrators of ethnic cleansing at least to the extent that the nation-states that emerged are now ethnically homogenous from region to region in the precise way envisioned by those who wanted Bosnia to become ethnically cleansed. To cite Toal and Dahlman, "That there is a now restored Islamic cultural landscape in Republika Srpska does not negate its origins as a secessionist project launched by figures that became indicted war criminals. The polity is founded on a racist Darwinian scenario, a hyperbolic Orientalist fear that 'Muslims' are 'conquering' Bosnia with their birthrate and planning to turn it into an Islamic state."[9] Toal and Dahlman describe the cultural process of objectifying difference in terms of "us" and "them," thereby transforming an ethnic identity group into an essentialized identity object for purposes of political subordination and exclusion. They write, "Essentialized enemy construction was and is used to fix an equally essentialized self, a long suffering 'Bosnian Serb' community that requires its own exclusivist space to survive such a plot."[10] The birth of the Republic of Srpska as a nation-state is based on a political culture of ethno-nationalism that divides ethnic groups from one another in exclusionary, separatist ways that reinforce the mutual dynamics of objectification. The result of the peace agreement is clear: "the ethnoterritorialism it institutionalized has entrapped Bosnia ever since."[11]

Sectarian Separatism/Exclusionary: The Case of Sudan and Southern Sudan

Nativism in the Darfur region of Sudan has "fed off desperation and grievance" combined with notions of Arab "racial" superiority, "ethnic" discrimination, and violence.[12] Sudanese nationalist ideologies have been predicated on Sudanization, that is, political-cultural transformations aimed at supplanting "African" culture with "Arabic" culture. Early Sudanization projects included "speaking Arabic, restricting the public role of women, using cash, dressing in the characteristic northern Sudanese manner . . . and shunning alcohol."[13] But by the early 1990s, Sudanization was not about "religion, nor language, and certainly not citizenship, but Arab identity through imputed Arab blood"; this "became the decisive factor in excluding the Other" from membership in the Sudanese nation and ideologically was applied to legitimate the violence against the Darfurians.[14] After years of oppression, Darfurians complained not that "the process of 'becoming Sudanese' denied them their own, unique cultural heritage," but rather "that the government in Khartoum was not treating them as full citizens of the Sudanese

state."[15] It was this kind of exclusionary Arabism that converted "disputes over camel theft or grazing rights" into the "systematic and ideological slaughter of one group by the other."[16] Perpetrators, particularly jihadist militias known as the *janjawiid*, participated in the ethnic cleansing of "African tribes" from the Darfur region, clearing the land for resettlement by "Arab nomads" in order to advance a racist, nationalist agenda enacted by and through the instrumentalities of mass political violence.

The ideological transformation of religion and sectarian identity constructions is not the only way liberal traditions in political culture become threatened or challenged. In instances of political culture gripped by communist class/totalitarian utopian visions, ideology turns on sets of distinctions among groups that appear to position them differently relative to distributive goods that by their very nature are limited. But the overall objective is to attain a level of conformity that perverts human individuality and does so in ways that operate according to the ideological metrics of total uniformity. In such instances, ideological objectifications work to transform questions of equity, discussed earlier, into justifications for political campaigns to bring about totalized equality. They seek absolute or totalized forms of equality in ways especially designed to suffocate those forms of difference that emerge as a result of political and economic freedom. Equity standards become converted into ideological justifications for political attempts to institute extreme measures of equality in sectors that include access to wealth, education, material goods, social services, urban dwelling, ownership of private property including farmland, and family status. Class ties become symbolized in terms of status and possession. High and low statuses often become symbolically represented in ways that position certain elite groups to gain consistent advantage. This represents a supreme irony: in the name of totalized equality fundamental inequalities arise. In Bolshevik and later Soviet Russia, the archenemies of the state, as ideologically constructed by the Communist Party of the Soviet Union, for example, were kulaks, the rich farmers who owned the private land on which many farm workers lived, particularly in the Crimea. According to Soviet ideological propaganda they were the enemies of the state that impeded progress toward the communist utopia, a land of complete or total equality in which all goods were to be produced and distributed equally for the good of all. The consequence was catastrophic. In the name of equality, the Soviet government annihilated the entire kulak class. It later turned to various segments of the population: urban educated professionals, former members of the Soviet military, entire sections of middle-class society, former members of the Communist Party, members of particular ethnic groups such as the Ukrainian people who were forced into massive starvation due to forced famine, and ultimately anyone, at any time, for

any reason. Identity constructions became arbitrary, fluid, and ever changing. It did not matter as long as it served the putative interests of the Soviet state as ideologically constructed by the clandestine services of the secret police charged with the tasks of totalitarian terror under the banner of the Communist Party of the Soviet Union. Such campaigns of terror seek to destroy any sense of privacy, intimacy, personal security, or social trust in legal or political order. The ideological vision used to justify this was a collectivized society not only in terms of Soviet agriculture but in ways that were aimed at the entire Soviet society as well. The ideology of totalized equality generated justifications for nothing less than a utopian effort to impose notions of "the many over the one" throughout Soviet Russia. Freedom and liberty as values in political culture gave way to the ambitions of achieving a totalized equality in which all needs were equally met for all members of the society at all times. This was done in the name of Soviet legitimacy, communist style. But the destruction of freedom and liberty meant the demise of individuality, privacy, personal dignity, and initiative. In their place came the instruments of Soviet terror, secret police, and the gulag, a penal method that spatialized the isolation of political prisoners, that is, those considered undesirable for any reason. These terror tactics combined with central planning produced a kind of cultural paralysis, a cynicism and despair, a system of utter corruption, an economy of scarcity, overproduction and black markets, and a degree of political depravity that ultimately led to the disintegration of the Soviet Union as a political formation. The loss of legitimacy of the Communist Party of the Soviet Union signifies the dangers of propagating an ideology of totalized equality as a justification for the elimination of certain classes of society in the name of a mythologized egalitarian utopia. Different political cultures of distinct nation-states promote and/or tolerate class differentials among groups of citizens in a variety of ways and to varying degrees. The quest for equity and fairness in terms of opportunity and access is critical, but this effort does not occur in the same ways everywhere. And it contrasts with the brutally enforced attempt to impose total equality on a society in the name of "the many over the one" or collectivization. Such political programs lead to the kinds of subnational conflict we have seen not only in the Soviet Union but also in Maoist China, in Cambodia under the genocidal regime of Pol Pot, and today in the Democratic People's Republic of North Korea (DPRK).

Political culture becomes transformed into ideologically constructed forms of legitimacy used to justify, first, sectarian exclusionary or separatist actions in cases where the sectarian and/or religious divides between identity groups becomes severe or extreme. In such instances, political objectives seek to achieve exclusionary zones of sovereign control. The aim is to control the entire sovereign territory of a

state in the name of one identity group over all others or to separate a portion of sovereign territory at the behest of one group wanting to be isolated from all others. In such instance, identity construction, territory, legitimacy, and ideology all combine in ways that tend to define nationality, ethnicity, and self-determination in terms of God, blood, or nature. This is the meaning of ethno-nationalism combined with ethno-territorialism. We have also seen how ideology frames class-based ethno-political violence in subnational conflicts. Often this is ideologically justified on the basis of collectivization and radical egalitarianism attached to utopian visions of society. The aim is to make political culture a monolithic screed of ideological conformity by means of systematic uses of terror that reduce all citizens to abject conformity, all in the name of totalized, that is, totalitarian equality. It does not work. In the name of class equality, class structures reinforce the privileged positions of an elite class. Collectivization of agriculture in Soviet Russia as well as Maoist China led to enormous human travail and suffering, not least on account of the genocidal violence it produced. In addition, totalitarian regimes often manipulate identity constructions in ways that engage ethno-nationalist features that contrive identity group differences for purposes of power and control. Soviet and Maoist experiences of collectivization in which private ownership of land and traditional forms of agriculture were destroyed in order to promote cultural revolutions demonstrate how identity constructions with respect to ethnic groupings can and do become objectified ideologically. When this happens, particular groups become objectified as the enemies of the state in ways that combine their class status with their ethnic features or identity. In the case of the Soviet experiences, Ukrainian kulaks, particularly those in Crimea, were hit especially hard; in the case of Maoist-led transformations of Chinese society, rural villages in regions with specific social/ethnic compositions were especially targeted.

Thus the study of political culture and of the making of the modern state frames the issue of legitimacy in ways that include the role of ideology. Ideological constructions of identity and legitimacy come together during episodes of totalitarian or authoritarian transformations done in the name of extreme or radical egalitarian objectives. But, as we saw in the case of political cultures gripped by sectarian or religious exclusionary objectives, communist or even egalitarian principles taken to political extremes lead to the destruction of equity and thus freedom. Under such conditions, political culture deteriorates into the devices of mass political oppression. Identity groups become readily objectified to serve repressive ideological interests. This misrepresents standards of equality; totalitarian forms of equality are profoundly destructive of the human spirit. This is the meaning of identity constructions in relation to totalitarian class legitimacy: personhood and civil society disappear.

Class/Collectivization (Communist) Ideologies

Class/collectivization ideologies reflect **socioeconomic positionality**. This is defined in terms of the arrangements that structure how privilege and disadvantage are organized in providing access to power, wealth, prestige, and even information. Class/collectivization ideologies framed the Russian and Chinese civil wars. These ideologies decrease emphasis on sectarian or religious values, although these might act as influences. Often, ideological values articulated include social leveling in the name of a communist party movement that tends to be replete with utopian aims that purportedly advance transformative political and social ideals. **Collectivist ideologies** such as those articulated in Soviet Russia, Maoist China, and Democratic Kampuchea pervert Marxist principles of class unity, agrarian communism, secular socialism, and national solidarity in order to justify the violation, concentration, oppression, and annihilation of objectified victims. Totalized notions of class purity become fused with supremacist ideologies of nationalism in ways that provoke campaigns that demand and sometimes actually attempt to exterminate purported internal enemies of the nation-state. Examples include the "Khmer bodies with Vietnamese minds" in the case of Kampuchea, the kulaks in Soviet Russia, and the "running dogs of imperialist capitalism" in Maoist China. Such ideological notions easily slide into calls for totalized leveling of the body politic in the name of absolute equality.

Class/Collectivization (Communist) Ideology in Soviet Russia

Stalin's efforts to transform the Soviet Union, for example, depended on a "constructivist task, as reflected in the catchphrase for it: 'building socialism.'"[17] Here "nationalism" became equated with "Bolshevism," encompassing both "patriotic devotion to one's own people and their positive national attributes" and "chauvinism, an overweening national pride and sense of superiority over other nations" that glorified "the socialism-building enterprise as a … mission in world history."[18] But Bolshevik nationalism readily incorporated class/collectivist elements, "disenfranchis[ing] all citizens who hinder[ed] socialist revolution."[19] In the name of collectivization, Lenin and his successors led "a war to the death against the rich, the idlers, and the parasites"—the so-called "enemies of the revolution"—that included "the sedentary old regime elites … priests, commercial traders, convicted thieves, former landowners … embezzlers, speculators, manipulators, tax-evaders, and swindlers, as well as people considered to be arrogant, rude, socially deviant, or immoral," all of whom

"shared the appellation 'class enemy'" and promoted "state terror" as a "legitimate instrument of revolutionary action from above."[20] As Tucker writes, "state terror is triadic.... [It requires] a political leadership determined to use terror for its purposes, [and] ... a minority chosen for victimization in so frightful a form that ... a far larger body of people, seeing what can happen to the victims, will be motivated to fulfill the leadership's purpose, which may be to render it quiescent or, alternatively, to induce it to take actions that it otherwise would not be disposed to take."[21] During the Second Revolution, the "victimized element was the 'kulak'" and the class/collectivist ideology that justified its annihilation was "dekulakization," the "liquidation of the kulaks as a class." Like others who were perceived to be "nonlaboring or parasitic," kulaks were "stripped of rights and classified as noncitizen aliens" by the Soviet government.[22] They were then "dispossess[ed] ... and, in very many cases pack[ed] ... into boxcars for dispatch to unknown distant destinations where they would, if they survived the trip (and very many did not), be forced to labor under wretched conditions on construction sites or in prison camps."[23]

But Soviet style class/collectivization also assumed a xenophobic dimension. As Golfo Alexopoulos writes, "in Stalin's Russia, aliens [disenfranchised noncitizens] were very often non-Russians."[24] Ethnic minorities including Germans, Poles, Estonians, Chinese, Kazakhs, Ukrainians, Uzbeks, Tatars, Turkmen, Ossetians, and Georgians, as well as Jews, many of whom lived on the periphery of the Soviet Union, were disenfranchised in greater proportions than ethnic Russians. For not only were ethnic minorities ideologically identified with capitalist economic practices, they "appeared culturally distinct from the enfranchised Russian citizenry" and were thus "often suspected of political disloyalty."[25] To prevent the "contamination" of the Soviet nation, these elements were often "disappeared" or, alternatively, annihilated outright in massacres, government-induced famines, and purges, all in the name of "national purity."

Class/Collectivization (Communist) Ideology in Maoist China

Like early Stalinist Russia, pre-Maoist China was "weak and divided" and Mao's first "national problems" were the "reunification of China and the expulsion of foreign occupiers."[26] Incorporating the Chinese military into the dual processes of revolutionary nation- and state-building, Mao and his successors favored an ideology that combined Marxist ideology with political mobilization, class struggle, anti-intellectualism, totalized egalitarianism, and xenophobia in order to advance a "Cultural Revolution." This was aimed at efforts that would purge

China and its Communist Party of "liberal bourgeois" elements threatening to undermine the purity of the postrevolutionary society. Calling upon students, workers, peasants, soldiers, revolutionary intellectuals, and party officials to "transform the superstructure" of Maoist China, the "Decision Concerning the Great Proletarian Cultural Revolution" instructed the proletariat to "meet head-on every challenge of the bourgeoisie in the ideological field ... [and to] overthrow those persons in authority who are taking the capitalist road, to criticize and repudiate the reactionary bourgeois academic 'authorities' and the ideology of the bourgeoisie and all other exploiting classes ... so as to facilitate consolidation and development of the socialist system."[27] The wave of violence and violation that ensued targeted millions of Chinese citizens who were ideologically objectified as "spies," "running dogs," "revisionists," "capitalists," or "imperialists," subjecting them to rape, torture, cannibalism, oppression, imprisonment, enslavement, and execution. Many were displaced, abused, starved, or worked to death in forced labor camps, while others were systematically annihilated in the name of political revolution and class struggle. Others were denunciated as "class enemies" and subsequently "bludgeon[ed] and dismember[ed]."[28] In this "People's War" against "capitalist" agents, ferocity symbolized revolutionary spirit; those who participated in the Cultural Revolution demonstrated their commitment to the Maoist movement by their merciless torment of class enemies.

Class/Collectivization (Communist) Ideology in Democratic Kampuchea

In Democratic Kampuchea, class/collectivist ideologies that were heavily influenced by Maoist egalitarianism fueled a fearsome desire for a return to a fantasized premodern communalism that portrayed "Vietnamese (and, to a much lesser extent, ethnic Chinese) as the quintessentially evil 'other'" who "were a threat to the racial purity and survival of the Khmer."[29] Having eradicated Kampuchea's ethnic Vietnamese population, however, the Khmer Rouge initiated a policy of genocidal annihilation against citizen-victims on the basis of their socioeconomic status. Obsessed with "hidden enemies burrowing from within," the government turned against ethnic Cambodians, particularly "new citizens," a category that included urban dwellers and collaborators of the Lon Nol regime; in Democratic Kampuchea, national belonging and citizenship became a function of class membership. In the name of purity and totalized egalitarianism, the Pol Pot regime mobilized those Cambodians who "felt that they were 'stepped upon' and 'dominated' by the wealthy and powerful," inciting "old citizens" to

participate in the corporeal torment and annihilation of those deemed unfit for membership in the Kampuchean body politic.[30] The Khmer Rouge claimed that "the party had conducted 'scientific analysis of the society' that revealed the 'true nature' of the socioeconomic situation," an analysis that legitimated widespread participation in a program of class-based torture and massacre. Such entrenched notions of "us" and "them" made elimination of "subversive" "new" citizens a matter of national security.[31] Khmer radio broadcasts explained the necessity "to draw a clear line between us and the enemy.... 'We' means our nation, people, worker-peasant class, revolution, collective system of the proletariat, cooperatives, trade unions, Revolutionary Army, and KCP. The 'enemy' includes all imperialist aggressors and lackeys of all stripes"; thus "we," the nation, were identified as members of the worker-peasant class whose patriotism and love for the nation shone from a deep commitment to the collective system, whereas "the enemy" was the capitalist class of unpatriotic aggressors and imperialist collaborators whose counterrevolutionary spirit and individualism made them betrayers of the Cambodian nation.[32] Because "enemies" were often identified not only by group membership but also according to the degree to which their behaviors conformed to party ideals and directives, the Khmer Rouge made allegiance to the party the primary condition for citizenship and turned the population of Cambodia against itself. Every citizen was under constant surveillance by agents of the state who determined which citizens were to be included in the Cambodian nation and which were to be eliminated. Khmer ideology encouraged its adherents to develop a "revolutionary consciousness" so that "anger for outside enemies, class enemies, and enemies burrowing from within" would facilitate their willingness to "work hard to research, investigate, seek out, and clean up these enemies."[33] As Alexander Laban Hinton writes, "the most overt way in which a person could display his or her revolutionary consciousness was a demonstrated willingness to ... ensure that the party line remained 'pure' [by annihilating] these subversive enemies," that is to say, to participate in the political project to protect and secure Democratic Kampuchea against "ugly microbes" that could do "real damage" and "rot [the nation] from within.[34] This language that objectifies others using imageries that conjure up disease, rot, and decay provides an example of how ideologically based identity constructions can and do attempt to demonize specific groups within the frames of the political culture of a "leftist" movement. As we now see below, demonizing an ethnic group for purposes of their annihilation was also practiced on the "right." Genocide and the Holocaust were not far behind.

A third pattern in political culture in which the meanings and values of nationality become ideologically destroyed emerges from the opposite end of

the political spectrum. This is also aimed at the violations of personhood in the name of a legitimacy that conflates nationality with ethnicity, not through class-based identity constructions, but rather through those ideologically linked to the supremacy of the state. Whereas totalitarian class equality is associated with political ideology from the "left," its ideological nemesis comes from the fascist or far right. "Right" and "left" are metaphorical terms for describing ideological predispositions that favor a certain set of values, beliefs, and attitudes over others, especially in ways that seek to legitimate political violence in subnational conflicts. As opposed to "the many over the one" in cases of communist class/totalitarian ideologies, (fascist) extremist/inclusionary ideologies justify virulent forms of violence against identity groups objectified and essentialized as internal enemies on the basis of "the one over the many." Fascist ideologies on the far right of the political spectrum totalize freedom, liberty, and the rights of the few over the many in order to promote definitions of nationality that are absolutely inclusive of a racialized group to the detriment of all other nationals. Political culture turns into a fascistic creed once it serves as the basis for an absolute inclusionary principle aimed at granting to only a segment of society the birthrights of nationality. The language of far right and/or fascist inclusionary ideology is laced with racism against others. Such racialized differences may turn on religion, as in the case of Aryan ideological doctrines advanced by the Nazis in relation to the Jews, whom they deemed not only genetically inferior but genetically nonentitled to German citizenship or nationality. In the case of those victimized during the Argentinean Dirty War, a security doctrine that was ideologically promoted in the names of both the state and the Catholic Church was applied with ferocious brutality to justify a program that involved the fierce eradication of hapless and innocent citizens who were deemed to threaten the security status of Argentina. The core of such contentions is found in the definitions and meanings attributed to nationhood and nationality and the extent to which political culture grounds difference in otherness. Fascist forms of extremist inclusionary ideology often act as the basis for determining the acid or litmus tests of the "rights to belong." In instances of extremist inclusionary ideology, the rights to belong are bestowed only upon "the one over the many," the one identity group perceived as superior and somehow deserving of citizenship, and as a result the only one with the rights to enjoy the freedom and liberty that come with it. Once liberty becomes ideologically totalized in this manner, the values of equity and equality are both driven out of the mainstream of political culture. "The one over the many" serves as an ideological justification for fascist and thus extremist political violence that stirs the ugly pots of internecine hate and violence across many political cultures in the making of modern nation-states.

Extremist/Inclusionary (Fascist) Ideologies

Fascist extremist/inclusionary ideologies often find themselves in search of nationalist forms of ethnic purity as a way of defining nationality. These ideologies attempt to racialize nationality and citizenship and in so doing essentialize group identity in ways that conflate being a member of the nation with a specific form of ethnic or existential identity. Political movements gripped by fascistic forms of extremist inclusionary doctrines often provoke intense forms of violence, not so much over who governs or over what constitutes legitimate authority, but rather over the purity of belonging as a standard not only of peoplehood but of nationality or membership in the nation.

As a result, the barrier to citizenship becomes ethnic, racial, or sectarian. Nationhood becomes ideologically constructed in purist terms and terminologies. Ethno-political violence in subnationalist conflicts aims to achieve extremist inclusionary or "inclusivist" forms of nationality or citizenship. Historically, this has often resulted in genocide and crimes against humanity. Fascist extremist/inclusionary ideologies reduce the enjoyment of nationality to members of a privileged group at the expense of others deemed unfit for membership in the nation on the basis of cultural, linguistic, religious, racial, ethnic, socioeconomic, or ancestral characteristics. By reducing nationality to sameness in heredity or biology, such ideologies eliminate space within the body politic for difference, distinction, and diversity. Individuals, who are often carriers of multiple identities, are prohibited from expressing this multiplicity freely and openly. Instead, "the demand [is] that the individual yield to social pressures to withhold, or deny, or efface, such intrasubjective multiplicity, since it is deemed a threat to the ideal of homogeneity."[35] As a consequence, the personal hyphen between ethnicity and nationality is collapsed in ways that absolutize national collective identity and belonging. This ideological dynamic converts nationality into a kind of ethnicized nationalism in which difference becomes fixed, oppositional, and adversarial. As Arne Johan Vetlesen writes, fascist, extremist, and inclusivist ethno-nationalist ideologies degrade identity groups so that persons are marked by "ethnic identities, physical-psychic carriers of ethnic identity . . . a marker of purity/impurity, own/alien, friend/enemy . . . [that] permit[s] no one to be neutral, unaffected."[36] Often beholden to fantasized mythologies of "lost glory" and thwarted "historical destiny," ethno-nationalist ideologies diminish the human condition to an existence of bare corporeality in the name of national purity. Whenever and wherever this occurs, inclusivist notions of "the authentic us" promote fascist extremist notions of alienation, prejudice, discrimination, contempt, and hate, leading ultimately to mass political violence.

Fascist Extremist/Inclusionary Ideologies in Argentina

Convened by President Raúl Alfonsín in December 1983, the objective of the National Commission on the Disappearance of Persons (CONADEP) was to investigate human rights violations committed by the military junta known as the National Reorganization Process, that is, by Jorge Rafael Videla's military-led government in Argentina between 1976 and 1983. The overall aim of CONADEP was to determine the fate of the *desaparecido*. This refers to the tens of thousands of Argentinean citizens who were listed as "subversive" by the junta, which was beholden to fascist ideologies and gripped by notions of "state security" and inclusivist nationality. In some cases, the actual disappearance of individuals identified with particular groups served as a tool to promote the political agenda of those seeking to exercise power in the name of an ideological construction of nationality that defined it in terms that circumscribed or limited citizenship to those who were absolutely pure in their commitment to state security as defined by the junta. This meant a form of nationality that was extreme in its inclusiveness. This is evidenced by the campaign waged by the junta against its own people. This campaign has come to be known as "The Dirty War." It led to mass numbers of tortured citizens as well as thousands of those now disappeared.

The word "disappear," while most commonly an intransitive verb, is used transitively in the context of ethno-political violence. Victims, often known in the Argentinean, Chilean, and Guatemalan examples as *los desaparecidos,* are said to "have been disappeared" rather than to "have disappeared"; their governments "disappeared" them, presumably forever. Forced "disappearance" removes victims from the political landscape. While they are certainly not alive in the physical sense, they are not definitively dead in the political or metaphorical sense. Instead they are gone, forced to dwell in a state of metaphorical limbo. Their absence carves an irreparable void in the hearts and communities of survivors, who are left to wonder about the fates of those whose bodies are never found and whose lives are erased from the public record, leaving the memories of those who knew them as the only evidence of their having existed at all. As a survivor from Operation Condor in Argentina recalls, "they were always saying, 'You don't exist. You're no one. . . . No one remembers you anymore.'"[37] In the words of another Argentinean *desaparecido,* "the first thing they told me was to forget who I was ... and that for me the outside world stopped right there."[38] As a result of the fascist extremist inclusivist ideologies applied by the junta as justification, thousands of innocent Argentine citizens were abducted, imprisoned, tortured, and assassinated (née "disappeared").

In its report entitled *Nunca Más (Never Again)*, CONADEP begins with a mournful disclaimer, for the testimonies collected by the Committee portrayed bodily torments so heinous as to challenge common understandings of human capacities for violence and violation:

> Many of the events described in this report will be hard to believe. This is because the men and women of our nation have only heard of such horror in reports from distant places. The enormity of what took place in Argentina, involving the transgression of the most fundamental human rights, is sure, still, to produce that disbelief which some used at the time to defend themselves from pain and horror. In so doing, they also avoided the responsibility born of knowledge and awareness, because the question necessarily follows: how can we prevent it happening again? And the frightening realization that both the victims and their tormentors were our contemporaries, that the tragedy took place on our soil, and that those who insulted the history of our country in this way have yet to show by word or deed that they feel any remorse for what they have done.[39]

The victims of the Argentinean junta were clergy, journalists, academics, trade unionists, and lawyers. They were men, women, and children who were selected for disappearance, torture, and extermination in accordance with the National Security Doctrine (NSD), an ideology that became "the yardstick by which all policies [were] measured [that served as] the beginning and end of politics."[40] In Argentina, the NSD "identified conspiratorial threats to national security and ... urged state leaders to engage in a form of permanent warfare against those security threats. The military's 'dirty war' against alleged enemies of the state, which resulted in the denial of individual and collective freedom, the routinized use of torture, and the death and disappearance of more than 15,000 individuals ... inspired [the government] to launch a campaign of state terror against its rivals."[41] Its ideology "rigidly derive[d] from an absolutist notion of war (or politics) that treat[ed] the enemy as unscrupulous and irredeemably immoral.... Since he or she will resort to any means to pursue ignominious ends, the enemy cannot be trusted to abide by negotiated settlements, or indeed be permitted to survive even as a vanquished member of society. Only the enemy's complete extermination would satisfy the absolutist thirst for total security, and only the unbridled use of state violence could ensure his or her demise."[42] Thus the national security doctrine served to "dehumanize whole categories of people and provide a quasi-religious rationale for their torture and destruction," not on the basis of racialized constructions of ethnicity or race, but on account of objectified notions of

political affiliation.[43] In the name of "security," tens of thousands of Argentinean nationals were brutalized and annihilated by agents of their own government.

The National Security Doctrine in Argentina incorporated **fascist** notions of centralized authoritarian state power and extremist nationalism. **Fascist ideologies** are predicated on the idea that races exist in a state of perpetual conflict and that the strong must assert themselves and cleanse the nation of impure, weak, and inferior "races" in order to survive. According to this fascist extremist inclusionary or inclusivist ideology, the "nation" acts as a unifying force but assumes a racist dimension that defines membership and citizenship according to biological determinism. In fascism, national identity is a totalizing force that essentializes "foreign elements" as "malignant parasites" to be excised from the body politic. Embedded in ideological constructions of "historical destiny" and national predominance, fascism is inherently racist and xenophobic, transforming citizens into "enemies within" whose annihilation is ideologically made to appear tantamount to the survival of the nation and the fulfillment of its predestined fate.

Fascist Extremist/Inclusionary Ideologies in Nazi Germany

In Nazi Germany, fascism elevated racist notions of biological supremacism, racial purity, and national solidarity to ideological predominance, placing particular emphasis on "racial hierarchies" that identified Germans or Aryans as the "master race," non-Aryan Europeans (including Slavs) as subhumans, and Gypsies and Jews as *lebensunwertes Leben* (life unworthy of life). This racist ideology justified the 1935 Law for the Protection of German Blood and Honor, which prevented marriage between Aryans and Jews, as well as the Reich Citizenship Law, which stripped all Jews of citizenship in the German state. Jews thus became "subjects of the state," deprived of the rights of citizenship and excluded from the German national community (*Volksgemeinschaft*). This essentialization of both Aryan and Jew would justify not only the doctrine that all German-speaking peoples should be unified in a single empire, but also the extermination of Gypsies, Jews, Slavs, and other "inferior" individuals and groups in Nazi death camps. Arguing that the Jews, in particular, were a "race of parasites" that "fed on national decay," the Nazis and their collaborators across Europe sought to annihilate the Jews as a people—a "race"—and thereby to secure glory, honor, and power for the German "race." In Nazi Germany, therefore, political violence was validated by a nationalist ideology that collapsed the hyphenated identities of modern political culture into the extremist totalities of existential nationalism and extremist

inclusivism. This attempted to fix forever the "natural" differences and distinctions between "pure" and "impure" "racial" groups.

Legitimacy and Identity

Mass graves resulting from ethno-political violence due to subnational conflicts are found throughout the world—in Rwanda, throughout former Yugoslavia, Cambodia, Burundi, and Darfur, just to mention a few instances. These graves serve as permanent testaments to the human tragedy that occurs whenever political-cultural linkages between nationality (or the values of citizenship and commonality) and ethnicity (or the values of ethnic identity and difference) collapse into a fantasized mind-set that ideologically privileges one national identity group within a nation-state to the exclusion of all others. Excluded identity groups emerge in political cultures once citizenship or nationality becomes a kind of insignia to be bestowed on a few groups but denied to others, especially on the basis of objectified, sometimes racialized, ethnic difference.

Ethno-Political Violence in Guatemala

The most heinous form of mass political violence occurs when states and their agents undertake to annihilate or exterminate populations of individuals deemed eligible for elimination on the basis of collective traits indicative of objectified otherness. Legal scholars use the term **genocide** to refer to these crimes. This concept, coined by Raphael Lemkin, refers to an act that is committed "with the intent to destroy, in whole or in part, a national, ethnical, racial, or religious group, as such," by means of one or more of the following strategies: "killing members of the group; causing serious bodily or mental harm to members of the group; deliberately inflicting on the group conditions of life calculated to bring about its physical destruction in whole or in part; imposing measures intended to prevent births within the group; forcibly transferring children of the group to another group."[44] When states undertake to annihilate a religious, ethnic, or cultural group on the basis of difference, all manner of unspeakable brutalities are unleashed upon victims. For so long as "they" exist as a collective grouping, the fusion between nationality and ethnicity resists total uniformity. Policies of catastrophic annihilation aim not only at political purity, but at a fantasized national ideal in which the hyphenated mediations between ethnicity and nationality in political culture vanish.

The Holocaust and the Rwandan genocide are commonly recognized episodes of systematic annihilation. However, genocide has also occurred in Armenia, Cambodia, Burundi, Bosnia, and Guatemala. The Guatemalan Commission for Historical Clarification has estimated that beginning with the outbreak of "internal armed confrontation in 1962" more than 200,000 civilians were killed or "disappeared" by agents of the Guatemalan government, including the military. Agents of the government also included "civilians to whom it delegated *de jure* or *de facto* authority to act on its behalf, or with its consent, acquiescence, or knowledge"; the Civil Patrol; the army's special counter insurgency force known as *Kaibiles*; the National and Treasury Police; "large land-owners who were granted police functions by the 1936 Penal Code"; and all "other third part[ies] that may have acted under the direction or with the knowledge of state agents."[45] Eighty-three percent of the identified victims were members of the Mayan community, which the army perceived to be a "natural all[y] of the guerrillas" and an internal enemy of the Guatemalan state.[46] The Commission reports that "the human rights violations perpetrated against [ethnic Mayans] demonstrat[ed] an *aggressive racist component* of *extreme cruelty* that led to the *extermination en masse* of defenseless Mayan communities purportedly linked to the guerrillas—including children, women, and the elderly—through methods whose cruelty has outraged the moral conscience of the civilized world.... These massacres and so-called scorched earth operations, *as planned by the State ... [and] committed by agents of the State, especially members of the Army,* resulted in the *complete extermination* of many Mayan communities, along with their homes, cattle, crops, and other elements essential to survival."[47] The Commission concluded that the massacres against the Mayan peoples from 1981 to 1983 constituted "acts of genocide" in which "there is evidence of ... savagery which preceded, accompanied, or occurred after the deaths of victims."[48] Moreover, "the Army destroyed [Mayan] ceremonial centers, sacred places, and cultural symbols.... Language and dress, as well as other elements of cultural identification, were targets of repression.... The legitimate authority structure of the communities was broken; the use of their own norms and procedures to regulate social life and resolve conflicts was prevented; the exercise of Mayan spirituality and the Catholic religion was obstructed, prevented, or repressed; the maintenance and development of the indigenous peoples' way of life and their system of social organization was upset.... Displacement and refuge exacerbated the difficulties of practicing their own culture."[49] The brutality unleashed upon Mayan victims by the Guatemalan army was so extreme as to prompt survivor and Nobel Laureate Rigoberta Menchú to remember the "bad times" in her villages as times when "evil men walk[ed] the earth and sadness [could] hardly be endured."[50]

Each historical episode of mass political violence is a unique combination of torture, torment, concentration, oppression, and/or annihilation. Throughout modern history and across the modern world, these dynamics become apparent whenever and wherever the commonality of nationality fails to anchor difference so that nationality becomes transformed into an exclusivist, inclusivist, or extreme nationalist form of existential purity. Whenever and wherever the hyphen between nationality and ethnicity becomes ideologically collapsed, the potential for mass political violence follows. In such moments, massive political violence produces intense and widespread human suffering in political theaters of cultural hell.

Part IV
The Holocaust, Genocide, and Crimes against Humanity

Political Culture in Violation of Personhood

Chapter 9
The Holocaust

The Uniqueness of the Holocaust

Germany's annihilation of at least six million Jews throughout Europe, reinforced by support from the states occupied by the Nazi military during the Second World War including France, Italy, Hungary, Romania, Poland, Czechoslovakia, Greece, and Austria, stands as an unprecedented level of systematic political violence against a minority of citizens in not merely one, but simultaneously across many nation-states. The Holocaust was perpetrated as a consequence of a political culture framed by the national history of Germany and defined by Nazi racist doctrines and limitless cruelty. But the instruments of death and torment developed in Germany were eventually applied throughout Europe. Sovereign nation-state after sovereign nation-state bore witness to campaigns to make Jewish citizens stateless so that they might be shipped to concentration camps or rounded up for purposes of annihilation. Herein lies the uniqueness of the Holocaust. Ideological objectification of Jewish communities and individuals went beyond the borders of sovereign Germany in a unique genocidal campaign that reached transnational proportions across several sovereign or municipal jurisdictions unlike any other historical instance in modern times. The Holocaust tragically demonstrates how ethnic affiliations and religious practices can be racialized and used as ideological justifications for the dehumanization and demonization of a people on the basis of minor differences made large by fraudulent mystifications.

Anti-Semitism within the Nazi Leadership

The anti-Semitism of leaders of the Nazi Party in Germany during the interwar period and World War II is well documented. For many years scholars have linked the systematic political violence perpetrated during the Holocaust to the effects of Hitler's personal role in fomenting virulent anti-Semitism in Germany. Hitler's hatred of the Jews may have stemmed from inner fears regarding allegations over a possible strain of Jewish lineage in his familial heritage, or perhaps it extended from his contempt for the Jewish doctor who failed to prevent the early death of his mother from cancer. Some psychoanalytic theorists suggest that Hitler's hatred for the Jews originated in the dread of anxiety and unworthiness. Robert Waite hypothesizes that Hitler's "fears were so many, so great, and so unbearable, he felt a great need to consolidate them all into one single fear that he could recognize, one that would explain all others, and one upon which he could release all his pent-up anger and hatred. He found it ... in the Jewish people."[1]

Whatever its source, as Neil Kressel writes, "if there was any one thing in which Hitler truly believed, it was anti-Semitism. When he said, 'The Jew's skull will be smashed by Germanic will,' twenty-one years before the construction of the death camps, he gave voice to his most sincere wish."[2] According to historian Lucy Dawidowicz, "the Jews inhabited Hitler's mind. He believed that they were the source of all evil, misfortune, and tragedy.... War and famine, financial distress and sudden death, defeat and sinfulness—all could be explained by the presence of that single factor in the universe."[3]

Hitler was, of course, not alone in his hatred of the Jews. Other Nazi leaders displayed similar rabidly extreme anti-Semitic beliefs and behaviors. As Ron Rosenbaum writes, Reinhard Heydrich

> had become so tormented by the fear of the "Jew within" that one night, in a drunken fit, he stared into a mirror, thought he actually glimpsed the shadowy Jew within somehow emerge in his reflection, and promptly fired his pistol into the mirror image, hoping to extinguish it. Unable to extinguish the doubt about a Jew within, the logic of this theory goes, Heydrich had to prove his purity by engineering the extermination of the Jews of Europe.... [As Himmler stated] Heydrich's devotion to the Final Solution came from the "fact" that he had "overcome the Jew in himself... and had swung over to the other side. He was convinced that the Jewish elements in his blood were damnable; he hated the blood which played him so false. The Fuhrer could really have picked no better man than Heydrich for the campaign against the Jews."[4]

In Heydrich we see the trappings of anxiety, the process of narcissistic self-rejection but also self-glorification, and his attempt to overcome this by objectifying Jews in ways that demonized them. To try to understand the Holocaust is to comprehend that the prejudices and even hatreds of a few individuals, however politically powerful, cannot explain mass atrocity and political violence. Explaining the Holocaust requires examination of the historic "moment" that set the stage for the takeover in Germany of the Nazi Party and the implementation of the Final Solution by ordinary citizens who, despite their lack of any particular sense of anti-Semitism, willingly participated in the systematic effort to annihilate the Jewish people.

The Preconditions of Genocide

Absent the particular historical conditions that provoked certain resentments and fears in what may be referenced as German collective consciousness in the early part of the twentieth century, particularly regarding Germany's defeat in the First World War, the anti-Semitic political ideology crafted by Hitler and later disseminated by the Nazi apparatus would likely have fallen on deaf ears. Prior to the rise of the Nazi Party, the pugnacious anti-Semitism so common across Russia and Eastern Europe failed to resonate with Germans, who had lived alongside their Jewish neighbors for generations, anchored in solidarity by a sense of common nationality if not common religion.

However, Germany was in nearly every way a latecomer to nation-state consolidation. It made the transition from dynastic kingdoms and principalities to a centralized modern sovereign nation-state later than its European neighbors. It industrialized later than rival European powers, leading to concerns about economic sustainability and prosperity. And it was among the last of the European states to secure an overseas empire, thus receiving the "leftover" colonies that provided very little in the way of resources but that remained costly to maintain. In the years immediately following its unification as a single nation-state, German national collective identity suffered from a sense of status insecurity borne by fears that it was falling behind other European powers that had long been established as unified nation-states. Beginning with the policies of Bismarck in the last years of the nineteenth century, Germany sought to catch up with other European powers, particularly Great Britain, by imitating their "modern" characteristics. Germany thus undertook to construct a large navy, a highly mechanized army, a prominent industrial sector, an (admittedly small) overseas

KEY CONCEPTS

Genocide

The term **genocide** was coined by Raphael Lemkin in 1944. It combines the Greek word *genos* (meaning race or people) with the Latin *cide* (meaning to kill). He created the word to refer both to the annihilation of the Armenians by the Turkish government during World War I and to the Holocaust committed by the Nazis against the Jews during World War II. Since 1944, numerous genocides and near-genocides or crimes against humanity have occurred around the world, including those in Indonesia (1965), Cambodia (1975–1979), Guatemala (1981–1983), Bosnia (1992), and Rwanda (1994), as well as others previously mentioned in south Asia during the partition of India and Pakistan and in course of the emergence of Bangladesh.

Since the Nuremberg Trials, the international community has considered genocide a crime against international order and humanity. On December 9, 1948, the General Assembly of the United Nations ratified the **Convention on the Prevention and Punishment of the Crime of Genocide (CPPCG)**. The signatories affirmed that genocide was a crime under international law, one they were now prepared to prevent and obligated to punish despite the roles of sovereignty and the norms of nonintervention in the international system. The Convention defined genocide as "any of the following acts committed with intent to destroy, in whole or in part, a national, ethnical, racial, or religious group, as such."[5] Genocide, conspiracy to commit genocide, direct

continued

empire, and a powerful centralized nation-state government in order to secure its position as a Great Power of Europe.

The First World War was Germany's chance to establish itself as the predominant political, military, and economic power of continental Europe. Having entered the conflict certain of its impending victory, Germany employed the most modern technologies and strategies against competitor European states. Its defeat in this great struggle, a defeat that left Germany militarily conquered, economically bereft, and socially humiliated, intensified the power insecurity that had characterized Germany in the years prior to the conflict. In the interwar period and during the Second World War, the German government would give new life to the desire to be advanced and powerful, transforming a prewar objective into a postwar obsession. Ultimately this translated into the genocidal campaign

and public incitement to commit genocide, attempt to commit genocide, and complicity in genocide were all deemed punishable crimes under the agreement. The convention was first enforced in 1998 when the **International Criminal Tribunal for Rwanda** found Jean-Paul Akayesu guilty of nine counts of genocide. Two days later Jean Kambanda, the prime minister of Rwanda during the genocide, plead guilty to genocide. He was sentenced to life in prison. The first state to be found in violation of the CPPCG was Serbia. Although the **International Court of Justice** ruled that the Serbian state did not commit genocide in Bosnia, it did rule that it failed to prevent the crimes against humanity waged in and around the city of Srebrenica and that it failed to transfer persons accused of genocide to the **International Criminal Tribunal for the Former Yugoslavia** for trial.

In the early 2000s the international community created the **International Criminal Court (ICC)** as a permanent tribunal to prosecute individuals for genocide, crimes against humanity, war crimes, and the crime of aggression. The **Rome Statute** that created the ICC adopted the definition of genocide from the CPPCG. It entered into force on July 1, 2002, for all signatories, but as of 2013 had not yet completed a full trial of anyone accused of committing genocide. The 122 signatories include almost all Latin American and European states, Australia, Canada, much of sub-Saharan Africa, Japan, and South Korea, but do not include the United States, China, Russia, India, or countries in the Middle East or North Africa. For this reason, the legitimacy and effectiveness of the ICC remains to be seen. As of late 2013, potential or ongoing trials focused on incidents in the Congo, the Central African Republic, Kenya, and the Ivory Coast.

within the national life of Germany to exterminate a people who had become inhumanly objectified as the cause of Germany's "primitive" backward condition.

The Treaty of Versailles, which ended World War I, established strict limitations on the German government, economy, and military that were designed to prevent the remilitarization of Germany. Germany lost key industrial holdings in Alsace-Lorraine, limiting German access to iron, coal, and steel. In addition, Germany was forced to pay reparations to France and Great Britain and, according to the terms of the now infamous "War Guilt Clause," to accept full responsibility for the First World War. Not only did these terms lead to a sense of national vulnerability and humiliation, they effectively limited the modernization that many Germans desired in their attempt to imitate the levels of military preparedness and economic prowess of the now victorious European powers. Thus, it was the historical conditions of

post–World War I Germany, intensified by the onslaught of the Great Depression, that set the stage for the rise of the Nazi Party and the Holocaust.

The German Nazi Party was founded in the years following Germany's defeat in the First World War. Built upon an ideology that emphasized the failure of democracy, the inadequacies of laissez-faire capitalism, the racial purity of the German people, and the inherent inferiority of "races" of non-German descent, Nazi rhetoric appealed to Germans who saw as contemptible the terms of the Treaty of Versailles, the policies of the Weimar government, and the prominence of Jewish Germans throughout the political, economic, and cultural fabric of interwar Germany. But despite the fact that the Nazi message appealed to the lower middle class—the farmers, public servants, and small businessmen—the party would not likely have attained widespread political power had it not been for the Great Depression. As Kressel writes of pre–World War II Germany, "freedom had not brought modern people a positive sense of their potentialities but had rather increased their sense of powerlessness."[6] Kressel continues, "these pressures ... had especially overwhelmed lower middle-class Germans" who became the rank and file of Hitler's organization.[7]

Thus it was the complete collapse of the German economy—the mass unemployment, the widespread business failures, and the hyperinflation—combined with the inability of the Weimar government and its dominant parties to formulate an effective solution that prompted widespread national support for the Nazi Party and brought Hitler and his political apparatus to power in 1933. Upon assuming control of the German government, the Nazi Party, its leaders, and its members were positioned to implement a campaign of radical modernization that would transform the German political apparatus, the German military, the German economy, and, most importantly, German political culture in ways that would lend themselves to the implementation of systematic applications of violence in the annihilation of the Jews.

Nazi Racist Ideology: Aryanism and Objectification

The Nazi Party advanced the idea of a German national community unified by the purity of the Aryan race, a national community free of social divisions and party lines and, most importantly, free of Jews (*judenfrei*). Though the Nazi Party gained support, particularly in southern Germany, from 1919 to 1923, popular enthusiasm fell sharply after the failed Beer Hall Putsch of 1923 and the subsequent imprisonment of the "face" and "voice" of the movement, Adolf Hitler. Following his release from prison in 1924, Hitler restructured the Nazi

Party, establishing a new leadership and tightening control over members and message alike. Thereafter, Nazi ideology elevated notions of racial purity, Aryan superiority, and anti-Semitism in ways that foreshadowed the political violence to come.

Nazi ideology racialized German nationality as belonging only to those who could prove Aryan genetic ancestry and "bloodlines." In doing so it sought to eliminate cultural and social space for an understanding of ethnicity attached to hyphenated or hybrid identity constructions. These might otherwise have been anchored to a political culture grounded by a sense of commonality among all German citizens linked together by a single nationality alongside various forms of ethnicity attached to cultural forms of difference. While ostensibly designed to foster national political and cultural unity, Nazi racialization of nationality limited the enjoyment of nationality, and ultimately citizenship, to members of a fantasized Aryan race at the exclusion of all others. On this basis, the Nazis constructed the myths of a fixed, naturalized, subordinated, and objectified "other" so that Jewish nationals in Germany would be made to carry the fault for German national failures, especially during World War I and the Great Depression. In time, Nazi ideology racialized the Jewish religion in ways that extended traditional forms of anti-Semitism into policies of objectification, concentration, and demonization. The ultimate aim was to perpetuate the illusion that in annihilating the Jews of Germany the German nation could be "purified" racially and genetically and made "clean" for Aryanism to reign forever. This was the absolute aim and intent of the Third Reich: to impose this eugenic racism in order to deny the Jews of Germany a political-cultural "space" for Jewish identity and to prevent any ethnicity of "difference" to thrive as a national community within the cultural frames of German nationality or nation-statehood.

Under the leadership of Joseph Goebbels, the German regime launched a massive propaganda campaign designed to establish the "natural" differences between Aryan Germans and Jews. This was done to dehumanize the Jews as a race set apart, and in order to assert that they were the party responsible for Germany's affliction and the very "race" whose annihilation would guarantee the survival and prosperity of the German *volk*. Through propaganda, the Nazis constructed a binary opposition between German and Jew that privileged Aryanism as the face of genetic superiority while subordinating Judaism as the face of the primitive other. Unlike the possible hyphenated identities that anchor ethnic differences to the commonalities of nationality and citizenship, the dual racializations of German nationality and of the Jewish religion made it conceptually impossible for an individual to be simultaneously "German" and "Jewish." This would facilitate the legal distinctions and exclusions that followed.

The Eternal Jew and other Nazi racist propaganda projects misinformed the German people that "in the course of centuries from the Oriental far eastern racial mixture with Negroid admixture the ultimate mongrelized Jews developed. Foreign from us Europeans born of totally different racial elements they differ from us in body and most of all in soul."[8] The Jew was objectified as a "group-thing" wholly separate and thus "naturally" and racially distinct. Nazi genetic mythology linked its racialized distortions of Jewish people to fears over how Jews would render the Aryan race impure by polluting it with the "Negro" elements. This not only built on Nazi anti-Semitism but fueled popularly held conceptions that persons of African blood were naturally and racially inferior to persons of white European blood. The Nazis associated the "Jewish race" with the death of nations, linking the "Eternal Jew" to the very turmoil faced by the German people in the years following the First World War. The Nazis spewed ugly forms of objectification replete with symbolic visual imagery in the propaganda films of the time to try to prove that Jewish people "infected" the souls of nations. The Nazi propaganda machine sought to demonize the Jewish people, portraying them as infectious so that their eventual annihilation would seem as necessary as the extermination of disease-carrying vermin.

Thus the Nazi regime devised exclusionary policies and applied a fraudulent set of nonscientific genetic practices purported to be able to distinguish between Aryan and Jew. Persons who could be identified as Jews on account of their religious practices or familial or cultural ties were quickly branded. On the basis of a made-up and delusionary "science," the Nazi bureaucracy developed a classification system to identify members of the Jewish people on the basis of racial features. Religious or ethnic affiliations critical to Jewish identity became factors in excluding Jews, but the Nazis reveled in their eugenic fantasies that emphasized physical and biological markers. Nazi pseudoscience also evaluated individuals suspected of being Jewish according to measurements etched on score cards reminiscent of op-scan metrics. The so-called data were fed into machines provided by IBM to determine whether the individuals in question were of the Jewish or Aryan "race." Once identified as Jewish, a person was forced to wear the Star of David on his or her clothing, a distinct message to members of the German, now Aryan, nation that such individuals were no longer nationals or citizens of Germany but rather a race apart.

The Nazi regime, having established the racial distinction between "German" and "Jew" and a system for the identification of the Jewish "race" throughout Germany, launched a second propaganda campaign. This was dedicated to the propagation of the notion that German Jews represented the "enemy within" Germany, an enemy responsible for Germany's defeat at the

end of World War I. At the core of this propaganda was the false assertion that the Jews had "stabbed Germany in the back." In fact, many Jews had served in the German army during the war with distinction and often with heroic valor. The Nazis argued that Jewish leaders were responsible for Germany's late consolidation, industrialization, and colonization; that Jewish bankers were responsible for the hyperinflation and economic collapse of the 1930s; that Jewish political leaders were the "November Criminals" who had "stabbed the German nation in the back" leading to the "false defeat" in World War I; that Jewish lawyers were responsible for the terms and conditions of the despised Treaty of Versailles; that Jewish politicians were responsible for the failures of the Weimar government during the interwar period; and so on. According to these misrepresentations the Jewish people alone bore responsibility for Germany's woes. This ignored the patriotism of German Jews. It disregarded the enormous contributions of the Jewish community in Germany to the pre–World War I modernization of Germany, to Germany's struggle during the First World War, and to the rebuilding of Germany during the interwar period. Once such lies were accepted, however, it would only be a step away for the Nazis to assert that complete annihilation of the Jewish "race"—first in Germany and later across Europe—would guarantee German national security, prosperity, pride, and survival. In this corrupted way, racial identification, spatial concentration, and ultimately industrial extermination became policies that were justified not only on the basis of anti-Semitic ideology, but also as a matter of national urgency linked to the continued existence of the German nation-state and its Aryan people. The Jewish "race" became the "enemy within" that had to be eliminated for the German people to become purified, and purification was necessary for the German nation-state and its people to survive in the modern world.

The Final Solution: Spatialization from Concentration to Annihilation

As the Nazi Party and regime gained increasing control over the state apparatus between 1932 and 1945, it incrementally but systematically eliminated the cultural and political "space" for German Jewish citizens in Germany. In 1933 Jewish doctors, lawyers, and businesses were boycotted under German law. In 1935 the Nuremberg Laws prohibited marriage between Jews and non-Jews, banned Jews from all professional jobs, forcibly segregated Germany's Jewish and non-Jewish population, required that Jews wear the Star of David, and, most importantly, stripped Jews of their German citizenship, thus legally abolishing

hyphenated forms of national identity construction. Nationality in citizenship became a matter of Aryan racial ethnicity and racial ethnicity was transformed into racialized distinctions. Also in 1935, long before the first deportations to concentration and death camps, the 1935 Reich Citizenship Law stripped German Jews of their German citizenship in order to draw the strict legal distinction between "nationals" and "Reich citizens" that afforded only the latter with full civil and political rights. Here is another example of how citizenship and nationality become linked together. The Jews were made stateless noncitizens on account of Nazi law and thus were no longer able to satisfy the normative standards of German nationality. But what were German Jews to do with the only nationality most had ever known or experienced? They were German nationals. But once their religious identity had become racialized so did their nationality. But a racialized nationality represented a contradiction in terms. Once stateless, German Jews lost all rights to enjoy citizenship and thus all the benefits of nationality. This was what the Nazis wanted: to make the Jews stateless and nonnational so that they were no longer able to participate in civil society on the road to ending their rights to civil existence. This provides another example of the dangers of combining nationality and ethnicity especially in ways that racialize identity constructions.

In 1939 the Night of Broken Glass (*kristallnacht*) marked widespread government-coordinated attacks on Jewish homes, businesses, and synagogues, indicating a transition from oppression to violence that would soon characterize Nazi policies toward members of the German Jewish community. In 1939 deportations of German Jews began, first to ghettos and later to concentration and death camps. As Elie Wiesel recalls, "from that moment on, everything happened very quickly. The race toward death had begun. . . . Jews were prohibited from leaving their residences for three days, under penalty of death. . . . A Jew was henceforth forbidden to own gold, jewelry, or any valuables. . . . Every Jew had to wear the yellow star. . . . New edicts were already being issued. . . . We no longer had the right to frequent restaurants or cafes, to travel by rail, to attend synagogue, to be on the streets after six o'clock in the evening. . . . Then came the ghettos," and then came the deportations to the camps.[9] At least six million Jews were killed by the Nazis in the Holocaust in an episode of genocide that represents the only historical example of the application not only of person-to-person killing, but also the use of industrial methods in the state-sponsored annihilation of an entire people, whether considered as a religious, ethnic, racial, or cultural group.

The Holocaust stands alone in its objective to eliminate all Jews everywhere by means of coordinated campaigns using modern technology, not just in Germany, but across many sovereign states. This process deployed a series of techniques:

the racialization of the Jewish religion; the incremental and forced displacement of Jews into ghettos and camps; the application of the German bureaucratic apparatus to the planning and execution of the Final Solution; the use of railroad networks to deport Jewish people objectified and dehumanized as "freight" bound for extermination; the use of cattle cars as the instrument and eventual symbol of the "box" of death; the application of assembly-line methodologies to annihilation; the use of gas chambers to expedite mass killing; and the utilization of crematoria and incineration pits to dispose of the remains of humans numbering in the millions. Racial objectification of a subaltern "other" in an attempt to justify the application of industrial technologies for the purpose of destroying an entire people demonstrates how the political culture of a nation-state can be taken to an extreme form. The consequence in Nazi Germany was that Jewish members of Germany's body politic, along with others such as Gypsies, homosexuals, and the disabled, were demonized and deemed humanly undesirable in accordance with Nazi eugenic fantasies. They became ideologically objectified and subjected to diabolical designs of mass murder. Their tragedy, stoked in the fate of satanic ashes, remains forever etched in historical memory.

The Nazi regime isolated the Jewish "race" within the body politic of the German nation-state, first by requiring that Jews wear the Star of David as a "racial" marker of difference and exclusion, and later by expelling Jews from their homes and relocating them to closed-off quarters or ghettos. This process again illustrates how racialized identity constructions culminate in efforts to dislocate, displace, and, ultimately, contain objectified victims within isolated spaces. The policies enacted upon the Jewish people ultimately took the form of complete extermination within spatially concentrated killing camps. The historical turning points from exclusion and concentration to annihilation began with the adoption by the Nazi regime of a series of policies known as the Final Solution (*Endlösung*). First established at the Wannsee Conference in 1942, held at a villa near Potsdam in eastern Germany, and chaired by Reinhard Heydrich, the Final Solution refers to the totalitarian effort at mass "purification" of the German Reich by means of the complete annihilation of a people identified (objectified) as such. This phrase, "as such," would later come to represent a critical component in the legal definition of genocide as stated in the **Convention on the Prevention and Punishment of the Crime of Genocide (CPPCG)**. In its pursuit of the Final Solution, the Nazi regime created a centralized apparatus or a "state" within the German sovereign state designed to oversee the annihilation of the Jewish "race" by the most efficient means possible. The Final Solution became the primary objective of the Nazi regime. Its objectives overtook and subordinated the established institutions of the German state that now provided Heinrich

Himmler and Heydrich with the resources necessary to identify, contain, concentrate, and eliminate the Jews. The implementation of the Final Solution fell to the *Kripo* (Criminal Police), who conducted mass arrests of Jews in the name of the German nation, as well as the Gestapo (Secret Police), the *Einsatzgruppen*

ALTERNATE PERSPECTIVES

Nationality, Nationalism, and Citizenship

The concepts **nation**, **state**, **nationality**, and **citizenship** each refer to separate but connected aspects of political culture, but it is not uncommon for these terms to be misused in everyday conversation or in the news media. For example, "state" and "nation" are almost always used interchangeably in colloquial speech. Similarly, many people use "nationality" when they mean "ethnicity" and vice versa. As we have previously noted, "citizenship" refers to the legal status of any person granted membership within a sovereign nation-state whereas "nationality" refers to the range of associations and affiliations that arise from the civil enjoyment of citizenship within a sovereign state.

Benedict Anderson's definition of nation is often cited in the literature on the subject. Anderson writes that a nation is an "imagined political community—and imagined as both inherently limited and sovereign."[10] Anderson states that these entities are imagined because while members of a nation do not know all the other members, each shares socially constructed ideas that are unique to and a product of that nation.

Nation-building is an ongoing challenge for modern states. It is not uncommon for national societies to construct exclusivist notions of national identity that prevent members of racial, ethnic, economic, or religious minorities from full membership in the nation. In addition, however, many states, particularly those that face ethnic, economic, or political turmoil, fail to extend the benefits of nationhood to all legal citizens of the state. They might create classes of citizenship that extend varying degrees of rights or privileges to citizens on the basis of their ethnic, racial, economic, political, or religious affiliation. Or they may deny some groups the benefits of citizenship all together. When this happens, when a state government strips a group of its citizenship on the basis of its difference, it becomes likely that the members of the stateless group will be targeted by the state apparatus for ethnic cleansing or annihilation. This was the case in Nazi Germany as well as in Rwanda, Cambodia, Armenia, and Bosnia.

("task forces" or "intervention groups"), and the SS (Black Order). They administered the concentration and death camps with the help of a wide range of bureaucrats who acted as a support structure for the Final Solution. These desk chair or bureaucratic genocidal perpetrators notoriously came to be personified by Adolf Eichmann. He eventually would argue at his trial in Jerusalem that he never personally killed Jews. Nonetheless, he was found primarily responsible for organizing the railroad system and schedule that carried so many innocents by cattle car to their torments and deaths.

Collective Death and Torment Become Normalized

The Holocaust was not perpetrated by the Nazi leadership alone. On the contrary, the systematic annihilation of more than six million Jews would not have been possible if not for the cooperation and active participation of thousands of rank and file Nazi soldiers, bureaucrats, and ordinary German citizens manifestly taken in by Aryan fantasies and the paranoid delusions of a demonized other threatening their survival. For this reason, the Holocaust cannot be explained merely by the anti-Semitic delusions of Hitler, Heydrich, and their associates. What, then, prompted so many German citizens to join in the task of annihilation?

Among the most famous of midlevel Nazi bureaucrats was Adolf Eichmann. He helped to pioneer the "I was just following orders" defense during his trial in Jerusalem. Eichmann was responsible for coordinating the deportation of the Jews from ghettos to concentration and extermination camps. He oversaw the train schedules, allocated resources and personnel, and facilitated the annihilation of a people toward whom he claimed to harbor no ill will. Hannah Arendt chronicled the Eichmann trial, producing a "report on the banality of evil." As Amos Elon writes in his introduction to Arendt's book, "evil, as [Arendt] saw it, need not be committed only by demonic monsters but—with disastrous effect—by morons and imbeciles as well."[11] Eichmann's "brainlessness" that "predisposed him to becoming the faceless bureaucrat of death and one of the worst criminals of all time" was compounded by his "moral and intellectual shallowness, his inner void."[12] He "personified neither hatred or madness nor an insatiable thirst for blood, but something far worse, the faceless nature of Nazi evil itself, within a closed system run by pathological gangsters, aimed at dismantling the human personality of its victims."[13] With Eichmann as an example, Arendt controversially distinguishes criminality from political evil. She does so by emphasizing the relevance of discursive practices symbolized by legal norms that undergird cultural as well as ideological meanings as opposed to the realities of what she calls the

"ordinary criminal, who can shield himself effectively against the reality of a non-criminal world only within the narrow limits of his gang."[14] Arendt writes that Eichmann "needed only to recall the past in order to feel assured that he was not lying and that he was not deceiving himself, for he and the world he lived in had once been in perfect harmony."[15] She goes on to emphasize that this self-deception was not particular to Eichmann but was instead a wholly cultural and ideological phenomenon. She writes that "the practice of self-deception has become so common, almost a moral prerequisite for survival, that even now, eighteen years after the collapse of the Nazi regime, when most of the specific content of its lies has been forgotten, it is sometimes difficult not to believe that the mendacity has become an integral part of the German national character."[16] But what was it that the German people had so deluded themselves about that made them willing to participate in the violence that Eichmann symbolizes? Arendt refers to a slogan, "the battle of destiny for the German people," that represents a rallying cry typical of German political culture during the Nazi regime. The slogan suggested "that [the Holocaust] was a matter of life and death for the Germans, who must annihilate their enemies or be annihilated."[17] Nazi political culture internalized, legitimated, and perpetuated the ideologies of collective objectification necessary to justify ordinary citizens' participation in massive political violence.

Arendt teaches us that when the perpetrators of massive political violence practice their horrible craft, they dive emotionally into a kind of sadistic stupor or state of mind and being that anesthetizes them against human empathy or feeling, let alone compassion. In a sense this is the key to an understanding of the inhumanity of perpetrators bent on genocide, crimes against humanity, wars of aggression, war crimes, or systematic gross violations of human rights. Such national or collective behaviors and state policies defy explanation and understanding. Yet they retain their significance precisely because they occur repeatedly in the modern history of the nation-state. Empathy and compassion for others are preeminently symbolic of what it means to be a human being among other human beings. Mass killing and torment—whenever and wherever they happen—represent practices of nation-states that contravene all shards of social benevolence. They are profoundly contrary to any shred of moral principle or attachment. The history of nation-states reveals that collective desire for social justice and humanitarianism, however powerful, surrenders repeatedly to moral indifference and spiritual hardness, as exemplified at the time of writing by the horrors of civil war in Syria and in Iraq. At such critical junctures, simple feelings for the plight and suffering of others become subsumed by the hard core of indifference and unfeeling. As Wiesel has eloquently argued, indifference is the greatest moral failure.[18]

Arendt describes Eichmann's moment at the Wannsee Conference where the Final Solution was determined as a "Pontius Pilate feeling." In the call to genocide issued by the Wannsee Conference, sanctioned as it was by "not only Hitler, not only Heydrich or the 'sphinx' Muller, not just the S.S. or the Party, but the elite of the good old Civil Service [who] were vying and fighting with each other for the honor of taking the lead in these 'bloody' matters," Eichmann found himself "free of all guilt," his doubts about "such a bloody solution through violence" having been dispelled.[19] Perpetrators become frozen cadaverous beings within the realm of their own spiritual psyches once any form of genocidal violence becomes implemented. The Nazi regime turned "morality" on its head by representing the Final Solution as "right" and all efforts to resist or impede the efficiency of the Final Solution as "wrong." This secured the support of the midlevel bureaucrats who managed the process. Eichmann continued to maintain throughout his trial that "whatever he did he did, as far as he could see, as a law-abiding citizen.... He did his *duty*, as he told the police and the court over and over again; he not only obeyed *orders*, he also obeyed the *law*.... In addition to performing what he conceived to be the duties of a law-abiding citizen, he had also acted upon orders—always so careful to be 'covered'—he became completely muddled, and ended by stressing alternatively the virtues and the vices of blind obedience, or the obedience of corpses, *Kadavergehorsam*, as he himself called it."[20] Indeed, Eichmann went to his death insisting that he had done nothing wrong, that he had broken no laws and spilled no blood but that he had instead executed his duties as a German citizen, officer, and patriot and thus lawfully to the best of his ability; that he might be found guilty of a crime, in this case the crime of genocide, on the basis of his actions was a concept wholly beyond his capacity to grasp.

When political violence at the behest of the political culture of nation-states is done, it is implemented collectively. Those who respond to the call to violent practices do so together, sometimes even beyond moral strictures in a realm of ideological practice, sanctioned by political culture, triggered by authority, and often galvanized by the energies of many other citizens who have succumbed to the calls of hatred. In genocide and crimes against humanity, heartless anonymity suppresses guilt, conscience, moral responsibility, humane obligation, and individual self-reflection in favor of goose-stepping armies or paramilitary gangs and thugs. The world today is witness to such events in the eastern parts of the Ukraine where Ukrainian nationality and Russian ethnicity come into conflict, in the Central African Republic between rival ethnicized groups acting in the name of Christianity or Islam, and in South Sudan where rival kinship groupings now ethnicized and impressed into military or quasi-militia service perpetuate

large-scale violations leading to the displacement of millions of persons. Such violent actions assume not only an ideological and political aspect but an aesthetic dimension as well, as demonstrated by uniforms, insignia, mass rallies, and rituals of bonding. This too contributes to a sense of self-evasion through collective practices that wash away individual conscience and compassion for others in favor of brutality and contempt.

Political violence is a spiraling descent into the currents of psychic iconography where fantasy and ideology, shaped by the aesthetic of public display and discursive hate, become the interpersonal realities of those who answer the call to perpetrate annihilation, crimes against humanity, or large-scale violations. This is the horror of horror in behaviors contributing to genocide and crimes against humanity—perpetrators come to think that they escape from moral responsibility as human beings in favor of a higher law that demands the transgression of the humanity of others. Perpetrators appear to justify genocide, crimes against humanity, gross violations of human rights, and war crimes on the grounds that such violence is pardoned by political cultures grounded in ideological sanctions and the authority of the nation-state. This represents a profoundly fraudulent misrepresentation of the relationship between personhood and collective political life. Political culture in the making of modern nation-states must not ever serve to justify the kinds of subversions of human agency borne by genocidal and inhuman violent actions.

Genocide and the Practices of Annihilation

After the German annexation of Poland, the Nazi government began the forced deportation of Jewish persons to concentration and death camps, thus transforming Nazi ideology into officially authorized public policy. The German bureaucratic organization created a language of euphemism as instructed by the dictates of the Final Solution. This referred to Jews by adopting a logistical language; as a result, Jews were referred to as "volume," "freight," and "weight" to be transported to central locations by any means. The Nazi regime established a vast array of internment, concentration, and killing camps throughout Europe. Overwhelmingly, concentration and death camps were located in Eastern Europe, primarily for practical purposes: first, most Jewish population centers were in Eastern Europe; second, the Nazis found willing collaborators among the governments of Eastern European nation-states and willing executioners (to use Daniel Goldhagen's phrase[21]) among the anti-Semitic segments of the populations throughout Eastern Europe; third, the Nazi regime sought to

"invisibilize" the Final Solution by locating many of the major camps outside of Germany. Charged with the task of annihilating the Jewish people of Europe, concentration and death camps became the instruments of death and torment in the execution of the Final Solution.

The Nazi regime used railroads to transport Jews to concentration and death camps. Thousands upon thousands of Jews were packed into cattle cars and were forced to endure oppressive heat or cold for days on end without food, water, or sanitation facilities. The hermetically sealed cattle car represented the harbinger of death and degradation for many Jews during the Holocaust, rail convoy after convoy. According to Wiesel, "a convoy of cattle cars was waiting. The Hungarian police made us climb into the cars, eighty persons in each one. They handed us some bread, a few pails of water. They checked the bars on the windows to make sure they would not come loose. The cars were sealed ... a prolonged whistle pierced the air ... the wheels began to grind.... We were on our way."[22] Other survivors of the Holocaust have similar memories. Ruth Minsky Sender writes, "on the tracks, freight trains are waiting. They are cattle cars.... To them we are animals.... They want to make sure that these animals cannot escape.... Days turn to night and nights into days again.... The stench of human secretion mixed with the sweltering heat makes it hard to breathe.... The buckets used as toilets are overflowing.... People faint from the smell, from the heat, from exhaustion."[23] Upon arrival in the camps, the living crawled from the cars; the dead were pulled out. For some the horror was over. For others the horror was just beginning. But for most horror found new meaning in the gas chambers and crematoria.

Upon disembarking from the trains, the Jews were sorted into binary categories—the first composed of healthy individuals or skilled workers who might live to form an army of slaves to labor in concentration camps; the second composed of the elderly, the young, the sick, or the weak who would go immediately to the gas chambers. Those selected for labor would endure physical torment as they were literally worked to death to advance the German war effort. Nearly starved, mercilessly beaten and whipped by camp guards, and subject to any form of sadistic torture devised by camp guards and commanders often acting in competition with each other to see who could devise the most cruel, the most satanic of agonies, prisoners served as a continuous stream of humanity with new arrivals replacing the dead, the sick, the injured, and the weak. One camp liberator of prisoners observed, "when you see them, there's nothing to distinguish them, you know. Shaved heads and sunken cheeks. There's no way. It's hard to even see them as human. Under the circumstances, you try to avoid seeing them too much. It's hard to do."[24]

Inside the concentration camps, the Nazi bureaucracy applied systematic branding on human flesh for purposes of identification and categorization. Each prisoner was tattooed with a number representative of homeland and arrival date. This designation replaced the prisoner's name for the remainder of his or her time in the camp. This desecration attempted to erase the names and thus the humanity of prisoners. Wiesel recalls this violation: "The three 'veteran' prisoners, needles in hand, tattooed numbers on our left arms. I became A-7713. From then on, I had no other name."[25] In response, some prisoners, like Riva Minska, clutched to their names as a lifeline. Years later Minska recalls the guards' orders interspersed with her own resolve to keep faith: "Prisoner Number 55082. Forget your name! Remember your number! How can I forget my name, Riva Minska? How will my family find me? How will we find one another when this is over? I must remember my number. But I must not forget my name. I must not let them wipe out my name."[26] Other prisoners, however, gradually found themselves reduced to the very numbers forced upon them by the Nazi apparatus. As Primo Levi wrote of a fellow prisoner, "He is Null Achtzehn. He is not called anything except that, Zero Eighteen, the last three figures of his entry number; as if everyone was aware that only a man is worthy of a name, and that Null Achtzehn is no longer a man. I think that even he has forgotten his name."[27] Levi referred to those prisoners who had lost the will to live, who had joined what he called the "living dead" as *Muselmann*, literally, those who had surrendered to the will of a power they recognized to be more powerful than themselves. The *Muselmann* is a prisoner who has lost the will to survive, who has given in to despair, anguish, and hopelessness. As Bronislaw Goscinki recalls of life in the camps, "You could see *muselmanner* everywhere: skinny, dirty figures, their skin and faces blackened, their gaze gone, their eyes hollowed out, their clothes threadbare, filthy and stinking.... They had no illusions about ever going home.... They did their work without thinking; they moved around without thinking, dreaming only of having a place in the line in which they'd be given more soup, more thick soup."[28]

But most Jews who were deported to the camps did not become prisoners. Instead they were killed en masse in gas chambers, their bodies disposed of in crematoria, in Treblinka, Chelmo, Maidenel, Belzec, Sobibor, and Auschwitz-Birkenau. Unlike concentration camps that killed primarily by means of attrition or corporeal torture, killing camps existed to annihilate Jews as efficiently and systematically as possible. These camps accomplished large-scale extermination by means of industrial methods and instruments in accordance with the logics of efficiency and industrial "production." According to a Treblinka guard, the camp would, during peak hours, "process" 12,000 to 15,000 Jews every day.

When asked to describe the process applied to the liquidation of the Jews, the same guard reported that a train would arrive at Treblinka station at 6:00 a.m., another at noon, and a third in the late evening. Thirty to fifty cars would arrive at once divided into sections of ten, twelve, or fifteen cars. On the tops of the cattle cars often were Ukrainian or Latvian guards, and on the platform were Jews from the Blue Squad as well as German and Ukrainian guards who expedited the unloading of the cattle cars. Jews, stripped of their clothes by the Red Squad, were herded into the "funnel," a corridor approximately thirteen feet wide bordered by barbed wire and screened by branches from pine trees that stretched between the train platforms and the gas chambers. Ukrainian guards armed with clubs and whips drove dozens of Jews into the gas chambers at a time. Dead bodies were often carried to the crematoria by other Jewish prisoners. Wiesel remembers, "not far from us, flames, huge flames, were rising from a ditch. Something was being burned there. A truck drew close and unloaded its hold: small children. Babies! Yes, I did see this, with my own eyes ... children thrown into the flames."[29] In two hours "it was all over."[30]

Survivors of the Holocaust bear the scars of political violence, their minds, hearts, and spirits standing as living testaments to the horrors of the Final Solution and to their resilient victory over it. From Nazi ideology that established a racialized binary opposition between "German" and "Jew" to the implementation of the Final Solution, Hitler's anti-Semitism represents an example of how the political culture of a nation-state can become genocidal in intent and execution. Had the Nazi Party, building on national collective anxieties, not captivated the German people and their culture, the Holocaust might not have become possible. Similarly, had the Nazi Party not gained control of the German state apparatus, it would have been unable to "sever," both legally and culturally, the linkage between the Jewish "race" and its German nationality. Absent control of the state, the Nazi Party could not have rendered the Jewish "race" stateless or without legal standing within the body politic of Germany, nor could it have crafted or enacted the Final Solution as official policy.

Political violence of this scale is often called a "crime against humanity," for in its aftermath the world is forever changed, never to be the same. The Holocaust applied the instrumentalities of the nation-state to the annihilation of a racialized, objectified, demonized "enemy within" the nation. This not only transformed the history of the political culture of nation-states, it also altered our understanding of what humanity is capable of doing. The Holocaust has imprinted itself on the memory of humanity. As Wiesel writes,

> Never shall I forget that night, the first night in the camp, that turned my life into one long night seven times sealed. Never shall I forget the smoke. Never shall I forget the small faces of the children whose bodies I saw transformed into smoke under a silent sky. Never shall I forget those flames that consumed my faith forever. Never shall I forget the nocturnal silence that deprived me for all eternity of the desire to live. Never shall I forget those moments that murdered my God and my soul and turned my dreams to ashes. Never shall I forget those things, even were I condemned to live as long as God Himself. Never.[31]

The victim of genocide is not only each and every affected individual. Murder is a crime against a victim, but the Holocaust was a crime against humanity itself. What is victimized is the very status of the human person, that is, the moral standing of personhood itself.

Chapter 10
Nativism and Genocide in Postcolonial Rwanda

On April 6, 1994, Juvenal Habyarimana, the president of the Republic of Rwanda and a member of the Hutu tribe, was assassinated. Within hours, members of Hutu militia began killing Tutsi in the capital city of Kigali. Over the course of the next 100 days, the violence spread from Kigali throughout Rwanda as Hutu militia brutally and systematically set about the task of annihilating Rwanda's Tutsi population. By the time the Rwandan Patriotic Front (RPF), the Tutsi army led by now-president Paul Kagame, drove the militia into the Democratic Republic of Congo and ended the genocide on Rwandan soil, more than 800,000 people, primarily Tutsi but also moderate Hutu labeled as Tutsi sympathizers, lay butchered across the countryside of this small African state.

In most instances of mass political violence, government officials and agents act against strangers, but in some circumstances executioners personally know their victims. In the case of the Rwandan genocide killers often knew their victims, sometimes intimately. The members of Hutu militias knowingly, willingly inflicted torment and death upon Tutsi friends, neighbors, colleagues, or family members as they sought to eradicate the Tutsi "race" from the Rwandan state. The Rwandan genocide thus represents a case study on how kinship identity constructions become ethnicized and racialized in a political culture in which existential attributes become the ideological tools of death and horror.

Colonialized Rwanda: Hutu and Tutsi before the Genocide

Throughout the nineteenth century, African dynastic chiefdoms became transformed in ways that reflected the power realities of European state relations rather

than indigenous understandings of legitimacy and discipline. In colonialism, European powers advanced their political cultures as representative of civilization itself and in doing so created the illusion of a superior European (modern) and inferior African (primitive). The devalorization of communal identity provoked the dynamics of mimetic desire on the part of African peoples who confronted the power and legitimacy of colonialism from the now-subordinated perspectives of honor and shame. The cultural superiority represented by colonialism became mystified at a terrible cost. Across Africa, and in this case within the Rwandan state, subordinated groups came to imitate those who appeared to be superior in ways that reflected the political cultures of the colonialist. The consequences ultimately proved fateful for Rwanda.

The 1884 Berlin Conference assigned Rwanda to Germany as part of German East Africa. The Germans did not exercise direct control over the Rwandan people but instead acted through the existing monarchy and feudal hierarchy, delegating power to local authorities. In the aftermath of World War I, however, Belgian forces took control of Rwanda and neighboring Burundi. The Belgians created a system of direct colonial rule, establishing a centralized power structure and transforming social, political, and economic norms according to colonialist pretexts. Central to this project was the racialization of Hutu and Tutsi identities.

When Europeans arrived in the precolonial Rwandan state, they found Hutu and Tutsi living together in a kind of postfeudal society in which codetermination underpinned their reciprocal relationship. In precolonial Rwanda, as Mahmoud Mamdani suggests, Hutu and Tutsi "spoke the same language, lived on the same hills, and had more or less the same culture … [though] they had yet to become one people."[1] Thus "Hutu and Tutsi lived together, not just as neighbors but also intimately, often through cohabitation, sometimes through intermarriage."[2] Theirs was a feudal society in which wives assumed the identities of their husbands, passing communal identity along patrilineal lines. "Hybrid" forms of family or group identity were avoided. Mamdani explains that in Rwanda a child took on "a unidimensional identity, that of the father, [while] the identity of the mother—whether Hutu or Tutsi—[was] systematically erased. So it happen[ed] that the child of generations of intermarriage and cohabitation between Hutu and Tutsi [came] into this world unequivocally Hutu or Tutsi … [thus] today's Tutsi need to be understood as children of mixed marriages who have been constructed as Tutsi through the lens of patriarchal ideology and the institutional medium of a patriarchal family."[3] Moreover, according to the patronage system that developed in precolonial Rwanda, Hutu clients often adopted the identity of their Tutsi patron. Although Rwandan feudal society appeared to exhibit a sharp distinction between Hutu and Tutsi, those designations were cultural

rather than biological. It was not only possible but likely that an individual born a Hutu would die a Tutsi and vice versa.

However, to Europeans, predisposed to view kinship cultures according to modern conceptions of "ethnicity" and "race," the Hutu/Tutsi distinction became constructed, not in terms of marriage, patronage, or lineage, but in terms of naturalized distinctions grounded in racialized notions of superiority and inferiority. The Belgians constructed race as "the marker dividing humanity into a few superhuman and the rest less than human, the former civilized and the latter putty for a civilizational project . . . [a] bipolar division of humanity [that would ultimately provide] the rationale for the elimination of entire peoples."[4] Upon taking control of the Rwandan state, therefore, the Belgian colonialists established a **racial hierarchy** in Rwanda. They fostered a cultural distinction between white Europeans who represented the superiorities of "modern" culture and black Africans who represented the inferiorities of "primitive" culture. In so doing the Belgians promoted the superiority of the Tutsi who represented the "potential" to be modern in contrast to the Hutu whom the Belgians treated as forever doomed to be primitive.

Thus Belgian colonialists perpetuated a racialized ideology that maintained that Hutu and Tutsi were two different groups with separate histories and separate racial origins. The Tutsi, the Belgians argued, were the superior "race" on account of their more European physical features—their more slender frames, their lighter skin, their more narrow facial features, and their more pronounced height. The Hutu, conversely, were an inferior, more African "race" on account of their more "primitive" physical features—their more squat bodies, their darker skin, their wider facial features, and their shorter stature. From the Belgians' observations of Hutu and Tutsi physicality emerged the **migration hypothesis** and the **Hamitic Myth**, explanations for the "racial" differences between the Hutu and Tutsi that would eventually serve as ideological justifications for genocide in the postcolonial period.

According to the **migration hypothesis**, Hutu and Tutsi migrated to Africa's Great Lakes region as different peoples of separate and distinct racial origins. This account of the Hutu/Tutsi historical and racial distinction relied upon the **Hamitic Myth**, a European fantasy indicating that "every sign of 'progress' on the Dark Continent was [the result of] a civilizing influence of an outsider race. This race of civilizers, it was said, were Caucasians who were black in color without being Negroid in race. [They were] the Hamites of Africa, separated from the Bantu, so-called real Africans."[5] In Rwanda, "the idea that the Tutsi were superior because they came from elsewhere, and that the difference between them and the local population was a *racial* difference [as opposed to a primordially

constructed sacred, ancestral, or metaphysical difference], was an idea of colonial origin."[6] This Belgian misconstruction of Tutsi superiority proved disastrous for Rwandan political culture for it advanced the notion that the Tutsi were a Hamitic people "mongrelized" by the native and inferior Africans but who were naturally and racially endowed with the potential to be a civilized people. This racialized conception worked to objectify relationships between Tutsi and Hutu for succeeding generations.

From Colonial Construction to Political Institution

The racialized distinction between Tutsi and Hutu may have originated as an ideological construct but it quickly assumed an institutionalized political, economic, and cultural role within the colonial Rwandan state. Centralized state institutions established by the Belgians to replace their feudal predecessors—from the state bureaucracy to the army and from schools to churches—were organized in ways that privileged Tutsi and subordinated Hutu. They elevated the Tutsi beyond their precolonial role as patrons and stripped Hutu from their precolonial standing. Moreover, in accordance with naturalized notions of race and difference, the colonial powers treated Hutu and Tutsi communal identities as fixed and unchanging. No longer could an individual be born a Tutsi and die a Hutu. Instead, each individual person was classified as Hutu or Tutsi and issued an identity card proclaiming his or her racial status. Like the Hamitic Myth and the state structure itself, these identity cards would eventually become tools of the *genocidaires*.

The Belgian colonialists appointed the Rwandan Tutsi as their clients in the colonial state, granting them positions of political power, legal authority, economic security, and social privilege. Feudal power arrangements, which placed both Tutsi and Hutu in positions of authority, were abolished and replaced with unitary government agents whose centralized, despotic, and often corrupt control stripped Hutu of their traditional status. In time even the Catholic Church advanced Tutsi superiority, giving religious legitimacy to cultural and political distinctions. Schools administered by the Catholic Church, which educated Tutsi as well as Hutu children, perpetuated the racial distinction between the two groups, privileging the former at the expense of the latter. The quality of the educations provided to Tutsi and Hutu differed. The result was that Tutsi were groomed for political, economic, social, and cultural leadership and Hutu were prepared for manual labor and service.

Over time political authority and governance became the birthright of the Tutsi "race," a far cry from the feudal governance legitimated by ancestry and

reciprocity. In the postcolonial era, the racial distinctions made natural and oppositional under colonial rule, along with the delegitimation of kinship values, would contribute to the subordination of the Hutu people and to the outbreak of genocidal violence in 1994.

In the aftermath of World War II, Belgium began to coordinate the Rwandan independence movement. In 1959 tensions between Hutu and Tutsi erupted in the Rwandan Revolution. Members of the Hutu emancipation movement began killing Tutsi, forcing more than 100,000 to flee to neighboring states. In the aftermath Rwanda experienced "the routing and dismantling of the Tutsi power at the local administration level . . . [as well as] broader constitutional and political developments that led to a transfer of governmental power from a Tutsi to a Hutu elite."[7] As a consequence, the Rwandan state "imploded in a revolution that pitted one section of the population (Hutu) against another (Tutsi)."[8]

Despite efforts by some political parties to transcend the colonial distinction between Tutsi and Hutu and to establish a Rwandan nationality in which all descendants of **Kinyarwanda** could unite their strengths in the building of a legitimated nation-state, Rwandan politics quickly became dominated by groups seeking to dismantle or perpetuate Tutsi privilege in the postcolonial era. When the Belgian colonialists left Rwanda in 1962 they instituted a "democratic" centralized state apparatus. Because the Hutu represented the majority of Rwandans, the postcolonial government became a Hutu-dominated structure. Tutsi were forced to either seek refuge in political exile in Uganda, Tanzania, Zaire, or Burundi or submit to the dictates of the Hutu government.

Nation-Building in Postcolonial Rwanda

European ideological legacies that established the Tutsi as a race that was nonindigenous to Rwanda and distinct from Hutu were quickly adopted by Hutu elites seeking to construct a Rwandan nation exclusively comprised of Hutu people. Because the Hamitic Myth had been accepted throughout Rwanda by Hutu and Tutsi alike, the Hutu were able to argue, quite logically and compellingly, for a postcolonial return to an authentic past—a reversion to a social order that predated the Tutsi invasion of Rwandan land and "enslavement" of the Hutu people. Thus, in the postcolonial political order called the First Republic, Tutsi were relegated to the status of resident aliens. Although they were permitted to reside in Rwanda, they were denied access to positions of political authority as well as many of the privileges of full citizenship. Nation-building in the First

Republic took on an exclusionary character as Rwandan nationality was racialized as Hutu. According to Mamdani, "Belgian power turned Hamitic racial supremacy from an ideology into an institutional fact by making it the basis of changes in political, social, and cultural relations. . . . The origin of the violence is connected to how Hutu and Tutsi were constructed as political identities by the colonial state. Hutu as indigenous and Tutsi as alien. The reason for continued violence between Hutu and Tutsi . . . is connected with the failure of Rwandan nationalism to transcend the colonial construction of Hutu and Tutsi as native and alien."[9]

The Second Republic transformed the colonial designation of the Tutsi as a race distinct from the Hutu to an ethnic classification more befitting a minority group within a modern nation-state. This redefinition changed the status of Rwandan Tutsi. They were no longer considered resident aliens wholly denied the political rights associated with citizenship. Instead, Tutsi in the Second Republic were permitted limited access to positions of political power. However, even under the leadership of the Second Republic, the Tutsi faced state-sponsored, institutionalized discrimination and subordination. Arguing that the Tutsi were a historically privileged minority, the Second Republic undertook to redistribute Tutsi wealth and to curtail Tutsi political participation. Moreover, Tutsi who had fled Rwanda were not permitted reentry. Nevertheless, under a banner of redress and reconciliation, the Second Republic rejected the Hutu nationalism of the First Republic and sought to create a Rwandan nation-state in which each ethnic group would have its own "space."

But by the late 1980s, amid economic crises and regional unrest, the Second Republic began to unravel. In 1990 the Rwandan Patriotic Front (RPF), a militia composed of primarily Tutsi Rwandans in exile, invaded Rwanda seeking repatriation of Tutsi Rwandans. The war lasted until 1993 and fundamentally changed the Rwandan political landscape. The growing Hutu Power movement, a radical Hutu nationalist organization, interpreted the invasion as an attempt to bring the Tutsi back to power in Rwanda. As a consequence, tensions between the Hutu and Tutsi escalated. After brutal fighting and RPF occupation of lands resulting in displacement of many Hutu residents, a tentative peace agreement, the Arusha Accords, was signed by the Rwandan government led by President Habyarimana and the RPF. As a concession to the RPF, the Rwandan government pledged to grant citizenship and travel documents to all Tutsi refugees in neighboring states who did not desire naturalization in their countries of asylum. However, even as the peace accords were under negotiation, proponents of Hutu Power began to assume greater political power and popular support.

ALTERNATE PERSPECTIVES

Domestic Political Conflict and Failed States

States that experience a high degree of internal conflict and instability are often called "weak" or "failed" states. Many authors argue that failed states emerge as a consequence of social or economic turmoil. However, Lothar Brock et al. argue that while social factors such as ethnic tension or religious strife are important for explaining conflict within a failed state, political circumstances are also key.[10] After analyzing the Democratic Republic of the Congo (DRC), Afghanistan, and Haiti, the authors were able to highlight political variables that contributed to conflict in already-fragile states. For example, in the DRC and Afghanistan, lack of central control over the state led to political infighting among subnational groups. In both cases the centralized state government failed to maintain its monopoly on violence. As a result, subnational militias undermined the state's authority and legitimacy. These groups include the Northern Alliance in Afghanistan and M23 in the Congo. In addition, the lack of centralized state control combined with an absence of national collective identity and strong tribal and/or clan affiliations among citizens resulted in long-lasting civil wars, ethnic violence, revolution, and rebellion.

Brock et al. also observed that the lack of strong state institutions often creates a cycle of ongoing domestic conflict that can often lead to international instability. Groups try to eliminate this cycle by engaging in what we call nation-building. But nation-building in these states is not based upon equal access to the privileges of nationhood. Instead, membership in the nation becomes the exclusive privilege of specific ethnic or religious groups. Ultimately, this only perpetuates the fragile nature of the state and sets the stage for more violence. In Rwanda, Burundi, and the Sudan, for example, attempts to define nationhood in ethnic terms resulted in genocide and ethnic cleansing. While social factors contributed to these episodes of mass violence, political values, dynamics, structures, and institutions were ultimately responsible for failure in state-building.

Hutu Power and Rwandan Political Culture

Hutu Power was rapidly becoming the dominant ideology in Hutu politics. At the core of Hutu Power ideology stood the Hamitic Myth—the notion that the Tutsi were a distinct race, nonindigenous to Rwanda, that should be eliminated

from the Rwandan nation-state. For those who shared in the ideology of the Hutu Power movement, Hutu were not merely the ethnic majority in Rwanda. As Mamdani argued, they *were* the nation. Given the events of the civil war, the Hutu Power political leaders were able to craft propaganda that would convince even moderate Hutu that the RPF sought not equal rights for Hutu and Tutsi within the Rwandan state, but rather a rebirth of the Tutsi dominance that had characterized the colonial era. Grounded in a falsified history of the Rwandan state, such propaganda provided the justification for genocide. As the Hutu Power radio commentators professed, "when people ask me, good listeners, why do I hate all the Tutsi, I say, 'Read our history.' The Tutsi were collaborators for the Belgian colonists, they stole our Hutu land, they whipped us. Now they have come back, these Tutsi rebels. They are cockroaches. They are murderers. Rwanda is our Hutu land. We are the majority. They are a minority of traitors and invaders. We will squash the infestation. We will wipe out the RPF rebels. This is RTLM, Hutu Power radio. Stay alert. Watch your neighbors."[11] As it prepared to annihilate the Tutsi population, Hutu Power ideology thus advocated a return to a pre-Tutsi Rwanda, a mythologized primordial past that had never existed. This betrayed the nativist underpinnings of the Hutu Power movement and the genocide that would unfold.

In colonialism, the institutions and values that governed kinship communities during the precolonial era often tend to be denied historical legitimacy. As a consequence, kinship communities become culturally subordinated and thus bereft of full recognition of the possibility of the legitimacy of their own political culture. This results in the belief, however false, that their future can only be defined in terms of their relationship to colonialism and its agents. Throughout the colonial era, Tutsi who imitated the European colonists and envied their notions of superiority projected their anxieties onto Hutus who represented the "backwardness" of kinship rule, while Hutus became jealous of the relationship between the Tutsis and the Belgians and projected that anxiety in terms of nativism. The Tutsi regarded themselves as superior because they had become "modern" while Hutus regarded themselves as superior because they had remained loyal to the disciplines of kinship and ancestral lineage. In the post–civil war era, this sense of Hutu superiority would be used to justify the annihilation of the Tutsi "enemy within" the Rwandan state.

Postcolonialist Rwanda experienced conflicts in political culture that revolved around the imagined return to an authenticity associated with the structures and disciplines of kinship. The past became glorified and "honor" became a justification for racialized identity. Thus the cultural conflicts in postcolonial Rwanda configured around objectified images of the **ethnicized other**, with the Tutsi

representing the depraved postcolonialist "face" of Belgian colonialism, and the Hutu representing the depraved loss of kinship honor.

A facile assumption sometimes guides interpretation of postcolonial conflicts and seems to assert that contemporary ethno-conflicts must be of venerable origin, that what is today has always been and must forever be—if Hutus hate Tutsis today, they must have always hated Tutsis and will forever hate Tutsis—it is an "ancient conflict." The inference drawn is that nothing can be done to abate it. Explanations of the Rwandan genocide do not point toward "ancient hatred." The outburst of genocidal violence stemmed from a socio-pathological attempt in political culture to seek a return to kinship values and discipline with vengeance toward the postcolonial clientist "face" of the colonizer. In nativism, segmented kinship groups that lived for centuries together according to kinship rules but that had become racialized under colonial domination seek a return to kinship "honor" but with deep resentments. As one Hutu Rwandan commented, "if [more Hutu] parents had really made their children understand that Tutsi have the same flesh as them and that their blood is the same as them, they wouldn't have dared to kill their fellow men in such a cruel manner. The people who took part in the genocide had learned from their parents that Tutsi are bad by nature and were created to die."[12] Anxieties provoked by this sense of ambivalence and cultural loss can lead to a glorification of the kinship past and mythological memories of tribal loss. In the Rwandan case, this promoted the eventual collective frenzy leading to genocide in which nativist narratives centered political culture on scapegoated objects of hatred and contempt. This provides a glimpse into a form of political culture gripped by **nativism**, a socio-pathological reassertion of the legitimacy of segmented lineage and kinship rule within the parameters of the modern nation-state that ethnicizes the identity groups forged during colonialism in ways that in turn racialize them during the era of postcolonialism. Nativism represents a postcolonial cultural yearning for a return to the primacies of segmented lineage tempered by the fires of nostalgia and resentment and transformed into the vengeance aimed at an objectified "Other" deemed as the mirror image of the colonialist. In nativism the Other is similar in terms of ethnic, racial, or national culture but becomes distinguished by markers of difference stemming from the colonialist experience. Political cultures captured by postcolonial resentments often conflate nationality with ethnicity. Nation-state-building becomes fraught with ethno-conflict once exclusionary forms of nationality squeeze out the forms of hyphenated identity that link nationality to ethnicity. As a result, Rwanda in the genocide becomes a Rwanda for Hutus alone. Just as Hutus were excluded from the colonial and postcolonial power structures, Tutsis became excluded—legally and physically—from Hutu conceptions of Rwandan nationality.

The Rwandan genocide is thus in part the postcolonial result of a socio-pathological attempt to restore "honor" through the relief of "shame" by spilling the blood of those whose "face" mirrored the face of the agents of colonialism. In nativism, kinship loyalty becomes perversely distorted into an ethnic superiority that demands the dehumanization of the objectified Other in the name of the honor of ancestral lineage. Honor becomes the excuse for the extermination of the Other. Hutu nativism represents a tragic desire of conflicted will: wanting to be modern but simultaneously wanting to return to kinship traditions and values. But efforts to relieve a collective sense of shame through violence are bereft of honor. No matter the justification, there is no honor in mutilation, slaughter, or eradication. And even if you annihilate the Other—the substitute for the colonizer—you cannot recreate the past, especially when, as in Rwanda, the desired past is a mythology, a nativist fantasy.

In Rwanda, Hutu nativism represented a cultural and political ambivalence toward the dynamics of nation-state-building. On the one hand, a pervasive sense of collective loss generated a profound antipathy toward the cultural features associated with modern nation-states. Hutu nativists reinforced the cultural attitudes and political perspectives associated with modern social affiliations including fixed, binary oppositional categories grounded in materialism. For example, while the Hutus rejected modern nation-state-building in the name of kinship discipline, they adopted the Hutu/Tutsi ethnic distinction and sought a Hutu nation-state. Try as it did to return to the legitimacies and disciplines of kinship rule, the nativist Hutu project was trapped by the structures, cultural conditions, and legacies of postcolonialism that had fostered binary cultural oppositions between "us" and "them." This worked to contradict the foundational rocks of citizenship and nationality as the anchors of commonality and ethnicity as an acceptable principle of difference. As Hutu extremists demonstrated, nativism in political culture can turn into a socio-pathological refuge for those torn between disciplines of honor, shame, and the lingering legitimacies of segmented lineage and the demands of modern governance in a political universe defined by sovereign nation-states.

Nativist Violence and the Rwandan Genocide

Even as the Habyarimana government worked on the cease-fire and peace accords, Hutu Power gained influence and appropriated governmental agencies to prepare for genocide. Machetes and rifles made in China were ordered and distributed to Hutu throughout the country. Materials necessary for the construction of roadblocks were gathered and placed at strategic sites throughout the country.

Government officials documented where Tutsi and moderate Hutu "accomplices" lived, taking a census of who was to be spared and who was to be annihilated so that the killing could be as efficient as possible. Local Hutu officials called upon their people to "gather with machetes for *umganda,* ostensibly to clear bush, then, with gendarmes present, sent them to kill their Tutsi neighbors.... The genocide would ultimately be presented as a community project."[13] Internally displaced and unemployed Hutu provided a strong base of support for the Hutu Power movement and militias. The genocidal tendency, born of defeat in the civil war, "re-created a sense of national unity—unity of the Hutu nation—and lived its moment of national glory through a shadowy 'struggle' in which it locked defenseless civilians into a deadly embrace. For the perpetrators of the genocide, the enemy within were the Tutsi and the Hutu political opposition, accomplices who had betrayed the national cause in the name of democracy. It is in this sense that the genocide was both a continuation of the civil war and a rupture with it."[14] Ultimately three groups were mobilized to participate in the mass killing of the Tutsi "race"—the victims of the RPF war, the refugees of ethnic violence sponsored by the Tutsi government of Burundi against its Hutu population (widespread accounts report that Hutu who fled the genocide in Burundi served as the most brutal executioners), and those Hutu who allowed themselves to be convinced that they would surely be victims if the Tutsi were allowed to assume political power in Rwanda. Feeding not upon "age-old hatreds" but upon national anxieties, Hutu Power made the oppression of the Tutsi seem a necessity for the very survival of Rwanda and, in particular, for the survival of the Hutu people. As Mamdani writes, "Hutu Power extremists prevailed not because they promised famers more land if they killed their Tutsi neighbors—which they did—but because they told farmers that the alterative would be to let RPF take their land and return it to the Tutsi who had been expropriated after 1959.... The [propagandist radio] stations 'were always telling people that if the RPF, the rebel Rwandan Patriotic Front, comes, it will return Rwanda to feudalism, that it would bring oppression.'... [The Hutu] heard 'over and over that the Tutsi are out to kill them, and that is reality. So they act not out of hate as fear. They think they have only the choice to kill or be killed.'"[15] The *interahamwe* were individuals acting as agents of a pseudostate government and organized into militia. They were legitimated on account of the widespread belief that the Habyarimana government had betrayed the Hutu nation and was, therefore, no longer representative of the sovereign political power in Rwanda. They then proceeded to implement a policy the objective of which was nothing less than the eradication of the Tutsi people from Hutu Rwanda. The postcolonialist political culture of a nation-state had become genocidal.

Armed primarily with machetes, the Rwandan Hutu militia killed with quick dispatch and speed, surpassing even the alacrity with which the Nazis were able to annihilate the Jews. But the methods of the Rwandan *genocidaires* differed vastly from those of their Nazi predecessors. In the Rwandan genocide, mass political violence was enacted personally and brutally with a passionate nativist fervor. Hordes of Hutu, often singing and dancing in ways reminiscent of a nostalgic past, swept through villages and slaughtered Tutsi, leaving their bodies to rot where they fell. Hutu women stripped Tutsi infants from the arms of their immobilized mothers, flinging them into the rivers to drown, forcing the mothers to watch them drown even as the Tutsi victims bled to death. Reports from settlements downriver of Rwanda spoke of bodies and body parts washing up on shores. Even the rivers themselves gradually took on a red hue. Linda Melvern writes, "an estimated 40,000 bodies [were] taken out of Lake Victoria. Thousands of bodies were floating down the Akagera River into Tanzania. In Kigali it was estimated 20,000 unburied bodies were lying in the streets."[16] We mention this to bear witness to the moral burden that such mass atrocity imposes.

While some Tutsi were killed in their homes, others in the streets, and still others along the banks of rivers, thousands were murdered en masse in churches, schools, hospitals, and other public locations throughout Rwanda. Tutsi found no refuge, even in traditional havens—the churches, the missions, the schools, and the hospitals. Some of the most horrific acts of genocide took place in maternity wards where Tutsi gathered under the delusion that no one would slaughter mothers and newborn babies. Across Rwanda teachers killed students, priests stood by while their parishioners were hacked to pieces before their very eyes, and doctors applied their knowledge of the human body to the annihilation of the Tutsi people. Sanctuaries became slaughterhouses, caregivers became executioners. As Mamdani writes, "those pledged to heal or nurture life set about extinguishing it methodically and deliberately. . . . Professions most closely associated with valuing life—doctors and nurses, priests and teachers, human rights activists—got embroiled in taking it."[17] Schools, overrun with Tutsi refugees, were quickly overtaken by Hutu militia who butchered Tutsi in classrooms, leaving their bodies to decay or to be eaten by roaming dogs. Churches were also targeted; in one instance, a Hutu worker was called upon to bulldoze a church "with the Tutsi crammed inside. The roof crashed down. A few Tutsi survived the razing of the church. Nearly one-third of the local Hutu population assembled to finish them off. They did so with machetes, spears, and sticks. . . . After demolishing the church [the worker] calmly asked the priests for the promised compensation for the public service he had provided."[18] Many Hutu who participated in the genocide similarly saw themselves as public

servants. Legitimated by propaganda that "this species of bad people [the Tutsi], the species called the inkotanyi ... these people should perish because there is no alternative. . . . 'Keep it up, mobilise, work, you the youth from everywhere in the country, come and work with your army, come and work with your government, to defend your country.'"[19] Reminiscent of the role personified by Adolf Eichmann in the Nazi regime, Rwandan genocidal killers referred to the violence as "work," casting themselves in the role of state employees. Far from committing crimes, these Hutu agents of the Rwandan state justified their actions in the name of service to their country; "genocide, after all, is an exercise in community building."[20]

Not only did the Hutu militias adopt primordial as well as modern weapons in their genocide of the Tutsi, perpetrators of the Hutu Power genocide co-opted sacred rituals from Rwanda's cultural history. Of particular significance was the cultural notion of "flow." Flow figured into notions of health and fertility. How a person symbolically entered the community depended on "flow." One of the earliest ritualized rites of passage in primordial Rwandan culture focused upon an infant's ability to be a productive member of the community. Symbolized by fecal excretion, an infant was accepted into the community as a social being only after demonstrating his or her ability to take (to consume) as well as to give (to excrete). Christopher Taylor explains that, in social terms, a body that was "blocked" (able to receive but not to give) "would be unable to participate in reciprocity," the very reciprocity upon which kinship communities depend for intergenerational survival and ecological sustainability.[21] In the nativist fervor of the Rwandan genocide, this flow/blockage symbolism was deployed as Hutu genocidal killers dismembered their victims, thereby blocking their flow of blood and/or life's energy.

Governments that promote mass political violence do so by rationalizing and routinizing the violence that is done. In the case of Rwanda, rationalization came in the form of propaganda that provided legal and ethical justifications for the annihilation of the Tutsi. For example, Hutu political leader Mugesera explained to the Hutu people,

> the opposition parties have plotted with the enemy to make Byumba prefecture fall to the Inyenzi. . . . They have plotted to undermine our armed forces. . . . The law is quite clear on this point: "Any person who is guilty of acts aiming at sapping the morale of the armed forces will be condemned to death." What are we waiting for? ... And what about those accomplices (ibyitso) here who are sending their children to the RPF? Why are we waiting to get rid of these families?... We have to take responsibility into our own hands and wipe out

KEY CONCEPTS

Responsibility to Protect (R2P)

The international community failed to stop genocides in Bosnia or Rwanda despite treaty obligations to intervene in cases of genocide. In 2014, Dutch courts found the Netherlands liable, during the days immediately before the genocide began, in failing to protect Rwandans who had fled into what they were told were safe zones under UN protection administered under Dutch military control. Even before this decision to compensate surviving Rwandan members of the families of the deceased, and in response to the failures demonstrated by the international humanitarian system, the United Nations General Assembly formally announced a new international doctrine at the UN World Summit in 2005: the **Responsibility to Protect**. Known as **R2P**, this norm stipulates that sovereign nation-states have the primary responsibility to protect their own citizens from violence and violation. However, sovereignty is not only a right, it is also a responsibility. If a state is unwilling or unable to end atrocities and mass killings within its boundaries, the responsibility to do so is transferred to the international community.

According to R2P, states have three responsibilities: to prevent humanitarian crises, to intervene in humanitarian crises where they occur, and to rebuild failed or tyrannical states in the aftermath of the crisis. To ensure that this norm would not be abused by global powers seeking to advance their own political agendas rather than the cause of human rights, the UN established an **order of authority** for R2P as well as **principles for military intervention**. The order of authority places the primary responsibility to protect civilian life on the host state. However, if the host state is unwilling or unable to intervene, the responsibility to protect passes to the UN Security Council. If the Security Council is unwilling or unable to intervene, the

continued

> these hoodlums. . . . The fatal mistake we made in 1959 was to let them [the Tutsi] get out. . . . They belong in Ethiopia and we are going to find them a shortcut to get there by throwing them into the Nyabarongo River. . . . I must insist on this point. We have to act. Wipe them all out![22]

The river thus came to represent a key symbolic metaphor in the political culture of Rwanda during the tragic days of its genocide; the river served "an important ritualistic function—that of purifying the nation of its internal 'foreign'

responsibility to protect passes to the General Assembly and from there to regional organizations, coalitions of the willing, and, ultimately, to individual states acting unilaterally.

The principles for military intervention establish the specific requirements for intervention. The Just Cause Threshold requires that large-scale loss of life or large-scale ethnic cleansing be confirmed in order to justify intervention. The Precautionary Principles require that intervention be a last resort, that intervening powers use proportional means to achieve their objectives, and that there be a reasonable prospect of success in any intervention. Finally, the Operational Principles require that the intervention force have clear objectives and a common military approach. Intervening states must emphasize the protection of the population rather than the defeat of any party to the conflict and must follow established rules of engagement. In addition, force protection cannot be the primary objective of any intervening state and the military leadership must coordinate with humanitarian organizations during operations.

Technically, all members of the United Nations are bound to act under R2P. However, thus far, R2P has been a weak norm in the international system. In 2011 the United Nations Security Council adopted a resolution approving military intervention in Libya under the R2P framework. Military action by the **North Atlantic Treaty Organization (NATO)** followed. However, the UN has not approved intervention in other cases, most notably Syria today in which nearly 200,000 citizens have been killed and millions internally dislocated or displaced in refugee camps outside Syrian territory. Challenges include persuading powers to act when necessary, preventing unjust or unnecessary intervention, and creating legitimacy for an intervening force. In the face-off between sovereignty and humanitarian intervention, sovereignty continues to reign supreme.

minority. . . . Rwanda's rivers became part of the genocide by acting as the body politic's organs of elimination, in a sense 'excreting' its hated internal other."[23]

Roadblocks also became a critical instrument in the Rwandan genocide and were linked symbolically to notions of flow and blockage. Roadblocks were the most frequent location of execution during the genocide. Erected ubiquitously by many different groups, roadblocks were nearly impossible to evade. At every barrier individuals were forced to show their ethnic identification cards; those identified as Tutsi were killed. Taylor writes, "barriers were ritual and liminal

spaces where 'obstructing beings' were to be obstructed in their turn and cast out of the nation. . . . There were scenes of inordinate cruelty. Often the condemned had to pay for the quick death of a bullet, while the less fortunate were slashed with machetes or bludgeoned to death with nail-studded clubs. In many cases victims were intentionally maimed but not fully dispatched. Beside the line of motionless corpses awaiting pickup and disposal lay the mortally injured, exposed to the sun and still writhing, as their persecutors sat calmly, drinking beer."[24]

Often Hutu targeted the parts of the body linked to movement—the legs, feet, and Achilles tendons—immobilizing victims so that they could be disposed of more "efficiently" and "conveniently." Moreover, it was not uncommon for the genocidal perpetrators to inflict corporeal torment on Tutsi digestive or reproductive systems. Tutsi, who were objectified as "blocking beings," were thus eliminated; the perpetrators removed "obstructers of the cosmic unity of the nation as that unity was imagined by the Hutu extremist elite: a purified nation with a purified, reified 'Hutu culture' expunged of all elements of 'Tutsi culture' and rid of all who would resist the encompassing powers of the state. The tortures not only killed their victims; they transformed their bodies into powerful signs that resonated with a Rwandan habitus even as they improvised upon it and enlarged the original semantic domain of associated meanings to depict an entire ethnic group as enemies of the Hutu state."[25] Hutu Power ideology was predicated on a return to the past, kinship, honor, and lineage but represented a modern political agenda in genocidal postcolonial experience. Despite rhetoric that glorified a return to a precolonial utopia, what the Hutu militia clearly wanted was not a return to the symbiotic feudal Rwanda in which Hutu and Tutsi shared power and lived alongside one another peacefully. Instead, the Hutu sought a modern, sovereign, centralized nation-state for Hutu, free of Tutsi altogether. Moreover, Hutu Power ideology was predicated on its acceptance of racialized notions of the Hutu/Tutsi distinction, a modern construction wholly different from the traditional constructions that attached Hutu/Tutsi identity to patrilineal segmented lineage and feudal patronage. Though the justifications and instrumentalities for the annihilation of the Tutsi referenced a mythologized primordial past, the genocide was undeniably a manifestation of a political culture deeply embedded in modern nation-state-building but wracked by postcolonial socio-pathologies. From notions of exclusion that now racialized nationality and stripped the Tutsi of the privileges, enjoyments, and protections of full citizenship in the Rwandan state, to the application of systematic, centralized, and state-sponsored corporeal practices that annihilated the bodies of the Tutsi people on the basis of their political identities, the Rwandan genocide, like so many other acts of mass atrocity and extreme political violence, entrapped the Hutu genocidal killers within modern constructions of cultural identity and political legitimacy.

Part V

Nation-Building and State-Building

Future Challenges in the Present

Chapter 11
The Struggle over Legitimacy

A Case Study of Afghanistan

Is Afghanistan Governable?

On September 11, 2001, the United States became the victim of four coordinated suicide terror attacks. Nineteen terrorists from the militant group Al-Qaeda hijacked four passenger jets. The first two planes were flown into the Twin Towers of the World Trade Center in New York City. Another plane crashed into the Pentagon in Arlington, Virginia. The fourth crashed into a field near Shanksville, Pennsylvania, after passengers attempted to regain control before it could reach its intended target, Washington, DC. Nearly 3,000 people died in the attacks.

Suspicion immediately focused on Al-Qaeda. The group's leader, Osama bin Laden, initially denied involvement, but in 2004 assumed responsibility for the attacks. In an attempt to bring bin Laden to justice, the United States began military operations in Afghanistan, a small, landlocked, central Asian country known to harbor the terrorist group and its leadership. By the end of 2013 the United States had killed or captured many of the leaders of the terrorist group, including bin Laden. But Afghanistan remained a conflicted state, wrenched apart by tribal and sectarian loyalties that impede the full integration of an Afghan nation into a singular political culture unified under the recognized and legitimated authority of centralized sovereign state institutions. In early 2014, as the United States prepares to withdraw its military forces, questions abound regarding the future of Afghanistan. Does Afghanistan have the potential to

emerge from its violent, fragmented past to join the international system as a stable nation-state?

History of Afghanistan

Afghanistan, officially the Islamic Republic of Afghanistan, is a central Asian country bordered by Pakistan, Iran, Turkmenistan, Uzbekistan, Tajikistan, and China. The territory known as modern-day Afghanistan has a long cultural, social, economic, and political history. Archaeologists have found evidence of human settlements dating back to 50000 BC and urban civilizations beginning around 3000 BC. The area has been a focal point of human migration and was once traversed by the Silk Road that connected China and the Middle East.

Although Afghanistan has been influenced by numerous dynastic regimes including the empires of Alexander the Great, Chandragupta Maurya, and Genghis Khan, the region has historically been dominated by a kinship group known as the **Pashtun**. In 1709 the Pashtun fought the Persian and Mughal Empires in order to establish the independent **Hotaki dynasty** near **Kandahar**. Since that time, the Pashtun have dominated Afghanistan. The Pashtun are the largest ethnic group in the country. They have historically ruled the region and they compose the majority of both the **Taliban** and the current Afghan government.

The Pashtun are the world's largest segmented lineage order. Several hundred tribes and clans constitute the Pashtun. The Pashtun today share a common language and governance structure but it is highly unlikely that they are all descended from the same origin. It is more plausible that groups migrating to the region assimilated into Pashtun culture, fusing Pashtun traditions with their own. Thus, the Pashtun represent a form of dynastic governance, an intermediary between primordial descent communities (now known as tribes or clans within the Pashtun "ethnicity") and a modern nation-state. Nevertheless, the Pashtun have historically been referred to as Afghans, that is, as a people descended from a common ancestor known as Afghana, purported to be the son of King Saul, making the Pashtun one of the twelve tribes of Israel, at least in terms of biblical legend. Although Pashtun culture predates Islam, today the Pashtun are primarily an Islamic people with some members claiming descent from the Prophet Muhammad himself. For a culture that believes that their legitimacy as rulers derives from the blood of their ancestors, a claim to descent from the Islamic Prophet is of particular importance because it fuses kinship legitimacy with adherence to fundamentalist interpretations of the Islamic faith. For the

Pashtun, government and religion cannot be separated since the latter is the source of legitimacy for the former.

In the late 1800s, Afghanistan served as a buffer zone between the British and Russian empires. Although the Pashtun had lost control of the Punjab region to the British, they were able to defend the heart of their territory from both the British and the Russian forces. The **Anglo-Afghan Wars** were fought as part of the **Great Game** that pitted these two Great Powers against each other. The Great Game, which the Russians called the **Tournament of Shadows**, represented a strategic rivalry between the British and the Russians for supremacy in central Asia. The British were concerned that the Russian Empire's expansion into the region threatened British control over India, by far the most valuable and important colony in the British Empire. The British were also concerned that Afghanistan would become a staging area for a Russian invasion of India. For this reason, the British began the First Anglo-Afghan War in 1838, with the intention of instituting a pro-British puppet regime in the state.

In 1838 the British East India Company invaded Afghanistan with a force of 16,000 British and sepoy regiments. They captured Kabul in 1839 but the Pashtun fought back and the army could not control the area around the capital city. In 1841 the Pashtun forced the British to retreat back to Pashawar. Although the British tried again to take Kabul, the Pashtun forced a complete retreat in 1842. Britain, arguably the most powerful state in the world at the time, lost nearly 20,000 troops to a small, poor, landlocked population of Pashtun warriors. Although the invading British force was able to conquer the Afghan capital, in what would prove to be indicative of future military campaigns in Afghanistan, it could not pacify the Afghan people and therefore could not hold the territory.

Fearing Russian territorial expansion in the region, the British again invaded Afghanistan in 1878. A British army of 40,000 soldiers attacked Afghanistan, forcing the Afghan leader to sign the **Treaty of Gandamak** in 1879. Although the Pashtun government retained sovereignty over Afghanistan's domestic affairs, it was made to cede control of foreign policy to the British. After the withdrawal of the British army, however, the Pashtun continued to fight. In September 1879 an uprising in Kabul killed the British delegation, thus reinstating the war. In October 1879 the British army defeated the Pashtun forces and occupied Kabul. But the Pashtun continued to attack British forces throughout Afghanistan. The moment the British subdued one part of the country, it faced attacks and rebellion in another. The British again withdrew. In 1893 the **Durand Line** between the British government in India and the Afghan Amir divided India from Afghanistan but also split the Pashtun tribal areas, with some remaining in Afghanistan and some ending up in modern-day Pakistan.

Afghanistan remained officially neutral during the First World War but it did accept a Turkish German envoy in Kabul as well as military assistance from the Central Powers. Convinced that Afghanistan should be an independent, sovereign state beholden to no one, the Afghan government took advantage of the British preoccupation with war to foment a rebellious movement culturally grounded in notions of tribal honor. As the victorious Allied powers began considering a peace settlement that prioritized popular consent and self-determination, the Afghan government demanded a seat at the Versailles Peace Conference. Although his request was denied, Afghan leader King Amanullah presented himself as a reformist and proclaimed his commitment to democracy, to ending forced labor, and to freedom from oppression, both foreign and domestic.

To unite the Afghan people under his leadership, King Amanullah invaded British India. In the war that followed, British and Indian troops drove the Afghan invaders out of India. However, the British suffered twice as many casualties as Afghanistan. In the aftermath of the war, Afghanistan emerged as a fully independent and sovereign state with control over both domestic and foreign affairs. The Afghan victory reinforced the emerging sense of Afghani nationalism. The Pashtun tribes, armed in the aftermath of the war, continued to resist the British along the Durand Line, protecting against retaliation and keeping the British at bay. But internal power struggles continued to divide the Afghani people and destabilize the emergent nation-state. In 1973 Mohammad Daoud Khan seized control of Afghanistan from his cousin King Zahir Shah, eliminating the Afghan monarchy and instituting a republican government. However, in 1978 the People's Democratic Party of Afghanistan assassinated Khan and his family. Known as the **Saur Revolution**, the PDP, known as the Afghan Marxists, took over the country. In response, many Pashtun joined the **mujahideen**, an opposition group dedicated to opposing this largely illegitimate, pro-Soviet government. When the Soviet government sent troops and supplies to support the Afghan Marxist government, the mujahideen fought against the Soviet military forces.

The mujahideen reflected the degree to which Afghan society remained beholden to the principles of segmented lineage. Associated with the Pashtun, the members of the mujahideen were governed by regional warlords who retained both the legitimacy and power necessary to conduct sophisticated military operations against the Afghani government and its Soviet supporters. Like the British in the First Anglo-Afghan War, the Soviets quickly learned that they could not hold the country. Even if they controlled the cities, the mujahideen employed seemingly indefinite guerrilla warfare in the countryside. More than 80 percent of Afghanistan was under the control of the local mujahideen leaders rather than

the central Afghan government. Loyalty and legitimacy thus shifted away from the centralized state and toward the fragmented local leadership. The harder the Afghan army and the Soviet forces fought to pacify the Afghan people, the more the mujahideen grew in support and numbers. In Pashtun-dominated regions, long-suppressed rivalries and subdivisions provided the basis for fragmented military leadership linked with the tribal **lashkars** (fighting forces). In non-Pashtun regions, minority communities looked to local, primarily Islamic, religious leaders whose networks provided the structure necessary to support military communication, mobilization, and resistance during the war. Moreover, as the increasingly illegitimate central government focused its efforts on the mujahideen, several regions of the country, such as Nuristan in the northeast and Hazarajat in the central mountains, lived in almost complete self-governing independence. Whatever national unity had existed in Afghanistan at the close of the First World War was eroded by this return to local, decentralized rule and tribal kinship discipline.

The mujahideen also received military aid and financial support from numerous countries, including the United States, Saudi Arabia, Great Britain, Pakistan, Israel, and Indonesia. It was during the Afghan Civil War that Osama bin Laden, originally from a wealthy Saudi family, became the leader and financier of the **Afghan Arabs** force that aided the mujahideen. This Arab fighting force would later evolve into the organization today known as Al-Qaeda. The Arab presence in Afghanistan would have enormous consequences in the years following the Civil War.

Having sustained enormous casualties and achieved few, if any, military objectives, the Soviet troops began to withdraw from Afghanistan in the late 1980s. After the withdrawal of the Soviet forces, the Afghan central government continued to face resistance from the mujahideen forces. The regime fell in 1992. Afghan parties agreed to a new power-sharing arrangement that would include general democratic elections and eventually created the Islamic States in Afghanistan. External forces, including those from Saudi Arabia and Iran, continued to undermine efforts to establish a strong Afghan nation-state. Iran supported a Shiite force known as *Hazara Hezb-I Wahdat* while Saudi Arabia supported the *Ittihad-I Islam*. Conflict between the two soon escalated into war.

Efforts to construct legitimate centralized state institutions were undermined by this subnational conflict and both Kabul and the countryside descended into chaos and anarchy. While the interim government tried to negotiate cease-fire agreements with the militia groups, it lacked both power and legitimacy and such agreements were regularly ignored. South Afghanistan fell under the control of local leaders and their militias. In 1994 the **Taliban**, a movement originating from *Jamiat Ulema-e-Islam* run madrasas (religious schools), emerged as a political

force opposing the local government. In 1994 the Taliban took over Kandahar, forcing the surrender of traditional Pashtun leaders. Its influence spread from there.

In late 1994 the warring foreign-backed militia factions were defeated by government forces. The Afghan secretary of defense, **Ahmad Shah Massoud**, attempted to create a new nationwide system of government dedicated to democratic elections and national consolidation—a state- as well as a nation-building enterprise—that would incorporate the existing factions, including the Taliban. However, the Taliban rejected this attempt to create a strong, centralized Afghan nation-state and refused to participate in the process, seeking instead to rule Afghanistan itself.

The Taliban attacked Kabul in early 1995 but were overwhelmed by Massoud's forces. With aid from Pakistan, however, the Taliban again attacked Kabul in 1996, this time forcing Massoud to retreat. The Taliban seized Kabul and established the Islamic Emirate of Afghanistan. According to the United Nations, the Taliban systematically massacred, tortured, and displaced civilian populations in its campaign to consolidate control over the northern and western provinces of Afghanistan. It was supported by Pakistani troops as well as by the successor to Osama bin Laden's Afghan Arabs, Al-Qaeda. The Taliban then began to systematically impose its fundamentalist interpretation of Islam upon the 70 percent of the country now under its control. It required that women wear the *burqa,* and banned them from public life and education. Arranged marriage practices were reinstated. Law and justice changed to reflect fundamentalist interpretations of Islamic teachings. For example, honor killings returned as legitimate forms of punishment and, under the Taliban, people accused of stealing lost their hands or arms without trial or due process.

Massoud continued his offensive against the Taliban, allying with former enemies to form the **United Front** (also known as the **Northern Alliance**). Together with Pashtun forces, the United Front controlled approximately 30 percent of Afghanistan's population and provinces. However, by 1998 only Massoud could defend territory against the Taliban. Within his region he established democratic institutions and protected human, and, in particular, women's rights. According to Massoud, "both men and women are created by the Almighty. Both have equal rights. Women can pursue an education, women can pursue a career, and women can play a role in society—just like men."[1] As Pepe Escobar wrote, "Massoud is adamant that in Afghanistan women have suffered oppression for generations. He says that 'the cultural environment of the country suffocates women. But the Taliban exacerbate this with oppression.' His most ambitious project is to shatter this cultural prejudice and so give more space, freedom, and equality to women—that they would have the same rights as men."[2] Through

education, Massoud sought to overcome tribal differences and historical prejudices in order to create an Afghani nation that could then legitimate democratic state institutions.

Massoud refused to accept a position in the Taliban-controlled Afghan government on the grounds of irreconcilable differences over political culture. As he explained, "The Taliban say: 'Come and accept the post of prime minister and be with us,' and they would keep the highest office in the country, the presidentship. But for what price? The difference between us concerns mainly our way of thinking about the very principles of the society and the state. We cannot accept their conditions of compromise, or else we would have to give up the principles of modern democracy. We are fundamentally against the system called 'the Emirate of Afghanistan.'"[3] In another interview he said, "There should be an Afghanistan where every Afghan finds himself or herself happy. And I think that can only be assured by democracy based on consensus."[4] In March 2001 Massoud sought to bring the Taliban into a political process toward nationwide democratic elections. Resentment against the Taliban, particularly among the Pashtun, festered, but support from Pakistan and Al-Qaeda kept the Taliban in power. Massoud sought assistance from the European Union in his campaign against the Taliban, warning that the Taliban and its supporters were a danger to global peace and stability. He also stated that he believed an attack on the United States was imminent. On September 9, 2001, Massoud was killed in a suicide attack undertaken by two Arabs posing as journalists. Two days later, Al-Qaeda attacked the United States.

Operation Enduring Freedom

In response to the September 11 terrorist attacks, the United States declared a **Global War on Terror**. During his address to a joint session of Congress on September 20, 2001, President George W. Bush announced a war on terror beginning with attacks on Al-Qaeda in Afghanistan. He demanded that the Taliban government in Afghanistan deliver Osama bin Laden to the United States and that it destroy Al-Qaeda bases in its country. On October 5, 2001, the Taliban offered to try bin Laden in an Afghan court but the United States refused. On October 7, 2001, the United States, together with its North Atlantic Treaty Organization (NATO) allies, launched **Operation Enduring Freedom**, military combat operations in Afghanistan.

On October 7, 2001, the United States began airstrikes in Kabul, Kandahar, and Jalalabad. The strikes were to target military sites and terrorist training

grounds and were to be accompanied by a humanitarian mission that would provide food, medicine, and other supplies to the Afghan civilians. Working with the Northern Alliance and Central Intelligence Agency (CIA) "assets" in the country, US forces damaged and destroyed many of the Taliban's air defenses, training sites, and command sites as well as much of its communications infrastructure. The CIA used their network of Afghan-born collaborators, left over from the conflict against the Soviets, to build small militia forces to fight the Taliban. When they asked these supporters who should be included in these militias, they often recommended their family members—brothers, cousins, and uncles. In Afghan culture, trust derived from blood, kinship, and lineage.

The war at this time went badly for the Taliban. On November 9, 2001, American-backed Northern Alliance forces captured Mazzari Sharif, a major transportation hub with two airports and supply routes to Uzbekistan. The Taliban abandoned the city to the cheers of civilians who recognized the legitimacy of the Northern Alliance and resisted Taliban rule. On November 12, 2001, the Taliban fled Kabul and within twenty-four hours all Afghan provinces along the Iranian border had fallen under the control of the United States, NATO, and the Northern Alliance. By November 16, 2001, the last Taliban stronghold in northern Afghanistan was under attack by the Northern Alliance and most Taliban forces had been forced back into their original heartland in southeastern Afghanistan near Kandahar. They concentrated their power at the Tora Bora cave complex, which the United States began bombing on November 16. By mid-December US-led forces captured Kandahar and Tora Bora and the remaining Taliban leadership fled into Pakistan.

As the Taliban sustained heavy damages, many Afghan cities and localities came under the control of foreign Al-Qaeda members. With the US-led victory of the Northern Alliance and other anti-Taliban militias, however, many of the Al-Qaeda leaders were forced to flee with their Taliban counterparts to Pakistan. The United States then faced a critical question. Having forced the government of Afghanistan into exile, who could provide legitimate national leadership for the Afghan people? To answer the question, the United Nations hosted the Bonn Conference, a meeting of Afghan leaders (not including the Taliban), neighboring states, and coalition representatives. The meeting ended with the establishment of an interim government, the Afghan Interim Authority, and the Petersberg Process, a political process toward a new constitution and the establishment of a new Afghani government. To maintain security and prevent a return of power by Taliban and Al-Qaeda forces, the United Nations authorized the International Security Assistance Force led by US general David Petraeus in Kabul and surrounding areas.

KEY CONCEPTS

Federations, Confederations, and Unitary Governments

States vary widely in their division of power among national and subnational (often called state) governmental agencies. These different political structures often represent practical solutions to the political, social, or economic pressures that besiege the domestic politics of sovereign states.

A **federation** shares power between a national government and the governments of partially self-governing states or regions. Powers are legally or constitutionally reserved either for the centralized government or for the states. However, the individual states are not sovereign. They usually possess no powers related to foreign policy and they generally do not have their own military forces. They do not make laws pertaining to citizenship nor can they enter into their own alliances with other national governments. In many cases, federations emerge from alliances between several independent, if not sovereign, states. Over time, however, these states cede specific powers, generally the ones we associate with sovereignty, to a centralized authority. Federations are common in many parts of the world. Post–World War II Germany, for example, established a federal system where power is divided among sixteen *Länder* and the German national government. Argentina shares power between the governments of twenty-three provinces and a national government while Mexico does the same between thirty-one constituent states and its centralized government. Russia, Brazil, India, Pakistan, Australia, Canada, and Nigeria also have federal systems of government.

A **confederation** is a political arrangement in which the constituent states hold the majority of the political authority while the national government's powers are very limited. The actual power balance varies widely among confederations. The United States began its history as a confederation with very powerful state governments and only a Congress at the national level. The national government was so weak that it was ultimately replaced by a federal system of government. Similarly, the Confederate States of America were a confederate system. Today, confederate states are rare. Switzerland calls itself a confederation and much of the political power is held by the twenty-six cantons. Although it is generally classified as a federal parliamentary republic, the cantons do have a high degree of independence and political autonomy, particularly when compared to their European neighbors.

A **unitary government** is one in which the central government holds all of the political power while local administrative units have only the powers that the central government chooses to delegate. Subnational units can be created or abolished and the scope of their authority changed by the central government. Most of the world's governments are unitary systems including France, Chile, China, Rwanda, and Saudi Arabia.

New Afghan State Institutions: The Karzai Government

The interim government represented the interests of four Afghani groups: the Northern Alliance; the "cypress group," a group of exiles with ties to Iran; the "Rome group," a group loyal to the former king Mohammad Zaher Shah who had been living in exile in Rome since being ousted in 1973; and the "Peshawar group," a group of primarily Pashtun exiles living in Pakistan. Not surprisingly given their historic leadership of Afghanistan and its people, the Pashtun leader, Hamid Karzai, became the leader of the interim government. The interim cabinet was composed of leaders from all four groups. Many of the leaders were still called "warlords" because they maintained private militias under their control.

According to the Bonn Agreement, the interim government would rule for six months before being replaced by a Transitional Administration. To facilitate the transition to representative democratic government, the interim government would convene the **Loya Jirga**, the traditional Afghan "grand assembly." The Loya Jirga would then appoint a Transitional Administration that would rule for a maximum of two years before being replaced by a fully representative government elected through free, fair, and open elections. For the sake of unity and stability, the candidates for president, including King Zahir Shah, put their support behind Karzai. He ran against Masooda Jalal, a doctor working with the World Food Program, and Mahfoz Nadai, an Uzbek military officer and deputy government minister. On June 13, 2002, the Transitional Administration held an election by secret ballot. To facilitate the voting process photographs of the candidates were shown adjacent to their names. Hamid Karzai won 83 percent of the vote, thus officially becoming the president of Afghanistan. His vice presidents and cabinet would heavily represent both the Northern Alliance and the Pashtun. They also represented the Rome group and incorporated Afghan citizens who were educated in exile in order to bring both legitimacy and expertise to the new Afghan government.

In 2004 President Karzai restructured his cabinet to include more policy experts and fewer warlords. Sixteen members of his cabinet held doctoral degrees and all had advanced training in specific policy areas. According to the Afghan constitution, the cabinet must be approved by the **Wolesi Jirga**, the lower house of the bicameral **National Assembly**. In 2004 and again in 2006, the Wolesi Jirga considered the cabinet appointments based on their qualifications as administrators rather than on their membership in an ethnic group or their status as leaders of kinship groups. And although several members of the Afghan cabinet have been accused of corruption, President Karzai and the Wolesi Jirga exercise oversight and expel members if necessary as they did in 2008 when they

removed interior minister Zarar Ahmed Moqbel, an official accused of both corruption and incompetence.

The Wolesi Jirga itself is an elected body with 249 directly elected delegates. Most members are elected for five-year terms by voters in Afghani provinces. Ten seats are chosen on a country-wide basis to represent an Afghan nomadic group, the **Kuchi**. The Wolesi Jirga is the primary legislative arm of the Afghan government. Sixty-four of the 249 delegates must be female. Although the Afghan constitution established state institutions and democratic procedures, Afghanistan is not a stable democratic state. Accusations of election fraud are rampant and low voter turnout undermines the legitimacy of the government. By far the most pressing problem facing the Afghan government remains the threat posed by the Taliban and Al-Qaeda.

Return of the Taliban

Members of the Taliban and Al-Qaeda began regrouping in the Paktia province in early 2002. Both groups planned to use the region as a base for launching insurgency and guerrilla attacks against US-led forces and the Afghan government, deploying the techniques the mujahideen perfected during their campaign against the Soviets. Using caves and tunnels to avoid capture and bombing raids, the Taliban and Al-Qaeda were able to coordinate forces and munitions for an offensive campaign. In late 2002 the Taliban called for a jihad (holy war) against the US-led coalition and the Afghan government. The Karzai regime and all who served in it were condemned by the Taliban as collaborators with the American infidels. The propaganda resonated with the Pashtun in Afghanistan's southern provinces, and although much of the Taliban support came from madrasas in Pakistan where the Taliban had originally arisen, it also began to gain Afghan support for its jihadist agenda. Bases were established along the Afghan-Pakistani border to train soldiers in guerrilla warfare and terrorist tactics.

The Taliban began an offensive campaign in Afghanistan in 2003. US forces were attacked by small groups of insurgents often using **improvised explosive devices**, or IEDs. Raids, ambushes, hijackings, and bombings increased in frequency and severity as the Taliban gained greater control over southern Afghanistan in 2003. The insurgency continued to spread through 2006. Although US and NATO forces in the region fought against the Taliban, exacting numerous casualties and tactical victories, the decentralized nature of the Taliban military organization made it nearly impossible to destroy. When confronted by US and NATO troops, the Taliban could retreat, regroup, and

retaliate. While US and NATO troops sought to destroy the Taliban in 2007, it launched attacks in southern Afghanistan. Civilian deaths and the hardships associated with war continued to drive the region's people into the arms of the Taliban, strengthening the group's capacities, legitimacy, and resolve. Although the United States increased its number of troops in Afghanistan by over 80 percent in early 2008, the Taliban continued to score important victories. On June 13, 2008, for example, the Taliban freed 1,200 prisoners from the Kandahar jail, 400 of whom were Taliban prisoners of war. Coordinated attacks continued throughout 2008. In 2009 the US commander in Afghanistan, General Stanley McChrystal, remarked that it would take 500,000 troops five years of fighting to defeat the Taliban definitively. He reported that the Taliban had gained the advantage as its power spread into the northern and western provinces. After the Taliban successfully disrupted the 2009 elections with attacks and intimidation, President Karzai requested that the United States enter negotiations with the Taliban to end the violence. The United States did not respond directly but announced in December that it was sending 30,000 more troops to Afghanistan to continue efforts to subdue a Taliban force with an estimated 25,000 dedicated soldiers.

By 2010, however, the United States began peace efforts. In January, Taliban commanders met with representatives from the United Nations to discuss terms. Later that month representatives from more than seventy countries and organizations met in London where President Karzai explained his plan to foster peace with the Taliban by inviting them to participate in the Loya Jirga. He proposed a new peacemaking organization called the National Council for Peace, Reconciliation, and Reintegration that would allow the Taliban and the Afghan people to learn to live with and respect each other. Here President Karzai used a language of forgiveness, of transcendence, of a future beyond violence, hate, and oppression in which legitimacy from a united Afghan nation would legitimate representative state institutions.

In March 2010, however, the Taliban reiterated its position, saying that it would not enter peace negotiations until all foreign troops left Afghan soil. In the meantime it continued its campaigns against US and NATO troops. In May 2011 US president Obama announced that Osama bin Laden had been killed in Pakistan. White House officials began talking about a withdrawal of American troops from Afghanistan in June 2011. In response, Ahmad Zia Massoud, Abdul Rashid Dostum, and Haji Mohammad Mohaqiq formed the **National Front of Afghanistan**, a reformation of the United Front (Northern Alliance) that fought the Taliban before Operation Enduring Freedom, to oppose a return of the Taliban to power in the name of the Afghan people.

Tensions between American troops and the Taliban heightened in February 2012 when US troops at Bagram Base burned copies of the Koran. Enraged crowds protested throughout the country, killing more than thirty people and wounding hundreds more. In March, relations further disintegrated when an American soldier left his base in the Panjwai District of Kandahar Province and eventually killed sixteen civilians, including nine children. While leaders in the Afghan government demanded justice, the Taliban promised revenge. For a people whose adherence to fundamental Islam is built upon kinship cultural traditions, a call for vengeance is not merely symbolic. It is grounded in honor codes that require blood as the payment to wash away shame. In the strictures of such a political culture, little space exists for mercy, rehabilitation, or personal redemption. Shame is forever and a call for vengeance will never be forgotten until honor is restored.

A Failed State?

In 2008 US secretary of defense Robert Gates stated, "There has to be ultimately—and I'll underscore ultimately—reconciliation as part of a political outcome to this [war in Afghanistan]."[5] Although he emphasized that peace negotiations would not include Afghanistan, he explained that "the exit strategy for all of us" would require cooperation between the Afghan government and the Taliban.[6] He went on to say, "The reconciliation would have to be on the Afghan government's terms and the Taliban would have to subject itself to the sovereignty of the government."[7] In 2010 US commander in Afghanistan General David Petraeus echoed Gates's comments, saying that the "ultimate goal" of the war in Afghanistan was to "enable the 'reconciliation' of the Karzai government with the Taliban."[8]

But progress toward reconciliation, peace, and stability appears to be at a stalemate. The Taliban refuse to negotiate as long as there are foreign troops on Afghan soil and the troops refuse to leave until an agreement between the Afghan government and the Taliban is reached. However, voices beyond the Taliban have also called for US and NATO troops to leave the country. In 2009 Malalai Joya, a former member of the Afghan Parliament, said, "Eight years ago, the U.S. and NATO—under the banner of women's rights, human rights, and democracy—occupied my country and pushed us from the frying pan into the fire. Eight years is enough to know better about the corrupt, mafia system of President Hamid Karzai. My people are crushed between two powerful enemies. From the sky, occupation forces bomb and kill civilians ... and on the ground, the Taliban and warlords continue their crimes. It is better that they leave my

ALTERNATE PERSPECTIVES

Anthropology and Social Psychology

Many of the ideas and linkages we have discussed are grounded in political science but are applicable across a wide variety of academic disciplines. Two disciplines, anthropology and social psychology, are directly relevant to our analysis and provide similar but distinct ways of understanding identity, culture, nations, states, and the making of the modern world.

Anthropology encapsulates a wide and diverse number of subfields, ranging from bioanthropology to cultural anthropology. Philip Salzman and Patricia Rice argue that what anthropologists have in common is their tendency to observe patterns. Salzman and Rice state that a pattern in "anthropology and social science more generally means a repletion of a social or cultural phenomenon—a belief, a practice, a custom, or an institution—over space or time."[9] For example, sociocultural anthropologists "talk to people about their ideas and values, observe people as they go about their lives, and monitor their activities." They then ask, "What patterns arise emerge over time, place, and context?"[10] Furthermore, anthropologists pay particular attention to cultural change, which is not necessarily the product of conscious processes, but may instead be the result of changing norms, values, and practices across generations. How and why societies and the people within them change represent fundamentally political questions with implications for domestic and international relations.

Social psychology, or the study of the individual as affected by the group, provides additional insight into many of the themes we have discussed. Social psychologists argue that culture stems from individuals' shared interpretations of their environment. Two individuals who interpret a social phenomenon in the same manner share the same culture. From this observation, social psychologists study culture in radically different ways. For example, cultural psychologists study cultural characteristics over a short period of time while cross-cultural psychologists analyze cultural changes over a larger span of time. Peter Smith[11] et al. note that cross-cultural studies in psychology are increasingly becoming the study of nations and of their inhabitants.

country; my people are that fed up. Occupation will never bring liberation, and it is impossible to bring democracy by war."[12] The United States and its allies are engaged in the process of withdrawing their troops in 2014 and will soon bring the US military presence to an end.

Some segments of the Afghani people fear that withdrawal of US and NATO forces will result in a Taliban takeover of the Afghan government. Today the Northern Alliance is prepared to oppose efforts to return the Taliban to power. Dr. Abdullah Abdullah, leader of the National Alliance for Hope and Change and political opponent of President Karzai, stated in 2010, "There are groups that are willing to fight to the death. Whether we like to talk to them or we don't like to talk to them, they will continue to fight. So, for them, I don't think that we have a way forward with talks or negotiations or contacts or anything as such. Then we have to be prepared to tackle and deal with them militarily. . . . The Taliban are not fighting in order to be accommodated. They are fighting in order to bring the state down." Abdullah went on to say, "At the moment, the people are leaving support for the government because of corruption."[13] At this point, therefore, neither Afghanistan's current government, sometimes cited as among the world's most corrupt regimes, nor the Taliban enjoys the legitimacy necessary to govern Afghanistan. Nonetheless, as the United States withdraws, hopes are raised that Afghanistan will finally emerge from a decade of war as a stable, sovereign nation-state, confronted with challenges threatening to pull it apart, but stable despite such forces.

For the purposes of a modern, sovereign, and consolidated nation-state, a political culture must legitimate centralized state institutions as well as promote cohesive nationality. The political culture of Afghanistan is grounded in only rudimentary concepts of centralized state legitimacy and national unity. Yet the preamble of the Afghan constitution does attach nation-state-building to Islamic traditions in ways that point the way to modern conceptions of nationality and statehood. It declares,

> In the name of Allah, the Most Beneficent, the Most Merciful, Praise be to Allah, the Cherisher and Sustainer of Worlds; and Praise and Peace be upon Mohammad, His Last Messenger and his disciples and followers. We the people of Afghanistan: believing firmly in Almighty God, relying on His divine will and adhering to the Holy religion of Islam; realizing the previous injustices, miseries and innumerable disasters which have befallen our country; appreciating the sacrifices, historical struggles, jihad and just resistance of all the peoples of Afghanistan, admiring the supreme position of the martyrs of the country's freedom; comprehending that a united, indivisible Afghanistan belongs to all its tribes and peoples; observing the United Nations Charter as well as the Universal Declaration of Human Rights; and in order to: strengthen national unity, safeguard independence, national sovereignty and territorial integrity of the country; establish an order based on the peoples' will and democracy; form a civil society void of oppression, atrocity, discrimination as well as violence,

> based on rule of law, social justice, protecting integrity and human rights, and attaining peoples' freedoms and fundamental rights; strengthen political, social, economic as well as defense institutions; attain a prosperous life and sound living environment for all inhabitants of this land; and, eventually, regain Afghanistan's appropriate place in the international family; have, herein, approved this constitution in accordance with the historical, cultural and social realities as well as requirements of time through our elected representatives in the Loya Jirga, dated January 3, 2004, held in the city of Kabul.[14]

The preamble thus emphasizes the need for congruence between state-building institutions and a unified Afghan nation.

Although the constitution created a series of state institutions, including a presidency, cabinet, bicameral legislature, and judiciary, those institutions have been tarnished by allegations of corruption and incompetence in ways that detract from their legitimacy. In addition, although the constitution establishes election procedures for national and provincial elections, disruptions by the Taliban and the general state of domestic unrest and instability have made fair, open, and democratic elections hard to achieve in practice. And although the Afghan constitution includes provisions for civil rights including life, liberty, privacy, peaceful assembly, and free expression and speech, and although citizens accused of a crime have the right to be informed of the charges, to representation, and to the presumption of innocence, these provisions protect citizens from their government. They do not forge cultural values based on the concepts of a unified political entity or national identity.

A possible solution is to shift the emphasis away from a strong, centralized Afghan government to focus on regional rule. A decentralized approach to Afghan governance could allow the central government to act as the power of last resort over a loose confederation of principalities each with their own culture, language, and government. President Karzai has prioritized governance at the provincial and district level. This represents a pillar of his reform agenda. Some observers have suggested that strong local authorities could better fight the Taliban than any centralized government because, given the history of Afghanistan's political culture, they alone could work to restore the Afghan people's hope for peace, security, and, eventually, economic growth and prosperity. But even such a set of objectives requires the Afghan government to perform the function of honest broker among the different regional and clan interests that compete for legitimacy, power, and resources within the country, including the recently discovered $1 trillion in untapped mineral deposits. And that cannot happen without cooperation at the national level.

Not only must the central government find ways to reconcile with the Taliban and its supporters, it must also ensure that reconciliation with the Taliban does not lead the Northern Alliance to plunge the country back into war. Here the Afghan government faces a critical challenge. If it engages in diplomatic negotiations, power sharing, and reconciliation with the Taliban, the Northern Alliance may condemn it for collaborating with the "enemy." The Afghan government risks the loss of vital support from the Northern Alliance if it were to concede Taliban control over the country or even its southern provinces. Part of the problem is that some Afghans, particularly those associated with the Northern Alliance, view the Taliban and its Al-Qaeda supporters as every bit as foreign to Afghanistan as US or NATO troops. The Taliban, after all, was born in the madrasas of northern Pakistan and spread into Afghanistan only to support the mujahideen in their fight against the Soviet invaders. Similarly, Al-Qaeda is the successor group to Arab fighters who joined the mujahideen against the Soviets and its roots are thus Arab and not Afghani. Although the Taliban can elicit support from the Pashtun in southern Afghanistan due to the fact that the Pashtun territory is split by the Afghan-Pakistani border, other regions of the country see it as a wholly illegitimate and nonnative influence in Afghan politics. But neither can the Northern Alliance afford to wholly exclude the Pashtun from the Afghan nation. For centuries the Pashtun were synonymous with Afghanistan's collective cultural identity. Just as space must be created for an Afghan citizen to be Kuchi Afghan or Uzbek Afghan or Tajik Afghan, space must be created for a citizen to be Pashtun Afghan.

Ultimately the problem comes down to legitimacy. Because there is no unified Afghan nation, state institutions lack the legitimacy that comes from congruence between nation and state. And because the state institutions lack legitimacy at the national level, legitimacy defers to subnational allegiances and loyalties, such as those to kinship, in the case of the Pashtun and the Taliban in the south, or to provincial authorities, such as the Northern Alliance in the north. In the end, the two groups do not speak the same language of political culture. The Northern Alliance, like the Afghan government, speaks in the language of states and nations, democracy and human rights, popular consent and rule of law. But for the Taliban the political dynamics associated with nations and states are themselves epiphenomenal, or secondary, to what matters the most—the blood lineage linking the Afghan people to the Prophet Muhammad and strict adherence to Islamic law in the name of honor discipline, intergenerational stability, and communal survival itself. For the Taliban, governance of Afghanistan takes on a nativist dimension that requires a return to the primordial values attached

to fundamental Islam with a vengeance toward all those who would undermine the sacred honor of the Afghan people.

Afghanistan has never had a secular government. As the constitution suggests, Afghanistan is, as it has been for centuries, an Islamic state. But what that means differs across the Afghan population. To the extent that strict adherence to Islam as it is interpreted by the Taliban acts as a form of exclusion that denies some of the Afghan people, including women and other Islamic sects, equal membership in the nation, it undermines nation- and state-building forces. But to build an Afghan government that does not appeal to the legitimacy of Islam is to build a government with no legitimacy at all. Nevertheless, the nativism represented by the Taliban impedes the political-cultural development toward Afghan nation-state-building. This is not to suggest that the Afghan people should sacrifice their religious, ethnic, or cultural identities in the name of unauthentic homogeneity. It means merely that if they are to enjoy the cultural status associated with a political formation recognizable as a nation-state, they must choose to ground their differences in the commonality of nationhood and to legitimate a centralized governmental authority through their unique political and cultural practices.

Conclusion

Nation-states represent living, breathing political cultures that are subject to change, influence, and reinvention. A certain mysterious quality pervades political culture. What it is depends on how it is experienced. This in turn is subject to great variation. Throughout this study, we have been concerned with the relationship between how the making of modern nation-states has influenced cultural constructions of collective identity and, in turn, how collective identities alter the cultures of nation-states within, between, and across their sovereign boundaries. These cultural dynamics differ but a few things have remained constant: the desire to belong, the need not merely for identity but to identify with a constellation larger than the self, whether kinship, ethnic, racial, religious, or sectarian, but in particular with political entities and formations that elicit allegiances among groups of people who see in one another something in themselves. When Americans say, "I pledge allegiance to the flag of the United States of America and to the republic for which it stands," this sense of allegiance to a certain kind of political "we-ness" is reaffirmed. But this act or practice is also a means of expressing a sense of "I-ness" or personal identification with the larger group, in particular, the sovereign United States, the nation-state that anchors collective political life. So too is this the case wherever allegiance to a national entity demarcated by sovereign boundaries of statehood is performed or symbolically experienced. This fateful tie binding individual and group identities to those configured around nation-states is itself an outcome distinctive of modern history. This series of results was never guaranteed but was rather the outcome of those processes, including the cultural dynamics that are described throughout this book.

What we have witnessed across place, time, and history is that collective belonging or attachment is never certain, nor is it universally shared in the

same ways. No study of the emergence of modern political cultures is able to do justice to the complexity among them. But modernity has revealed a set of constants: the gradual but persistent emergence of centralized states or forms governance; the exclusionary ways in which geographic space has become the province of state boundaries; and the paramount role of popular consent and/or, in its absence, continuing struggles for legitimacy in the relationship between governing institutions and citizens who to varying degrees imagine themselves as "nations." Although political culture may be conceived as something immaterial or elusive, what emerges clearly throughout our exploration has been the role it has played in the forging of the contemporary political realm. This speaks to the precarious ways nation-states have arisen as the invented artifacts of political processes. Political culture and the making of modern nation-states are a story about the contingent consequences of history, not the revelations of necessity that were fated to become realized over time.

Nor is the picture that we have painted necessarily "pretty" in this regard. On the contrary, in many cases, the injustices and conflicts we see in the world today represent the continuing residues of the postcolonial cultural forces released by and through the decades associated with the history of global and internal colonialism. Over and again we have been witness to the various forms of cruelty and suffering that attended and continue to mark the making of the modern political world. These may be understood as the consequences, sometimes direct and sometimes indirect, of Western colonial expansionism. The political cultures of sovereign nation-states have emerged through contacts involving political domination and oppression, economic exploitation and impoverishment, geographic dislocation, and cultural displacements. The study of political culture demonstrates how deeply hurtful the erosion of all forms of bonding and belonging based on natal or genetic ties is. It appears that humanity reveres its forms of biological belonging, the ties of blood and kinship, family and ancestry. In a sense, the bonds and ligatures that grow from birth and extend through death are ever-present as influences in personal and group identities and they are so in ways that influence political cultures everywhere.

In many instances the making of modern nation-states has either destroyed or threatened the survivability of such cultural values and institutions. In a more concrete way, these dynamics have weakened the bases of legitimacy on which "the power of the fathers," or the patrimonial rule of traditional communities divided by descent or segmented lineage, depended. As we have seen, this has provoked a wide range of dysfunctional, even painful outcomes, not the least of which are such phenomena as failed states and nonhistoric national cultures; corruption and clientism; dysfunctional mimesis and the racialization of kinship

leading to genocidal rage and crimes against humanity; spatial politics leading to racist patterns of group isolation; ethnicized and thus racialized color codes of discrimination; genderized forms of sexual violence; and intersectarian violence. Despite this, or perhaps on its account, the sovereign nation-state as a political formation and culture remains the foundational principle of modern political history.

This book has depicted the overall results. The political geography of the earthly planet is now configured around the spatial boundaries of sovereign nation-states. In a sense, world-geographic "space" is now the spatialized "place" of sovereign legitimacy divided into more or less exclusive zones but that remain to varying degrees highly dependent on one another. But the question remains as to how to interpret the dynamics of legitimacy. Once the legitimacy of governance no longer reverts to stories or narratives of nature, blood, birth, and death, where does it turn? Of course, generations continue to be "born into" nations, but nations exist as the legitimating mechanism of states not because of nature, but on account of the particular ways governance is ritualized and symbolized in contemporary political culture. Birth and natality may represent a component of these performative and symbolic practices, but only a part. What political culture and the making of modern nation-states reveal is the demand that the ties of legitimacy between nations and states be demonstrated ritually and symbolically by means of celebrations, festivals, anthems, flags, and a wide range of monuments.

The amalgam between nation and state thus reflects a deeper construct, one that brings to the foreground the tensions within specific political cultures or polities between constructs of difference or diversity and those embedded in notions of affinity. Modern political affiliations across virtually all political cultures reverberate according to the tensions that exist among citizens or resident "aliens" in terms of cultural divisions and class cleavages. The terms we use to describe these distinctions, such as nationality, ethnicity, race, religion, gender, age, geography, linguistic majority and minority, etc., are all a part of the great mosaic that makes up the richness of now-globalized political cultures. But they can and often do resound to the resentments and even objectifications that eventually culminate in the "weakness" of centralized governing institutions or with the inability of a people to conceive of themselves as part of a historical nation.

Political legitimacy depends on numerous factors, but, ultimately, none is as important as what is in the human heart and political imaginary. How and in what ways do a people constituted as such "believe" in the processes that govern their lives? How do they give expression to such beliefs that one might call political faiths? Under what circumstances do events on the ground reveal crises and

conflicts over the internal structures permitting the consent of the governed to be asserted? When does the power of the nation-state intrude on citizens in ways that undermine its capacity to govern at all? These are the questions pertaining to the study of comparative politics, political psychology, and sociology. But the question of culture runs through them as to why, how, and with what effects political cultures and imaginaries become constituted and practiced.

If political culture is experienced, it is practiced. Thus, political culture may finally be understood not as given or received, but rather as practiced or exercised. Like any exercise, it demands disciplines and regimes. It generates obligations of time, effort, and even self-sacrifice. That these may be rewarding, freely offered, and personally confirming, or alternatively imposed, demeaning, and personally hurtful goes to the very core of legitimacy and how it is experienced. But the practices or exercises of legitimacy critical to the sustenance of national political cultures in the modern world are now experienced through performative and symbolic manifestations of national political culture. Often these expressions are taken for granted. That this is the case speaks to how deeply they are embedded in the cultural values that lend meaning and a sense of significance to citizens whose political identities are shaped by them.

National symbols instill patriotic bonds and sentiments of national belonging. They confirm the stature of popular consent and nationhood as supreme values in state legitimacy. How such symbolic practices function relative to the legitimacy of centralized state or sovereign governing institutions depends on the degree to which the members or citizens of any national political culture know or recognize "commonality" among themselves amid their differences. In all cases, the symbols and ceremonial rituals serve to reinforce either the solidarities or the divisions and cleavages such as they exist within any polity at any given time. Thus, they can become the cultural instruments of peace and reconciliation or of conflict and division depending on the policies of power elites and/or ideological beliefs and attitudes within general populations.

Examples of symbolic rituals and discursive or ideological practices proliferate. They are composed of national holidays and commemorative national days. Some holidays remember the founding of the nation-state; others commemorate veterans of wars or conflict, or those fallen on behalf of the nation-state. Most political cultures maintain certain burial places or a national network of regional cemeteries to honor those who are remembered as "the greatest generation." Monuments to the founding "fathers," "mothers," or "daughters" of the nation abound. Statues and monuments are sometimes erected on isolated knolls; in other instances, they are situated in the midst of the capital or major urban centers. Commemorations of the founding and founders of nations; memories

of wars, revolutions, and civil conflicts; and testimonies of sacrifice by past as well as present generations all attest to the process of transforming the political cultures of nation-states into metaphysical meanings endowed with sacred value. Some might speak of the "sacralizing" of the nation-state, that is, the attempt to envision the emergence of modern sovereign nation-states as a manifestation of a political theology. The irony is that once political theology becomes endowed with strong influences in national political cultures, the "we-ness" of nationality turns into the metrics of "us" and "them" nationalism in ways that readily demonstrate human capacities for self-righteous hatred, contempt, and violence.

One is tempted to wonder how the spirit of political theology informs the human spirit in politics as we look at rising anti-Semitism, racism, and anti-immigrant sentiment in Europe today; as we turn to attempts to understand the depth of violence that assails so many national cultures throughout the world today, for example, in Syria and Iraq, in the Central African Republic, in the Sudan and South Sudan, in Somalia, in cyclical conflicts between Israelis and Palestinians, to mention but a few; as we look at fierce and politically inspired conflicts over the sovereignty of a nation-state such as that in Ukraine. Such questions take us beyond the realm of political culture into a discussion of political metaphysics or religion or political ontology or the study of being and the human condition writ large.

What we have attempted to explore here is the relationship of cultural constructions of collective identity with respect to the central organizing political formation of contemporary history, the modern sovereign nation-state. We have done so to understand the ideological, discursive, and ritualistic practices that inform how peoples have come to know and interpret themselves symbolically as collective or political formations.

At the core of our study of political culture and the making of the modern nation-state remains the elusive but fundamental concept of legitimacy. The performances and rituals of patriotic duty and national celebration reaffirm the peoplehood of nations. When such performative practices remain fragile, as in cases of failed states, cultural divisions seem unable to transcend intractable political conflict. The consequence is that the nation-state as a political-cultural formation no longer functions as a civil society bounded by what one might call sovereign integrity. Both Syria and the Central African Republic illustrate this today in stridently painful ways. Thus, symbolic practices can become the cultural instruments of peace and reconciliation or they can become transmuted into the instruments of disarray, conflict, and division depending on the policies of power elites and/or the predispositions of general populations.

Despite their constants, such dynamics continue to change. A global human community is now emergent among all the "localizations" of cultural identity. Political cultures will adjust to these processes and influences as they must. As never before, political conflict and culturally inspired forms of violence anywhere and everywhere become the centerpieces of a digitally formatted information universe. But the question is, with what impacts? Peace, justice, and reconciliation are just words, but they too constitute aspects of political culture, at least in principle. The processes illustrated by this book demonstrate how political cultures and the making of modern nation-states have remained subject to a range of influences, not the least of which are the imaginaries that inform not only political but also moral values and ethical commitments. How to transfigure these political imaginaries toward the making of a sustainable world; how to foster values that celebrate differences within political cultures defined by sovereign nation-states; how to nurture understanding of the profound commonalities that bind all human beings together—these are questions beckoning the global future.

Notes

Chapter 1

1. Astronomers Without Borders, "Moon and Culture," www.astronomerswithoutborders.org/programs/all-programs/685-moon-and-culture.html.

2. Ibid.

3. Terry Eagleton, "Ideology and Its Vicissitudes in Western Marxism," in Slavoj Žižek, ed., *Mapping Ideology,* London: Verso, 2012, 223.

4. Ruth Benedict, "Patterns of Culture," in Edward Weisband and Courtney I. P. Thomas, eds., *Nations & Nationalities: Cultural Constructions of Collective Identities,* 8th edition, Boston, MA: McGraw-Hill, 2008, 28.

5. Ibid., 27.

6. Joan Riviere, "On the Genesis of Psychical Conflict in Earliest Infancy," in Melanie Klein et al., eds., *Developments in Psychoanalysis,* London: Karnac Books, 2002, 43.

7. Rollo May, "Contributions of Existential Psychotherapy," in Rollo May, Ernest Angel, and Henri F. Ellenberger, eds., *Existence: A New Dimension in Psychiatry and Psychology,* New York: Basic Books, 1958, 50.

8. Ibid., 51.

9. Paul Tillich, *The Courage to Be,* New Haven, CT: Yale University Press, 1952, 39.

10. Ernest Becker, *Denial of Death,* New York: Free Press, 1973, 89.

11. Ibid., 120.

12. Ernest Becker, *Escape from Evil,* New York: Free Press, 1975, 4.

13. Becker, *Denial of Death,* 92.

14. Ibid., 120.

15. Erik H. Erikson, "Sioux Child Training," in Edward Weisband and Courtney I. P. Thomas, eds., *Nations & Nationalities: Cultural Constructions of Collective Identities,* 8th edition, Boston, MA: McGraw-Hill, 2008, 64.

16. Ibid.

17. Gary Allen Fine, "Symbolic Interaction: An Introduction," in Edward Weisband and Elana DeLozier, eds., *Nations & Nationalities: Cultural Constructions of Collective Identities,* 6th edition, Boston: McGraw-Hill, 2005, 18.

18. Maria Montserrat Guibernau, *The Identity of Nations,* Cambridge, UK: Polity, 2007, 11.

19. Ross Poole, *Nation and Identity,* London: Routledge, 1999.
20. Ibid., 20.
21. Ibid., 18.
22. Ibid., 25.
23. Ibid., 23.

Chapter 2

1. Becker, *Escape from Evil,* 7.
2. Ibid., 45.
3. Ibid., 28.
4. Ibid.
5. Ernest Van Den Haag and Ralph Ross, *Passion and Social Constraint,* New York: Aldine Transaction, 2006, 107.
6. Becker, *Escape from Evil,* 7.
7. Maasai Association, "Maasai Ceremonies and Rituals," www.maasai-association.org/ceremonies.html.
8. Tepilit Ole Saitoti, "My Circumcision," in Edward Weisband and Courtney I. P. Thomas, eds., *Nations & Nationalities: Cultural Constructions of Collective Identities,* 8th edition, Boston: McGraw-Hill, 2008, 51.
9. Suzanne Ruggi, "Commodifying Honor in Female Sexuality: Honor Killings in Palestine," in Pinar Ilkkaracan, ed., *Women and Sexuality in Muslim Societies,* Istanbul: Women for Women's Human Rights, Kadinin Insam Haklari Projesi, 2000, 126.
10. Human Rights Watch, "Administrative Detention Undermines the Rule of Law in Jordan," 2009, www.hrw.org/node/83254/section/6.
11. Human Rights Watch, "Honoring the Killers: Justice Denied for 'Honor' Crimes in Jordan," www.hrw.org/reports/2004/jordan0404/1.htm.
12. Ibid.
13. Katherine Zoepf, "A Dishonorable Affair," *New York Times,* September 27, 2007, www.nytimes.com/2007/09/23/magazine/23wwln-syria-t.html?pagewanted=all.
14. Ibid.

Chapter 3

1. Jack Maes, "From Religion to Tales of Old: A Little Thing Called Love," *Washington Times,* August 20, 2012.
2. Matt. 16:18–19 (King James version).
3. David Landes, "Culture Makes Almost All the Difference," in L. E. Harrison and S. P. Huntington, eds., *Culture Matters: How Values Shape Human Progress,* New York: Basic Books, 2000, 3.

Chapter 4

1. Benedict Anderson, *Imagined Communities: Reflections on the Origin and Spread of Nationalism,* London: Verso, 2006, 6.
2. Ibid., 7.
3. Ernest Gellner, *Nations and Nationalism,* Ithaca, NY: Cornell University Press, 1983, 1.
4. Anderson, *Imagined Communities,* 7.

5. Ibid., 83.

6. Gellner, *Nations and Nationalism*, 1.

7. UN Treaty on the Prevention of Genocide, https://treaties.un.org/doc/Publication/UNTS/Volume%2078/volume-78-I-1021-English.pdf.

Chapter 5

1. Elliot Jaspin, *Buried in the Bitter Waters: The Hidden History of Racial Cleansing in America,* New York: Basic Books, 2008, 7–8.

2. Richard Rodriguez, "On Becoming Chicano," in Edward Weisband and Elana DeLozier, eds., *Nations and Nationalities: Cultural Constructions of Collective Identity,* 6th edition, Boston: McGraw Hill, 2005, 266.

3. Ibid.

4. Ibid., 267.

5. Ibid.

6. Eithne Luibheid, *Entry Denied: Controlling Sexuality at the Border,* Minneapolis: University of Minnesota Press, 2002, 34.

7. Mary Matsuda Gruenewald, *Looking Like the Enemy: My Story of Imprisonment in Japanese-American Internment Camps,* Troutdale, OR: New Sage Press, 2005, 15, 14.

8. Ibid., 23.

9. Ibid., 26.

10. Ibid., 47.

11. Ibid., 87.

12. Ibid., 213.

13. Ibid., 217.

14. Ibid., 221.

15. Rogers Brubaker, *Ethnicity without Groups,* Cambridge, MA: Harvard University Press, 2004, 133.

16. Andreas Wimmer, *Ethnic Boundary Making: Institutions, Power, Networks,* Oxford: Oxford University Press, 2013, 50.

17. Peter Behrens, "It's About Immigrants, Not Irishness," *New York Times,* March 16, 2012, www.nytimes.com/2012/03/17/opinion/its-about-immigrants-not-irishnesss.html.

18. Ibid.

19. Peggy McIntosh, "White Privilege: Unpacking the Invisible Knapsack," www.amptoons.com/blog/files/mcintosh.html.

Chapter 6

1. Jane Elliott, "A Class Divided," *Frontline,* 1985.

2. William Peters, *A Class Divided: Then and Now,* expanded edition, New Haven, CT: Yale University Press, 1987, 15.

3. Ibid.

4. Ibid.

5. Ibid., 21.

6. Ibid., 22.

7. Ibid., 23.

8. Ibid., 25.

9. Ibid., 29.
10. Ibid., 30–31.
11. Ibid., 31.
12. Ibid., 36–37.
13. US Census Bureau, "Overview of Race and Hispanic Origin: Census 2000 Brief," 2000, www.census.gov/prod/2001pubs/c2kbr01-1.pdf.
14. Ruby K. Payne, *A Framework for Understanding Poverty,* Fourth Revised Edition, Highlands, TX: aha! Process, Inc., 2005, 9.
15. National Poverty Center, "Poverty in the United States: Frequently Asked Questions," www.npc.umich.edu/poverty/#4.
16. Ibid.
17. Ibid.
18. The Poverty Site, "United Kingdom: Low Income and Ethnicity," www.poverty.org.uk/06/index.shtml?2.
19. Robin Marty, "Wisconsin Equal Pay Law Repealed Because 'Money Is More Important for Men,'" The Women's Rights Cause, April 7, 2012, www.care2.com/causes/wisconsin-equal-pay-law-repealed-because-money-is-more-important-for-men.html#ixzz1rZHFRXZn.

Chapter 7

1. Frantz Fanon, *The Wretched of the Earth,* New York: Grove Press, 1963, 111.
2. Ibid., 171.
3. Ibid., 97.
4. The Fund for Peace, http://global.fundforpeace.org/.
5. "Columbus and the Native Americans," Hartford Web Publishing, www.hartford-hwp.com/archives/40/182.html.
6. Adam Hochschild, *King Leopold's Ghost: A Story of Greed, Terror, and Heroism in Colonial Africa,* Boston: Houghton Mifflin Company, 1998, 72–73.
7. Ibid., 73.
8. Ibid.
9. Ibid., 74.
10. Ibid., 101.
11. Ibid., 119.
12. Ibid., 119–120.
13. Caroline Elkins, *Imperial Reckoning: The Untold Story of Britain's Gulag in Kenya,* New York: Henry Holt and Company, 2005, 10–11.
14. Ibid., 12.
15. Ibid., 14.
16. Ibid., 18.
17. Ibid., 19.
18. Emily Wax, "Growing Beyond the Pull of the Tribe in Kenya: Nairobi Teenagers Find New Unity in Contemporary Culture, Even as Old Ties Persist," *Washington Post,* September 18, 2005.
19. Ibid.
20. Ibid.
21. Ibid.
22. Avraham Burg, *The Holocaust Is Over We Must Rise from Its Ashes,* New York: Palgrave Macmillan, 2008, 161.

23. Ibid., 162.
24. Ibid., 161.
25. Ibid., 162.
26. Ibid., 162–163.
27. Mahmood Mamdani, *When Victims Become Killers: Colonialism, Nativism, and the Genocide in Rwanda,* Princeton, NJ: Princeton University Press, 2002, 11.
28. Prevent Genocide International, *News Monitor for September 2001,* www.preventgenocide.org/prevent/news-monitor/2001sept.htm.
29. Burg, *The Holocaust Is Over*, 161–162.

Chapter 8

1. Stefan Wolff, "Conceptualizing Conflict Management and Settlement," in Ulrich Schneckener and Stefan Wolff, eds., *Managing and Settling Ethnic Conflicts,* London: C. Hurst, 2004, 1.
2. Monica D. Toft, *The Geography of Ethnic Violence: Identity, Interests, and the Indivisibility of Territory,* Princeton, NJ: Princeton University Press, 2003, 32.
3. Gerard Toal and Carl T. Dahlman, *Bosnia Remade: Ethnic Cleansing and Its Reversal,* New York: Oxford University Press, 2011.
4. Sri Lankan Ministry of Defense, "LTTE Defeated; Sri Lanka Liberated from Terror," May 18, 2009, www.defence.lk/new.asp?fname=20090518_10.
5. TamilNation.Org, "Sinhala Sri Lanka's Ethnic Cleansing of the Eelam Tamils," accessed May 19, 2009, www.tamilnation.co/indictment/index.htm.
6. Human Rights Watch, "Sri Lanka: Government Abuses Intensify: Killings, Abductions, and Displacement Soar and Impunity Reigns," August 5, 2007, www.hrw.org/en/news/2007/08/05/sri-lanka-government-abuses-intensify.
7. Ibid.
8. Toal and Dahlman, *Bosnia Remade*, 5.
9. Ibid., 307.
10. Ibid., 307–308.
11. Ibid.
12. Julie Flint and Alex de Waal, *Darfur: A Short History of a Long War,* London: Zed Books, 2005, 40.
13. Ibid., 14–15.
14. M. W. Daly, *Darfur's Sorrow: A History of Destruction and Genocide,* Cambridge, UK: Cambridge University Press, 2007, 260.
15. Flint and de Waal, *Darfur*, 15–16.
16. Alex de Waal, "Tragedy in Darfur: On Understanding and Ending the Horror," *Boston Review,* October/November 2004, www.bostonreview.net/BR29.5/dewaal.php.
17. Robert C. Tucker, *Stalin in Power: The Revolution from Above, 1928–1941,* New York: W. W. Norton and Company, 1992, 28.
18. Ibid., 41.
19. Golfo Alexopoulos, *Stalin's Outcasts: Aliens, Citizens, and the Soviet State, 1926–1936,* Ithaca, NY: Cornell University Press, 2003, 16.
20. Ibid., 17; Tucker, *Stalin in Power*, 27.
21. Tucker, *Stalin in Power*, 174.
22. Alexopoulos, *Stalin's Outcasts*, 24.
23. Tucker, *Stalin in Power*, 175.

24. Alexopoulos, *Stalin's Outcasts*, 57.

25. Ibid., 59, 60.

26. "Maoism," *Encyclopedia Britannica,* 2009, Encyclopedia Britannica Online, accessed October 22, 2009, www.britannica.com/EBchecked/topic/363444/Maoism.

27. "Decision Concerning the Great Proletarian Cultural Revolution, Adopted on 8 August 1966 by the Central Committee of the Chinese Communist Party," official English version, www.rrojasdatabank.info/16points.htm.

28. Steven Béla Várdy and Agnes Huszár Várdy, "Cannibalism in Stalin's Russia and Mao's China," *Eastern European Quarterly* 41, no. 2 (2007): 12–13, www.paulbogdanor.com/left/cannibalism.pdf.

29. Alexander L. Hinton, *Why Did They Kill? Cambodia in the Shadow of Genocide*, Berkeley: University of California Press, 2004, 215, 217.

30. Ibid., 59.

31. Ibid., 53.

32. Khmer Rouge Radio Broadcast, "Who Are We," reprinted in Hinton, *Why Did They Kill?*, 211.

33. Hinton, *Why Did They Kill?*, 82.

34. Ibid., 261, 147.

35. Arne Johan Vetlesen, *Evil and Human Agency: Understanding Collective Evildoing,* Cambridge: Cambridge University Press, 2005, 161.

36. Ibid., 212.

37. Margurite Feitlowitz, *A Lexicon of Terror: Argentina and the Legacies of Torture,* Oxford: Oxford University Press, 1998, 51.

38. Ibid., 51.

39. CONADEP, *Nunca Más (Never Again), Part I: The Repression,* 1984, http://web.archive.org/web/20031013222229/nuncamas.org/english/library/nevagain/nevagain_004.htm.

40. David Pion-Berlin and G. A. Lopez, "Of Victims and Executioners: Argentine State Terror, 1976–1983," unpublished manuscript, 10.

41. David Pion-Berlin, "The National Security Doctrine, Military Threat Perception, and the 'Dirty War' in Argentina," *Comparative Political Studies* 2, no. 3 (October 1998): 383.

42. Ibid., 398.

43. J. Patrice McSherry, "Operation Condor: Clandestine Inter-American System," *Social Justice* 26, no. 4 (December 1999): 66.

44. International Criminal Court, *Rome Statute,* 2002, www.un.org/law/icc/index.html.

45. Commission for Historical Clarification: Conclusions and Recommendations, *Guatemala: Memory of Silence*, http://shr.aaas.org/guatemala/ceh/report/english/concl.html and http://shr.aaas.org/guatemala/ceh/report/english/conc2.html.

46. Ibid., http://shr.aaas.org/guatemala/ceh/report/english/conc2.html.

47. Ibid., emphasis added.

48. Ibid.

49. Ibid.

50. Rigoberta Menchú Tum (Maya) and Dante Liano, *The Girl from Chimel,* Toronto, Ontario: Groundwood Books, 2005.

Chapter 9

1. Robert G. L. Waite, *The Psychopathic God: Adolf Hitler,* New York: Da Capo Press, 1977, 39.
2. Neil J. Kressel, "Mass Hate: The Global Rise of Genocide and Terror," in Edward Weisband and Courtney I. P. Thomas, eds., *Nations & Nationalities: Cultural Constructions of Collective Identities,* 8th edition, Boston: McGraw-Hill, 2008, 378.
3. Lucy Dawidowicz, quoted in ibid., 378.
4. Ron Rosenbaum, *Explaining Hitler,* New York: Harper Perennial, 1999, 293.
5. UN General Assembly, *Convention on the Prevention and Punishment of the Crime of Genocide,* 1948, www.hrweb.org/legal/genocide.html.
6. Kressel, "Mass Hate," 382.
7. Ibid.
8. *The Eternal Jew,* 1940, directed by Fritz Hippler.
9. Elie Wiesel, *Night,* New York: Hill and Wang, 1985, 10, 11.
10. Anderson, *Imagined Communities,* 6.
11. Hannah Arendt, *Eichmann in Jerusalem: A Report on the Banality of Evil,* New York: Penguin Books, 2006, xi.
12. Ibid., xiii.
13. Ibid.
14. Ibid., 52.
15. Ibid.
16. Ibid.
17. Ibid.
18. www.historyplace.com/speeches/wiesel.htm (1999).
19. Arendt, *Eichmann in Jerusalem,* 114.
20. Ibid., 135. Italics in the original.
21. Daniel Goldhagen, *Hitler's Willing Executioners: Ordinary Germans and the Holocaust,* London: Vintage, 1997.
22. Wiesel, *Night,* 22.
23. Ruth Minsky Sender, *The Cage,* New York: Simon Pulse, 1986, 139–140, 144, 145.
24. *Shoah,* 1985, directed by Claude Lanzmann.
25. Wiesel, *Night,* 42.
26. Sender, *The Cage,* 175.
27. Primo Levi, *Survival in Auschwitz and the Reawakening: Two Memoirs,* New York: Summit Books, 1986, 42.
28. Bronislaw Goscinki, reprinted in Giorgio Agamben, *Remnants of Auschwitz: The Witness and the Archive,* New York: Zone Books, 2002, 168–169.
29. Wiesel, *Night,* 32.
30. *Shoah.*
31. Wiesel, *Night,* 34.

Chapter 10

1. Mamdani, *When Victims Become Killers,* 52.
2. Ibid., 53.
3. Ibid., 53, 54.
4. Ibid., 77.

5. Ibid., 79.

6. Ibid., 80.

7. Ibid., 104.

8. Ibid., 105.

9. Ibid., 88, 34.

10. Lothar Brock, H. Holm, G. Sørensen, and M. Stohl, *Fragile States*, Cambridge, UK: Polity Press, 2012, 93.

11. *Hotel Rwanda,* United States: Metro Goldwyn Mayer Home Entertainment, 2005. For a documentary record of Hutu Power Radio Transcripts, see http://migs.concordia.ca/links/RwandaRadioTranscripts.htm. This quotation encapsulates the substance of Hutu Power Broadcasts, as represented in the film *Hotel Rwanda.*

12. Linda Melvern, *Conspiracy to Murder: The Rwandan Genocide,* New York: Verso, 2004, 192.

13. Mamdani, *When Victims Become Killers*, 194.

14. Ibid., 207.

15. Ibid., 191.

16. Melvern, *Conspiracy to Murder*, 220.

17. Mamdani, *When Victims Become Killers*, 228.

18. Mark A. Drumbl, *Atrocity, Punishment, and International Law,* Cambridge, UK: Cambridge University Press, 2007, 1.

19. Melvern, *Conspiracy to Murder*, 208.

20. Philip Gourevitch, *We Wish to Inform You That Tomorrow We Will Be Killed with Our Families: Stories from Rwanda,* New York: Picador, 1998, 95.

21. Christopher C. Taylor, "The Cultural Face of Terror in the Rwandan Genocide of 1994," in Alexander Laban Hinton, ed., *Annihilating Genocide: The Anthropology of Genocide*, Berkeley: University of California Press, 2002, 148.

22. Gerard Prunier, *The Rwanda Crisis,* New York: Columbia University Press, 1995, 171–172, reprinted in ibid., 159.

23. Taylor, "The Cultural Face of Terror," 159, 160.

24. Ibid., 161.

25. Ibid., 168.

Chapter 11

1. Marcela Grad, *Massoud: An Intimate Portrait of the Legendary Afghan Leader,* St. Louis, MO: Webster University Press, 2009, 310.

2. Ibid.

3. Piotr Balcerowicz, "The Last Interview with Ahmad Shah Massoud," 2001, www.orient.uw.edu.pl/balcerowicz/texts/Ahmad_Shah_Masood_en.htm.

4. Susan Martin, "The Man Who Would Have Led Afghanistan," *St. Petersburg Times,* September 9, 2002, www.sptimes.com/2002/09/09/911/The_man_who_would_hav.shtml.

5. Mike Mount, "Gates: U.S. Would Support Afghan Peace Talks with Taliban," CNN.com, October 10, 2008, http://articles.cnn.com/2008-10-10/world/gates.taliban_1_afghan-security-forces-afghan-government-afghanistan?_s=PM:WORLD.

6. Ibid.

7. Ibid.

8. "Petraeus: Reconciliation with Taliban Is Ultimate Goal for Afghanistan's

Future," FoxNews.com, August 25, 2010, www.foxnews.com/politics/2010/08/25/petraeus-reconciliation-taliban-ultimate-goal-afghanistans-future/.

9. Philip Salzman and Patricia C. Rice, *Thinking Anthropologically: A Practical Guide for Students*, 3rd edition, Upper Saddle River, NJ: Prentice Hall, 2011, 7.

10. Ibid., 6.

11. Peter B. Smith et al., *Understanding Social Psychology across Cultures: Engaging with Others in a Changing World*, London: Sage, 2013, 56.

12. Travis Lupick, "Suspended Afghan MP Malalai Joya Wants NATO's Mission to End," Straight.com, November 12, 2009, www.straight.com/article-270310/vancouver/afghan-activist-wants-natos-mission-end.

13. National Public Radio, "Abdullah Abdullah: Talks with Taliban Futile," October 22, 2010, www.npr.org/templates/story/story.php?storyId=130757482.

14. *The Constitution of Afghanistan*, www.afghanembassy.com.pl/afg/images/pliki/TheConstitution.pdf.

Bibliography

Agamben, Giorgio. 2002. *Remnants of Auschwitz: The Witness and the Archive.* New York: Zone Books.

Alexopoulos, Golfo. 2003. *Stalin's Outcasts: Aliens, Citizens, and the Soviet State, 1926–1936.* Ithaca, NY: Cornell University Press.

Anderson, Benedict. 2006. *Imagined Communities: Reflections on the Origin and Spread of Nationalism.* London: Verso.

Arendt, Hannah. 2006. *Eichmann in Jerusalem: A Report on the Banality of Evil.* New York: Penguin Books.

Astronomers Without Borders. "Moon and Culture." www.astronomerswithoutborders.org/programs/all-programs/685-moon-and-culture.html.

Balcerowicz, Piotr. 2001. "The Last Interview with Ahmad Shah Massoud." www.orient.uw.edu.pl/balcerowicz/texts/Ahmad_Shah_Masood_en.htm.

Becker, Ernest. 1973. *Denial of Death.* New York: Free Press.

———. 1975. *Escape from Evil.* New York: Free Press.

Behrens, Peter. 2012. "It's About Immigrants, Not Irishness." *New York Times,* March 16. www.nytimes.com/2012/03/17/opinion/its-about-immigrants-not-irishnesss.html.

Benedict, Ruth. 2008. "Patterns of Culture." In Edward Weisband and Courtney I. P. Thomas, eds., *Nations and Nationalities: Cultural Constructions of Collective Identities.* 8th edition. Boston: McGraw-Hill.

Biersteker, T. J., and C. Weber. 1996. *State Sovereignty as Social Construct.* Cambridge, UK: Cambridge University Press.

Brock, Lothar, H. Holm, G. Sørensen, and M. Stohl. 2012. *Fragile States.* Cambridge, UK: Polity Press.

Brubaker, Rogers. 2004. *Ethnicity without Groups.* Cambridge, MA: Harvard University Press.

Burg, Avraham. 2008. *The Holocaust Is Over We Must Rise from Its Ashes.* New York: Palgrave Macmillan.

"Columbus and the Native Americans." Hartford Web Publishing. www.hartford-hwp.com/archives/40/182.html.

Commission for Historical Clarification: Conclusions and Recommendations. 1999. *Guatemala: Memory of Silence.* www.aaas.org/sites/default/files/migrate/uploads/mos_en.pdf.

CONADEP. 1984. *Nunca Más (Never Again), Part I: The Repression.* http://web.archive.org/web/20031013222229/nuncamas.org/english/library/nevagain/nevagain_004.htm.

Connor, Walker. 1994. *Ethnonationalism: The Quest for Understanding.* Princeton, NJ: Princeton University Press.

The Constitution of Afghanistan. www.afghanembassy.com.pl/afg/images/pliki/TheConstitution.pdf.

Daly, M. W. 2007. *Darfur's Sorrow: A History of Destruction and Genocide.* Cambridge, UK: Cambridge University Press.

Danieli, Yael. 2005. *The Trauma of Terrorism: Sharing Knowledge and Shared Culture.* New York: Routledge.

Dawidowicz, Lucy, quoted in Neil J. Kressel. 2008. "Mass Hate: The Global Rise of Genocide and Terror." In Edward Weisband and Courtney I. P. Thomas, eds., *Nations and Nationalities: Cultural Constructions of Collective Identities.* 8th edition. Boston: McGraw-Hill.

"Decision Concerning the Great Proletarian Cultural Revolution." 1996. Central Committee of the Chinese Communist Party (official English version). www.rrojasdatabank.info/16points.htm.

de Waal, Alex. 2004. "Tragedy in Darfur: On Understanding and Ending the Horror." *Boston Review*, October/November.

Drumbl, Mark A. 2007. *Atrocity, Punishment, and International Law.* Cambridge, UK: Cambridge University Press.

Eagleton, Terry. 2012. "Ideology and Its Vicissitudes in Western Marxism." In Slavoj Žižek, ed., *Mapping Ideology.* London: Verso.

Elkins, Caroline. 2005. *Imperial Reckoning: The Untold Story of Britain's Gulag in Kenya.* New York: Henry Holt and Company.

Elliott, Jane. 1985. "A Class Divided." *Frontline.*

Erikson, Erik H. 2008. "Sioux Child Training." In Edward Weisband and Courtney I. P. Thomas, eds., *Nations and Nationalities: Cultural Constructions of Collective Identities.* 8th edition. Boston: McGraw-Hill.

The Eternal Jew. 1940. Directed by Fritz Hippler. Film, 62 min.

Fanon, Frantz. 1963. *The Wretched of the Earth.* New York: Grove Press.

Feitlowitz, Margurite. 1998. *A Lexicon of Terror: Argentina and the Legacies of Torture.* Oxford: Oxford University Press.

Fine, Gary Allen. 2005. "Symbolic Interaction: An Introduction." In Edward Weisband and Elana DeLozier, eds., *Nations and Nationalities: Cultural Constructions of Collective Identities.* 6th edition. Boston: McGraw-Hill.

Flint, Julie, and Alex de Waal. 2005. *Darfur: A Short History of a Long War.* London: Zed Books.

The Fund for Peace. http://global.fundforpeace.org/.

Gellner, Ernest. 1983. *Nations and Nationalism.* Ithaca, NY: Cornell University Press.

Goldhagen, Daniel. 1997. *Hitler's Willing Executioners: Ordinary Germans and the Holocaust.* London: Vintage.

Gourevitch, Philip. 1998. *We Wish to Inform You That Tomorrow We Will Be Killed with Our Families: Stories from Rwanda.* New York: Picador.

Grad, Marcela. 2009. *Massoud: An Intimate Portrait of the Legendary Afghan Leader.* St. Louis, MO: Webster University Press.

Grant, Rebecca, and Kathleen Newland. 1991. *Gender and International Relations.* Bloomington: Indiana University Press.

Greenfield, Leah. 1993. *Nationalism: Five Roads to Modernity.* Cambridge, MA: Harvard University Press.

Gruenewald, Mary Matsuda. 2005. *Looking Like the Enemy: My Story of Imprisonment in Japanese-American Internment Camps.* Troutdale, OR: New Sage Press.

Guibernau, Maria Montserrat. 2007. *The Identity of Nations.* Cambridge, UK: Polity Press.

Harrison, Lawrence E., and Samuel P. Huntington, eds. 2000. *Culture Matters: How Values Shape Human Progress.* New York: Basic Books.

Hinton, Alexander L. 2004. *Why Did They Kill? Cambodia in the Shadow of Genocide.* Berkeley: University of California Press.

Hochschild, Adam. 1998. *King Leopold's Ghost: A Story of Greed, Terror, and Heroism in Colonial Africa.* Boston: Houghton Mifflin Company.

Human Rights Watch. 2004. "Honoring the Killers: Justice Denied for 'Honor' Crimes in Jordan." April. www.hrw.org/reports/2004/jordan0404/1.htm.

———. 2007. "Sri Lanka: Government Abuses Intensify: Killings, Abductions, and Displacement Soar and Impunity Reigns." August 5. www.hrw.org/en/news/2007/08/05/sri-lanka-government-abuses-intensify.

———. 2009. "Administrative Detention Undermines the Rule of Law in Jordan." May 26. www.hrw.org/node/83254/section/6.

Hutchinson, John, and Anthony David Smith, eds. 1994. *Nationalism.* Oxford: Oxford University Press.

Inayatullah, Naeem, ed. 2010. *Autobiographical International Relations: I, IR.* New York: Routledge.

International Criminal Court. 2002. *Rome Statute.* www.un.org/law/icc/index.html.

Jaspin, Elliot. 2008. *Buried in the Bitter Waters: The Hidden History of Racial Cleansing in America.* New York: Basic Books.

Kressel, Neil J. 2008. "Mass Hate: The Global Rise of Genocide and Terror." In Edward Weisband and Courtney I. P. Thomas, eds., *Nations and Nationalities: Cultural Constructions of Collective Identities.* 8th edition. Boston: McGraw-Hill.

Landes, David. 2000. "Culture Makes Almost All the Difference." In Lawrence E. Harrison and Samuel P. Huntington, eds., *Culture Matters: How Values Shape Human Progress.* New York: Basic Books.

Levi, Primo. 1986. *Survival in Auschwitz and the Reawakening: Two Memoirs.* New York: Summit Books.

Luibheid, Eithne. 2002. *Entry Denied: Controlling Sexuality at the Border.* Minneapolis: University of Minnesota Press.

Lupick, Travis. 2009. "Suspended Afghan MP Malalai Joya Wants NATO's Mission to End." Straight.com, November 12. www.straight.com/article-270310/vancouver/afghan-activist-wants-natos-mission-end.

Maasai Association. "Maasai Ceremonies and Rituals." www.maasai-association.org/ceremonies.html.

Maes, Jack. 2012. "From Religion to Tales of Old: A Little Thing Called Love." *Washington Times*, August 20.

Mamdani, Mahmood. 2002. *When Victims Become Killers: Colonialism, Nativism, and the Genocide in Rwanda.* Princeton, NJ: Princeton University Press.

"Maoism." *Encyclopedia Britannica.* Encyclopedia Britannica Online. Accessed October 22, 2009. www.britannica.com/EBchecked/topic/363444/Maoism.

Martin, Susan. 2002. "The Man Who Would Have Led Afghanistan." *St. Petersburg Times*, September 9. www.sptimes.com/2002/09/09/911/The_man_who_would_hav.shtml.

Marty, Robin. 2012. "Wisconsin Equal Pay Law Repealed Because 'Money Is More Important for Men.'" The Women's Rights Cause, April 7. www.care2.com/causes/wisconsin-equal-pay-law-repealed-because-money-is-more-important-for-men.html#ixzz1rZHFRXZn.

May, Rollo. 1958. "Contributions of Existential Psychotherapy." In Rollo May, Ernest Angel, and Henri F. Ellenberger, eds., *Existence: A New Dimension in Psychiatry and Psychology*, pp. 37–91. New York: Basic Books.

McIntosh, Peggy. "White Privilege: Unpacking the Invisible Knapsack." www.amptoons.com/blog/files/mcintosh.html.

McSherry, J. Patrice. 1999. "Operation Condor: Clandestine Inter-American System." *Social Justice* 26 (4).

Melvern, Linda. 2004. *Conspiracy to Murder: The Rwandan Genocide.* New York: Verso.

Mount, Mike. 2008. "Gates: U.S. Would Support Afghan Peace Talks with

Taliban." CNN.com, October 10. http://articles.cnn.com/2008-10-10/world/gates.taliban_1_afghan-security-forces-afghan-government-afghanistan?_s=PM:WORLD.

National Poverty Center. "Poverty in the United States: Frequently Asked Questions." www.npc.umich.edu/poverty/#4.

National Public Radio. 2010. "Abdullah Abdullah: Talks with Taliban Futile." October 22. www.npr.org/templates/story/story.php?storyId=130757482.

Nelson, Scott G. 2011. *Sovereignty and the Limits of the Liberal Imagination.* New York: Routledge.

Özkirimli, Umut. 2000. *Theories of Nationalism.* New York: St. Martin's Press.

Payne, Ruby K. 2005. *A Framework for Understanding Poverty.* 4th edition. Highlands, TX: aha! Process, Inc.

Peters, William. 1987. *A Class Divided: Then and Now.* Expanded edition. New Haven, CT: Yale University Press.

Peterson, V. Spike, ed. 1992. *Gendered States: Feminist (Re)Visions of International Relations Theory.* Boulder, CO: Lynne Rienner Publishers, Inc.

"Petraeus: Reconciliation with Taliban Is Ultimate Goal for Afghanistan's Future." FoxNews.com, August 25, 2010. www.foxnews.com/politics/2010/08/25/petraeus-reconciliation-taliban-ultimate-goal-afghanistans-future/.

Pion-Berlin, David. 1998. "The National Security Doctrine, Military Threat Perception, and the 'Dirty War' in Argentina." *Comparative Political Studies* 2 (3).

Pion-Berlin, David, and G. A Lopez. "Of Victims and Executioners: Argentine State Terror, 1976–1983." Unpublished manuscript.

Poole, Ross. 1999. *Nation and Identity.* London: Routledge.

The Poverty Site. "United Kingdom: Low Income and Ethnicity." www.poverty.org.uk/06/index.shtml?2.

Prevent Genocide International. *News Monitor for September 2001.* www.preventgenocide.org/prevent/news-monitor/2001sept.htm.

Prunier, Gerard. 1995. *The Rwanda Crisis.* New York: Columbia University Press.

Riviere, Joan. 2002. "On the Genesis of Psychical Conflict in Earliest Infancy." In Melanie Klein, Susan Isaacs, Paula Heimann, and Joan Riviere, eds., *Developments in Psychoanalysis.* London: Karnac Books.

Rodriguez, Richard. 2005. "On Becoming Chicano." In Edward Weisband and Elana DeLozier, eds., *Nations and Nationalities: Cultural Constructions of Collective Identity.* 6th edition. Boston: McGraw-Hill.

Rosenbaum, Ron. 1999. *Explaining Hitler.* New York: Harper Perennial.

Ruggi, Suzanne. 2000. "Commodifying Honor in Female Sexuality: Honor Killings in Palestine." In Pinar Ilkkaracan, ed., *Women and Sexuality in Muslim Societies.* Istanbul: Women for Women's Human Rights.

Saitoti, Tepilit Ole. 2008. "My Circumcision." In Edward Weisband and Courtney

I. P. Thomas, eds., *Nations and Nationalities: Cultural Constructions of Collective Identities.* 8th edition. Boston: McGraw-Hill.

Salzman, Philip C., and Patricia C. Rice. 2011. *Thinking Anthropologically: A Practical Guide for Students.* 3rd edition. Upper Saddle River, NJ: Prentice Hall.

Schneckener, Ulrich, and Stefan Wolff, eds. 2004. *Managing and Settling Ethnic Conflicts.* New York: Palgrave Macmillan.

Sender, Ruth Minsky. 1986. *The Cage.* New York: Simon Pulse.

Shoah. 1985. Directed by Claude Lanzmann. Film, 566 min.

"Sinhala Sri Lanka's Ethnic Cleansing of the Eelam Tamils." TamilNation.Org. Accessed May 19, 2009. www.tamilnation.co/indictment/index.htm.

Smith, Peter, Ronald Fischer, Vivian L. Vignoles, and Michael Harris Bond. 2013. *Understanding Social Psychology across Cultures: Engaging with Others in a Changing World.* London: Sage Publications.

Sri Lankan Ministry of Defense. 2009. "LTTE Defeated; Sri Lanka Liberated from Terror." May 18. www.defence.lk/new.asp?fname=20090518_10.

Taylor, Christopher C. 2002. "The Cultural Face of Terror in the Rwandan Genocide of 1994." In *Annihilating Genocide: The Anthropology of Genocide.* Alexander L. Hinton, ed. Berkeley: University of California Press.

Tickner, J. Ann. 2001. *Gendering World Politics.* New York: Columbia University Press.

Tillich, Paul. 1952. *The Courage to Be.* New Haven, CT: Yale University Press.

Toal, Gerard, and Carl T. Dahlman. 2011. *Bosnia Remade: Ethnic Cleansing and Its Reversal.* New York: Oxford University Press.

Toft, Monica D. 2003. *The Geography of Ethnic Violence: Identity, Interests, and the Indivisibility of Territory.* Princeton, NJ: Princeton University Press.

Tucker, Robert C. 1992. *Stalin in Power: The Revolution from Above, 1928–1941.* New York: W. W. Norton and Company.

Tum, Rigoberta Menchú, and Dante Liano. 2005. *The Girl from Chimel.* Toronto, Ontario: Groundwood Books.

UN General Assembly. 1948. *Convention on the Prevention and Punishment of the Crime of Genocide.* www.hrweb.org/legal/genocide.htm.

US Census Bureau. 2000. "Overview of Race and Hispanic Origin: Census 2000 Brief." www.census.gov/prod/2001pubs/c2kbr01-1.pdf.

van den Haag, Ernest, and Ralph Ross. 2006. *Passion and Social Constraint.* New York: Aldine Transaction.

Várdy, Steven Béla, and Agnes Huszár Várdy. 2007. "Cannibalism in Stalin's Russia and Mao's China." *East European Quarterly* 41 (2). www.paulbogdanor.com/left/cannibalism.pdf.

Vetlesen, Arne Johan. 2005. *Evil and Human Agency: Understanding Collective Evildoing.* Cambridge, UK: Cambridge University Press.

Waite, Robert G. L. 1977. *The Psychopathic God: Adolf Hitler.* New York: Da Capo Press.

Wax, Emily. 2005. "Growing Beyond the Pull of the Tribe in Kenya: Nairobi Teenagers Find New Unity in Contemporary Culture, Even as Old Ties Persist." *Washington Post*, September 18.

Wiesel, Elie. 1985. *Night.* New York: Hill and Wang.

Wimmer, Andreas. 2013. *Ethnic Boundary Making: Institutions, Power, Networks.* Oxford: Oxford University Press.

Wolff, Stefan. 2004. "Conceptualizing Conflict Management and Settlement." In Ulrich Schneckener and Stefan Wolff, eds., *Managing and Settling Ethnic Conflicts.* London: C. Hurst.

Zoepf, Katherine. 2007. "A Dishonorable Affair." *New York Times*, September 27. www.nytimes.com/2007/09/23/magazine/23wwln-syria-t.html?pagewanted=all.

Index

About the Authors

Edward Weisband is the inaugural Edward S. Diggs Endowed Chair Professor in the Department of Political Science at Virginia Tech. Throughout his career, Professor Weisband has devoted his primary attention to teaching and pedagogy and is nationally recognized for his distinguished contributions to teaching, especially of introductory subjects. In 1983, he was promoted to Distinguished Teaching Professor, a rank above full professor, by the State University of New York (SUNY). In 1987, the Council for the Advancement and Support of Education (CASE) selected him as the Gold Medal Finalist in its National Professor of the Year competition. Professor Weisband was also named by CASE as the New York State Professor of the Year during the same year. He initiated the proposal to establish the Diggs Teaching Roundtable and Teaching Scholar Award at Virginia Tech, a program that has emerged as a form of major recognition of teaching excellence and as an important Virginia Tech faculty forum to explore pedagogical approaches and instructional methods. He is the recipient of the Virginia Tech Sporn Award for excellence in teaching introductory subjects. Professor Weisband has authored, coauthored, edited, and coedited numerous books, monographs, and articles on normative standards and accountability, including *Turkish Foreign Policy: Small State Diplomacy and Great Power Politics*; *The Politics and Economics of Cooperation: A Free Trade Association among Canada, Britain and the United States*; *Secrecy and Foreign Policy*; *Foreign Policy by Congress*; *Word Politics: Verbal Strategy between the Superpowers*; *A Paradigm of Lockean Liberalism: The Ideology of American Foreign Policy*; *Resignation-in-Protest: Loyalty to Team versus Loyalty to Conscience in American Public Life*; and *Global Accountabilities*. In addition, he has edited or coedited three texts, *Teaching World Politics: Contending Pedagogies for a New World Order*; *Poverty*

amidst Plenty: World Political Economy and Distributive Justice; and *International Political Economy: Navigating the Logic Stream.* Professor Weisband has presented numerous papers abroad and has recently completed a study on perpetrators of genocide and mass atrocity.

Courtney I. P. Thomas is a Visiting Assistant Professor at Virginia Tech. She is the author of *In Food We Trust: The Politics of Purity in American Food Regulation* (University of Nebraska Press) and the coauthor of *International Political Economy: Navigating the Logic Streams, an Introduction* (Kendall Hunt). She is the proud mother of Sonya, Marie, Bettie, and Levi.

Printed in Canada